THE
IMPERIAL
ANIMAL

Tout être vivant est aussi un fossile

—Jacques Monod

THE
IMPERIAL
ANIMAL

LIONEL TIGER & ROBIN FOX

An Owl Book

Henry Holt and Company • New York

Published by Henry Holt and Company, Inc.,
115 West 18th Street, New York, New York 10011.
Published in Canada by Fitzhenry & Whiteside Limited,
195 Allstate Parkway, Markham, Ontario L3R 4T8.

Library of Congress Cataloging-in-Publication Data
Tiger, Lionel, 1937–
The imperial animal.
Reprint. Originally published: New York :
Holt, Rinehart and Winston, 1971.
"An Owl book."
Bibliography: p.
Includes index.
1. Sociobiology.   2. Social evolution.   3. Sex differences.
4. Behavior evolution.   5. Power (Social sciences).
I. Fox, Robin, 1934–   II. Title.
GN365.9.T52   1989   304.5   89–7446
ISBN 0-8050-1154-4 (pbk.)

Henry Holt books are available at special discounts
for bulk purchases for sales promotions, premiums,
fund-raising, or educational use. Special editions
or book excerpts can also be created to specification.

For details contact:
Special Sales Director
Henry Holt and Company, Inc.
115 West 18th Street
New York, New York 10011

First published in hardcover by
Holt, Rinehart and Winston in 1971.
First Owl Book Edition—1989

Designed by Nancy Tausek
Printed in the United States of America
1   3   5   7   9   10   8   6   4   2

CONTENTS

FOREWORD

by Konrad Lorenz

To DO justice to this important book in a foreword I must go far afield.

"Nature and Spirit—one doesn't talk like that to Christians; that is why they burn atheists, for such phrases are most dangerous." Goethe's joking lines evoke the wall separating nature and the human spirit—a wall which unfortunately is as strong today as it was then, dividing those who seek understanding into two groups (important thinkers have even described it as two cultures) which face each other as strangers, if not indeed as enemies.

This separation stands in the way of that demand for *self-knowledge* raised by the philosophers of ancient Greece. We *know* today for a certainty that man, like all other living creatures, owes his existence to a historically unique process of evolution. If one wants to understand fully his characteristics and attainments, one must know something about their origins and development. Just as the art historian who wishes to understand all aspects of a cathedral built over a long period of time must know something about the history of architecture—and conversely may learn much about that history from the particulars of its construction—so the researcher needs a thorough knowledge of human evolutionary history if he would come to an understanding of man.

It has long been taken for granted that the study of man as an animal, with all of his physiological functions, must be examined with the heuristic techniques and methodology of natural science. On the other hand, the notion that human *behavior* is based on inherited "programs" firmly established in the course of human phylogeny runs into bitter opposition. Many naturalists will not attempt the study of human behavior, especially social behavior, because as scientists they seek in principle to avoid value judgments, and because this is not possible when the subject of observation is ethical and moral behavior. Philosophers of an idealistic bent consider the human spirit (in the sense that Goethe ridiculed it) as something diametrically opposed to nature, and thus fundamentally unapproachable with the tools of natural science. Between these two, and equally alienated both from nature and from the spirit—not to say unnatural and dispirited—is the view of the behaviorist, to whom people are born *tabula rasa*. This is to say, they possess nothing in the way of inborn modes of behavior or reaction unique to their species, but have only "conditioning," the acquisition of particular reflex actions, with which to master their environment.

All three of these perspectives are generally accepted; all three are to blame for today's lack of knowledge about the characteristics and attainments of man as a species. ("Human nature" is often referred to, but never examined.)

Until very recently we ethologists, along with very few others, were the only ones striving for a scientific understanding of man, including his unique cultural accomplishments. Now in the camp of the anthropologists and sociologists two extraordinarily powerful allies have appeared: Lionel Tiger and Robin Fox. They come from quite another side and work with very different methods, but their goal is the same. More important, their motivation is the same: They see that humanity as a species is in danger and that many of the dangers threatening it derive from inherited norms of behavior unique to the species—those "adaptations to yesterday" which today, under greatly changed circumstances of human life, may prove harmful.

In the present book they give a convincing, simply stated description of just what innate programs of behavior are, how they are actualized under varying circumstances, where their survival value for the species lies, and how and why they may lose that value under certain conditions. The far from simple pedagogical problem of presenting these ideas in an understandable fashion is masterfully solved.

To abstract what is universally human from the great diversity of culturally conditioned forms, the authors borrow from the methods of modern linguistics. In the same way that Chomsky and Lenneberg used the comparative study of language to arrive at the abstraction of universal rules of grammar applicable to all languages of all peoples, Fox and Tiger are seeking a "biogrammar" of human behavior. In addition to the norms of innate behavior, this includes the regularities of culture—the readiness to acquire, transmit and store traditional knowledge—comparable to the rules of language discovered by the linguists.

The authors carry out their most ambitious project in an exemplary manner. Their task requires of them a comprehensive knowledge—not only in their original fields of anthropology and sociology, but also in ethnology, general biology, and ethology. The things they have to say about biology or ethology that I am competent to judge are so convincingly correct that I have great trust in their general reliability. Moreover, their every word bespeaks both common sense and a healthy human understanding.

This is not to say that this book will not raise storms of emotional indignation from many sides or that much dirt will not be slung at its authors. That the opponents will throw mud clearly shows their lack of munitions for scientific argument. The knowledge-inhibiting wall between nature and spirit *must* be torn down, no matter how fiercely philosophers, behaviorists, or even naturalists defend it. Truth is on the side of those who batter this wall (with their heads, if necessary) as one fact makes clear: The defenders are of many different opinions among themselves, while we who rebel against the separation of nature and spirit are all of one mind. Indeed, we say almost word for word the same things—and considering the differences in our intellectual backgrounds, this is most remarkable!

Before writing this, as a sort of inner preparation, I read another foreword, one my friend and teacher Julian Huxley wrote more than twenty years ago for one of my books.

Only if we know and face the truth about the world, whether the world of physics and chemistry, or of geology and biology, or of mind and behavior shall we be able to see what is our own true place in the world. Only as we discover and assimilate the truth about nature shall we be able to undertake the apparently contradictory but essential task of reestablishing our unity with nature while at the same time maintaining our transcendence over nature.

Reading these words, it came to me how few we were then, twenty years ago, we who worked on that "essential task." Reading Tiger and Fox, one cannot escape the feeling that truth is on the march and that the evil wall between nature and spirit is beginning to crumble.

Max Planck Institut für Verhaltensphysiologie
Seewiesen, Germany

TRANSLATED BY *Robert Rockwell*

INTRODUCTION

Twenty Years On

WHEN AN author, or in this case two authors, consider the new introduction to a reissue of an early and controversial work, they are inevitably torn between the pleasures of revenge and the satisfactions of skillfully modest self-congratulation. We shall try to eschew the former and go easy on the latter, which will not be difficult since the results have in their way been modest enough. It could hardly have been otherwise, since the two young authors we look back upon were trying for nothing less than a total revision of the behavioral sciences and the creation of a new ethic. We were trying to change the world in the same spirit that we had changed our own worlds, leaving our native lands and striking out anew in a land which, with all its faults, appeared to be open to new ideas. We did all this with a naive honesty that now astonishes us; but in so doing we stumbled— two innocent and recent immigrants—into the empire of ideology.

We had no predetermined political or philosophical program when we wrote this book. The changes we advocated appeared to us to be compelled by the overwhelming data we were faced with, data of which we were the accountants and translators. But quickly after the book's appearance it became clear that in the narrowed eyes of too many we were bad people. Pro-aggression and warfare, anti-female, advocates of unfettered capitalism, enthusiasts of the primordial—

moral throwbacks in a greening age. What a surprise! since we had always done our lessons, maintained tolerably clean fingernails, met our classes on time, and were earnest about good grammar and lucid argument. Of course we saw ourselves in no way the energetic villains we evidently were for some reviewers, correspondents, irritated colleagues, and a hive of others. We helpfully wrote letters to literary editors, protested to journals, populated seminars and after-class bars, confident that one more fact, one more measured and generous statement of the position, would win the day. Surely no one *preferred* misinterpretation and unfair calumny? Surely the brisk refreshment of scientific truth would bring a smile to the scowling face of the most curmudgeonly of our new, unwanted enemies?

But it was not to be. In fact, the more that we corrected their often puzzling misrepresentations, the more that we pointed out the factual errors, the more that we conclusively refuted their bizarre connection of our carefully documented and argued words to the unsavory positions listed above, the more irritated, angry, and abusive they became. It was soon obvious that we had trodden on some very sensitive toes. As far as the owners of these delicate digits were concerned, there was no room for argument. They didn't want to know. They wished we would roll over and die, or at least shut up and go away. As we puzzled over the nature of our grievous offense, we came to understand that our bright-eyed effort had a significance wider than we could have realized at the time: not because of its specific content, but because it raised an issue that the voluble opponents did not want raised, much less discussed and debated. We found out that the world could not be changed by pointing out truths to honest scholars, because the very definition of truth was at issue. No amount of fact and argument would help because *ex definitione* our premises were so deeply in error that we could not even approach the truth.

Obviously this was not the only style of response to *The Imperial Animal* otherwise we wouldn't be here, on these pages. The book was translated into many languages; it was widely reviewed and adopted by book clubs and instructors of college courses. It sold enough copies to induce publishers to invite us to top-grade lunches and even permit us to pay for our own a few times a year. There were some wonderful reviews and some thoughtfully skeptical ones that nevertheless identified the positive strengths not so much of the book as of the argument it sought to urge. Our effort to build an accessible bridge between biology and the social sciences was treated seriously, and some commentators thought we were brave, if also perhaps oft intrepid. Frankly, we were so full of ourselves that this we expected. We had tried to do a lively and decent job and thought we had succeeded. When others perceived this, clearly there was order in the universe.

What puzzled us were the other, the angry responses. The people who liked what we had done seemed to like it for the right reasons. Those who didn't like it did so for what were to us quite the wrong reasons. Sometimes it seemed there were no reasons at all. Very little criticism was leveled at our specific ideas, and as the reader will see, some of them were radical enough at the time. To oppose the busing of schoolchildren to achieve racial balance in schools was blatant and major heresy in the heyday of civil rights. This was more or less passed over. Instead we were accused of such things as "reviving social Darwinism," "male chauvinism," "biological reductionism" (a great favorite), "militarism," "genetic determinism." One exuberant English reviewer even compared our book to *Mein Kampf*! (Our solicitor advised us that the review was so confused it would be difficult to discern sufficient clear motive to sustain the necessary charge of malicious intent. Anyway, we were told, neither the writer nor the publication had sufficient pounds sterling to cover the costs if we won.)

The reader of the foregoing cheery pages may be forgiven for being as surprised as we were. But this was truly and in some cases even sincerely what critics *saw* in the book. It was like an intellectual inkblot, obviously, whose vague outline, if one did not pay attention to the details of the argument, *suggested* these things to a hasty reader; things so reprehensible that the details did not matter. What was being condemned was a genre, a kind of thinking, a way of looking at the world, a theoretical orientation, a broad aesthetic, a weltanschauung, or whatever you want to call it. We were being attacked for what was assumed were our philosophical and ethical motives. Our pained denials were dismissed as disingenuous or dishonest. We had stumbled onto one of the large issues that divide the Western intellectual world in which the establishment position is clear, if not always stated clearly or even consciously understood. To describe this position we can do our own name-calling in turn: Skinnerism, empiricism, cultural relativism, behaviorism—nurture's triumph over nature; man's absolute control of his destiny in the age of space travel, an age when sociologists would write the new edition of Diderot's *Encyclopédie*.

Perhaps one reason we were as baffled as we were about all this was that we emerged rather unsuspectingly onto an already rather volatile battlefield. Lorenz-Ardrey-Morris and their lib-rad opponents had fully aroused the bystanders and the media. Even though we were approaching these issues as card-carrying members in good standing of the social sciences, and even though our earlier joint publication had been rather equably received, both *Men in Groups* two years earlier and *The Imperial Animal* were greeted as bellicose warriors in a critical struggle.

Nevertheless, the real question remained: Was the cup of human genetic legacy half full or half empty, or was there anything in the cup at all? We had tried to integrate two clearly useful, clearly thriving, clearly appropriate approaches to the complexity of behavior. We took for granted the importance of the variation in behavior that complex animals, including us, would display. We also took for granted the importance of the genetic structure that in varying degrees affects all animals, including us, even to the remarkable extent of categorically causing them to die.

We were hardly so ingenuous as to deny there was a nature-nurture controversy, but we blithely assumed that with our evolutionary approach to behavior we had neatly begun to solve it. We had borrowed this from the ethologists, whose credo, as far as we could see, was that while there are innate predispositions to behavior, these need social or cultural releasers in the environment for their full expression. We wanted to identify the predispositions and look at human culture as a set of appropriate or inappropriate releasers.

Obviously we did not approach this in a totally arbitrary or impressionistic manner. We worked to a rather careful, if necessarily general or crude plan. We took particular social institutions such as politics, economic activity, education, and so forth, and tried to define a "primate baseline"—what aspects of the behavior of other primates did we share with them as a result of common evolution? This established, we moved on to examine the results of our peculiar evolution away from the common baseline, and in particular the role of the transition to a hunting and gathering way of life. We asked what it was that the "transition to humanity" had effected. How had it capitalized on and how had it changed the primate baseline? Then we examined recent and contemporary behavior and institutions to see where and how today we may capitalize on or distort our primate and hominid legacy. We continue to insist that this is a more modest and realistic approach than that of utopians or perfectionists with their fabulous prescriptions for ultimate human happiness. We thought and still think that before anyone tells man what to do, he or she should find out what man is, what he wants, what he needs. If the law of gravity is an imposition, it doesn't help to deny or ignore it. Figure it out, then invent airplanes.

What was so wrong with that?

What was wrong was that we had raised the issue at all. As far as the establishment was concerned, our effort to settle the issue boasted no virtue. Surely it had been settled by John Locke in 1690 and was now principally raised by bad people who were, whatever their overt professions of innocence, interested covertly in re-introducing the heresies that Locke had banished with his equally baffling tirade against doctrines of "innate ideas"—most of which no one on record had ever held.

Perhaps from time to time the liberal-environmentalist establishment feels it necessary to stamp out attempts to re-raise the issue that for them is metaphysically settled. John Stuart Mill took disproportionate years of his life to refute the philosophy of the dull, unreadable, and otherwise unremarkable Sir William Hamilton precisely because he feared the pernicious influence of those ideas the Lockean revolution had banished. He had another buzzword: intuitionism. After World War I, L. T. Hobhouse castigated what he described as "The Metaphysical Theory of the State," pounding the idealists in the name of that same liberal-progressivism. We became the latest puzzled victims of this long-standing campaign to refuse even to accept that there was an issue.

In fact, we came to see that the whole behavioral science establishment, from its foundations by Durkheim in Europe, and Boas and John B. Watson in America, was in peculiar reality an ideological enterprise devoted to promulgating a metaphysical truth: the truth of cultural relativism in its various disguises. Against this truth we had sinned. In consequence, there was little hope that our specific arguments would ever receive a fair hearing.

It was also our ambiguous luck that our book appeared when one particularly militant version of this truth enjoyed a noisy airing: modern feminism. We assert nothing in the book that is anti-feminist in the broad sense that it demeans women or suggests anything but an equal and complementary role for women in human affairs. However, it does suggest that various male-female differences are real and that significant consequences flow from this reality. None of our concrete arguments was attacked, but pilloried was our mere sug-

gestion that all sexual differences in behavior do not stem from socialization, and implicitly from a male conspiracy against women—
women who are men's friends, daughters, wives, mothers, co-
workers, political leaders, political supporters, customers, vendors.
Our crime was to *raise the issue*, a damn issue that had already been
settled. We were criticized not as bad scientists, which at least offers
the possibility of interesting negotiation, but as heretics, which wet-
blankets the whole party.

Plainly, this was not and is not solely a scientific issue, because
there are political, religious, economic, and related consequences, at
least for many people, to the view that there may exist certain
relatively constant behavioral propensities in the human genetic system. For such people, any amount of genetic fixity calls into question
the option human communities have to effect social change, create
new forms of society, point toward new psychological attitudes—in a
word, to create the various utopias that illuminate the efforts of
worthy people seeking progress in the world. To admit any degree of
genetic influence appeared to challenge the freedom of imagination
and ambition of political and moral leaders.

It became clear that the issue went far beyond our book when four
years later E. O. Wilson's *Sociobiology* was greeted with the same
outbreak of scorn, calumny, outrage, ferocity, and partisan passion.
In detail, our two books were very different—which Wilson was at
pains to point out in his Introduction. While kindly praising our
effort as "unquestionably correct" and displaying "brilliant clarity,"
he sought to distance himself: his was to be a work of scientific
hypothesis testing, while ours was "advocacy." We admit cheerfully
to the charge, since we were indeed trying to effect a "scientific
reorientation" (in Robert Merton's terms) rather than seeking a full-
fledged scientific theory. Although we did hope such a unified theory
might emerge, we did not feel confident enough to say exactly what
it might be. We simply suggested where it might come from. But
Wilson's efforts met with as little sympathy on the ideological bat-
tlefront as ours, even though he had a battery of indisputable and
extensive "science" behind him that we lacked. His critics were, if
anything, more furious. It seemed that the better the science of
evolutionary behavior got, the more threatening it was to THE
IDEA.

This is perhaps a good time to answer the question many of our
readers have asked in the past: What is the relation of your work to
Wilson's? Where do you stand on "sociobiology"? First we must get

clear what the latter is, since in the popular press it has now come to mean *any* efforts of this kind, and we are repeatedly referred to as "sociobiologists." We don't mind such an appellation—we have used "biosocial science" or "biosociology" ourselves (Fox had edited a book called *Biosocial Anthropology*)—but to those inside science, it refers rather to a precise kind of theory of evolutionary behavior.

Readers will note that we cited the early work of W. D. Hamilton on the evolution of altruism. We were much impressed by its elegance and power and were probably the first social scientists to be so. But we saw it as limited to the explanation of the genetic basis for a particular trait. We failed to see that it could be generalized. Wilson saw how it could. He combined his previous work on insects (Hamilton's prime examples) with his insights (derived ultimately from the great population geneticists of the thirties) and the exciting, newly emergent work of Robert Trivers. The impressive, generous result was a theory of the evolution of behavior in general. It was all to be tied in to Hamilton's idea of "inclusive fitness"—that creatures not only tried to reproduce their own genes but also strove to encourage the reproduction of such genes in other individuals who were close to them, i.e., genes belonging to relatives.

Voilà! Anthropologists who had historically specialized in studying kinship were right all the time. It is the central feature not only of society but also of evolution. So they had been accomplishing not only good ethnography but also basic biology! Needless to say, THE IDEA had most anthropologists scurrying off in panic, because the theory implied that there was an evolved genetic element in such behavior.

We regarded this extension of insect genetics with great interest. But we were initially skeptical (and remain so) about its usefulness as a general theory of social behavior. It often threatened to explain everything and therefore sometimes did not seem to explain very much. It was interested in ultimate causes of behavior, which are hard to "prove." We were interested in more proximate or directly obvious mechanisms that were the residue of evolution. Nevertheless, we welcomed the attempt as a far-reaching and brilliant incursion of biology into the responsible interpretation of behavior, including human behavior. It seemed to us to justify our "advocacy"; after all, we had advocated just this endeavor for social theory.

If we had reservations about specific applications, these were within the system of ideas, not reservations about the attempt itself. We had had similar reservations about the "application" of ethological ideas to human behavior, which was often done with little regard for the details of human social systems and the accumulated knowledge of the social sciences. But again, we heartily welcomed the attempt. What we advocated was at least the trying out of all such theories to see where they would lead us. Without this trial there could be no judgment.

But to the ideological critics there could be no trial. The judgment was already in. Despite his attempts to "distance" himself, Wilson and his followers got, if anything, worse treatment than we enjoyed.

What, you might ask, of our "followers"? Who were they? Where were they? They were at once few and many, depending on how they are defined. Insofar as we helped bring Wilson and Hamilton together, and had earlier—in 1966—made our own ambitious evolutionary incursion into the social science field, we could claim the Wilson effort as part of our "following"—although in this case it was really more of a parallel development. But there was a great difference. We had not proposed a specific theory or method. We were eclectic, looking for material wherever we could find it. We advocated synthesis, an art rather than a science since it has no particular method. Synthesis depends on the imaginative creativity of the synthesizer. You cannot teach it; you can only feed information and ideas to students and hope that some of them will come to it themselves. If not, at least they will add to the stock of knowledge. But this does not produce a "school." Anyway, neither of us could find tolerable the role of intellectual guru. Against our nature. We had always been mavericks ourselves, and we encouraged the maverick student— especially the one who disagreed with us. Our immediate students at Rutgers produced some brilliant work. But they were too few to constitute a following, and also we kicked them out into the world to fend for their intellectual selves rather than rehiring them to produce an inbred and cozily agreeable department. We were almost masochistic in this, insisting on hiring a whole bunch of anthropologists at Rutgers who didn't agree with us but who did represent the broad spectrum of the discipline.

However, an extraordinary opportunity of a more leveraged kind was presented to us to promote the very eclecticism we favored. Mason Gross, who had retired as president of Rutgers and was appreciative of our work and fond of us as intellectual rebels, took over the Harry Frank Guggenheim Foundation and asked us to help him develop a program for it. Suddenly we were asked to become precisely the kind of characters who had with granite noncomprehension refused to give us the money for the research we wanted to do. But as research directors of the foundation, and with the support and guidance of an able and adventurous board and the brisk insight of Gross as president, we quickly established a highly practical and influential way of affecting the direction of the science in our field— we spread the bucks around.

We approached the matter with self-conscious ingenuousness. We had no printed forms and the simplest of application procedures. We gave money to individuals, virtually never to institutions. We did not provide overhead funds to universities for their general use to support their corps of vice presidents, and our standard reply to officials who wrote from universities complaining about this policy was to invite them to tell their faculty members that they could not receive their H. F. Guggenheim grant. Not one university finally turned down a grant, of course, and recipients appeared to appreciate the emphasis on what they did with their brains rather than with their office managers.

Our major challenge was that the fields in which we were to operate were poorly or at best subtly defined. Flexibility was essential. So was an eagerness to explore what might at first seem unrelated to issues of human violence and inequality, because sometimes the connections became obvious and useful only later. For example, one eventual recipient, Jonathan Winson of Rockefeller University, called to say he wanted to study nightmares, which with undue confidence we pronounced beyond our scheme. Until we slept on it, and the next day called him back to begin discussion of what became a fascinating, fundamental study of brain functions, memory, evolution, and the Freudian theory of the meaning of dreams.

The upshot of all this was that within a few years we came into contact with a fascinating invisible college and were able to facilitate the work of scientists and scholars willing to endure unsentimental scrutiny of often unpleasant and always controversial elements of human and animal behavior. *The Imperial Animal* was our explicit point of departure for this. In a real sense the grant program in part was our scientific and educational contribution—as if we had a school or institute to which people would come. In effect, we went to them. The result was a list of grantees which—we are candidly willing to admit—gave us an enormous sense of accomplishment and also a peculiar sense of wonder at the way genuine intellectual work may sometimes inform issues of the greatest complexity. Among the people whose work we were able to abet in ways they thought useful were David Barash, Jack and Patricia Barchas, Jerome Barkow, Colin Beer, Mark Bekoff, Joel Berger, Thomas Bever, Gerald Borgia, Napoleon Chagnon, Michael Chance, Ivan Chase, James Chisholm, Peter Collett, Peter Corning, John Crook, Martin Daly and Margo Wilson, Richard Dawkins, Irven DeVore, Mildred Dickeman, Ellen Dissanayake, Paul Eckman and W. Friesen, Gary Emory, John Fuller, Benson E. Ginsberg, Patricia Goldman-Rakic, Jane Goodall, James Gould, David Hamburg, Steven Harnad and H. Steklis and Jane Lancaster, William Irons, Nicholas Blurton Jones, D. Kahneman and A. Tversky, Arthur Kling, Melvin Konner and Marjorie Shostak, Jeffrey Kurland, Jean Laponce, André Lecours, Robert Jay Lifton, Jane Lockhard and Robert Adams, C. J. Lumsden, Wade Mackey, Peter Marler, Peter Marsh, Roger Masters, Alan Mazur, Bruce McEwen and Robert Sapolsky, Michael McGuire, Jacques Mehler, Andrew Meltzoff, Desmond Morris, Fernando Nottebohm, Gordon Orians, Craig Packer and Anne Pusey, John Pfeiffer, Charles Poletti, Michael Potegal, Michael Raleigh, Stanley Rothman, Dorothy and Robert Seyfarth, Joseph Shepher, Edward Shorter, Albert Somit, Helen Strausser, Donald Symons, Herbert Terrace, Robert Trivers, Sherwood Washburn, Samuel Wasser, Beatrice and John Whiting, Edward O. Wilson, Jonathan Winson, Alexander Yanov. Other scholars participated in the various conferences we organized or sponsored in the United States and Europe.

We mentioned that *The Imperial Animal* was our explicit point of departure, and this had to do with our employers, Rutgers University. As we have already noted, Mason Gross had been its president, and when he retired, he was asked to become president of the Guggenheim Foundation. Its field was not his field—he was a philosopher—and he explored the matter further. He read B. F. Skinner's bewildering *Beyond Freedom and Dignity* and found it unhelpful, but then read our book and decided that it dealt precisely, and for him usefully, with the matters the foundation was to explore. Thus the book in a very real sense generated and sustained a great deal of the energetic work in the biology of behavior that characterized and was solidified in the 1970s. In the (understandably kind but perhaps nonetheless discerning) words of one of our grantees, we "kept the biosocial enterprise afloat" at a time when the established foundations, with an unhappy mixture of ideology and timidity, were unwilling or afraid to do so.

Intellectual life does not stand still. Our book was not intended as any kind of final statement but was a summary of what we felt germane at the time. It was open for future development in evolutionary exploration of human behavior. It was not a textbook on how these sciences should be used, but an invitation to pursue any and all approaches that might tell us more about the proximate physiological causes of behavior and the ultimate evolutionary explanation for their existence.

Perhaps we were overly enthusiastic about pure ethology at the time. After all, here was an avowed evolutionary science that was nevertheless concerned with explanation of *social* behavior, and we were social scientists. However, as it has turned out, perhaps to the surprise of many ethologists themselves, ethology appears to have become almost exclusively or at least most successfully a science of communicative behavior—of the signs and signals from animal to animal that are the basis for social systems. The book also lacked certain other ingredients that were to prove crucial. For one thing, it had not much detailed and codified sense of the ecological context of behavior. While we recognized the importance of ecological variation, we had neither a real way to integrate this into our analysis nor a real commitment to develop one. The rapid recent development of the science of ecology has added a vital component. Any new theorizing must take ecology into serious account.

In two other areas there have been such rapid strides that it is hard to keep abreast: cognitive sciences and neuroscience. While we announced in Chapter 9 that the great step was "from the simple life to the symbol life," we did not deal effectively with the latter. Perhaps we were consciously combating the idea that man as a symbol-using animal was somehow exempt from the rules of natural selection—the dominant social science orthodoxy of the time. Developments in these fields, however, show clearly that symbol-using behavior can be analyzed as part of man's biological heritage. This means that we could now write the chapter on the "symbol life" that was difficult in 1969, and in addition we would have sympathetic developments in the modern philosophy of mind to aid us.

We have to add endocrinology to this list of crucial developments. Many of the hypotheses in the book can now be tested by data from the burgeoning sciences studying hormones and behavior. It is clear that the body is the arena for a host of secretions and messages which with remarkable complexity and yet effectiveness mediate between physical experience and social behavior. Now we know that not only does physiology affect behavior but vice versa: the judge pronounces more severe sentences when his digestion is perturbed, but the behavior of his digestion can be as readily affected by the social life around him. The skin is not an envelope but a means of transmission from inside to out and back again.

Some of these lacunae have been remedied in our later work where we have striven to advance the study of the human biogrammar separately in directions related to our personal, rather than our joint, interests. Tiger tried to relate the exciting new work on neuropeptides and behavior to the perennial problem of how humans cope with their own self-consciousness. His *Optimism: The Biology of Hope* was an attempt to see how in a world of probable change and inevitable death, we seek to endow our lives and our societies with meaning and expectation. But the book broadly rooted this search not in the symbolizing process itself, as social science is wont to do, but in the evolution of an endorphin-governed process in the brain that makes all this cultural baggage possible. He joined with the late Joseph Shepher in studying that crucial experiment in planned living, the kibbutz. Their *Women in the Kibbutz* showed how the biological pressures discussed in Chapter 3, "Bond Issue One: Women and Children First," exert themselves in a situation where they are being denied by social utopianism.

Fox continued to push into the area he shared in common with the structuralists—the nature-culture divide—by exploring the whole range of primate kinship to find what the "baseline" really was in this area of social life (*Biosocial Anthropology*). He then examined the social science orthodoxy that the incest taboo was the crucial cultural invention in the transition to humanity, and found it wanting (*The Red Lamp of Incest*). In the process he formulated an evolutionary theory for the origin of mental categories (related to the evolution of incest prohibitions) which enabled him to pursue, in a series of articles, the "natural" basis for human category systems. (In this he drew heavily on the aforementioned work of Jonathan Winson on the relation between memory and emotion, and on the work he did with Jacques Mehler in *Neonate Cognition*.)

Both authors have continued to wrestle with the problems of ethics and social policy that they tackled with perhaps rash confidence in the original. In *The Manufacture of Evil: Ethics, Evolution, and the Industrial System*, Tiger considered a triangle of forces: an Upper Paleolithic hunting-gathering species evolved to the small community; an ethical system operating the planet which by and large derives from the convulsive transition from hunting and gathering to pastoralism and agriculture; and a massive-scale industrial system barely ten generations old which has produced no indigenous ethics of its own. What is the result of such a stressful discontinuity? In *The Search for Society: Quest for a Biosocial Science and Morality*, Fox pursues the issues of the philosophical origins of the empiricist prejudice against doctrines of the innate, and the consequences for our view of ourselves and the future of the knowledge of our ancientness as a species.

Obviously a concern with social policy was never far from the surface of our book, and in many places it is the stuff of the book itself. Permit us to consider two issues on which we had strong assertions to make about the link between biology and our kind of society. One is gender, and the other is the relationship between economic organization and theories of human nature.

Perhaps it was inevitable that *The Imperial Animal* would enter the gender debate with disproportionate tumult because Tiger's *Men in Groups* had been the occasion of much hot but ill-lit discussion about the "social construction of gender." Nevertheless *The Imperial Animal* sought to broaden the argument by demonstrating the linkage between primate kinship systems and human ones, and by inferring a realistic connection between what men and women had done in the past to reproduce and survive and what they were doing now. We concluded the work world had been organized principally for men and that women would lose out in the race for equality if it was assumed they were identical with men. Quotas were one answer, which we approved, because in an alternative system, women as usual would be the losers. However, events overtook us ever more quickly, and we could not have foreseen how rapidly women would move into the labor force and where they would move. But we did foresee that this move would not be without serious and chronic difficulty unless decent ways, which worked and felt good, were available so that women could be mothers as enthusiastically as producers.

The contest between production and reproduction remains as hard fought and poignant as ever, though in a way it is being settled *faute de mieux*: more women are having fewer children. This may be a good thing in ecological terms, but it is not self-evidently the result of glad free choice. One certainty is that birth rates in the industrial communities are at historic lows, and it remains our suspicion now as it was our assertion twenty years ago that this is all about the inter-action of a complicated urgent biology and a self-assured heartless industrial system. Zookeepers esteem zoos in major measure by how successfully their residents reproduce. Where does the Human Zoo stand in the ratings?

One of the issues we fumbled rather painfully was trying to under-stand the relationship between evolutionary theory and contempo-rary economic reality. To our surprise, while berating us on most other issues, our liberal progressive colleagues applauded our com-mitment to a mixed welfare economy. Gratifying as this was, it is clear to us now that we had not understood then the motivations involved in acquiring wealth and those involved in redistributing it. If we had, we might have announced that the small family firm in a totally competitive economy was the ideal situation for maximizing our human potential. In this case, we might not have been so kindly treated. But the present popularity of this model and its rapid and obviously successful rise even within socialist redistributive systems should give us pause.

What apologists for capitalism gleefully point to as a vindication of their system may in fact be more a vindication of an evolutionary view that sees the kinship unit as basic to the whole phylogenetic process. After all, the theorists of capitalism have always taken the individual consumer or the firm as such as their units, not the family and the family firm. At least one view of the newly popular econom-ics of the market sees it as actively engaged in the destruction of the family farm and firm. Indeed, an almost hysterical opposition to "nepotism"—which is nothing more than kin selection in action—has characterized the growth of meritocratic, anonymous, universalistic economies and polities, whether socialist or capitalist. Were we doing this book again, and were we intrepid enough, we would tackle this issue much more aggressively and with much greater confi-dence. We would certainly expect to do better than the economists, whose mathematical calculations may be correct but are about the wrong things to start with and lead to inevitably wrong policy sug-gestions. Perhaps it was the social and intellectual turbulence of the 1960s which sufficiently intimidated us that we failed to rise to what we now see as an interesting challenge.

We could go on with the book's lacunae, but there is a limit to the usefulness of this enterprise because it is always relative to the reader's interest. If you are a sociologist, you will notice what is missing from that perspective; if a biologist, a psychologist, a historian, or a podiatrist, you will find gaps to be filled. This is good. The book was meant to provoke such reactions.

On the other hand, we are grateful to notice, almost daily, that both the perspective we urged and some of our specific recommendations have passed into the general currency of informed discussion. And many of these were ideas that were ignored or ridiculed or dismissed as self-evident nonsense at the time. We mentioned our opposition to busing to redress racial imbalance in schools. We saw this as a cowardly imposition on children carried out by adults who were unable to settle their issues of equality in a sensible fashion. Now it is commonly agreed, except by die-hard unreconstructed sixties liberals, that the experiment has failed and that something else will have to be done to give inner-city black children a fair shake. Again, for example, on the issue of mothers and children and their mutual bonding, we were sunk in a sea of feminist indignation which saw only abortion and day care as relevant issues. What is more, the medical establishment was either indifferent or opposed. Now there is a whole literature on mother-infant bonding, and the medical authorities have shifted their position significantly to allow hospitals to encourage rather than to thwart this natural process. And while day care is still a sacred cow and the route to salvation for many, it is at least now not unthinkable to investigate seriously its effects on children; indeed, this is being done.

We could mention several areas in which our scorned ideas of 1971 have become commonplaces of today's academic and public dialogue. Tiger's term "male bonding" seems to have passed into the language much as "inferiority complex" did. Again, our assertion that it was the quality of crowding, not the sheer density, which affected rates of violence was disputed by even those ethologists who otherwise approved our approach. Since then it has been announced as a "new" theory with considerable fanfare and hype, and generally accepted. We don't wish to point fingers. We are not after the priority prize in any of these matters. It is enough that our innocent deductions from the facts as we saw them are now agreed to be at least testable hypotheses and not simply errors of ideology. It heartens us, for instance, that on opening almost any serious health book today we come across passages like this:

Even if we are not 100 percent sure that a high-fiber diet helps prevent most of the diseases listed, common sense directs us to eat in a manner more closely resembling that of our ancestors, who were rarely bothered by these problems. Their diet consisted primarily of vegetables, whole grains, legumes and fruits. When meat was consumed, most evidence suggests that it was low in fat because it came not from deliberately fattened animals, as our meat does, but from animals that roamed long distances looking for food. (William Manahan, M.D., *Eat for Health*, 1988)

This splendid advice is attributed to "common sense." All we can say is that today's common sense is yesterday's ridiculous theories. This may seem a minor example, but it illustrates the penetration of evolutionary thinking down to the level of medical "common sense"—something that surely didn't exist in 1971. All in all, both at the highest scholarly levels and in everyday thinking, people are now much more inclined to ask the commonsense question: how would our ancestors have done it, and how does this relate to how we are doing it today? It is the inverse of the commonsense view that we grew up with that dismissed our evolutionary past as irrelevant and the investigation of it as immoral.

Above and beyond this we have seen an upsurge of concern for the survival of the species as a whole—the development of a "species-centered ethic" that we advocated. Again, this now seems so obvious, given the horrendous nature of our contemporary planet-wide problems, that it is assuming the mantle of a new orthodoxy, of a new "common sense." Thus what was dismissed as reactionary determinism twenty years ago turns out to be a radical necessity in the beleaguered world of the dawning 1990s. Our plea to treat ourselves as an endangered species, and hence to ask seriously "what kind of species are we?" seems less off the mark today than it did then. Even so, we still have to persuade the majority of our behavioral science colleagues that the only way to answer this question is to examine our evolutionary history. But the urgency of the issue will not wait upon their conversion. We had better ask that question, and ask it properly, if we are going to be around to do any behavioral science in the future. And if the scientists won't ask it, then the public will ask it for them. People are tired of seeing experts fiddle while the planet burns and their eternal optimistic belief in the omnipotence of science and technology is wearing a little thin.

One thing that strikes us forcefully in trying to assess the continuing relevance of our book is this: when we wrote it, although there was much dispute as to details, there was no dispute about the basic *scientific* nature of the argument we were all engaged in. While an intellectual slugfest was conducted, it was assumed by everyone concerned that what was at issue was the scientific status of what we were at. Harsh critics condemned us for being "unscientific" while enthusiasts saw us as creating a "new science," but no one questioned that this was the issue. This is not the case today. We are faced in the social sciences with an often less than dignified flight from science. This came about for many reasons, high among them the disillusionment with the prevailing school of functionalism which had dominated for so long that it seemed more than a school to some: it was the only possible form of social theory. It did not, however, deliver the scientific goods any more than behaviorism was doing in psychology. But while the psychologists responded by trying to develop a better scientific theory (as in cognitive science), the sociologists and anthropologists responded by throwing in the scientific towel. The anthropologists in particular were hoisted on their own relativist petard. Having preached moral and cultural relativism, they were helpless when the doctrine was turned against them and their own forms of analysis and explanation declared to be local folk science with no universal validity.

If our work continues to have a message, then, it is to reinforce a commitment to a scientific theory of society, but not one based on arbitrary functionalist premises. Our theory, or potential for theory, is rooted in the neo-Darwinian synthesis, rooted in natural science pure and simple, and not in some erroneous analogue of same. As such, it stands out as a clear, almost puritanical protest against the tides of hermeneutics, deconstructionism, critical theory, interpretive and symbolic anthropology, and all the other "humanistic" approaches to social behavior currently so fashionable. These are bound to founder on the rocks of their own arbitrariness. We would be the last to deny the influence of ideology even on natural science, but like our predecessors, we see this as something to be avoided, not erected into a theoretical virtue. We do not feel that because human beings have motives, intentions, and meanings, this exempts them from susceptibility to a scientific understanding. On the contrary, these human capacities have an evolutionary history as "hard" as the organs and skeletons of their bodies. If the latter can be "explained," so can they. The scientific paradigm was a hard-won victory, and it is a hard and uncompromising taskmaster. We sympathize with those who find it too demanding but if they can't stand the proverbial heat they should leave the proverbial kitchen.

Obviously in the twenty years since the book was written, the facts have changed, the theories have changed, and the world has changed, but what has not changed is your authors. We remain very different people in our approaches to life and learning and the societies we try to cope with. We began this project with no prior agreements about how to vote, why to vote, what to do about inheritance, housing the poor, taxing the rich. Mostly, as a matter of private record, we disagree; but we were out to get neither ourselves nor a chum elected nor an opponent banished from the polity. We didn't even know who our opponents were. One of us could even understand cricket; the other remained lamely baffled. We differed then, as now, politically, culturally, and personally.

This is worth stressing, since when two people write a book this integrated, there is a tendency to regard the authors as intellectual clones. One of the questions we are most commonly asked is "How did you write it?" This doesn't puzzle us, since we did it, but it does seem to baffle readers who know us. It is not just a technical question of joint composition—we'll come to that—but of the melding of views. The conclusions and recommendations seem so confident that they must, people insist, emanate from two minds in perfect concord.

This is news to us. The reason for whatever confidence that does inform the book is that far greater time was spent discussing each issue—the data to bear on it, the possible interpretations—than on the smooth assertion of political, religious, ideological, or even aesthetic certainties. We followed the argument, not walled it in or stormed it. We are both fortunately protected by sufficient intellectual confidence and work experience to assume that any challenge to a statement or opinion will send neither of us sobbing for recuperative haven. We could scorn positions while admiring their feckless proponent. We could admire the elegance of an argument while dismantling its basis. Each could accept six straight, better arguments from the other without thinking this made the tiniest difference to his respective value to the enterprise and without allowing the temporary winner to think he had to buy the after-hours booze of consolation.

Please give credit to the theory. We were fortunate to have a fertile, elaborate, exquisitely worked out theory of behavior and its evolution which was rooted in the generous intellectual hospitality of the Darwinian perception. We were its servants, and glad to be. There were new data, there was a world changing every day, there were exciting theories that seemed to promise a better understanding of more human behavior in a way that made both scientific sense and gave some hint of more civilized and fairer social arrangements which knowledge could help provide. Given this, what is the point of egoism, or solipsism, or dreary self-assertion? Of course there is none, and it was a joy to be able to focus in helpful concert with someone else on the substance of a problem and its solution not on its style or reputation.

A few notes more. We shared the whole process of the book as we shared exactly the money it earned, the perquisites it provided such as travel, and what approval or calumny it secured. This is easy to comprehend, but what appears to cause more people more puzzlement is how two people could actually write a book together. Did X write one chapter and Y the next? Did bold X really write it while surly Y wielded a fierce editorial pen? Did X do the recitative about monkeys and Y the aria on newborns?

No. We both had one sacred rule. Every single sentence had to be written with both perpetrators present. We followed this same rule in writing this new introduction. No taking home of manuscripts, no dividing up of chapters. Either could rewrite anything and rewrite everything, so much so that eventually we forgot totally who started and finished what, whose idea was this and whose caveat that. In the end what occurred was a kind of improvisation rather like jazz. A theme would be announced, worked over, run through and worked over again, to the point where the separate instruments blend into one sound. While the separateness is there, it is submerged in the joint product—which becomes the only thing that matters. We had fun writing it; we hope you have fun reading it. We also learned more through writing it together than we could ever have through solitary research. There is probably a moral in this about the biology of social behavior, a moral for the reader to draw.

1.

BEGINNING
BIOGRAMMAR

WE KNOW OURSELVES surprisingly well. The isolation of the individual is neither final nor merciless. We are none of us truly isolated; we are connected to one another by a web of regularities and by a host of shared, deep-seated certainties. People age, and their behavior changes. Males and females differ; their interaction and their separateness are trying, necessary, and exciting. Confident of these regularities, people seek to define their own special reproductive and erotic lives. Children are noisy and full of needs. Parents confront these needs with an astonishing certainty, and a hard—if superficially sentimental—commitment to a process they themselves started. Powerful people strut, and though the notion of power is as offensive to some as the strutting, there continue to be powerful people who continue to strut. There will always be black limousines; it is only the people in the black limousines who change. There will always be someone hunching in those seats in the same confident, heavy way. Humans need food, and from that need a breadwinner speaks to his fellows with a silent eloquence. A mother with her child makes demands that are universally acceptable to even the most ruthless despot or doctrinaire reformer. That bond is the expression of a wealth of understandings and the assertion of a forceful dictate: babies are important, growth is good; the mother and child are icons for our unspoken statements about the value of living

1

and persisting. In each small circle of people—wherever—there is the same pleasure and involvement in what is represented by the simple notice attached to the gates of palaces: "A child, Prince Henrik Fynn, was born at 9:30. . . ." The fact of birth is its own statement, widely understood.

The purpose of this book is twofold: to describe what is known about the evolution of human behavior, and then to try to show how the consequences of this evolution affect our behavior today. To do this we must draw from zoology, biology, history, and genetics. We must use the sophisticated techniques and many materials of the social sciences—the techniques with which, as social scientists, we are most familiar—to place man in the broad context of the natural world. The real and intellectual pressures forcing us to see ourselves as an endangered species demand an expansion of the vision of the social sciences. They demand a skeptical review of how we explain our political behavior, our economies, our leisure, our forms of education, and the recurring tragedy of war.

As conventionally trained students of human behavior we know we can explain a great deal with the techniques we conventionally use. But not enough. The sciences of behavior have an incomplete concept of what governs and constrains human action. They fail to take seriously enough the possibility that there is an authentic "human nature" —that just as we can define *Homo sapiens* by how he looks, we may be able to define him by the way he acts and by the social structures he sustains.

Viewing man as an endangered species helps us to focus on the most serious failure of social science—the failure to deal with the species as a whole. This is strange when we consider that in dealing with other animals we treat a species as an entity, a whole, a unit of evolutionary history; something that has come into the stream of organic life by a natural process, has adapted or failed to adapt, and, if it has failed, passed out of that stream again into the museums and preserving bottles.

A species often deals itself a bad hand, and we are no exception. But we are unique in that we can understand ourselves as a species. It is to this introspective and yet objective task that we address ourselves.

How do we achieve this understanding? Given a species of butterfly, and faced with the questions What is this species about? How did it get that way? Why does it do the things it does? What are its chances for survival?—how do we set about finding the answers? And will the techniques that will help us find them for our butterflies help us at all when we apply them to so elaborate an animal as man?

Zoologists and evolutionary biologists have led the search for such answers ever since Darwin revolutionized biology with his decisive concept of natural selection.[1] Species are not immutable; new species develop out of old ones; mutations in the genetic material which favor survival are preserved. The end product of such an evolution is, very simply, every contemporary species. Their anatomy and physiology are the result of trial and error and the sifting of genes over countless generations. A species is what it is because of the pattern of successful adaptation built into its genes. It is programmed to grow and develop in a highly specific way, and the program is transmitted from generation to generation in the genetic code. If we know enough, on the one hand, about the contemporary condition of a creature, and, on the other, about its evolutionary history, we will be able to answer the deliberately naïve questions: Why is it like it is? Why does it do what it does?

It is like it is because of the history of its adaptational strategies.[2] It does what it does because this behavior has paid off in the struggle for survival. But there is always the possibility that altered circumstances will make the strategy obsolete and even detrimental. If the obsolete strategy persists, the result is extinction. The adaptational strategies of the human species have clearly been highly successful, but their success seems in danger of backfiring. The circumstances *created* by these adaptational strategies are such that they cannot be *maintained* by them. The analogy with the hydrogen bomb is all too clear: the super weapon is so powerful that, if used, it will destroy everything—including the user.

If we are to begin to understand the impasse we have created for ourselves, we have to look at ourselves as a species—as the end product of a particular path of evolution. We have to look at the form of our bodies and the related structure of our behavior and ask: What is it for? What were the adaptational strategies that produced it? What were the circumstances that caused this particular mode of moving or behaving to be selected? Is the behavior that was selected still appropriate to life today? And if it is not, what can we do about it? We know that the striding walk—a form of locomotion peculiar to our species—was an adaptation to hunting life on the savannas.[3] But how much of our behavior is similarly adapted?

These are not easy questions. It is not even easy to know the right way to set about asking them. A good deal of conventional wisdom both inside and outside the sciences would deny the validity of an essentially biological approach. Nonetheless, man is just one species among all the others. As long as he reigned confident over the others, he could declare his independence of nature and get away with it. Now, when he is faced with his own possible demise, he has to recognize his commonality with the other species in at least this one unavoidable respect: that no species is sacrosanct—either it adapts or it disappears. There is, therefore, only one intellectual route left for a judicious appraisal of our future: coming to terms with the process of our own behavioral evolution in the past.

To this end we must try to discover the regularities of human behavior—of the behavior of man in society—and to understand them in terms of the adaptive significance they have had. Scientists have looked for regularities before and found them, but they have not necessarily put them into an evolutionary context. They have not seen them as end products of our evolutionary history; they have not treated man as a species, but as a conglomerate of diverse populations, nations, cultures. We are less concerned here with the differences than with the overwhelming similarities—what zoologists would call the "species specific" behavioral regularities that characterize all men at all times and that stem from the very nature of the animal species—*Homo sapiens*—we are dealing with.[4] For it is an article of scientific faith among Darwinians that any regularities that characterize a species must exist because of their adaptational significance in the evolution of the species. If we then ask how a species evolved and what the changing circumstances were that it was adapting to, we can begin to understand what on the surface often appears to be a bizarre piece of anatomy or a decidedly odd item of behavior. So, in asking these questions about the social behavior of man, we need whatever help we can get from the evidence of fossils and from the discoveries of social scientists about the uniformities and variations in our social systems.

To add to this explanatory mix the things we have in common with animals is at once to complicate by adding more data and yet to simplify by insisting that certain features of our behavior have already been observed and explained in other species. This is not a matter of seeking attractive analogies between human and animal ways, but of insisting that we are animals still and that things that are true for the rest of nature hold true for us too. In looking at how various species use, for example, complex social arrangements in the struggle for survival, we learn something about the use of society as an adaptive strategy, about its successes and its limitations. If men are men everywhere, so that studying one group of men will reveal something about all men, so animals are animals everywhere, and learning about the adaptational patterns of one species will tell us something about the processes of adaptation in all species. Including our own.

Our point of departure, then, is to treat man as an alien species, one whose behavior is as strange as an unknown foreign language. Faced with an unrecorded language, the linguist assumes very little except that the phonetic patterns can be recorded accurately, that the minimal units of meaning—the phonemes—can be isolated, and that ultimately the grammar of the language can be analyzed. He knows this because, however much the languages of mankind may differ in content, there has to be a regular relationship between the phonemes, morphemes, clauses, and sentences; and if the relationship is regular, then the code can be cracked.

But why this universal regularity? Because we are one species, and our spoken language—our particular and unique form of communication—is a common biological heritage. It is one of the end products of our evolution that demanded its own very complex kind of communication system. But every species has a system of communication that enables the animals to signal to one another their moods and intentions. And in every species it is the totality of the behavior of the animals that constitutes the communication system.[5] Ours is no exception. That we speak grammatically and behave in regular and predictable ways are both outcomes of our common evolutionary history rooted in our biology. A species tends to "enjoy" doing what has been important to its survival: sex and eating are the two most obvious examples. We enjoy both our verbal and our behavioral languages. And this enjoyment is matched by our intense curiosity, our drive to understand what our behavior is saying, our delight in exploring the behavioral biogrammar.

Biogrammar? Each species has a repertoire of signals—postures, gestures, movements—to communicate what the animals feel and what they plan to do. When a young Gelada baboon intrudes into the personal space of an irascible elder, the latter affects what looks to be a huge yawn but what is, on the contrary, a warning display of canine teeth and red gum tissue meant to intimidate the careless youngster.[6] When one herring gull lands on another's territory, the situation instantly becomes ambiguous. Male and female gulls look more or less the same to one another. The intruder may be either a challenging male to be fought, or an enterprising female to be courted. If the newcomer stares head on, it is a signal for a fight; if it wags its head, it is an invitation to seduction.[7] If one of the wives of a Hamadryas baboon strays too far and shows a friendly rump to a roving bachelor, her overlord will chase her and bite her on the neck—a part of her anatomy well enough padded to prevent damage but sensitive enough to remind her that, for better or for worse, she is part of an exclusive mating group.[8] If a human being gives something—real or incorporeal —to another, something will be given back. Even the Spanish beggar gives his blessing in return for alms.[9] A female chimpanzee who has left her band to give birth to a new member does not simply rejoin without ceremony. She approaches the old males of the band with hand outstretched in a begging gesture; the old males touch her palm or stroke the back of her neck; only then will she rejoin the females of the group.[10]

All these examples, taken more or less at random from the behavioral repertoires of various animal species, may vary in complexity as one ascends the scale of evolution. But for any species a set of predictable transactions could be drawn up to show how they interact or occur in sequence, how they can be modified, under what circumstances they will be applied, and, finally, how they help the species survive. The total repertoire of possible behaviors of any species is sometimes called the "biogram."[11] But this is a static list; to understand how the elements in the list are related, we need to know the rules that govern the relationships. For although the language of behavior is readily intelligible to whatever species speaks it, it can seem no more than gibberish to the outsider. A foreign language is an unintelligible stream of noise to a nonspeaker, who, however, armed with a grammar, can begin to make sense of it, to isolate elements, and eventually to put them together and communicate. In short, he learns the rules. In order to understand the language of behavior, we need a comparable set of rules for the biogram—the biogrammar, a relatively small word on which hang all the major questions of social science.

These rules describe the principles on which the language of behavior works, though they offer no certainty as to what individuals are going to do. The actual watchfulness and relative viciousness of the hamadryas male will vary from one to another and from circumstance to circumstance, but the response to provocation will invariably be the neck bite and not something else. The form and content of human gift-giving vary enormously, but behind each of its many manifestations the ground rules of reciprocity operate just as surely as the rules relating subject to predicate lie behind all the rich and unpredictable outpourings of Romance languages. Within the limits set by the rules, there is room for eloquence as well as plain speaking. Even those who like to say how much they hate the crabbiness of perfect grammar must observe its rules. If they did not, their words would fail to make sense to anyone else.

If the rules of language are not observed, verbal communication breaks down, and the result is gibberish; if the rules of behavior for a species are not observed, social communication breaks down, and the result is behavioral gibberish. Most people want—and need—to understand one another. They try, as hard as they can, *not* to talk gibberish. But at the behavioral level, in their own species at least, they seem constantly to verge on breakdown.

In this book we want to search for some of the principles on which behavioral literacy should be based.

To do this we have to discover those elusive ground rules and those elements of human behavior that are the lexicon of social action. Here we run into the controversy that has plagued the social sciences since Darwin first forced on us the recognition of our cousinship with the beast. Can the underlying structure of behavior be *bio*grammatical, rooted in the biology of the species? Can elements of our own behavior be compared with the animal biogrammar?[12]

To a large section of the social-science establishment such a comparison would be anathema—however obvious it may be to the intelligent animal lover. But, again and yet again, man *is* an animal. He has evolved as other animals: he is a vertebrate, a mammal, a member of the order Primates. How, then, can the same principles of analysis that we apply to the study of the animal kingdom at large not be applied to him?

Once upon a time people actually doubted that there was any *physical* continuity between humans and animals.[13] This is astonishing to us now, and yet it appears likely that it will seem equally bizarre in fifty years that many sensible people—even many of the scientists paid and trained to know better—claimed that there was no significant and analyzable continuity between the *behavior* of humans and other animals. It isn't only a view of man that is involved, but rather a whole sense of nature and the process of living things and the system

of beings—in other words, a world view which encompasses a man
view. The artist Francis Bacon paints decomposing slabs of meat,
obscene popes, people whose flesh is already almost part of the air surrounding them; in their state of nature even the envelope of their skin
is gapingly open. Bacon's vision is that all animals exchange being
with their whole environment; nothing is crisp and particular, everything blends. The digestive guts of a chimpanzee and of a man are both
wet and colorful, and both are arenas for the interaction of chemicals
and food. If we are related so irrevocably in our very centers, it is
going to be hard to argue that we are unrelated at the extensions of
those centers—our behavior. The duke and the chimp are fellow
citizens in the democracy of nature. What unites them is as important
as what divides them. The distinctions which obviously do exist are the
more intriguing and important precisely because the duke and the
chimp both share the inexorable fact of a common primate, even mammalian history.

In fact, the only way we can understand the exact nature of the
distinction between man and animal is by first looking at what they
have in common. It has long been held, out of ideology, ignorance, and
just plain fear, that man is unique in the animal world, that the difference between him and brute nature is a difference not of degree but of
kind. A comforting abyss separates the semidivine human from the
dumb brute—no matter that the demigod has the body of a brute.
For brutes, so goes the catechism, do not have souls or minds, reason or
foresight, wisdom or culture, language or opposable thumbs, fire or
any one of a host of attributes that set man "above" nature, exclude
biology in favor of culture, and enable him to "triumph" over mere
animality.

Man's body is unique; so is his behavior. And in both his body and
his behavior the uniqueness represents very special biological adaptations built in by the exacting process of natural selection. The point
is not that man has shed or risen above his primate nature, but, simply,
that he is a unique primate with a unique primate nature. But every
species is unique in its specializations—that is, after all, how we tell
them apart; and it is often easier, if they are closely related, to tell
them apart by their behavior than by their anatomy and physiology.[14]
Behavior is as much a part of the evolutionary process as anatomy.
The head-wagging of the herring gull is as essential to its survival and
success as its wings are. It is *how the animal performs* that determines
its chances of survival. Sexual anatomy is ingeniously adaptive, but it

is sexual behavior that determines which characteristics will appear in the next generation; the magnificence of an individual hamadryas baboon's genitalia will not ensure it genetic immortality unless it manages its neck-biting act successfully.

The uniqueness of man's body does not represent a difference in kind between him and his primate cousins. It represents a series of often trying specializations. The most obvious of these is permanent bipedalism.[15] Other primates are able to walk on two legs, but most of the time they do not. Man made this change as he adapted to a hunting life on the hot savannas. His spine straightened, his pelvis narrowed, his ankle bone solidified, his buttocks expanded, his head balanced precariously on top of the spine. The outcome of all this was the striding walk—the most efficient and least fatiguing way to cover long distances.

In the same adaptive context the frontal lobes of the brain grew in both size and complexity; the outcome of this was an increase in intelligence, articulate speech, greater learning capacity, foresight, and the overall ability to process more and more complex data.[16] But the other primates have brains with frontal lobes, too. The other primates have spines and a pelvis, too. They are different because they have specialized differently in response to different evolutionary problems. The gibbon has specialized in long arms and the ability to swing gracefully through the trees; the gorilla in great size and the ability to digest stems and roots; the baboon in quadrupedalism, large canines, and high speed; man in bipedalism, the striding walk, and the enlarged brain.[17]

Even so, these anatomical specializations in a sense have a kind of either/or quality not always found in behavioral differences. Either a primate has a large brain or he does not; either a primate has the striding walk or he does not. The physical differences are thus clear-cut, whereas, with the exception of language, the behavioral differences are not. Everyone except the hardiest fundamentalists understands that bodily continuities exist and are even obvious. But our suspicion is that behavioral continuities are even more obvious. No one saw the anatomical continuity between man and the other primates, because no one looked for it. The feeling that there is a great and unbridgeable gulf between human and animal behavior also has resulted from a failure to look closely and think comparatively. A theoretical blindness about physical structure has been replaced by a theoretical blindness about behavior.

Of course we have cultures, of course we have symbols, of course we have Beethoven, Stravinsky, and Paul McCartney; clearly, we are the only species with the Koran, the Bible, the Torah, and the Communist Manifesto. And of course we boast a plastics industry, supersonic fighters, remedial-reading courses, custom-made jewelry, Ferraris, and crêpes suzette. We are the only primates who make things and then lose them and then dig them up and place them in museums.

And surely no one has a more complicated (and probably unworkable) educational system in all of nature. No one but a human could take our kinship systems seriously. We are perhaps the only species that selects certain especially endowed females for purposes of communal worship because of their sexual magic. And certainly the only species that covers those very sexual organs whose energetic exercise we seem to crave and in which we seem to have a particular if private pride. Only people plant flowers.

But what can be expected from this kind of animal? We do these things because these are the things that this animal does. Given an animal endowed with the biological capacity to produce and attach itself to symbols, we can confidently predict a range of bizarre outcomes. Endow our hamadryas baboon with the same capacity, and the simple neck-biting procedure would burgeon into weird, beautiful, or grotesque variants. In one community the punishment might take the shape of attaching the errant wife to a painted post by a collar made of carved ivory fitted with spikes; in another there might be a ceremonial public humiliation in which the chief of the band cut off the transgressor's hair and branded her neck with a red-hot sword; in yet another the husband might lead her around the camp in a halter while the women of his harem sang ribald and satirical songs; in another she might be hanged by the neck until dead. The only limit to the variety of punishments would be the limits of the imagination of the species.

The same can be said about the rituals of courtship. Everywhere in human society this activity is carried on. In some places girls put hibiscus flowers behind their ears, in others they put on a date's fraternity pin, but everywhere they announce by symbolic devices of one kind or another that they are in the running and ready to run. The content of courtship practices may vary a good deal, but the process itself is universal.

At first glance the bewildering variety of customs suggests that humans can invent any kind of culture with any kind of processes.

But on closer scrutiny it turns out that while the variations are almost endless, the themes are restricted in number, and are, in all cultures, the fixed points on which the system turns. The story can be told in many different ways, but the plot and the characters remain the same.

Universal processes, however, do not necessarily have universal results, nor do they give birth to identical institutions. This holds true even in the plant world; the same plant going through the same life processes will look totally different at maturity, according to where it was grown and what the history of its growth has been. But it *is* the same plant. In the same way, human culture can flower and wither. But because we are the kind of animal we are, there will be fixed points in the culture's development and routines which are as predictable as the neck bite of the baboon.

We inevitably produce culture, and culture inevitably varies from population to population. Of course, human beings will do human things, and baboons will do baboon things. Dealing with this variation is a problem, because the ideology dies hard that the division between us and the brutes is that brute behavior is passed on genetically, while ours is passed on culturally—by processes of teaching and learning, couched in symbols and particularly in language. This ideology has it that the little baboon is born with a bundle of genes to guide his life down to the last detail, and that, though learning will play some part in his behavior, the use of symbols, foresight, and the application of intelligence will not. He will bite his consort's neck because his genes tell him to, not because his culture has made it a rule. He will collect a harem because the instruction to do so rests in his genetic code, not because polygamy is an invention of his tribe and one of its laws. He will adopt young female infants as prospective brides because this is one of the things baboons cannot help doing, not because child betrothal is encouraged by his religious code.

Not only is this an oversimplified view of animals—particularly of our nearest relatives—but it poses an unreal dichotomy. Here it is useful to employ a term of polite abuse: the "culturalist" view. This assumes that the human infant is a *tabula rasa*—a blank slate—unencumbered with the imperative, instinctive demands that manipulate animals. All the infant has is intelligence—and the capacity to learn anything it is taught. Thus, goes the claim, any culture can write anything it likes on the blank slate, limited only by physiology and the laws of learning discovered by behavioral psychologists. Of course, the culture cannot demand that the infant fly or lay eggs or live underwater. It must reinforce learning properly, through reward and punishment, in order to condition the organism to conform to the mores of the clan, tribe, class, or nation involved. The organism is a receptor and capable of learning anything that is properly fed into it. It will break down only if the conditioning process is ineptly applied. There are, in this view, theoretically no limits to the learning process, and the incredible and arbitrary variety of human cultures testify to this. What is more, in this ideology *all* cultures are invention. They may rest on certain universal needs and emotions but these have little specific effect. It is argued, for example, that the sex need does nothing to explain why some cultures are monogamous and others polygamous. (The fact that whatever the rules, all cultures are adulterous, and that it is the women who get punished, is overlooked.) In this theory, the need for food (or "hunger drive") does not explain the variety of food taboos, nor the need for shelter the incredible variety of human architecture.[18]

At the level of specific content this view is perfectly true. It has been suggested that the existence of a grammar does *not* enable us to predict what people are going to say; it tells us only how they must say it in order to be understood. So the question has to be faced: Are the only rules of human behavior those of learning psychology, or is there something else in human beings that produces regularities that, despite their surface differences, crop up in society after society?

Again, the comparison with language is useful. On the *tabula rasa* principle, all language must be learned by the processes of imitation, reward, and punishment. But modern linguists argue that this is an impossible position to sustain—as any parent will quickly understand. Linguists like Chomsky and psychologists like Lenneberg argue that the capacity for grammatical speech is somehow "in" the brain, as the capacity to walk is somehow "in" the body, and matures as the child matures.[19] The child learns because it has a cerebral *language-acquisition device* that enables it to learn rules for the production of sentences it has never heard before. The device enables it to process data and deduce rules. Most importantly, the rules of child speech are not just poor imitations of adult grammar; they are based on rules of sentence production appropriate to the child's level of maturity.

Thus every child has the capacity for grammatical speech, and is ready to be programmed with whatever specific grammar its culture provides. The specific grammars are many and various, like the cultures in which they are used. There is no "explanation" for why one grammar does what it does, as opposed to any other. Nevertheless the speech patterns of all languages are known to operate on a few basic principles, which linguists have identified. The grammatical patterns may well also be reducible in this way once what Chomsky calls the "deep structures" of all languages are known. Then we can write the "universal grammar," which will tell us the principles on which all particular grammars rest. Even at this point in our understanding, no language exists that a linguist cannot record with the universal phonetic alphabet in the first place and analyze with universally applicable techniques of semantic analysis in the second. This can be done, because, despite the variety of surface grammars, languages are all doing the same job, and in a limited number of ways.

In the same way, *all* the rest of human culture lies in the biology of the species. We have a *culture-acquisition device* constraining us to produce recognizable and analyzable human cultures, just as we must produce recognizable human languages, however varied the local manifestations may be. Just as a child can learn only a language that follows the "normal" rules of grammar for human languages, he can learn only a grammar of behavior that follows the parallel rules of the biogrammar. Of course, in either case, a departure from normal grammar may be tried, but the likelihood is that it will end only in gibberish.

This view of human behavior is very different from that of the culturalists or the behaviorists. It makes the organism an active, searching, and stubborn participant in the learning process, rather than just a receiver; it suggests that the teacher is as moved to teach in a certain way as the pupil is to learn. The slate here is not blank at all; it is doing a lot of its own writing.

If all behavior, including linguistic behavior, is simply the result of cultural conditioning, then the logical conclusion is that if ever a new generation were cut off from tradition, it would be unlikely to invent one again. In this view, human culture does not stem in a direct way from human nature, but is, rather, a precious accumulation of unique skills and knowledge that must be passed on or be lost.

But is it? As far as language is concerned, at least two monarchs in history have had their doubts. Would untutored children speak, they asked? The Egyptian Psamtik I (in the seventh century B.C.) and James IV of Scotland (in the fifteenth century of the Christian era) are both reputed to have tried isolating children at birth and leaving them to grow up without human communication, to see what language, if any, they would speak. Perhaps King James's pious hope that it would be Hebrew may have been somewhat optimistic, but his belief that they could invent a language without ever having been taught one is theoretically justifiable. This invented language, although totally different from any known to us, would be analyzable by linguists on the same basis as any other language, and thus translatable into all known languages.

The experiment can be extended. If our children could survive and breed—still in isolation from any cultural influences—then eventually their descendants would produce a society and culture recognizably human in all its details. But even if its content differed from any we have so far seen, even if it had different gods, devils, and theories, bizarre marriage rules and obsequies, its scheme could be identified by biogrammarians. Its status structure could boast untold absurdities and countless seemingly trivial distinctions. But there would be a status system and it would therefore not be trivial. Perhaps the culture would subject its young to ferocious ceremonies of initiation. But there would be ceremonies, and they would be initiated. It could use or treat schizophrenia in wholly unexpected ways; but a biogrammarian would recognize the type and note it down in his rapidly expanding behavioral lexicon. Such things, and more, would be there because *Homo sapiens* is the kind of animal he is.

And if the feral children-parents, Adam and Eve, could survive and breed despite their isolation from the influences of culture, we can be reasonably sure that they would do a predictable variety of things: they would spawn a society with laws about incest and how and whom to marry; rules about property; habits of taboo and ritual avoidance. They would defer to the supernatural and try to control it in some regular fashion. They too would have their initiations; they would foment courtship ceremonies and fuss elaborately about the adornment of young females. Men would do certain things which excluded women; in some of these all-male associations secrecy would hold the members together as surely as prison walls. Some intriguing form of gambling would probably go on. Weapons and tools would be made. Our biogrammarian would be sure to find the following, too: myths and legends, dancing, psychosis and neurosis, adultery, homosexuality, homicide, suicide, loyalty, desertion, juvenile delinquents, senile fools, and various shrewd practitioners to cure or take advantage of the various ills from which communities and people suffer.

This picture of the behavioral infrastructure of human societies may seem little more than a tridimensional comment about human reality—that we became this way, we are this way, and we will be this way for a long time still: a human is a human is a human. But it is not so simple as that. To understand it we must turn to the new data and theory which permit us to insist on the continuity of human experience over long periods of time, and to assert the real effect of biological control even though the weight of our intellectual history and the aggressive optimism of our progressivist leaders deny us the ambiguous luxury of attributing at least some of what we are to . . . what we are.

Without any exposure to cultural traditions, our isolated tribe would develop very specific and highly complex cultural patterns, and probably very quickly—a matter of a few generations, once they got a language going. And they would do this for the same reason that the baboons produce a baboon social system in captivity —because it is in the beast. Baboons—primates—humans have not only a very general physical capacity to learn, they have a programmed preference to learn some things rather than others, and to learn some things more easily than others.

It is not *instincts* in any old-fashioned sense that are at issue here; initiation ceremonies and male rituals are not "instinctive." They emerge from the biology of an animal programmed to produce them, once it is given the appropriate stimuli. Without these stimuli, there will be no behavior, or only a modified or distorted form of it. The human organism is like a computer that is set up or "wired" in a particular way. It is always in a state of readiness —at successive points in the life cycle—to process certain kinds of information and to produce certain kinds of information. To be sure, the information has to be of a specific type in order to be processed, but its content can vary a great deal. Once the information is received, the computer stores it and goes onto the next task. If the system is confused—if, for example, adult programs are fed to adolescent computers—then the fuses blow and there is risk of breakdown. This analogy pushed to its logical conclusion would yield a bizarre science-fiction world in which computers fed one another information—thus simulating the human condition. Only when they were synchronized would the system run smoothly.

This model of human behavior, although stark, really does differ decisively from that favored by either instinctivists or culturalists. To the instinctivists, behavior resulted simply from the manifestation of innate tendencies like "maternalism," "self-abasement," and "acquisitiveness." The theory failed because it ended up as little more than a list of ever-more-specific human attributes.[20] Culturalists hold that if cultures are similar it is because the same basic "needs," or "functional prerequisites," must be met in them all, and because the laws of "conditioning" are universally applicable.[21]

But an alternative, if more moderate, view may be offered in the biological context: that is, that the human organism is "wired" in a certain way so that it can process and emit information about certain facts of social life such as language and rules about sex, and that, furthermore, it can process this information only at certain times and only in certain ways. The wiring is geared to the life cycle so that at any one moment in a population of *Homo sapiens* there will be individuals with a certain "store" of behavior giving out information at another stage to others who are wired to treat this information in a particular way. The outcome of the interaction of these individuals will be certain "typical" relationships.

There is nothing specific in the genetic code about initiation ceremonies for young males. There are no instructions about circumcision whizzing around the bends of the alpha helix. But neither are male initiation ceremonies pure cultural inventions—results of the free activity of the intellect. They occur because we are biologically wired the way we are. We can predict how older and younger males in a community will relate to one another because of the way their wiring allows them to be programmed and to program them in turn. In postadolescent males the genetic message is one of sinister and often undirected rebelliousness; this threatening information is received by older males, whose steadier hormonal systems go into a reaction and insist on containment. So all societies find ways of taming and using the young men and of forcing them to identify with the system. There is, theoretically, a variety of ways of doing this, but relatively few are used. Not only does it appear that we have to stick to the grammar, but to a relative modesty of vocabulary and expression as well.

Of course, the particular transaction between older and younger males called initiation does not always result in a specific ceremony; but it is always at the very least a process. Young braves are subjected to it; so are graduate students, junior executives, apprentices, novices in religious orders, even outlaw gangs. Of course, the initiation need not always "take": for example, one might argue that some of the difficulty universities throughout the world are having with the simple problem of discipline—let alone the more trying one of actually teaching and discovering—is that as a system of initiation, the university is far too arbitrary, unsatisfying, and undemanding for the young men concerned. No brave would count it a particular honor to triumph in history at Berkeley or Bombay. The challenge is somehow unmanly and the challengers themselves vaguely laughable and inept. It now seems to take a special faith to accept the value of the life of the mind; a good many twenty-year-olds lack the faith and reject the challenge. The university crisis is a good example of feeding the wrong program at the wrong time to the people. Perhaps more explicit, ceremonial, and physical initiation processes would "solve" the problem (though these are clearly unfashionable at present). Perhaps they will not. Nonetheless, we may have to be prepared as a community to consider novel and unexpected ways of reordering our educational practices to accord more faithfully to the biogrammatical dictates, to which—our suggestion is—we have to yield at least a little or endure a lot.[22]

We have confidently asserted that identifiable propensities for behavior are in the wiring. Unless we look to divine intervention, these got there by the same route as they got into the wiring of any other animal: by mutation and natural selection. One of the sturdiest theories in science, widely and agreeably accepted, is that animals vary along a normal curve in a number of respects, and that selection occurs in terms of this curve. Taller giraffes could secure more food and consequently reproduce more and better offspring—which is why they developed long necks. Early turtles with hard backs could survive their enemies by withdrawing behind a shelter of their own; they lived to endow their successors with this specialized characteristic. The broad outlines of the theory, and the process, are clear and indisputable: biological change results from a knowable and known procedure.[23]

This is easily seen when physical characteristics change through selection. More subtle and more exciting is the matter of behavioral evolution, which the science of ethology has forced us to recognize as a central issue.[24] We can readily see that species can be defined physically, but as we get better information about how they behave in natural settings, we begin to see how they can be classified behaviorally. The implication here is important: regularities of behavior are as predictable and discernible as the color of plumage and the shape of eggs. But how is this regularity controlled? Why is it that, while almost anything can happen in principle, only a limited and specialized set of actions occurs in practice?

Back to the wiring, and back to the new data we have about genetics and the control of living systems. Though we have known for many years how genetic systems worked, breaking the genetic code—the structure of the DNA molecule—allowed a rather hardheaded species to see with its own eyes how the life of an animal was controlled by facts of nature as comprehensible as a computer program.[25] The genetic code *is* a program, and it *is* a way of transmitting a program from generation to generation. DNA is immensely complex in itself and in what it does, but its overriding work is carrying from the parents to the offspring a program that includes behavior as well as body shape, color, and sense of smell. The most obvious program is the life cycle itself, which is both profoundly physical and profoundly behavioral at the same time.[26] The caterpillar turns into a butterfly in an astonishing display of life-cycling. The human infant begins to smile at a predictable time, and the boy soon loses his shrillness and darting lightness and becomes a character more uncertain, more portentous, more annoying to his elders. He is, without doubt, a different creature, and all at once subject to forces even free will and the force of government cannot hold back. His behavior changes as it is programmed to do. He is wired so that this will happen, and indeed not only human boys but also young males in many other primate groups suffer the scorn of their elders and the uncertainty of a transition from one difficult role to another. It is as much a behavior as dying. The geneticist J. Z. Young once defined death as "what happens when there is no longer a program to repair the program to repair the program to repair the program . . . etc., etc." It is unnecessary to labor the point that living involves successful programs and that successful behavioral programs are as much a result of natural selection as the opposable thumb and the reproductive differences between men and women.

The unique outcome of the human wiring is human cultural behavior, with its rich symbolic content, its complex social traditions,

and its nongenetic mode of transferring information from one generation to another. But how did the human animal get wired for culture
in the first place? The theory used to be that, for some reason or
other, at some time or other, the human brain expanded to the point
where it was capable of producing first symbols and then culture.[27]
This no longer seems plausible.[28] Our little-brained ape-man ancestors
of two million years ago—with skull spaces no larger than a gorilla's
—were doing cultural things. For a start, they were making tools
of bone and stone.[29] At first glance this may not seem a great leap
forward (after all, the rudiments of toolmaking occur in chimpanzees),[30] but it implies that these creatures were organizing their experience in a manner that was already typically human. They had
diverged from the rest of the primates as surely in this respect as in
the upright stance and the splayed big toe, and this divergence was
a consequence of the momentous transition from vegetarianism to
systematic hunting. It was *after* they started doing cultural things
that the brain grew in size and complexity[31]—for the making of
butchering tools to deal with the proceeds of cooperative hunting
implies foresight and planning, a complex system of cooperation, and
a division of labor that in turn presupposes some fairly advanced
form of communication.[32] Obviously there was a selective advantage
to cultural behavior, as in the clear cases of the hard shell of the
turtle and the neck of the giraffe. There was a premium on an animal
which could learn a lot and learn it quickly and which did not
depend too heavily on direct instructions from the genes for each
item of behavior. Selection favored the smarter animals, and they
in turn bred smarter ones still, whose skills and cunning enabled
them to survive and flourish. But this process constantly created a
new environment for the human animal—an environment of its own
making. Once the animal became dependent for survival on speech,
for example, selection would favor whatever mutations produced
some improvement in the speech organs;[33] if the variable were imagination, selection would operate in the same way. The genetic
qualities that favored scientific activity or associative learning,
"general intelligence" or the ability to inhibit present gratification
in anticipation of future wants, or the propensity to obey rules, would
be subject to selection as much as the muscular qualities that facili-
tated the striding walk.[34]

Obeying rules is important: the animal had not only to do things,
but *not* to do them as well.[35] It was beginning to shed its dependency
on the precarious certainty of instinct, but it still had to get done—

somehow—the jobs that instinct did for other animals. It substituted customs and habits, but these had nonetheless to be obeyed like instincts, and they had to be almost semiautomatic to be successful.[36] Selection, then, clearly favored those creatures with a propensity to obey rules, to feel guilty about breaking them, and, generally, to control their sexual and aggressive tendencies enough to let otherwise recalcitrant individuals form a working society. In a real sense, this yielded citizens more effective for the evolving human social group and its evolving cultural patterns. Selection put into the actual wiring those qualities and propensities that made for a successful social and cultural animal. It left a lot of variety, of course —that is nature's way.

What happened was that culture itself became a selection pressure that favored animals with attributes which served a culture-bearing creature.[37] Man became dependent on cultural modes of surviving: the more capable of cultural behavior he was, the more he prospered. And the result was an animal that is not only the producer of culture but its product as well. It is not surprising that man is driven to produce that which produced him.[38]

In sum: we behave culturally because it is in our nature to behave culturally, because natural selection has produced an animal that has to behave culturally, that has to invent rules, make myths, speak languages, and form men's clubs, in the same way that the hamadryas baboon has to form harems, adopt infants, and bite its wives on the neck.[39]

We fail to appreciate this infrastructure of our cultural behavior because our perspective on ourselves as a species is chronically limited. To most of us a generation is a long time. How many people can grasp with any constructive imagination the period of a life span? To all of us the period of known history is a very long time and fades into indistinction with the advent of civilization. But that five thousand years which is civilization is, in evolutionary terms, as but an evening gone. From the perspective of the evolution of the species, nothing much has happened in that period except an unprecedented rise in population. It is just an episode. Given the right perspective, everything is just an episode. The order of Primates, our order, is a seventy-million-year-old episode in the history of the mammals—itself an episode in the history of the vertebrates, itself an espisode in the history of organic life. The line leading to man probably broke off from the other primates more than twenty million years ago,[40] while indisputable remains of our ape-man ancestor—*Australopithecus*—date back some five and one-half million years.[41] The first upright and big-brained human—*Homo erectus*[42]—is usually credited with about one million years of history. *Homo sapiens* is half a million years old, while the appearance of truly modern man—*Cro-Magnon*—dates from forty or fifty thousand years ago.[43]

This is our time scale for the evolution not only of physique but also of social behavior, emotions, patterns of learning, loving, and hating. Stored in the older parts of the brain are all those codes and messages held over from that ancient time—the heat of the jungle past and the long drag on the Pliocene savannas. Surrounding and coming to terms with this old brain is a new brain forged mostly in the cool-to-icy environment of the Pleistocene and the touch-and-go battle with the snaking ice.[44] And since then? Fire is maybe half a million years old; agriculture at least ten thousand years; large settlements five thousand; elaborate cities three thousand; steam power and industrial explosion a mere two hundred. Nuclear man appeared yesterday.

If we made an hour-long film to represent the history of tool-making man, industrial man would flash by in a few seconds at the end—he would barely be seen. Yet it is only the flashy and tortured complexity of industrial man that is so often taken to be truly human. Or, at best, we use civilized man as our model. But civilized man is an evolutionary afterthought. We remain Upper Paleolithic hunters, fine-honed machines designed for the efficient pursuit of game. Nothing worth noting has happened in our evolutionary history since we left off hunting and took to the fields and the towns—nothing except perhaps a little selection for immunity to epidemics, and probably not even that.[45] "Man the hunter" is not an episode in our distant past: we are still man the hunter, incarcerated, domesticated, polluted, crowded, and bemused.

We have overtaken ourselves with those fantasy structures called civilizations, and with the sheer overpowering growth of our numbers. For most of our hunting past—for ninety-nine percent of our history —the population of the species stayed steady at about one million. With the dawn of agriculture it leaped to one hundred million. Since the advent of industry it has reached 3,700 million, and by the year 2000 it will be 7,000 million. A creature evolved for living in bands of 50 or so cannot but have problems with such a series of population explosions and their organizational consequences. Most of what we take for granted in human nature is in fact an end product of the pathological events attendant on the incarceration of our hunting selves. We are all in this together, treading on one another's toes.

Without a grasp of this perspective we will never understand ourselves or our societies or the sustaining and yet undermining role of our culture-producing brains. We have to make the imaginative and unsettling leap into understanding that *agricultural and industrial civilizations have put nothing into the basic wiring of the human animal.* We are wired for hunting—for the emotions, the excitements, the curiosities, the regularities, the fears, and the social relationships that were needed to survive in the hunting way of life. And we are wired basically on a primate model. This primate wiring was adjusted and readjusted for over seventy million years before we emerged as distinct from the rest of our order. In this perspective even the forebrain is an afterthought. The cerebral cortex struggles with a heritage it did not ask for and has frequently wished aloud it did not have.[46] "What art thou, O Man, when thou art full of lust?" said an anguished prophet. What, when thou art full of compassion, or ambition, or the urge to exchange, or the pleasure in taking risks, or the skill in dealing with associates, or the compulsion to explore, or the need to be talked to?

Ours is a heritage stretching over millions of years of the primate hunting past and capped by a recently acquired symbolizing brain. Yet we are still living inside our own skulls and feeding on our fantasies. When we see how helpless we are to prevent war and civil violence, when we rail against the pollution of our air and rivers, when we find ourselves unable to bridge the gap of understanding between old and young, when we watch our cities fall into greater and grimier decay, when we come up against the seemingly inexorable nature of racial conflict and religious prejudice—when, in short, we look at or hide from the progressively awful spectacle we present to ourselves, we can react only in terms of what our intellect offers us as alibis. We blame the decline of monopoly capitalism, the communist conspiracy, the military-industrial complex, the corruption of the powerful, the permissiveness of parents, the viciousness of the right or the subversiveness of the left, the falling away from God, affluence, imperialism, racism, Marxism, the cult of youth, overpopulation, the shadow of the bomb, and the innate brutality of man.

But in the cold eye of nature we are just another species in trouble. This has happened before, and there were no conspirators to blame then. If a species fails to adapt, it does not survive. It is finally as simple as that. It did the tyrannosaurs no good to blame one another for their failure. They could not adapt to reality, and they became extinct. If and when we are gone, our quarrels about which of us was to blame will merely seem funny—except that there will be nobody there to laugh. We are the first species to hold in its own hands the power to affect consciously its own survival. But this can be achieved only if we know ourselves as a species, and, more important, *sense* ourselves as a species, and, in the last resort, *act* as a species in the interests of the species as a whole.

2.

POLITICAL
NATURE

WE USUALLY THINK of politics as a highly specialized affair involving special people called politicians, an affair that, moreover, touches people at large only when their votes are wanted or their taxes are collected. We harbor a regiment of people called political scientists who carefully inspect what politicians do, and who develop ideas about something called the "political system." But in our earnestness we have forgotten what it is all about, and why, in the first place, we have politics at all.

Analogies are often drawn between human and ant societies.[1] There are, to be sure, striking similarities—such as division of labor, caste system, and domestication of other creatures—but the analogy breaks down at one fundamental point: human societies are political, and ant societies are apolitical. The social order of an ant colony is genetically fixed. Workers are workers, drones drones, queens queens, soldiers soldiers, and so on. Workers cannot usurp power in the colony, because they are genetically programmed to be workers and nothing else. There can be no redistribution of power, of place, and, most importantly, of breeding ability, and therefore of contribution to the genetic pool. This is a critical difference. Politics involves the possibility of changing the distribution of resources in a society—one of which is the control over the future that breeding allows. The political process—the process of redistributing control over resources among the individuals of a group—is, in evolutionary terms, a breeding process. The political system is a breeding system. When we apply the word "lust" to both power and sex, we are nearer the truth than we imagine. In the struggle for reproductive advantage, some do better than others. It is this that changes the distribution of genes in a population and affects its genetic future. This is a world of winners and losers, a world of politics—of the haves and the have-nots, of those who have made it and those who sulk on the sidelines.

God was notably astute in arranging Eden: there was one male and one female and no politics. The question could not arise of who had access to Eve and who had sons and daughters, and who could see in a small living creature a reassuring echo of his own existence. Politics as a process began when the wicked snake competed with Adam for the loyalty of Eve, when innocence was lost because good and evil—that is to say, the possibility of choice—sharply disrupted what promised to become one of the most tedious perfections of all creation. From that time on, the species has been irretrievably concerned with who can marry whom and with the relationship between position, property, and productive copulation.

The result of the reproductive struggle is a social system that is profoundly hierarchical and competitive. And if human politics exhibits a constant tension between the communally valued ideal of equality and the privately valued aim of happy inequality, then this is simply a reflection of our evolutionary history. The imaginative brain —our means of pursuing this equality—developed long after those deeper primate motives devoted to the pursuit of unfair shares and an unequal access to control over genes and privilege. This ancient pursuit, however, had its own set of ground rules, and we are heirs to its inhibitions as much as to its lusts. To compete we must cooperate as well as fight. To dominate we must be merciful as well as ruthless. We must be, in a word, political. Our own political behavior and ideologies should be explored in the context of Aristotle's dictum that man is, *by nature*, a political animal; that he is the only animal with empires, justice, and formalized welfare, but that he remains an animal nevertheless.

Society has been an important weapon in the struggle for survival of many animal species.[2] It is, of course, possible to survive by adopting the solitary life—except for brief mating periods—but it is also something of a dead end. The beginning of society is gregariousness, but that alone is not enough. Fish and birds flock, ungulates wander about in herds, but often they have only the rudiments of society. The individual members respond to one another, not so much as individuals as other members of the flock or herd moving in certain directions and taking up certain space. A herd or flock or school is like a wave in which the members are drops of water: the flock undulates and ripples in response to the attraction of food or the sense of danger, but it is not more than a rudimentary society. A true social system begins to emerge when animals develop contrasting but complementary roles within the group.

The simplest example is the male-female pair. Societies emerge when pairs form constituent units of larger groups and where relations between the pairs—usually spatial or "territorial"—become elaborated. The example is well known of the colonies of birds in which males stake out territories first, then are joined by females, then each pair defends its nest site and its young. In such arrangements, some males do not get territories and some females do not get mates.[3] Those who miss their footing on the merry-go-round of marriage are banished to the peripheries of the society and do not mate. If they die before breeding, their genes will not join the common pool of the species's genes, and future generations will be stamped with the characteristics of their successful rivals. Mutations favorable to the successful acquisition of nest and mates would be selected for. Included in these mutations would be the physiological basis of successful aggression on the one hand and, on the other and just as important, a successful bonding, in this case with the mate. Animals able to drive off rivals and retain females with ease would be at a distinct advantage; the characteristics favoring this, such as size, agility, coloring, aggressiveness, and sex appeal, would be favored reproductively and passed on. This is not a simple matter of aesthetics or animal flirtation: it is a sober business which, alternately in leaps and subtle sifting, changes the course of evolution by producing new species and modifying old ones.

Competition for scarce resources—food, nest sites, mates—is the basis of society and the stuff of politics. But the simple nest-site competition is not very complex; no really ingenious political system can be seen to come out of it. The basic processes, however, are there—competition, inequality, exclusion, bonding. In any competition, someone wins and someone loses; a relationship of dominance and subordination is set up. If the subordinate is excluded, the matter quickly loses its interest as far as the forging of political systems is concerned. But if the dominant and subordinate animals remain in some relationship to each other, and if the dominance and subordination continue to be recognized, and if, further, the subordinate animal is itself dominant over yet another animal, then the rudiments of hierarchy emerge, and a political system now exists.[4] It is a system of inequalities in that those at the top get more than those lower down (including such intangibles as freedom of movement); it is a system of politics in that changes in status can take place—indeed, this is what political systems are about.

This conversion of status into reproduction has an historical aspect; it has always been a way for information about one generation's experience to become part of the reality of the next. It is, in the technical and aesthetic senses, the biological rendering of history. In this context, there is no generation gap, just an inexplicably cumulative and effective bridge whose gatekeeper is none other than the ubiquitous Politics. Hence the political process is not only about the existential business of feeling powerful, being vain, leaving a room in which one's low status is an embarrassment. The very intensity of these status fights masks their implication for the future.

We ourselves have by and large lost sight of the place of politics in the arrangement of our genetic future. We remain caught in the process and seek both power and genetic immortality without trying to formulate the relationship between the process and its consequence, and without caring—if we do figure it out—that the heat of the moment is defined by its effect on the cold facts of the species's future. Only when mating and politics affect major fortunes and conspicuous lineages—as with aristocrats and feuding families or tribes—do we pay explicit attention to genes and power. Otherwise, like the gourmet wholly unconcerned about vitamins, we partake and enjoy. What the human species in particular has become obscures many of these relationships. But in many primate systems the constituents remain, and it is these that must first be isolated and described.

Because there is considerable variety in primate political organization, we can only summarize some of the most general characteristics, those common to a large variety of systems.[5] However, it must always be remembered that man has had a peculiar evolutionary history during which he has evolved features peculiar to him as a species. Because he is a gregarious, terrestrial primate with a history of savanna living, it will help us to look at other terrestrial primates with a similar history and see what adaptations have ensured their success.[6]

One hurdle must be cleared at the outset. It was thought for a long time that the primal social bond that held primate societies together was the constant sexual interest of the members in one another.[7] In many ungulates—the red deer, for example—the sexes mix only during the breeding season, when the powerful stags gather harems of females and defend them. Once the season is over, the stags form an all-male group or become solitary, the females with the young in turn form their own group, and the sexes thus part company. It used to be thought that primates bred all year round. This, it was claimed, was the real difference between them and other mammals, which, like the red deer, formed a total male-female society only during the rutting season.[8]

This theory would have sexual attraction as the basis of politics. Without constant sex there would have been no enduring society whose politics could become a matter of dispute. But this is not so. Many primates that maintain year-round societies do not engage in year-round sexual activity. Thus, a male is not ensured perpetual sexual bliss by being at the top of the primate hierarchy, even though he will indeed be more likely to breed than his inferiors. Which reinforces the point: politics is about genetics, not sex per se. The more powerful animal gets a better chance to perpetuate himself genetically rather than simply a better chance to indulge in sybaritic excesses. This raises a second point: if constant copulation is not the reward, and hence the goal, of power, then power must be attractive in itself. At the risk of seeming anthropomorphic, we can hazard a guess that animals strive for dominance because they want to be dominant. A dominant animal moves more freely, eats better, gets more attention, lives longer, is healthier and less anxious, and generally has a better time than a lowly and peripheral animal. To escape from the gloom of peripherality into the aristocratic confidence of the central hierarchy must be its own reward. The effective outcome of this, aside from the apparent pleasure, is simply that while all males get a chance to copulate, only the more dominant get a chance to breed. This is the point around which the whole social system revolves: who does the breeding?

A typical savanna baboon troop has an average of forty members. How the troop organizes itself can be seen in its spatial arrangements both at rest and on the move, more typically the latter. The group moves about all day foraging for food—mostly grass—and each member fends for himself. At the center of the group are the dominant males—never more than about six adults, however large the troop. Around them cluster the females and the young. Spread out around this central core are the "cadets"—the more junior males who are candidates for the central hierarchy. The peripheral males are confined to the edges of the group; here these animals which have left their mothers and moved to the borders are joined by some older males that have not made the central hierarchy. The males of the central core act as bosses, defenders, policemen, and leaders in a complex set of actions and inter-actions. Within the hierarchy there are coalitions of animals, usually two or three, which, when acting in concert, can outrank any individ-ual, no matter how strong. This system has great advantages to a troop moving across the savanna. The peripheral males—the most expendable—are at the edges, where they are most likely to encounter predators and give the warning. The mothers and young are near the big males. In the event of danger from lions or leopards, for example, the big males will come out and threaten and usually succeed in driving off the foe. A large male baboon with his huge sharp canines is a formidable fighting animal, and even carnivores hesitate to risk wounds that might prove fatal.

A group like this has to be disciplined in order to survive, and this discipline is maintained by the ranking system. For example, the large males will tolerate little quarreling within the group and will quickly stop fights between females and juveniles. Furthermore, the attention of the lower-ranking animals is directed mostly toward the top male. Among the ranking males there is very little fighting over food, space, and females. Once the ranking order has been determined, threats are enough to maintain it: a fierce baring of the canines will put a sub-ordinate in its place very quickly. The ranking pattern therefore tends to be very stable over time. Palace revolutions do occur from time to time, and older males are ousted, but it is remarkable how long a dominant male can hold his position, even when he has grown old and lost his teeth and could easily be defeated by a better-equipped junior. The habit of obedience dies hard. On the other hand, some animals that are individually quite dominant do not seem to have the taste for leadership; some achieve power only to discover they do not like it. They leave the band and become "solitaries." Sometimes they return for brief periods to play among the peripherals, but most of the time they prefer their own company. This often happens to males at the top when for some reason the group gets very large.

In a large group there are subunits of female relatives and their young, which also act in some sense as coalitions. The females have their ranking too, even if it is not as clear and is more volatile than the male hierarchy. These subunits of females—for example, among the baboonlike macaques—can themselves be ranked. The ranking of females is important, since the sons of high-ranking mothers stand a better chance of making it into the hierarchy than do the sons of lowlier females. Perhaps this is because the high-ranking mothers are nearer the dominant males and are able to keep their youngsters with them longer. The sons of the hoi polloi move out to the edge as early as one year after birth, but the aristocrats can stay in the court circle for two or three years. The big males learn to recognize and tolerate them, and they themselves learn that they are born dominant. Their mother can probably outrank even some of the males; the youngster becomes accustomed to seeing animals flee from him; and the emotional tone and confidence of a dominant female are his to share.[9]

The males without this privilege must sit it out at the peripheries, playing their games when young and cautiously testing out their strength as they get older. They will either push into the central hierarchy of their own band, leave and try elsewhere, or die. The death rate among peripheral males at puberty is very high: as many as half their number will never see adulthood. Again we have a weeding-out process favoring not only the strongest but also the most confident, controlled, cunning, and in some ways cooperative males. They must cooperate with other males in many ways; they must pull in the female vote. A top male who is totally unacceptable to the females may not keep his position. He is subject to too much female harassment. And the big males will win female approval only if they indulge and supervise the infants of the community.[10]

The nonhierarchical animals carefully watch their bosses. Rather than sex, this may be the clue to the cohesiveness of primate groups. The lower animals seem to be programmed to pay attention to the dominant animals, who, however, pay little attention to them and gaze off into the middle distance with relative indifference unless challenged or disturbed. Peripherals are so apprehensive they will often abandon the very food they are eating in order to focus all their attention on the dominant males.[11]

Who gets paid attention to can apparently help to change the structure of a troop. Animals display different capacities for dominant behavior—which, like intelligence in humans, is not uniformly distributed through the population. Unusually dominant animals are not necessarily the ones that can win the most fights, but often those that can get the rest to pay attention to them. The dominant animal is by definition the one to whom the rest pay the closest attention. And within limits the group will take an animal at its own evaluation. Thus the dominant animal is the one that behaves most like a dominant animal and can convince the others that it is. This is why a strange animal can often usurp the top position in a group. His novelty value is a great asset in getting attention and also explains why, once dominant, an animal can remain dominant for a long time: it is hard to get attention diverted from it.

How does this affect the female population? What matters in the system is who does the breeding.[12] This is what being top animal means in genetic terms. Females go through a monthly cycle of sexual behavior—the estrous cycle. During and just before menstruation, they are not sexually receptive, and the males are not interested in them. But for a few days in mid-cycle they go into heat—a kind of sexual mania—when they solicit the attention of the males. This solicitation— the presenting of the hindquarters—is aided in some species by spectacular swellings and colorations of the genital areas. While they are actually in heat, the females will be appropriated by a dominant male, who will try to monopolize them. If he is successful, he will be the only one to copulate with them during this period. Since this is their time of ovulation, it follows that he will be the only one to impregnate them.

Before and after this peak of estrus, the dominant male is more or less sexually indifferent and will often let inferior males mount the females. Everyone copulates; only dominants propagate. The genetic composition of the group in the future is heavily determined by the breeding privilege these high-ranking animals exercise. They control not only the present of the group, but its genetic future too.

These are some of the features of baboon and macaque social structure. The social systems of many terrestrial primates do *not* have the concentric structure described here. But whatever the details of the system, certain underlying processes are obvious despite the diversity of surface structures, and can be easily summarized.

The system is based on hierarchy and competition for status, which determine access to resources and the privilege of breeding.

The males dominate the political system, and the older males dominate the younger.

Females can be influential in sending males up the status ladder; and their long-term relationships to one another are critical for the stability of the system.

The dominant males keep order among the females and juveniles; they are nurturers and protectors of the young.

Cooperation among males is essential; coalitions of bonded males act as units in the dominance system.

The whole structure is held together by the attractiveness of the dominants and the attention that is constantly paid them.

Because of this, charismatic individuals can upset the hierarchical structure, and by the same token, retain power.

It will be quickly apparent that these rules apply to human beings as well as to many of the other primates. Of course, there are differences: humans differ from baboons, as chimpanzees differ from gorillas. But the basic biogrammar is there, in which we can recognize many of the syllables of our common behavioral language. The point is that human communities are fundamentally concerned with the same things as other primate communities—surviving, perpetuating the group, defending it, keeping some social order, using the environment reasonably constructively, and just generally muddling through. The woman with a baby or the pasha bidding weary good-bye to a representative of his harem may think they are serving themselves and their own pleasures and vanity. They are, but they are aiding and abetting the species even more directly than themselves: the reason they get pleasure in what they do is that pleasure and survival are linked; our most primitive hedonisms are episodes in nature's scheme for making sure that animals do what is necessary for their survival.

Human political systems are based on hierarchy and competition for status; it remains an ardently sought political ideal to divorce ascribed or inherited status from control over resources. But not only have most states failed to wither away, they have prospered. The encompassing grip grows rather tighter of pettily differentiated hierarchies doling out pettily or even grandly differentiated payments and perquisites. Hierarchies lend coherence to whatever systems of government humans create; competition for status is to social process as sexual attraction is to reproduction. That sex and status are connected should not surprise us: the primate quest for high status seems more pervasive and persuasive in practice than the human quest for equality is in theory. This is not to deny the importance and complexity of political idealism and its effect on the sundry forms of human politics. It is only to suggest that the earlier primate passion for preeminence in terms of which reproduction occurs still underlies and inhibits our political idealism.

But why have any hierarchies at all? To pontificate about original sin would be neither original nor helpful, and the whole effort of blaming unfortunate patterns of social life on some forms of dispensable nastiness would exercise the moral muscles beautifully but provide no answers, and no insights into reality. No matter how hard and how often we rail against them, the affections for difference in status are also part of our primate structure, part of our "primative" reflex to be higher rather than lower. We refine this reflex endlessly; we humiliate others; we are rank-makers and flag-planters. We create a god to whom *we* can be subordinate. So committed are we to the notion of hierarchy that even our mightiest leaders must subserve something or someone. We set about formulating governmental systems that are retained by boundaries of territory or of group. But then we spill over these boundaries and become a highly specialized kind of primate, one who creates out of the stuff of a local hierarchy the basis of an imperial apparatus. By the use of symbol wedded to underlying propensity, we strive to control huge areas of land and large groups of people. That we accomplish and justify this is an ambivalent tribute to our humanness and our brain. That we want to at all is a predictable outcome of our evolution as primates.

No one would affirm the necessity of hierarchies nor be so foolish as to argue that when a man loses his empire he loses his humanity. But it must be understood that the process which gives rise to empire is the very same process that primates engage in simply in order to exist and persist. The hierarchical encounter and the rank order are the cells out of which whole and larger systems are built.

What can be the relationship of hierarchy to such quintessentially human structures as empires, bureaucracies, and ideologically committed political parties? What happened was a change of gear. Our earlier hominid ancestors had lived a simple primate life with a society compounded of the elements we have described. They too roamed the savannas in search of food, but at some point they made a breakthrough: they abandoned total dependence on vegetable food and took to hunting—small game at first, but later bigger and bigger animals and in ever greater quantities.[13] They invented tools and weapons, fire and clothing, and the whole complex of culture. To do this they had, as we saw in Chapter 1, to improve their brains in feedback with their improving skills as hunters and weapon-makers. The improved brain was capable of novel symbolic processes, but it was working on the same material. The symbolic processes enabled the evolving hominid hunters to create political structures that overstepped the boundaries of the troop even as they continued to use the same raw material.

A very simple example serves to illustrate this. When primate groups get too big they split up into two groups, usually of about equal size. There are upper organizational limits to the troop—as we have seen, forty or fifty individuals is just right, as in human hunting groups. The primate groups that split become, in effect, two new breeding groups; if they are still in close proximity, they establish at once a dominance-subordination relationship. But that is the limit of their continuing association.[14]

Human groups also split; it is clear that those of our evolving hunter ancestors did. But their capacity to make symbols would enable them to do several additional things. They could, on the one hand, continue to trace genealogical relationships to one another and remain united as kin, even though they were divided as ecological units. On the other hand, they could share a common name and gather for ritual activities that would be unique to them and bind them as one clan. Often a worship of common ancestors would serve as the operative religious code—a very effective way to maintain continuing identity. In the primate groups the males move around from group to group, but when they leave a particular group they are effectively lost to it. Human hunters—both males and females—can and could move around too, but their identity with members of the parent group would not necessarily be lost, since they would bear a common name and be able at all times to conceptualize their relationships and rights with those of their group of origin. In this way, although ecological considerations as inexorably divide expanding human groups into fragments as they do groups of baboons, symbolic processes can weld them together into clans and tribes. Even among hunters and gatherers who have to be dispersed, as many as between one thousand and five thousand people can be linked by language and kinship and common ritual.[15] In this way, they are able to respond to the symbols rather than only to the persons. To a male baboon of one troop, a male baboon of another is simply another male baboon—and thus a potential threat. The human tribesman, on the other hand, is able to ascertain whether or not the other male is a member of the same tribe. If he is, is he a member of the same kinship group? Is he a close or distant kinsman? Is he a relative to be joked with or avoided, avenged or even murdered? The human tribesman responds to the man not only as an individual but as a representative of a category of persons.

Clearly the ability to bind otherwise fragmentable groups gave an enormous advantage to the humanizing hominids. Their ever-growing hunter bands became the most effective and efficient predators on the face of the earth. Their ability to exploit an environment multipled n times, and very rapidly too. What this uniquely human feature did—and the point cannot be overstressed—was to reorganize the basic material of the ancestral primate political system. It added no new words to the vocabulary of politics. Its contribution was a new way of organizing the words into more ambitious sentences and paragraphs. It enabled us to elaborate and categorize, to define and analyze. And, as culture began to make more and more demands, it enabled us to think up more and more complex criteria of rank, so that, for example, eloquence might well be as important as strength, and the great speaker—for the speaking primate—could be as likely to reach high office as the great hunter. Territories could be mapped, instead of demarcated by physical approach and retreat; relations between neighbors could be formalized by agreements. Internal order could be coded in rules, laws, and maxims, and enforced not only by the patience of the strong and the consent of the weak but also by the fact that the agents of the law are themselves constrained by the rules of the group.

This change can be seen aesthetically, as the longest-running ballet in history. The choreography of the movements of the animals—man and prehuman—depends on the same scheme. There is attraction between the animals. They seek one another out, sit with one another, cluster in coveys, range together, and reproduce. If they are successful, the groups increase in size, and this very success forces the group to split, to start the process all over again. Baboons do this, and they have colonized Africa so extensively that there are now more of them than people. Humans danced to the same basic choreography: they moved together, interacted, had babies, grew, and with overpopulation found new continents, new hearths, another human colony. The rhythm is slow and measured; the individuals move with the stateliness of creatures knowing that it takes a whole lifetime to live a whole lifetime; the components of their lives are inexorably linked with the components of the lives of others.

Yet the colonies remained linked. That is the great human invention, the new melody and color in the dance. The groups still cluster together, fondle babies, laugh at jokes, and worry about keeping dry. But a web of symbols and reminiscences called history now binds them. The first human empire was just down the road; our great leap forward was a quiet amble to see the People of Other Village, *and we knew them and could state our connection.* It was an intimate empire, based on our astonishing knack for spacing ourselves out to keep physically healthy at the same time that we bound ourselves together to preserve the richness of our society. We kept both our primate inheritances, body and group, but we found a way of expanding our societies, though our bodies remained substantially the same—except for our heads, which we filled with brain tissue, in good part to keep track of our extended web of people and ideas about people. We became superlative primates; the breeding system that was so effective that we had to colonize also yielded the political skills necessary to make empires of separated groups, make theories of society out of the way we treated with our neighbors, make gods out of what we thought we shared in common, and make primate order out of human symbol.

The transition is subtle, but it can and should be explained. The political process in its evolutionary setting is a breeding process—part of the system of natural and sexual selection. Power equals self-perpetuation—or at least some more throws of the dice, a statistically better chance of contributing disproportionately to the gene pool. When the system of power and perpetuation comes to include not only genes but also material goods and hereditary privileges, the matter becomes much more complicated. We inherit a system in which males strive for dominance; we have seen how this perpetuates their genes; differential access to food, females, and security are the objects of the game. The human innovation is to add to this a conscious striving to perpetuate the nongenetic heritage as an end in itself: power, goods, office, and influence—as well as offspring—become the counters in this new version of the old game.

The crucial aspect of the new politics is the divorce of the ends of the game from its motivations. The deep motives of the participants stem from the system of selection in which they evolved—the hierarchy-dominance-breeding system. But the ends are no longer simply the dominance of the genetic structure of the future, though this has certainly played its part in human politics. In Australian aboriginal societies, for example (and there are many cases just like this), the most successful males collect the most wives and contribute unequally to the gene pool. King Ismail of Morocco (1672–1727) is said to have fathered 1,056 children from "countless" concubines and wives.[16] But as society increased in density and complexity, sexual dominance ceased to be much of a genetic issue. Natural and particularly sexual selection continued and indeed continues to operate, but not primarily through hierarchical politics. Even the *droit de seigneur* did not ensure the overlords a monopoly of genetic power. In fact, the situation soon reversed itself, and the poor and oppressed began to outbreed their masters.

Power became divorced from the control of the genetic future of the population, and fastened instead onto the control of material goods and the symbolic future. The leaders could not ensure that they controlled the future merely by peopling it with their own offspring; they had to ensure that their offspring controlled the future by having the monopoly on wealth and power. The same basic motive power that moved our primate ancestors and hominid forebears flowed into a new political system, but because of the move to symbolic operation, no longer occupied the same niche in the natural order of things. Politics was thus severed from its evolutionary role—with consequences both benign and malignant.

Control over the power and wealth of future generations, however, was, and to a large extent still is, linked to breeding through systems of succession and inheritance. If an aristocratic class controls the system, then the only way to participate in that control is to be or become a member of that class. This "breeding elite" differs from primate breeding elites: it is an elite of the "well bred" or properly fathered which links genes to power in a peculiarly human way. Human societies have the same problems of stability and perpetuation that their nonhuman cousins have. Some kind of aristocratic system is a common human answer to these ancient evolutionary problems. For human society has a conscious concern with continuity and the preservation of stability—not things that seem to actively trouble our primate cousins. The processes that give stability and order to primate groups have already been described; now we should see how the aristocratic principle manifests, supplements, or negates these principles in human society.

By an "aristocratic principle" we mean any system of domination based on hereditary position—what Max Weber would have called a "traditional" system of political domination.[17] Continuity is provided simply and effectively by allowing heirs of aristocrats to be aristocrats in their turn. Since legitimate heirs are a special resource, aristocratic families are usually very careful about their women and the general control over reproductive capacity that women represent. There is no doubt that women have always been important counters in the political game; the fate of empires can turn on the marriages they make and the potential heirs they carry. The aristocratic way assures stability, but at the risk of stagnation, since there is no guarantee that the heir will be competent—a common and vexatious problem of monarchical systems. But aristocracy nonetheless taps some of the basic primate processes. For a start, it is avowedly based on a system of inequalities and often on an exquisitely graded hierarchy. All men may in theory be equal before God in some ultimate sense, and the meek may very well inherit the earth, but in the meantime society is fixed on a rigorously rank-ordered basis. As long as one stays within the system, the only way to achieve power is to make an aristocratic claim to legitimate authority, either by being born noble, by being ennobled, or by managing to sustain a claim to legitimate nobility. Challengers to thrones before Perkin Warbeck and after had to claim that they were the true heirs of some dead and undisputed monarch; Pugachev had to claim that he was in fact Peter III, and most claimants to the English throne had, for some tortuous reason, to prove descent from John of Gaunt.

Yet even within the central hierarchy of an aristocratic system, there is a quite ferocious competition for effective power. The position of king or chief may well be fixed, but the system is rare in which all power effectively resides in one person. It does happen—oriental despots did flourish—but even there the power play among the elite was considerable.[18] The central hierarchy of high aristocrats played power politics among themselves, but at the same time they joined forces to keep at bay any peripheral groups that sought to usurp aristocratic power; and there were always such groups—serfs, burghers, peasants, free knights—harassing the central core. What Disraeli fondly referred to as the "aristocratic settlement" had to be preserved.[19] But inside the boundaries drawn around nobility, the gloves were off. Thus both hierarchy and competition were incorporated into the system. Membership of the central hierarchy was relatively stable, and with this the group as a whole was assured stability and continuity, but the members of the central hierarchy could give expression to the need to strive for dominance and maintain it.

The maintenance of dominance in such a system was based on the one hand on coercion and threat, and on the other on established habits of deference. Effete aristocracies could often last for a long time after their real power had evaporated. They could even continue to exercise great influence, although formally stripped of much of their legitimate authority. Both ethnographers in Africa and historians in Europe have noted that, remarkably, rebels in feudal-type societies rarely challenged the feudal principle itself. Peripherals who moved in to challenge did not want to change the system—merely the personnel who ran it. The impulse is to accept the established hierarchy—which enhances stability and makes matters easy for the dominants, who can maintain their dominance largely by ritual means. Ultimately, of course, there is the threat of force—the primeval canine tooth—but most of the time subordinates will defer to badges of rank and thus to those who wear them.[20]

Babies born to aristocrats are "superior" immediately. Babies born to commoners are what they are and no more. The aristocratic system possesses the distinct advantage—in terms of maintaining formal stability if that is what is wanted—of being able to induct members of the society into the pattern of dominance right from birth. When two men meet after one has known for thirty years he would be king and the other that he was only a commoner, the encounter must reflect a habit hard to break, even with the best intentions in the world. His Royal Highness and Mr. Smith may, in terms of some theory or other, be brothers under their respective skins, but in their habits as animals, one takes precedence *as a person*, and the other defers. Aristocrats are people. They are even primates; perhaps a useful analogy can be drawn with those primates whose birth from a high-ranking mother makes it much more likely that they themselves will become dominant. One animal learns to dominate as another learns to serve. There is no reason to believe, as far as dominance is concerned, that the human primate learns less than baboons; we can be sure that he learns even more. So the duke is more appalled by being crowded—he needs more space, and usually gets or is given it. First-class travel gives you more room to move. And the duke expects not only room, but that people will make room. It is a habit learned young, which dies hard.

Aristocrats know all the primate tricks—particularly those relating to what Michael Chance has called "attention structure." Dominant primates get looked at most; they are the focus of attention, and also the center of the group's social structure. It is not clear—nor does it really matter—which comes first. What matters is that leadership and

visibility are closely linked, and that human attention structures—
while infinitely more complex and symbolic than the other primates'—
nonetheless can be identified and their functions for politics made
clear. Consider the dramaturgy of aristocracy—the forms of address,
the styles of clothing, the seating plans, and the very dining halls
themselves.[21] The architecture is made to impress as much as to shelter,
and to be definitive rather than merely serviceable. The round of life
celebrates the status and pomp of the aristocracy, the more visible the
better. Perhaps it is true that tourists crowd around to peer at Greenwich Village hippies just as avidly as they flow around the rails of
Buckingham Palace. But they go to Greenwich Village and Buckingham Palace for different reasons, and they react differently when the
Queen appears or disappears than when even a queenly hippie girl
makes an entrance or a sign. It is too easy to scorn the tourists at both
places. They are real people who choose to spend their time and energy
this way; it is expensive to gape at foreign palaces. Nonetheless, they
willingly place themselves, in terms of the attention structure, in a
position of subservience, along with autograph hounds and consumers
of gossip columns. It is beside the point to say that this is a good or
bad thing or that aristocracies are better or worse than other systems.
The point is that many of the components of primate systems of hierarchy and deference can be seen in the attention-structure efforts of
aristocrats.

Of course, aristocracies and similar traditional systems of dominance
can be challenged and overthrown like any other political systems. In
the context of our earlier distinction between primate politics, which
have to do with differentiation and acknowledged hierarchy, and
human politics, which have to do with the search for equality and
humane management, we can quickly understand the special attraction
of primate politics for aristocrats.

In other words, aristocracy is more primitive than democracy. This
primitiveness is effective not simply because aristocrats are integrated
into a well-protected and economically overprivileged social class, but
because humans appear to find satisfaction in such an enticing display
of dramaturgy and stability. This deference may be extremely expensive to those who defer. But in the business of being inferior and
superior, we do not begin from scratch, but rather draw on an elaborate
repertoire of already broadly programmed ways of showing those differences of status it seems we are compelled to show. The inflexible
and consistent connection of all this with the way we evolved as a
breeding species confirms our connection with our own prehistory. It

also suggests that, despite our noble wishes, there are limits to how much we can affect our circumstances by our will, and our community by our goodwill.

Despite this, there is a sense in which democratic arrangements are even more "primitive" than aristocratic ones. The primate political system is based on ruthless but ritualized competition for power. Though some systems have some hereditary elements (the advantages gained by the son of a high-ranking mother), it is on the whole true that all young males are thrown into the pool of potential leaders and have to work their way to the top. In primate groups, perhaps the basic feature and certainly the most important is competition for status. This plays a part in aristocracies too, but the very nature of the hereditary principle acts to play it down by defining the over-whelming majority of males as ineligible for the competition. These males may succeed in local status competitions, but it is not the same thing: being best archer or best sackbut player in Walton-on-Thames is a poor substitute for being Lord of the Marches. Aristocracy capital-izes on those primate features that favor long-term stability—the "stability of the dominance hierarchy"—and the principle of a central hierarchy as a focus of attention and cohesion. But it reduces the feature of competition as far as the whole population is concerned. Democratic regimes in effect open up the status competition to greater numbers of people, but they base the competition on a principle of rotating leadership unknown among primates. To some extent, while a dominant primate male cannot hold effective power without the con-sent of the governed, he does not depend on this consent to achieve office. Democratic politicians battle with one another as ruthlessly and with many of the same tricks as their primate counterparts, but ulti-mately they get to the top by getting votes, not by physically defeat-ing their rivals.

It may be instructive for us to look at the voting system as a con-ventionalized, or ritualized, competition. The primate wins his battles and maintains his position chiefly by bluff. He convinces his opponents that it is not worth their while to take him on physically, and they defer. To listen to the speeches of candidates during an election is to believe that the victory of the opposing party will lead to nothing short of national if not cosmic disaster, not to mention the personal misery and poverty of each and every voter. But what happens in-stead? Each side counts heads, and when one side sees that the other has more physical support, it backs down, leaving its opponent the field, but continues to harass it and wait for another opportunity to challenge. Votes are the canine teeth and threat display of democratic politics.

Democratic regimes are faced with the problem of continuity, and usually settle it by having as the focus of the attention structure some person or institution who persists despite changes in the effective leadership. This person or institution can be a constitution, a supreme court that is not elected, a president who is "above" politics, or a constitutional monarch as titular head of state. Political theorists trying endlessly to define the significance of this concept of "head of state" have been given pause by the seeming paradox that the most stable democracies are constitutional monarchies.[22] A student of attention structure would immediately recognize the value of Queen Elizabeth, not as a technical element in the British constitution, but as a persisting focus of national attention who can be venerated while prime ministers are despised. One of the problems with the American presidency is that it confuses these two roles: one must respect the office while possibly despising its holders. There is always a fair chance that the near-half of the population who voted against the victorious candidate may do just that.

Democracies cannot escape dealing with the same primate problems as the aristocracies they overtly disparage and often secretly envy. And despite their egalitarian theories, they often generate very similar structures. In the same way that they intensify the status competition, they stress the attention structure, and here they have a lot of the primate heritage going for them. For example, the dominant male is visible and an object of intense interest and observation. The cohesion of the group depends on this structure of attention. The attention is competed for, and the dominant animal is the one who can get it. He is not born with attention directed toward him—although a high-ranking mother can help to draw some—but has to compete for it either as a rugged individual or in consort with bonded male companions. The democratic politician is in somewhat the same position. If he wants to get to the top, he has to be visible, has to get attention and hold it, in open competition with other politicians. Of course, like his well-born primate cousin, he can start with great advantages. A common explanation for the success of the Kennedys was that the best way to get to the top is to start there. This beautifully illustrates the point that it *is* attention that counts. Whatever his merits as an individual politician, a Kennedy (or a Rockefeller or a Roosevelt) starts with more than his fair share of almost hypnotized attention from the voters. Yet he still has to compete, and is not—as would be the case if this were an aristocracy—handed office on a plate simply because he is his father's son.[23]

We can see that aristocracies, oligarchies, plutocracies, tyrannies, despotisms, democracies, and all other forms of political dominance, despite their obvious overt differences, all work according to the same basic processes. They differ in the way they institutionalize the basic features, and how they emphasize different parts of the primate political biogram. For example, tyrants and despots exploit the virtues of a strong dominant male; but they make the mistake of trying to wipe out the competitive arena so essential to the successful running of a dominance system. Aristocracies see the virtues of the stability of the dominance hierarchy and allow for competition within it. But they make the mistake—by severely restricting entry to the arena—of permanently frustrating the peripherals. The most successful aristocracies, the ones that have survived in even attenuated forms, are those that have freely admitted new members on the one hand, and readily demoted old members on the other. In this way they have avoided becoming castes or closed estates. A familiar example of this process is the British system, in which younger sons did not receive titles, and often married into the bourgeoisie, while wealthy burghers, and recently men of talent, have been admitted to hereditary peerages. An aristocratic-democratic compromise has thus been reached, in which socialist leaders become earls and viscounts, and the younger sons of peers become socialist Members of Parliament.

In theory, the perfect system would be a true democracy, not because it renders all men equal, but because it gives them an equal chance to become unequal. An aristocracy, on the other hand, allows them only an unequal chance to become unequal. Inequality is the goal of both systems, and democratic ideology and theory only become self-defeating when they confuse the democratic process with egalitarianism. Egalitarianism is often the stated goal of democratic idealists; indeed, it is often adopted as a symbolic structure (*Mr.* President, *Comrade* Stalin, *Citizen* Robespierre), but here the possible hiatus between symbol and action is the most glaring—a continuing testimony to the human capacity for self-deception that is at once necessary and disastrous. Necessary because without it there would be no democratic ideals; disastrous when it comes between us and a proper understanding of the limits within which those ideals can operate.

A political society is more than just a system for integrating unequal organisms (although it is that); it is a system that allows organisms to strive for inequality—a system rooted in the evolutionary
process.[24] What true democratic theory advocates is simply that the
basis for this striving should not be arbitrary, that the criteria for
being a competitor should not be fixed at birth by class, sex, or color;
that people should be allowed to dominate other people on their merits
and not on the basis of factors beyond their control.

The ground rules of the political biogrammar become clear: organisms are unequal in their capacity for dominance; they strive to dominate one another; they should have a roughly equal chance to compete
in this process. These are not statements of any particular political
ideology—they are in fact compatible with several; they are statements about the animal and the conditions of its evolution, and any
political system is going to have to face up to them. Most systems
operate this way anyway, even though they may have overt ideologies
to the contrary. If they do not, they are doomed to fail. If a system
denies effective competition, it will frustrate its best talents and
stagnate.

There is another set of ground rules, apparently contradictory, that
have to do with the necessity that rulers be regarded as competent and
merciful. It does a leader no good to be visible and authoritative if
he is always widely regarded as improvident and tyrannical. All
primate leaders must attend to infants and females and successfully
respond to the challenges of both the outside environment and the
social disruptions within the group. This is the least they must do. If a
community permits a total and antisocial incompetent to lead it, it may
not survive to tell the story of its political misjudgment.

Human populations also suffer from the slovenliness, avarice, and
callousness of their leaders. It is small consolation to tell a shanghaied
soldier or a half-starved peon that his splendid warrior king is winning
lands galore from the perfidious enemy or building the world's most
glorious marble palace. It takes judgment on the part of leaders to appear dominant enough to be treated as dominants and yet not affirm
too relentlessly the subdominance of their followers. Everyone always
says that all taxes are too high; yet, for the most part, they are paid,
and whatever dissent there is is restrained and formal.

Nonetheless, there have been occasions when the venality, incompetence, and simple greed of leaders have driven the imperial animal
to the elaborate gamble of revolt, of revolution, of desperate anarchy

made tolerable in the present only by the prospect of a more perfect union of all people when the rottenness is expunged and the inequities balanced back. We can expect revolutionary action or wish from young people—that is an old and honorable part of the political process; old men can be so boring, so rich, so full of the rectitude of their own customs, and the young male primate in particular has little time for them and their works. The exceptional act of revolution which is human specifically involves mature males without power confronting mature males with it. That is bitter, and that is remarkably troubling to communities. It is a military truism that civil wars are the most severe and perplexing of all. And well they might be, for they affirm that the community has failed to find within the common symbolism of its former unity reason enough to stop the killing of opponents once friends if not kin. Civil wars are in this sense just extended revolutions—a coup that failed but an impetus that remained.

No almighty formula could possibly apply to all the problems that arise from uncertainty about competence, hierarchy, authority, tenderness, ruthlessness, and mercy, which in varying proportions compose the biogrammar of the politics of the imperial animal. The most complex judgments come into play in deciding who should be leader, and for how long, and under what circumstances, and why. In principle, the institutions of most societies are supposed to serve the exercise of this judgment, though they often prevent its free emergence and almost always add a baffling rigmarole. As primates we are constantly making political judgments, constantly looking to the center, constantly buzzing around the central hierarchy. This hierarchy too looks outward—through agents of tyranny such as brutal police, secret police, debt collectors, and, *in extremis*, the army. Politicians are intensely sensitive, if only to one another. They may learn of their standing from agents or opinion pollsters or regional advisers, or from actual encounters with their constituents. They must be aware all the time of their problematical link with the people they represent and lead, but upon whom they also depend for their income and sense of mighty place. It is no accident that kings have castles with heavy walls and secret passages, that presidents have conspicuous guards, that a Swiss bank account is as much part of the dictator's kit as his control of contracts and of guns. That leaders are loved or respected or at least equably tolerated is no guarantee that they will be safe.

This brings us to the question of change in political systems. Primate systems do not change basically unless some evolutionary mechanism operates to produce new behavior. But certain processes in primate society give us clues to the seemingly inexplicable and often frightening upheavals that can take place in human groups, and often do. Attention structure is a rule in the grammar of stability. But this is a two-edged weapon, for if attention can be taken away from the dominant animals, then the hierarchy can be changed. On a small scale, every grade-school teacher knows how dangerous is the child in the class whose antics—often of an incredible sophistication—so easily divert the class that the authority of the teacher is strained and often seriously threatened. The same tension and unseemly panic can be seen on a larger scale among political figures of established dominance when a prophet arises from nowhere and begins to draw vast crowds with a doctrine that threatens not only the politicians' persons but also the very system of dominance to which they are committed:[25] this may be a system in which they can rise and fall, but it is also one whose rules they know and play by, and whose familiar rhetoric and pomp they enjoy and crave.

Such disruptive people who claim no authority other than their own vision have been called "charismatic" personalities.[26] Their doctrines are many and various, their inspiration profoundly mystical, as was Christ's, or harshly secular, as was Lenin's. What they have in common is a refusal to work within the established order of dominance, and a recurrent claim to a "higher" good to which they owe their allegiance—the coming of the kingdom of God, the triumph of the proletariat, or whatever. The body social has been pumped full of such injections of idiosyncratic energy, but only the few that "take" always have other things going for them. The process is uniformly the same: the zealots capture the attention of the masses or of a revolutionary elite, and eventually overthrow the established system. This they do ostensibly with ideas, and although ideas can be—and are—important, it is the processes that operate irrespective of ideas or ideologies that concern us here.

It may well be that of all processes of social change, those that depend on the vehicle of a charismatic leader for their effectiveness are in a real sense the most rudimentary. Whether the leader is good or bad, provident or irresponsible, sacred or secular, there seems always to be a ferocity of interaction and personal intensity in his relationship to his followers and in their commitment and response. It is an almost desperately indulgent act—to claim that one has the truth or the only plan or scheme to change the world forever. Such a claimant must be

willing to traffic with his constituency with all his most skillful resources as a political animal. There can be no babbling about constitu-
tions here, nor any memos about conciliation. Just as the archetypal
siren provokes in a host of men the taste of promised love, so the
charismatic leader must promise and offer instantly to his followers
an incontrovertible sense of the drama of his energy, the majesty of his
vision, and their special blast of fortune in joining with him at this
critical time for this critical purpose. Charisma requires for its perpetuation a commitment of people's full time and complete political heat,
and needs nothing more than a touch of indifference to kill it. The ideas
of the leader and the promised land he holds out are important, but
they are to the structure of the social relationships as the tracery is to
a flying buttress.

If the participants in a charismatic drama may not understand
what moves them, neither do social scientists. Max Weber used the
term "charisma" to describe the form of dominance that derived its
legitimacy not from tradition or rationally established legality but
from the personal authority of the leader; he was well aware that he
was dealing with something beyond sociological explanation. Sociologists might be able to explain some of the conditions under which
charismatic figures rose and operated successfully. But they could not
explain the nature or peculiar effectiveness of the leader-follower
bond that was involved. Weber recognized this as a phenomenon that
had passed "imperceptibly into the biological."[27] And we can see why.
What is involved is one of the most basic of all biosocial processes,
one that is rooted in the evolutionary struggle for dominance within a
population. The paying of attention to a dominant animal is both the
basis of political society and the major mode of its dynamics. Millions
of years of biopolitical evolution have programmed the primate to be
ready to pay attention to dominant animals, provided the right cues
are given; the natural variety within their populations has ensured
that individuals with superdominance potential will be thrown up in
each generation. It is as unlikely that all of these will achieve leadership positions as it is that a community will discover all its Ein-
steins—but they remain a pool of threatening potentiality.

A leap of the imagination is necessary to see that the massive events
of political upheaval gather their primitive energy from the same
evolutionary source as sexual ardor. But the power and the passion
of a leader for his followers, and the passion of the followers for the
beloved voice and presence, are of the same stuff as the agony of a

lover for his mistress. Both are products of that blind, persistent struggle for dominance and reproductive advantage that is the primal energy of evolution in the animal world. A beautiful woman who arouses a man's lust, and a religious leader who inspires fanatical devotion, are *both* playing the oldest game of all.

There is an infrastructure to all political activity, which we share in part with the other primates and in part with our species-ancestors. Our politics, like our digestion, have biological components. Though an elaborate and vexatiously variable series of options is open to the political animal, there are certain central points which remain determinable. After all, if history is important, then it must count for something that most of our history was spent in small groups of perhaps thirty to fifty individuals and that presumably our political motivations, responses, and controls are adapted to cope on that scale and with that intimacy. In this context, and for this animal, it becomes an act of political extremism to create bureaucracies. Bureaucracy as a theoretical system, and bureaucracies as undeniable and pervasive realities, constitute both a tribute to our exquisite skill of social organization and a caricature of our capacity to create quiet brittle lunacies in the name of reason.

Large-scale bureaucratic organizations are constantly criticized for their inhumanity and impersonality; they are charged with reducing individuals to numbers, computerizing social relationships, overorganizing their conformity-obsessed members, and eventually producing anomie, ulcers, delinquency, anxiety, and wife-swapping. And yet no other form of organization can cope effectively with the overarching problems of a system that goes beyond the face-to-face.[28] Bureaucracy stands at the opposite pole to charisma, with hereditary systems hovering between. The bureaucrat owes his dominance position to formal qualifications; it is not his person that is deferred to, but his office. This replacement of person with office is, as Weber saw, the major characteristic of formal organization, and as inevitable as it is unprimate and inhuman.[29] Unprimate because primate politics are personal politics; eyeball-to-eyeball politics—literally. There are no primate officeholders, only primate individuals.

The paradox is that in order to survive, the human animal has to employ a mode of social organization that in many ways negates all those features that have brought him into the exalted position of needing such an organization in the first place.

Behavior evolved in a social context marked by intensive relationships in hunting communities of thirty to fifty people; we have been
hunters for ninety-nine percent of our existence, and it was in this
context that our behavior was selected, and to these ends. One component of this inheritance is our skill in dealing with human relations
on a small scale. The housewives' kaffeeklatsche, the poker players'
evening out, the gang of adolescent boys, the cabals in the Senate, the
PTA, the local Democratic club, the party cell, the men's hut, the
office clique—are the small groups in which we excel and find satisfaction and fulfillment. But when we move to higher levels of bureaucratic
organization we lose our sense of scale and rapidly move out of touch
with our own human natures. It is the comparatively new and relatively untried organ called the cerebral cortex that makes it possible
for us to organize ourselves beyond the intimate. No wonder the fruits
of reason are sometimes sour. The big brain with its power of unlimited
symbolization puts big organization within our grasp, but in grasping
it we lose our grip on just those social processes we are so sensitively
equipped to handle. When students seek commitment, relevance, and
contact, when workers become alienated, when psychiatrists advocate
fulfilling relationships, when we curse Big Government and abhor the
impersonality of bureaucracies, we are trying to affirm the value of our
skill at intimacy and the heartlessness of those who appear to condemn us to live and work in dehumanized ways. Our revolt against
bureaucracy is really a revolt of nature against antinature, of all our
evolutionary skills against a system that is their negation.

The small groups we can handle so well may be trying, but at least
the problems they present are not insoluble. But when we go beyond
groups of about fifty, we can no longer relate in a face-to-face way;
we have to relate to symbols of the group or its parts: Department X,
Platoon 6, Division 9. We first respond to the symbols rather than to
the occupant of the office, whom we may not know at all as a person
and who may know us only as a case in a file. Yet we do respond to
the large office, to the quiet and seclusive waiting room, to the executive with the alert chauffeur, to the person with "in-chief" attached to
his title. We are willing spectators of the drama of political presentation. The students of Columbia University who sat in its president's
office and smoked his cigars were not so much scorning the man himself
as they were the circumstances that gave a stranger such apparent influence over their education and their sense of personal well-being.
Had they, without knowing his specific place and function, met him in,

say, a boutique or a billiards hall, such preemptive antipathy would almost certainly not have marked their encounter. This simple point has its ramifications; how else could the students attack a system than by focusing on the local conditions of the man who led it? And yet how else could a man take a high place in a rich endeavor than by assuming all the symbolic trappings that this and other cultures attach to dignitaries? Officials spend considerable time protecting themselves as persons against those with whom they interact as officeholders. Hence the rule book, and hence the justified charge that systems are more important than the very people to whom the systems are alleged to cater.

And yet we have so far found no other good way to encourage warmly personal relationships in impersonal systems. Sociologists were right to make the important distinction between formal and informal organization; there is a conflict—an elaborate and eventful one. Bureaucracies are inhuman because large-scale rule-abiding organizations require the denial of the quick kinetic primate interpersonality which we crave and which in the web of nonformal encounters we try to recreate. The office party is a revealing event, not simply in its apparent aphrodisiac effect; it is a ritual that makes an ironic statement of the strains of being one kind of officer or another. Here are all these people, full of valences and antipathies, normally controlled by the rules of work and the etiquette of organization; yet the party offers that possibility of reversal which anthropologists describe; the day of the lords of misrule; the day when the king is mocked, when the "officers" serve the "men."[30] But there is an even deeper reversal going on, too: the structure is overturned or mixed up. For a careful, limited few hours bosses are just people, employees just men and women with rights to the same full grasp of a human occasion as anyone else, particularly the bosses.

The office party is a dramatic enough example of a continuous and pervasive process—the process of conflict between the established routines of "bureaucratic politics" and the pressures of "primate politics." One of the central sources of disillusion that political idealists may experience in contemplating political life is the extent to which personal situations—such as friendships, allegiances, kinship ties, even racial, ethnic, and class patterns—appear to govern political and bureaucratic appointments and activity, and seem to intrude into the theoretically ordered impersonal system. We are trying to play politics with the wrong rule book—but we have no alternative.

The frustrations felt by most people who deal with bureaucratic organizations are as real and justified as the criticisms they provoke.

But they stem from deeper causes than are commonly recognized—from the fact that we are trapped in a form of political organization that is contrary to our political natures yet necessary for our social survival. Millions of years ago the ants managed to program such a form of organization into their genes; in consequence, their social systems are infinitely better organized and much more efficient than our own. But, again, ants don't have politics. Man seeks to combine primate politics with insect bureaucracy, to reinvent consciously what the ants evolved genetically. It is no wonder that there is revolt against this unnatural reversal of the natural trend of our behavioral evolution. Why, then, do bureaucracies survive at all? Why do they not constantly fail?

The answer takes us even further into paradox. Bureaucracies certainly negate major principles of primate political behavior. But they also tap deep human motivations, particularly those that have to do with dominance. This gives the players in the bureaucratic game a feeling that the old rule book is still in operation. They are teased into thinking that primate politics are still being played. Senior members of large organizations occupy large personal spaces into which intrusion is forbidden without rituals of submission (such as making an appointment, waiting in the outer office, etc.) that send out strong signals of dominance and attention. Loyalty and orderliness so essential to organizations are aspects of pack hunting.[31] So are the sense of belonging and the hostility to outgroups. So is the sense of hierarchy and competition. Yet formal organization sends out recognizable cues from the repertoire of primate politics at the same time that it denies the participants the right to play the person-to-person game that is what those politics are about.

If bureaucracy were simply a denial of humanity, it would have no success at all. Both its successes and its frustrations lie in the fact that it uses human motives to inhuman ends. That people constantly feel in some deep way *cheated,* and eventually alienated, by this double-bind situation is not surprising. Bureaucracy is an infuriating tease; it may constitute a career, and structure a life, but it is less life-enhancing than many of its members and clients want. Bending its rules is only infidelity, and not emancipation. Bureaucracy has a human face that is too much like a passport photo.

In its conservatism, bureaucracy reflects a general problem of human political systems that it is both trying to confront and hazardous to avoid: how to change, and how much. These are problems that every community has to face—even those communities that give the appearance of not changing, and even those changing so quickly that their members find it hard to root even their own social experience in sufficiently tangible realities to feel continuity from one year or decade to the next. The problem of change is based on a regularity of the species perhaps as predictable and necessary as that there will be some short and some tall, some fat and some thin, some fast and some slow: in every community there will be some who are eager and vitalized when change occurs and others who are cautious and hold on to the present and the past inherent in it. This difference in attitude toward change cuts across class, creed, party, and even age group. It is the difference between the innovator and the conserver, the hearth-watcher and the explorer.

In "Beginning Biogrammar" we saw the importance in human evolution of the development of inhibition and the capacity to obey rules. If culture was to replace instinct, this had to happen. But, like all the other potentialities under discussion—dominance, sexuality, intelligence, etc.—the capacity to obey rules is distributed on the normal curve. There are those so constituted that no amount of socialization will ever turn them into men in gray flannel suits, while there are others who seem to be enveloped in this unlovely material from birth. Of course, training has a great deal to do with the development of a conforming or a rebellious personality. But it is equally clear that all animals are different from birth: some of Pavlov's dogs were very difficult to condition, and most experimenters have encountered the "impossible" rat that just has to be discarded. Strains of easily trainable or recalcitrant animals can be bred.[32] The set of differences is ultimately located in the central nervous systems of the animals.[33] It seems inevitable that there will be more conformists than rebels; this is nature's only sensible strategy, since nature is essentially conservative. Most mutations, whether genetic or cultural, are deleterious. Even those that are favorable are favored because they help to maintain a traditional way of life rather than because they lead to new possibilities. Thus the strong fins of the Devonian lung fish—the first fish to venture onto land—were selected for because they enabled the fish to get back into the water. In some of the fish—those that stayed ashore longer than the others—the fins eventually became legs, and so the land animals were born. But legs were originally devices to keep us fish rather than to turn us into animals.[34] When man substituted custom for instinct, the same pattern continued to apply. There has to be a balance between stability and persistence in social systems. On the one hand there are well-tried customs and institutions, and on the other the need for innovation in changed circumstances. The weight is on the side of persistence—of the wisdom of group experience embodied in those customs that have existed from "time immemorial." Innovation is more readily accepted if it tends to preserve the status quo than if it threatens to disrupt it.

Again, nature has not left this to chance and the vagaries of learning; she has ensured that a majority of us shall be predisposed to conformity and caution through a vigorous incorporation of the rules of the tribe into our own personalities. On the other hand, there are always those who resist socialization to help innovate, rebel, and otherwise buck the system. Most fall by the wayside, but occasionally, when times are propitious, their innovative behavior pays off. They may be radical politicians, bloody-minded intellectuals, criminals, religious maniacs, unconventional artists, military geniuses, visionary poets, reformist priests, revolutionary philosophers, or simply men in the street who have the courage and the need to say no to the gray mass of those-who-follow-the-ways-of-our-fathers.

Philosophers of history as well as sociologists and psychologists have noted this distinction. But in this biological context it becomes a natural process in the fullest sense, inasmuch as it reflects a principle that runs throughout the evolution of organic life, a principle as true for our species as for any other—that a species is essentially conservative but that it must allow for innovation. To strike a balance between these two forces is the quintessential evolutionary challenge. A species that provides for a wide variety of characteristics is clearly better off than one that gambles heavily on a few. The balance, however, has to be in favor of conservation. In a species like ours, heavily dependent on learning and socialization, the balance is struck by providing a large pool of overlearners and a smaller pool of restless, "undersocialized" innovators. This biological polarization lies behind all the great movements of class war, national conflict, and party feuding. It does not necessarily correspond to the "conservative-radical" distinction as it is culturally defined; it cuts across these institutional systems: there are nonconformist conservatives and rigid radicals. But at times in the history of tribes or nations it can crystallize and form the basis for conflict and opposition. This may be one reason for the heat, the acrimony, and the ardor of political encounter—and for the antipathy of rednecks and longhairs to each other.

If a broadly biological process is implied by the fact that there is a predictable quota of radicals and back-looking hard-liners in any group, or even that group dynamics urge such a divergence, then the attitude we can have to political systems becomes somewhat clearer. Absolute dictatorships that depend upon one man for their procedures and goals will probably fail—except by escalating force—in the task of keeping some reasonable social order that provides members some satisfaction and some dignity. And the other extreme, structures in which everyone is required to be a proponent of change, will experience difficulty too. The world is a hard place even for those who wish it otherwise and can present plans to make it better. Neither the perfection of God nor of Stalin, Perón, Napoleon, or Lucky Luciano can totally mask the dynamic realities of change that mark all living systems. Nor can the perfections of the kibbutz, the urban commune, the Scandinavian state, or the wholly permissive classroom solve all problems. There will always be the question of what to do with innovations—once enthusiastically made by admirable predecessors—that are now stultifying and in disharmony with the new realities. And it is not a counsel of despair to say that when hatred and loathing form the only bridge between the judges and the accused, between the pigs and the yippies, between the socialists striving for higher taxes from the rich and the businessmen picking shreds of steak from their teeth after banquets, something is going on more influential and conscribed than any of us can know. It is all part of a complex drama of preservation and repair, flurried by a new sortie in a new direction, by the fear in retreat and the dawning pride of discovery. It is not only a conflict between heart and stone, between wisdom and theory, or an engagement between people who understand and love human potential and those who fear the proneness to folly in a complex species. In another sense it may all be as predictable and banal—and hence glorious in the way the baffling change of seasons is glorious—as that some are tall, some short, some fast, some slow. The importance of this encounter between finders and keepers is an invitation at best for us to indulge both our sympathy and our understanding, without loss of ambition for the species or affection for our friends.

The science of politics should have the preeminence in the scheme of moral sciences that Aristotle gave it, and for the same reason: man is, by nature, a political animal.[35] Our approach is basically different from that of the pre-Darwinian sage. The political process has been offered as *the* basic natural process in its evolutionary role as part of the organization of sexual and natural selection.

Sex and politics are two sides of the same evolutionary coin, but we have lost sight of this both as a species and as theorists of our own behavior. What textbook on sexual behavior treats it as a political process? And what primer of political science recognizes that its subject matter is a derivative of a biological theme as fundamental as the struggle for reproductive success? What politician sees his own compulsive energy as fired by the ancient impulses of sexual competition? What lover sees his amorous pride as part of the necessary comportment of the successful mammalian politician? Our political institutions draw their strength and energy from the motives of the old breeding systems. But they offer very different rewards. It is scarcely surprising that reasonable systems fail because people behave unreasonably.

3.

BOND ISSUE ONE: WOMEN AND CHILDREN FIRST

THE YOUNG MOTHER pushes the empty stroller along the sidewalk while her small child stumbles and lurches ahead, testing, as well as his legs, his ability to move willingly away from his mother's body. She is about five yards behind, and mother and child smile with certainty at each other. He runs ahead another two yards—but perhaps he is too young for that, because a signal of alarm is on his face now. As if on some firm elastic rope tied to her child, the mother moves forward; mother and child now move physically toward each other. They are both keen and vital during this small circumstance. They are both almost intrinsic to each other; they are really part of each other's being. Were they minerals, we'd call them magnetized. Because they're people, we say "They love"; because they are animals, we know they must have this group-of-two, just as to walk we need the use of two legs, and to carry, the use of two arms. It is no accident that mother and child do what they do: it is as highly predictable and as much a feature of the life cycles of both as are puberty and growing old.

Around their campfire on the night before a raid on the enemy, a group of Crow Indians, mostly young males, is engaged in cutting up a sausage. As each brave cuts a piece off the sausage and passes it on to the next man, he recites the names of all his lovers since the last raid. He does this with complete honesty, even though the list may include the wife or daughter of a comrade. There is pain in an older man's eyes as his wife's name is recited more than once, but he makes no move. A young man hears his mistress named and flinches slightly, but he takes his piece of sausage and recites unhesitatingly in his turn. On any other occasion this knowledge would have driven either man to anger and retaliation. But this is the night before a raid. At dawn these men must stand together against their enemies; they must fight together, and possibly die together. So on this evening they reaffirm their bonds as men, asserting that their relationship as warriors in a war party supersedes all others, and in particular their relationship with women. Once a man has recited his list of names, he is free forever from retaliation on that score; the slate is wiped clean. The warrior band is freed from the contamination of sexual jealousy and can go about its essentially male business. War and fighting and the hunt have always been the business of human males, just as the protection of the troop is the business of male primates. Women are always a potential source of disruption to the unity, loyalty, and trust necessary to comrades in arms. Far from belittling the strength and importance of women, this affirms it. It is important enough to everyone to be made the focus of the only ceremony which precedes the day during which men must trust one another or maybe die, and even die despite the forces generated by their certainty and by their collective yearning for a triumph.[1]

In the children's house of a kibbutz surrounded by Israeli desert and stimulated and formed by socialist ideals, a group of boys and girls between seven and ten years of age play together. They learn the skills and facts and theories appropriate to becoming functioning adults in communities committed to prosperity, growth, and egalitarian integrity. Every day they eat together and play the same games and compete and cooperate, and sleep in the same rooms every night. They see their colleagues-in-growth more often than they see their parents; with the cruel and yet implacably positive demand for insight which children can afford, they come to know one another's fears and competence, and to share hilarities and scorn.

The expectation of the "system" and the hope of the adults is that the children will mature sexually and marry formally and raise more children, to enlarge the area that is not desert. This is a reasonable expectation. The sociological "law of propinquity" is that, all other things being equal, young men and women marry young men and women who live nearby rather than far away. This law is followed—except in the kibbutz.[2]

Here there is an antibond: friendship in childhood seems to prohibit love in maturity. The boys and girls who grow up together rarely marry: once they are adult, only a tiny number of them break the routine of general familiarity to enter into intimacy and the attempt to maintain a special sexual valence in the context of general social links. One kind of bond seems, in a surprisingly uniform and profound way, to preclude another. Perhaps familiarity does not really breed contempt—but it does not appear to breed at all. There may be a lesson in this: that it is difficult to have more than one kind of major bond with another person. It is therefore difficult for brothers and sisters to marry; despite the myth of Oedipus, it is difficult for sons to have sexual intercourse with their mothers; despite the current myth of many cultures, it may be difficult for parents also to be lovers. We do know that it appears to be virtually impossible for Israeli boys and girls raised in egalitarian and committed groups to form that smallest-group-of-all which bears children and rears them.

A lovers' quarrel has just ensued. The lovers are alarmed at their own capacity for hostility, and frightened at the ensuing sense of loss. Never had they realized how closely bound they were to each other than when faced with the possibility of breaking the bond. What is worse, they cannot pin down the source of the anger: she says it is his possessiveness, he says it is her coquetry. But they know that it come from something deep that at once draws them inexorably close and yet builds up tensions and fears bound to erupt sooner or later in accusation. But her tears move him to pity, so that he wants to protect her; his bafflement moves her to compassion, so that she wants to comfort him. Soon they apologize, embrace, and laugh. It is an old story. We are spared from further elaboration by the very banality of the event we are describing.

All social acts are patterned. They are as nonrandom as our physical structures. The patterns of social relationships into which they are formed can be predicted and explained. They are major regularities of the species—of any species. They can be called bonds. What dogs feel for their masters is an example of what bonding is about. What parents feel for their children is another example of this bonding; what parents do for their offspring is yet another feature of a process to which humans, like other social animals, are prone. This process of social bonding encompasses the formation and maintenance of certain relationships that appear to be stimulating, easy to learn, and in some cases necessary for the general health of the individuals concerned— to say nothing of the well-being and persistence of whole communities.

Human social life is not anarchic; it is not random; it is not capricious. With which woman or man or workmate or best friend we bond may be capricious, particularly for transients and dwellers in large cities. But that we will bond at all, and within certain definable limits, is no less "part of the wiring" than our bodily structure or our growth patterns. This is both true and a truism; yet perhaps it permits us to build a model of a human society that accommodates both willful choice and biological constraint. It allows us to say that the human being not only will proceed through a definable life cycle but also will engage in social relationships—of foreseeable intensity and meaning— with predictable categories of people of predictable ages. Our behavioral biogrammar underlies not only how we will act but how we will interact and with whom.

Though it is far from our intention here to revive the essentially false image of "society as a physical body," we want now to try to show how our interactions are as nonrandom as the shape of human heads and the rate of people's metabolism. There may be as much variation in behavior as there is variation in the size of physical items and the rate of physical processes: both are subject to similar basic rules. Not only human will and the dictates of social culture, but other regularities too, determine how people live gregariously, with whom, and why.

When the origins of the central political process—in essence the process of sexual selection—were discussed in "Political Nature," the basis of bonding was linked to evolution. A species can get by without much bonding. Flocks and herds and schools of fish are notable for the interchangeability of their members: one individual is by and large substitutable for another, as far as any individual is concerned. Such species can be very successful, but like breeding systems with asexual reproduction, they restrict their options and reduce the amount of variety on which natural selection can work. A true social system, as we saw, begins when animals respond differentially to other members of the species as individuals. They begin to *select* other members for specific kinds of relatively permanent interaction. In many animals this is related to territory. A creature defending its area reacts to other creatures as enemies. It is usually the male who defends the area, but, for reproductive and rearing purposes, he has to be joined at some point by a female. He responds selectively to this female as an individual, not simply as any female of the species. Insofar as their relationship has any degree of stability—either over a breeding season or for life—they can be described as "mates," and we can watch a fundamental bond in action. The mates are closely attached to each other. They drive off intruders, perform ceremonies, rear and protect their young, build nests, feed each other, and indulge in a host of intimate grooming and ritual activities that are not promiscuously shared but exclusive to the bonded pair.

A great deal of their ritual has to do with the tricky problem of reducing potential aggression between them. The male is initially hostile to all intruders. If he is to mate at all, he has to come to terms with his potential female partner. In providing sometimes elaborate ritual behavioral mechanisms for reducing potential aggression, nature has also provided the bases of successful bonding. The ceremonies that initially reduced the chances of a fight between mating couples become the means whereby the mates learn to recognize, tolerate, and finally to prefer each other to all others. As Lorenz points out, the fact that love and hate, passion and aggression, are two sides of the same coin is something built into the very nature of the bonding process. Indeed, it is only when a species is, for example, territorial and aggressive that bonding of this kind can begin.[3] Unless there is something to force the animals apart, there is no reason to evolve complicated means of bringing them together. Unless the conditions of life provoke mistrust, there is no need for ways of ensuring trust. This may reflect a biological principle: that the more highly developed the species, the more likely there is to be a high degree of individualism and aggressiveness, and hence of mistrust, and consequently of bonding. If it is indeed *Homo sapiens* who is the most highly developed, then it stands to reason that all these factors should be maximized in his behavior.

Our first example of the bonding process was the mating, or "pair" bond. But there is an even more fundamental bond that all mammals at least have to respect—the bond between mother and child.[4] Even in those mammalian species without pair bonds, where mating is brief and where the sexes part immediately after the mating season, the association of the young with the mother remains important. This is particularly true in all those species where the young are relatively dependent. Whether or not the pair bond will figure significantly in the social system seems to depend on factors associated with territoriality on the one hand, and the nature of the protection needed for the mother and young on the other. In some cases the mother and children can fend for themselves. The breeding season of the hamster, for example, lasts only about a week. During this time the males invade female burrows and then retire to their own. The mother and babies stay in the maternal burrow during the brief maturation period, after which the young disperse and the process starts all over again. With slower-maturing young this is not so easily arranged. Sometimes, as with wolves, pairs form and rear the young together. But with many ungulates, like the red deer, a group of females with their offspring, led by an older hind, form the ongoing social unit. Males associate with these "harems" only at the rutting period.

The reason behind the invariability of the mother-child bond in mammals—as compared with the extreme variability of the male-female bond—is very simple: suckling.[5] Mammals after all are by definition the animals that suckle their young. With this evolutionary innovation the basis is laid for a greater development of sociality than can be found elsewhere in nature. This in turn follows from the longer period of dependency and immaturity in mammalian young. The young of an animal that mature quickly are fully formed both physically and socially at an early stage. Those that mature slowly have plenty of time to *learn* their sociality and incorporate greater variety into their behavior. As we go up the phylogenetic scale of mammals, we find several trends: life span increases; the gestation period becomes longer; the period of immaturity lengthens; the suckling period is extended; the size of the litter decreases until single births are most common. All these factors conspire to delay the maturity of the young animal as long as possible, to prevent his becoming fully formed too quickly.

In all these matters man is the supermammal. He does not achieve this by somehow overcoming or denying or surpassing his mammalian nature, but by exaggerating it.[6] Of all mammals it is man who capitalizes most on the biological particularities of his order. This means that he exaggerates the *behavioral* characteristics—an increase in learning ability dependent on the greater size and complexity of the brain, an even more pronounced period of mother-child dependency, a greater emotional lability, a more elaborate sexuality, more complex play, more spectacular aggressivity, a greater propensity for bonding, a more extended system of communications, and so on. But all this rests on the bedrock of the mother-child bond, itself a product of the live-birth-and-suckling syndrome that is the defining characteristic of the zoological order to which we belong.

The mammalian mother has to suckle the child so that it can live, flourish, and eventually breed. But again, the higher we mount the scale of mammalian complexity, the more it becomes true that something other than simple feeding is involved in the mother-child relationship—particularly when, as with bottle-feeding, actual suckling is unnecessary. The further we move from the governance of primary instincts into the arena of learned abilities, the more it becomes essential for the slowly growing young animal to get its learning *right*. A great deal of its most important learning occurs early and involves those experiences that will provide the foundations for further learning. Since this is the time when the young will be intensively suckling, nature has no option but to make the mother-child bond the matrix for the basic learning processes of the maturing animal.

Simply on the basis of what we know about the social mammals in general, we can predict that if the mother-child bond does not go right, the unfortunate youngster may never get any of his *other* bonds right. The first instruction in the program says: "Form a close and emotionally satisfying bond with the mother; when completed, move on to form x number of bonds, in the following order." Ultimately the "nonbreeding" bond with the mother has to be transformed into a "breeding" bond with a member of the opposite sex. If the initial instructions are not properly followed, the rest of the program may be jeopardized and emerge in an attenuated or skewed form. At worst the wrongly programmed animal may not be able to breed at all and thus be lost to the gene pool; at best it may breed but put the programming of its own offspring in danger.

Sometimes nature tries to make sure of the bond by relatively mechanical means. These, like all instinctive mechanisms, have the advantage of sureness—but they can also go disastrously awry because of their otherwise advantageous rigidity. The idea of "imprinting" is now firmly established in both the ethological literature and the popular imagination.[7] In some animals (*e.g.*, most species of duck) the young learn quickly and dramatically to associate with the first moving object of a given size and color that they see—or even more generally with any larger object that they encounter at a specific period in their development. They will follow and respond to this object in predictable and specified ways. The "object," of course, is almost always their mother, but if for some reason it is something else, the program is totally and irreversibly confused, and a duckling may become attached to a dog or an ethologist or a scientist's boot. The unfortunate creature accepts this object as of its own "species"; once the animal matures, the inexorably confused program instructs it to mate with the only other member of its "species," with comic and yet pathetic results. Zoo animals, to the distress of zoological societies and breeders, thus fixate on their keepers and fail to breed with their own kind. But this is rare. Usually the creature makes the appropriate fixation, and often this is ensured by such devices as having mother and child isolated for a period immediately after the birth. This is common in mammals and gives time for the bond to be formed exclusively with the mother animal, who will then be followed incessantly, turned to in danger, and generally used as a base providing security for forays into the outside world.

Ethologists, with some accuracy, have established "critical periods" during which various types of imprinting take place in various species. But even if the "learning" involved is not of this rather dramatic and rigid character—as is the case with higher mammals—it is nevertheless like it in that it must take place at certain times and in certain ways, and that its outcome determines to a large extent the future performance of the creature. For example, some infants for some reason may not take easily to food, and some mothers may be unwilling or temperamentally incapable of suckling or otherwise feeding them. As we have noted, these characteristics will simply not reproduce themselves in the gene pool if the infant dies or later cannot breed. And, again, the infant may be permanently damaged in a behavioral sense because it has not learned the first rule of the behavioral biogrammar that allows him or her to go on.

This sounds drastic, and it is. There is a striking similarity between behavioral "malnutrition" and food malnutrition. It is now absolutely clear that children deprived of good food—chiefly the substances contained in milk—when they are very young can never wholly recover. For one thing, their growth rates are adversely affected.[8] This has evident consequences for other features of their development. Also, it has been shown recently that the lack of protein in the newborn's diet inhibits the little body's development of myelin, which is necessary if brain cells are to form in the appropriate sequence.[9] Brain damage results as surely from deprivation in the first weeks and months of life as it does from a concussion later.

Development is also closely tied to social patterns, and there is a close connection between behavior and food—one without the other will not do. There is no point in going into an attractive restaurant staffed with capable and friendly waiters who do not serve food; it is just as unpleasant to eat good food in an environment in which one is harassed and abused. For the infant it is a far more desperate matter. Children in orphanages get the food but not the behavior; infants of loving but poor parents may get the behavior, but they will not get the food.[10] In both cases, if the children live to become adults they will be less effective and more frail than their counterparts who were raised by competent mothers and given suitable food.

Our proposal is that the mother-infant bond precedes all others in time—which is obvious—and is the basis for the development of the other bonds that humans are "programmed" to be likely to have. What is the evidence for a statement both so simple and so portentous of complexities to come?

The maladjusted adult has frequently been traced back to the disturbed child, and the disturbed child to the unloved infant. Psychoanalysts argue among themselves about the most vulnerable period of the mother-child relationship.[11] Some favor a late date, some argue for the first few months, some stress the moment of birth itself with its attendant traumas, while still others look into the darkness of the womb—which does in fact contain a living child capable of psychic upset. In any event, the child *is* born in a very "fetal" state—one of the means of extending its dependency and hence its maturation period. But all agree that basic disturbances in the early stages will adversely affect proper passage through the later ones. Many of these explanations and arguments seem overelaborate. A convergence of work in child psychiatry and the study of animal behavior suggests that something rather simple is behind all this, even if the simplicity is disguised by the jargon term "separation trauma."[12] Nature intended mother and child to be together. It is at once as simple and as profound as that. If they are separated when the bond should be forming, it forms imperfectly, if at all. The child suffers a deep sense of loss and even physical distress. And though the mother may not be clear about what has happened to her, she too may suffer—from feelings of depression and inadequacy.

The mother is totally essential to the well-being of the child. Remove her, and its world collapses. This dependence is based on the suckling tendency of mammals, but it does not wholly hinge on food. It is largely a matter of emotional security, of which food is but a part.

The human mother is a splendid mammal—the epitome of her order. Her physiology is more highly developed for suckling behavior—with permanent breasts, for example—than any of her cousins, except domesticated ungulates bred specially for milk-giving. But more than this, she is, like any other mammal, emotionally programmed to be responsive to the growing child. Her whole physiology from the moment she conceives is changed not only to accommodate the sheer business of parturition but also to cope with this physical extension of her body for years after the event. Animal experiments have shown that the softness and texture of the mother—and even her smell—are more important to the child than simply her milk supply, although without the latter, in most "wild" conditions, it would not live. Primate infants deprived of real mothers will adapt best to mechanical substitutes that are alike in *texture* to their real parent, in preference to those that simply provide milk but no warmth.[13]

Whatever the value of the substitute, the young animal, psychically, is permanently damaged by the separation.[14] The male may never learn to relate to females, with the consequence that his sexual identity will be confused.[15] The female will almost certainly fail in her task as a mother by ignoring her own offspring, as she was ignored herself.[16] Anyone who has seen the grief, the listlessness, the obvious and heart-rending despair of infant monkeys deprived, in an experiment, of maternal care, will echo the sentiments of the man who performed the experiment. He declared: "Thank God we only have to do it once to prove the point."[17]

The point is proved time and time again in human society. Brief separations of mother and child are bad enough, but excessive separations are devastating. Nature is ruthless about this. In the case of some animals, if the mother is not able to find the child immediately at birth, respond to its cries, and above all, lick it from head to foot, she will treat it as a stranger and refuse to suckle it when it is later presented to her.[18] Yet in the name of sanitation we risk tampering with this delicate system by taking babies away from their mothers on the maternity wards moments after they are born. Monkey infants that lose their mothers develop all the characteristics of autistic children, even to the endless rocking and crouching—with little chance of becoming fully functioning adults. Our orphanages and nurseries are full of children wholly or partly so deprived who also rock and grieve and make only painfully insecure adjustments to the adult world.

The practice of taking infants from their mothers during the first five days of life is an example of the acceptance of hygiene and comfort as of greater importance than the possibility of behavioral disruption—if this is even considered. In some of the most sophisticated and admirable places on earth—the wards of excellent hospitals—newborn organisms emerge from their mothers' wombs in a demanding and exciting process to face a suddenly novel environment containing unmuted sounds, swirls of unfamiliar air, and the impressive movements of hands and bodies. Often the mother of such a confused and needy creature is drugged and will sleep for many hours after this first potential social encounter with her child. The neonate itself may be somewhat under the influence of her drugs and in any event will be quickly removed in a plastic basket from her presence to a ward of a dozen or two similar creatures, many crying, all under high light, and all handled by skilled nurses—part of whose professional skill must be that denial of the special treatment which seems to mark how women treat their own children as opposed to the children of others. The child will be labeled by a card on its container, and some mothers will confuse their own child with another, and the more naïve among them will question their competence as mothers: if they cannot even recognize their child, how can they possibly cope with it?

This plight has to be seen in the context of the improved health of mothers and infants. It is probably true that there are important advantages to having the mother rest after the single most trying of all predictable human actions. The question here is about the effects of systems—which are perhaps useful for mothers and certainly efficient for hospitals—on the essential bond between mother and infant. On theoretical and empirical grounds there is a real and disturbing possibility that—with effects difficult to measure—some human babies and their mothers encounter in the act of birth a fact of technology and custom that may make more uncertain the elaboration of a bond begun *in utero,* a bond severely interrupted at just that point when presumably some forceful re-creation of the certainty and strength of uterine environment is most necessary.

The mother-child bond is the basic instruction in the human bonding program, and the ground rule of the human biogrammar. If this rule is not learned, the human may not learn to "speak" behaviorally, just as, if he does not learn the difference between subject and predicate, he will never be able to handle the verbal grammar. What he "learns," essentially, is the ability to make successful bonds in general. Bonds depend on feelings, and the mother-deprived child is most commonly described as "affectless"—lacking the motive power to love or care. It is here that the groundwork for "emotional maturity" is laid: that the child will eventually become an adult capable of the full sexual experience and of complete parental behavior. In general, he learns to be confident in his own ability to explore; he develops self-confidence and security. Young monkeys with mothers will move off to enjoy the pleasures of curiosity, whereas maternally deprived monkeys will be afraid to. Successful bonding in later life depends to a great extent on this tendency to explore. This program of security/exploration is so easily interfered with—especially in "advanced" societies—that a large number of people end up by making only partial adjustments in all these areas, to the detriment of their social relationships.[19]

It is just as important to note that the instructions are also quite precise about the termination of the bond—which begins with the gross physiological act of weaning and ends with the transference of emotional ties onto peers and mates.[20] If the mother ignores the instructions to terminate the bond, the results can be just as disastrous as if the child continues to talk baby talk into adulthood: its chances of communicating effectively with other adults are severely curtailed. "Maternal overprotection"—the continuation into adolescence of the relationship appropriate to childhood—extends the mother-child program to a time when the "child-child" and "child–other-adult" programs should be coming into play.

It is not necessary here to pursue the *content* of the mother-child bond, once it has been established as the basic bond. Whatever else a linguistic system does, it has to have some means of sorting out subject from object. Whatever else a social system does, it has to have some means of ensuring the security of the relationship between mother and infant until at least that point when the infant is independently mobile and able to survive with a reasonable chance of reaching adulthood. There are many and various ways of doing this. Within any animal species they tend to be uniform, but across species, as has been seen, they are very diverse. Within the human species, given the biological adaptation of culture, there is also diversity—but within very narrow limits. And the diversity revolves around this basic dyad as a fixed point in a changing social universe. The languages are exotically different, but the basic grammar is always the same.

The mother-child bond offers a model for other bonded relationships in which humans and other social animals engage. The model implies that social responses of a surprisingly complicated kind involve genetic programming. These patterns, far from reflecting simple "instinctive" needs, are directly social; their stimulus, operation, and consummation depend upon the existence of other members of the species and their actions. This is really the heart of the ethological approach; social interactions reveal the evolutionary history and biology of an animal as much as its digestive processes and means of movement do.

In this context we can reexamine some of the more common human relationships. Perhaps this will clarify the limits of variation and the intricacy of the special process of affiliation that marks us as the particular animal we are. So let us turn to some of the other strategic bonds between members of our species, in order to understand better how these "social organs" have worked in our history and how they are expressed today.

The claim that the mother-child bond is the basic one might appear paradoxical, if not repetitious; after all, it is preceded by sexual intercourse—which implies that the mating bond preceded *it*. But the answer to this is that the mating "bond" may or may *not* have preceded it—it does not have to. A simple act of copulation which need last only ninety seconds is all that is necessary to start the mother-child process.

But a mating bond is convenient to ensure food and protection for the mother and child at a later stage. Protection is what the whole business is about. In other species and many human societies, the mating bond as such is not activated to this end. There are many alternatives. Among deer, as we have seen, a group of self-sufficient females provides this envelope of provision and protection.[21] Even when the "harems" form during the rutting season, the stag does not in any sense control the group—he is preoccupied with repeated copulation on the one hand and driving off rival males on the other. The harem generally responds to the leadership of the old female; once his inseminating function is completed, the male leaves for the rest of the year. Sometimes the mother and young can survive without any help at all—as with the hamster. In other cases a troop organization takes over as the envelope or shell, as with elephants or trooping monkeys. Here the whole group is responsible for the mother-child units within it. All the males and mature childless females surround and protect the nursing mothers. Many bonds are activated in this way, but in none of these cases is the mating bond more than a brief episode.

The bond, once activated, can take a number of forms. With some carnivores, such as wolves, pairs form for life, develop "packs" with the offspring, and enter a cycle of family development.[22] Alternatively, as with hamadryas baboons, "harems" (each male may have four or five females) are collected, which last for a lifetime and not just a rutting season.[23] Among the anthropoid apes there is the unique case of the gibbon, which lives in treetops and defends territories. On each territory a mated pair jointly repels intruders and disperses its young as soon as they are mature.[24] In all these primate groups the mother-child unit is a "constant." What varies is the degree of involvement of the mate. In most cases of pair formation the key determinants are ecological—the unit of male-plus-female (or females) and offspring is the optimum unit for survival. Where these ecological conditions do not hold, a species is unlikely to make much of the mating bond.

What is true across the range of mammalian species is true across different populations of the human species. Because of the brilliant biological adaptation of culture, human societies can create different rules. They can adapt various customs to fit different ecological niches, and need not wait for natural selection to program them genetically. They have to observe a number of grammatical ground rules—one of which has already been explored here—but they can use a variety of languages. Each human population protects and provides for its mother-child units; but whether or not the father stays "home" is another and highly variable matter. The strategy of the father staying home has been commonly adopted because human cultures can capitalize on the powerful motivations aroused by courtship, especially during the volatile and intense period of puberty. These motivations can then be changed into powerful bonding patterns associated with parenthood. The combination can produce a relatively lasting set of bonds that make up what we commonly refer to as the "family."

But it is revealing that societies always seem to find it necessary to surround these "natural" bonds with a host of legal provisions and sanctions to make them stick. This is not the case with many consanguine bonds: people do not have to enter into contractual obligations to be made someone's sister, but they do have to have a "contract" to become someone's husband or wife. It is arguable that without all the legal safeguards a much more fluid mating and family system would prevail; indeed, there are many instances where this is so.

This is a central point. Many social scientists want to maintain that the "family" is in some sense a "natural" unit like the "family" of the gibbon and is based on a similar "pairing-for-life" instinct.[25] When people persistently behave differently, they are accused of failing to live up to their natural obligations, and we speak of breakdown, neuroses, the crisis in the family, etc. Our interpretation is exactly the opposite.[26] What the "family" as a unit does is artificially to cement together, with social conventions and legal rules, one subset of the possible sets of bonds that can be used as the envelope for the mother-child unit.[27] In many senses this parental bond is the most fragile, even if the most common, of such arrangements, since it involves bringing together two people not previously related and predicating the success of their relationship on the relatively temporary emotional ties that flood through them and between them in the courtship stage. Most societies that use mated pairs as the basic units do not dare to leave the necessary stability of the family to the vagaries of adolescent emotion. They "arrange" marriages without regard to such emotion, but with the continuity and stability of the unit in mind.

It is nonsense to assume that the only kind of "parental" bond possible in the human species is between sexual partners. Yes, the mother has to be impregnated, but her impregnator need not be the male who provides the provision and protection for her and her young. There is another bond more fundamental in some ways, and just as logical—the bond between brother and sister. This is an asexual bond that grows up over the years and is in some sense ready-made for the task of parental care. It does not involve the setting up of a new and risky contractual relationship, but can draw on already existing trust and deeply developed obligations. In some human societies, the weight of responsibility for a woman and her children rests with her brothers. Her sex life is separate from her parental role. Usually she has a series of lovers more or less attached to her. To call such systems exceptional is to beg the question: they represent a logical and viable alternative that, while relatively rare, works well in certain circumstances. The mating relationship and the security relationship are simply not allowed to coincide.[28]

In other cases the two types of bond—blood ties and mating ties—may both be partly activated. Some aspects of security can be associated with the mating bond, and so shared with the brother-sister tie.[29] The most common arrangement here is for groups of related women to live together and to depend for some things on their brothers and sons, and for other things on their husbands and sons-in-law. Again the brother-sister tie is permanent and continuous (one cannot divorce a brother), while the husband-wife tie is relatively loose. The ecological factors are uppermost here. It is quite possible for the female households to live without reliable and continuous male support. There is no need for the mating bond to be protected by a weight of sanctions, since intermittent male help will suffice. Men therefore tend to float about between households, and while some marriages can be long-lasting, many are short-lived. This is sometimes described as a system with a "high divorce rate," but this description is very ethnocentric. It is more accurate to see it as a high turnover of mates.

A similar solution involves groups of related females as the envelope, but with no real institution of marriage. "Boyfriends," or whatever they may be called, can meander through the system, but the women can get by without them; they exist to satisfy sexual and emotional needs, and not to protect and provide. Sometimes the women are simply self-sufficient, or sometimes, in good primate style, the society at large assumes the role of protector.[30]

Here the chief function of the mating bond is not to ensure the security of the mother-child unit; it is a natural device for bringing together the healthy young males and females on whose sexual enthusiasm rests the survival of the group. The bond is as much the result of maturation and biological "wiring" as puberty is. It is so strong that virtually all communities create rules to control its incidence; rarely is sexual intercourse completely random and unrelated to measures of social inhibition. In fact, a lot of work goes into keeping pairs apart.

In quite dramatic contrast, most societies create elaborate and formidable rules to keep the pairs together, once they have mated. Far from representing the intrinsic normality of the mating bond, these rules suggest how precarious it really is. The great variety and depth of customs surrounding kinship and marriage are not expressions of an innate and ready tendency to form families: *they are devices to protect the mother-child unit from the potential fragility of the mating bond.*

This is diametrically opposed to the agreeable fantasy that families will live happily ever after if only they will love each other more in some fine romantic fashion. The parental bond is not the mating bond; recalling and evoking the mating bond may embellish and stimulate the parental one, but it is still not the same thing. The traditional Indian scheme reverses this procedure. Marriages are arranged by elders to suit the needs and structures of the overall community. It is possible that the couple may not have met before their elaborate wedding commits them to each other for life. But then the assumption is that for perhaps a year they will do very little, and spend a great deal of time learning about each other both socially and sexually. The elaborate manuals of sexual technique—such as the *Kama Sutra*—which surprise many Euro-Americans by their earnestness and invention, are guides in a situation in which the equivalent of courtship happens *after* the equivalent of mating.[31]

In examining the biogram of primate politics we tried to see how far the human primate was governed by, or transgressed, this set of ground rules. We sought to clarify the relationship between breeding systems and political systems. Here we are considering the primate breeding system in its human manifestation, and accordingly we should outline the rules of the primate breeding biogram.

In itself the primate breeding biogram falls within the mammalian parameters already described, sometimes pushing them to extravagant extremes.[32] But however much variety we find in the politico-breeding systems of the higher primates, certain features are outstanding. For one thing, in direct contrast to the ungulates, both sexes associate the whole year round in relatively closed groups. As we have seen in "Political Nature," this was once attributed to year-round sexual activity, which kept the males interested in the females.

But this is too simple. Even in groups that have marked breeding seasons on the ungulate pattern, the association of the sexes is not sporadic but continuous throughout the year. This is all clearly related to the adaptive functions of the group as a defense mechanism in the struggle for survival—particularly against the more dangerous carnivores. Because they lacked, among other things, the ungulate specializations of speed and large numbers, the primates on the plains had to stick together if their little breeding groups were to survive. The protecting and controlling functions of the males, and the constant attention paid them by the females, are what ensure the heterosexual bond among the savanna monkeys rather than year-round sexual delectation.

In all the higher primates the males and females are sexually intrigued by one another only at certain times.[33] When the female is menstruating or pregnant she is not an object of interest. As she approaches ovulation (the midpoint of her menstrual cycle) and recedes from it, she herself initiates sexual activity by soliciting the attention of males through sexual presentation. Despite the sometimes spectacular genital swellings and colorings that attract male attention, it is certain that her ripeness is judged by smell rather than sight.[34]

In the typical baboon group, the dominant male takes over the ovulating female at peak estrus to form with her what primatologists call a "consort" relationship.[35] For a short period—from a few days to a week—he directs all his attention to her and she to him. They groom each other incessantly, and copulate often. Once the honeymoon is over, she is thrown back into the pool of females. Others may have a chance to mount her, subject, of course, to the whims of the alpha male. She, however, grows less and less interested, gradually ceasing to take part. Thus, for a brief while at her peak of sexual receptivity she is the exclusive "property" of one male; but before and after this she becomes the relatively asexual property of the group at large.

There are variations on this pattern. Baboons in the dry desert, faced with different survival problems, have to be relatively puritanical in their sexual lives.[36] However, chimpanzees in their forest paradise can afford greater sexual freedom. The desert baboons have as the subunit of their large herds the individual "harem." Here each successful male has several females that he has "kidnapped" as infants, then mothered and nurtured, and so "bonded" to himself by a fairly elaborate process. Even so, he has to keep them near him and faithful by administering neck bites when they stray adulterously toward the eager young males on the periphery; and so they soon learn the close limits of their sexual options. It is the female who inevitably gets punished in primate society for her failure to attend exclusively to the sexual needs of her consort. The marauding male is ignored by the irate cuckold. But even the arrogant dominant male will allow an "apprentice" younger male to join the group and eventually succeed him as harem leader. This scheme makes the otherwise brief "consort" relationship into a year-round structure by this spectacular method of attaching females to a particular male or males. It is into these units that herds split up in the dry season. Ecologically this is the most efficient organization for such a harsh and demanding environment. Out of the basic primate biogram emerges thus a "polygamous" unit by means of a particular version of the bonding process. The difference between the two systems, however, is one of emphasis. In some sense, even among the savanna baboons, the females continue all year to "belong" to the alpha male of the group. Since he has ultimate control over their sexual activity, he can allow himself the luxury of tolerating other males around in a way that his desert cousins cannot. The hamadryas baboon in the Ethiopian desert, for example, will tolerate only his apprentice near his females, while his chacma cousin on the plains will tolerate a larger number of subdominant males. The basic program is put to different uses in the two cases, but in both it remains true that the male is only sexually interested, and the female only sexually receptive, at certain points of the cycle.

Defensive measures and ecological pressures are not so prominent among the forest chimpanzee.[37] Once a female goes into heat, the whole band of males will pursue her and copulate with her in turn. The order of copulation may be determined by dominance, but everyone participates. The chimpanzee, we have to conclude, is incurably promiscuous. But here again sexual interest depends on the cycle of the female; it is she who initiates the activity. This is one end of the primate scale of sexual behavior; the consortship of the savanna baboons is yet a stage further toward some kind of assignment of mates; the harems of the desert baboons are the extreme of this process, in which a new bonding mechanism—kidnap-adoption—is utilized to make the consort relationship virtually permanent.

The gibbon must be mentioned here. He alone forms nuclear families, and so is dear to the hearts of those who want to derive Euro-American mating customs from a primate source. But the gibbon never came down from the treetops to which he fatally overadapted with his fantastic brachiation abilities. He is a rather large animal, and in order to survive in his treetop habitat, he had to adopt territorialism; students of gibbon behavior have calculated that a gibbon territory will support only a pair of adults and their young. Thus, the only system open to him is that of pair formation. Once they are mobile, the offspring are ejected from the territory, like young birds from the nest. After this they fend for themselves. There is nothing here to suggest a forerunner of a human situation, as the gibbon is much more like some birds or some of the prosimians than like his ape and monkey cousins who took to the ground.[38]

In all these cases the constant again is the mother-child unit, and all the variable systems are just strategies to protect it. In all of them the female has a cycle of hormonally controlled receptivity that governs male sexual interest in her. In varying degrees, females are attached to males for longer periods, according to the specializations of the species. The intensity of this attachment has to do with the degree of tolerance a male will show toward other males in his personal space. When females are in heat, they will present promiscuously, and the male therefore has to establish his exclusive right to copulate with them. So, along with the female cycle, there are two other factors:

male rights to copulate, which depend on dominance, and the establishment of male rights to exclusive attention for varying periods. But in all cases there remains constant a degree of protection for the results of the copulation: there is always an envelope for the mother-child unit. The primate system differs from the ungulate system in its year-round association of males and females: the protection of the mother-child units is a full-time function of primate males.

There is an important contrast here with pair formation among the carnivores. A number of investigators have stressed the fact that the human primate became carnivorous and his social organization should therefore be compared with that of the pack of hunting carnivores.[39] But what became omnivorous (not carnivorous) was a previously largely vegetarian primate. This was undoubtedly a major shift and did not have a background of millions of years of carnivorous experience built into it. The great cats and the hunting dogs fixed on their specializations earlier and built them into their genes. One of their strategies was classical "pair formation," in which animals at puberty mate for life, sometimes eventually forming packs with their offspring, or sometimes, like the gibbon, sending out their young to fend for themselves. Whatever the ground-dwelling primates did in their transition to hunting and regular meat-eating had to be manufactured out of the primate biogram.

To see what they did in fact do, we have to look at the end result—ourselves. To what extent have we, in the course of our particular evolution as a species, made radical changes in the biogram, and to what extent, in preserving it, have we molded it to suit our particular needs? At least one change has been offered as being fairly spectacular: the estrous cycle of sexual activity has been "lost," and with it the essential dominance of hormonal control over female sexual behavior.[40]

But this can be examined more closely. We are led to believe that the structuring of human sexual behavior is predominantly sociocultural; the fact that sexual activity results in the biological fact of procreation is somehow abstracted from what is an otherwise non-biological business. And also that females are not governed or even indirectly influenced by the estrous cycle, because they do not exhibit the extravagant coloration of the other primates' estrous displays, and because there are no evident human equivalents of the heady quest for intercourse that marks the rhythm of the primate sisterhood. The upshot of this is that the menstrual cycle is purely physiological in effect and utterly nonsocial in implication. This may be so, but if it is, it is curious, since a sensible biological rule is that breeding—which is never left to chance—is always mediated and stimulated by a set of signals and states of readiness that are not left to chance, either.

However, there is suggestive evidence that the menstrual cycle of the human female serves at least some of the functions of the general primate cycle, through the variation and subtlety in the expression of these functions are of a quite different order. (Assuming, that is, that primatologists who study the sexual behavior of the subjects perceive all the features of mating encounters. Of this we cannot be confident— for example, the crucial role of smell in primate sexual attraction has only recently been appreciated for the central mechanism it is.[41] There may be others; the fact that we cannot easily imagine what they could be is neither here nor there, and is chiefly another restatement of the reality that one of the useful things scientists do is find things they did not expect to find, or even look for.) This estimate of the possible importance of the menstrual cycle for the human female de- rives from the general idea that any important bond in the animal world is served by some mechanism that ensures its occurrence and abets its success. But if the courtship or mating pattern is such an important one—and our stubborn breeding proclivities even in an era when children are not an economic asset seem to support this view—there are probably some features of the bond that are like the other primates'.

Undoubtedly, cortical additions and modifications are important and consequential. It is true that human females are permanently able to engage in sexual relations and always susceptible to particular blandishments of circumstance and person. This is how they are able to behave, but it is not clear that this describes how they do behave.

One is tantalized by evidence like the following: if we do not inquire about subjective feelings and urges, but simply count objectively what primatologists refer to with characteristic indelicacy as "copulatory success," we find that human females are more likely to copulate more often at the midpoint of their cycles, when they are ovulating, than at either end of the cycles. There is a slight rise in the frequency of copulation just before the onset of menstruation, and there is a clear peak in mid-cycle. The curious thing is that the curve of human female copulatory success and that of the macaque monkey (for which the most data are available) are identical—a rise toward midpoint, a fall-off, and then a slight rise before the menstrual period begins.

The clustering of copulatory acts at the midpoint of the cycle is equally true, though less well documented, for all other primates.[42] Just as for the other primates, the physical cycle of the human female is accompanied by a behavioral cycle. This cycling is not as obvious in the case of humans—even to the individual women who routinely fail to anticipate cyclical changes in their moods and predispositions. But our prediction is that if we managed to get fair reports of both sexual activity and sexual feelings, we would find that, despite variations in class, culture, climate, and protocol of sexual relationship, there was a central tendency for women to want, and to have, sexual intercourse far more when they are likely to conceive than when they are not. That this might surprise some people is itself surprising. The menstrual cycle is related in part to hormone levels, which we know influence behavior in general and sexual behavior in particular. In normal conditions the production of hormones in the female system is tied to the reproductive cycle. Why, after all, should the existence of sexual hormones be unrelated to the sexual process? What we see in this cyclical business is yet another feature of the general phenomenon that physical processes are related to social ones, and that this is especially so where the sexual interaction is concerned.[43]

A particularly dramatic piece of evidence for this involves that sense of smell so important in the sexual signaling system of primates. Women, it seems, increase by fantastic proportions their ability to detect the odor of musk (and strong odors generally) during ovulation.[44] At this behaviorally intense moment in their cycle, they need, in order to detect its presence, only a small fraction of the amount of musk scent needed at either end of their cycle. That increased sensitivity to odor should correlate with increased sexual excitement makes excellent primatological sense. Not only is the sense of smell affected, but so is clarity of perception. In the three days immediately preceding and following menstrual bleeding, human females display an array of behavioral disturbances.[45] Menstruation is signally influential. No woman needs to be told this, and most men have felt its impact. When her sexual excitability runs down and her body readjusts to prepare for the ejection of the unfertilized eggs, she suffers from considerable perceptual confusion, and fails in tests where she has to discriminate the relevant from the irrelevant.[46] (These tests have been conducted largely by men, who have not so far tried to find out if women are better at discrimination performances when they are ovulating. They should be, in the same way that they are better at detecting certain odors. For at this point they are keyed up to perform one of their essential mammalian female tasks to the best of their ability—getting themselves impregnated, and presumably by males they prefer over others.)

The female's perceptual confusion as she moves toward the turbulent monthly episode is accompanied by a rise in her propensity to accidents,[47] nervous disorder and mental breakdown, criminality,[48] inability to work and concentrate, poor performance in examinations,[49] and a general if relative dislocation of normal routines. It appears that the more sensitive researchers become to these special factors, the more related they turn out to be to more behaviors in general.

Throughout this whole debate on what humans are really like in their sexual bonding behavior and what implications this behavior has for "families," there is a vital non sequitur, a constant tendency to leap from animal *behavior* to human *institutions*. Thus an observer of human behavior can argue that although many marriages, in America for example, fail, most married couples stay together, and that this illustrates the "strength of the pair bond."[50] But it does not necessarily illustrate anything of the kind. In societies without divorce laws, where separation is wholly at the discretion of the individuals involved, separation is much more common than permanence. What the figures for the United States show is that the institution of marriage—a contractual legal institution that binds couples together and allows them to separate only at considerable cost and with considerable trouble and sometimes penalty—can be made to look successful in the purely statistical sense. On the other hand, when we look at what human creatures *do* about their sexual and mating behavior, we may again find that the difference between them and their primate relatives is of degree only.

This is not to underestimate the importance of the male-female bond, ephemeral, buttressed by legal conventions and customs, and secondary to the demands of the mother-infant bond as it is. There is one sense in which it is crushingly important to individuals and central to the mating arrangement of communities. Two individuals formerly capable of sustaining a round of activities and of living in their own skulls and in terms of the needs which they can fulfill for themselves become inordinately and troublingly attached to each other. The ardor of this need is most easily observed in adolescents—but adolescents are not the only ones who bond fully and single-mindedly. At some time or other something happens to nearly everyone so that he focuses all his attention on another person, from whom he in turn demands attention of the same dire and exhausting kind. Every act, every word, every touch, is a marker for the lover's insistence that this encounter is particularly blessed. Shaw once said that "Love consists in overestimating the difference between one woman and another." But perhaps when one makes the personally revolutionary move of becoming attached to another person, one must be convinced that the object of this disruptive act is not only desirable but unique as well.

This is very dramatic, but the encounter itself is dramatic. It has to be. The bond that unites people to breed is altered by the very circumstances and effect of its success—that persons marry and bear young. But the way of uniting them in the first place is so strong and demanding that people want to re-create it. Thus, many try to have a second honeymoon, to relive the "first date" or the first love, or somehow to recapture that mixture of innocence and imperious demand that is agonizing at the time but nonetheless thrilling in anticipation or in memory.

The dilemma is clear enough, especially for adolescents, who have spent extremely important years with their mother and other kin and have estimated their movements in terms of these familiar realities. But now they are sexually mature: there are hormonal storms and physical eruptions, changes in cosmetic and hair pattern; legs suddenly grow too fast and control too slowly. Reputation among peers and little tides of childish fashion were important to them. But they grow out of the home base, out of whatever family structure there was. Now, with considerable speed, boys and girls become males and females; the sexes divide in corners at parties or gatherings, only to engage in the central arena, where the dancing is, in an increasingly fierce and troubling way. It is suddenly very hard to ask parental advice; rumors about the appropriate conduct of sexual-social relationships circulate freely. Young girls become worrisome to their parents. Young males become objectionable to the dominant males, who cannot countenance their emotional storms, their increasingly embarrassing demands for opportunities for drama, heroism, and participation in sexual action. Among baboons at this point the emerging males are as far from the center of the group as they are ever likely to be. They form little groups of two or three, and are bitten by the dominant males as they steal around the females.

This "peripheralization"—this being pushed out to the fringes—is equaled by the new, urgent desire to get to the center, both to be among the dominant males and to have access to the females. Among humans, there is this same interest in the females, the same wariness as in baboons. The human male and female have complex social cues to take, elaborate ritual paraphernalia and notions to carry with them in this little odyssey from one defined system of bonds given by their progenitors to another, which they will have somehow to create for themselves.

Adolescent males suffer confused instructions from the old program: become mature; remain dependent; show affection to girls and hardness to boys; accuse the dominants of being too powerful, yet admire their power; and perhaps begin dimly to shape out some way of reproducing. The job of reproducing is easy and fast and also immensely pleasurable. But reproduction, like justice, must not only be done, it must be seen to be done. Some social analogue of the actual or potential copulation must be established—the fraternity pin, the hibiscus behind the ear, the exchange of love fetishes or food. It is hard to become a sexual adult rather than a nonsexual needy child; the strength of the emotional interactions involved reveals both the intrinsic difficulty of reproductive bonding and its central importance to the persistence of the group and the actual life cycles of its members.

The various "instructions" the pubertal organism receives at this point are among the most complex it will receive in its whole life cycle. The adolescent is being told to go through the painful business of terminating the mother-child bond, and the only slightly less painful process of establishing heterosexual and unisexual bonds outside the immediate circle of kin. The young male is also being instructed to make forays into the male competitive arena, with the double outcome of establishing himself as a potentially successful breeder and a likely candidate for a position in the male hierarchy—two positions that have always been closely related in evolutionary history.

The establishment of the mating bond can be seen as a direct successor to the consort behavior described for the primates. It is clearly unlike the territorial pair-bonding of the gibbon, or the "parent-surrogate" bonding of the hamadryas baboon, although parent-child elements do enter into it in part. In its structure it is much more like the relatively exclusive and very intense consort pairing that characterizes those savanna-dwelling primates, who are perhaps the best evidence so far mustered for the proto-stages of our own sexual evolution, and whose female sexual cycle resembles that of human females.

The heterosexual bond in our prototype primate has two phases. There is the constant year-round association of the males generally with the females generally, and all the noncopulatory elements of protection, control, cooperative care of the young, and grooming that go with it. This is punctuated by periods when females are sexually receptive and the object of competition among the males, with the dominant animal or animals taking priority. While the consort period lasts, the relationship between the animals is relatively exclusive, and their attention is directed almost exclusively to each other. Indeed, this emphasis on selective attention is the most obvious of the consort relationship.

The normal progress of this bonding episode is well established. The female first obtains the attention of the male by *visual* means—the coloring of the genital area. The male follows and inspects, chiefly with his nose. From this develops a *tactile* encounter involving grooming and mounting. Finally, if all these stages go well, there is the consummatory act of copulation. In between copulations there is a great deal of repetition of these stages, particularly grooming. Again the animals pay exclusive attention to each other, the male pausing only to drive off rivals. The period of sexual intensity wanes along with the interest of the male. Finally the female returns to the other females, and the male goes about his normal business, which is largely conducted in terms of his fellow males.

But his relationship with the female does *not* cease with the diminution of his intense sexual interest in her. She is still a female of his breeding group, and still under his control, care, and protection. She is like the wife of a polygamous sultan who, whether she is in favor with her master or an outcast among the eunuchs (males made physiologically peripheral), remains his property. But no primate male ever *provides* for his partners. The element of the parental or protective relationship in the male's bond with the mother-child units should not be overlooked.

In human courtship—the method by which the mating bond is established—much the same features and sequences occur, although they last, in some cases but not always, for a longer period than the maximum time of sexual receptivity.[51] Courtships can be brief and explosive or long and subdued, but they go though a well-established sequence. First the boy sees and is attracted to the girl; he then follows and approaches, and since he is human, uses speech. Tactile communication of a preliminary sort should come next, then copulation itself. In the intervals between copulations there will be repetitions of parts of this sequence, with a good deal of emphasis on tactile and verbal communication.

The bonding period will be characterized by the same qualities of intensive and exclusive attention between the partners that are found in the primates; this is a constant source of amazement and delight to the partners, and of sentimental pleasure or cynical amusement to the onlookers. During this period the male is extremely possessive of the female. He displays her and himself to other males, whose challenges he is ever ready to fight off. This is the "normal" procedure.

It is interesting that all the sexual behavior described as "pathological" involves fixation at one point of this sequence or the omission of various stages.[52] Thus the voyeur is stuck at the visual stage and the frissoneur at the tactile stage; and the rapist leaps literally from the sight to the act without going through the rest of the sequence. It is no surprise that failure to follow the correct program is related to the initial failure of the mother-child bond. Thus the success of the mating bond is in itself dependent on the success of the initial bond and does not automatically emerge as a "pair bond" on the carnivore or bird pattern at puberty. Only the message to try to form such a bond in the appropriate sequence is transmitted at this confusing and exciting time.

Like its primate counterpart, this bond is not necessarily either long-lasting or exclusive. Both longevity and exclusivity are contingent factors. It is true that the bond is usually exclusive for a time, but, as it is highly dependent on novelty for its effectiveness, it can and does very often wane rapidly when the partners seek fresh adventures. Its exclusivity, too, is a problem. Humans find it well within their capacity to bond successfully with more than one partner. This is not promiscuity—although humans can be as promiscuous as chimpanzees if they wish and have the opportunity. It is simply a question of having more than one partner with whom the courtship sequence has been successfully accomplished. Very often it is not only social sanctions, but time, energy, and resources as well that limit the possibilities of multiple bonding, which, however, can and does occur. Thus a male may take on the responsibility for protecting and providing for one mate, or as in polygynous societies, more than one, and these potentially parental duties may keep him around—especially if he is susceptible to legal sanctions. But his interest in novelty is not necessarily any more extinguished than it is in his savanna-monkey counterpart. Nor is his need to express dominance through display of subservient females—a need he will satisfy in fantasy, even if he does not in fact, through fear, devotion, or simple confusion about what he is supposed to be doing.

He will not only express dominance in fantasy but in fact, even if the factual situation excludes the element of sexual intercourse itself. For polygamy has to do with power rather than with sex. An alpha male *controls* his females and thus demonstrates his dominance; his erotic acts are less significant than his political ones. Even our latter-day bureaucratic polygamists can do this by the (theoretically) asexual method of controlling bevies of typists, research assistants, secretaries, nurses, receptionists, and other more or less skilled females. Perhaps the dominant male may hint that his bureaucratic control is also sexual and that the formal relationships which indicate his power as an official are matched by his intimate relations which suggest his power as a male. But this is relatively unimportant. What matters is that dominance is marked by increasingly exclusive control over female services.

Of course, as with all hierarchical relations, there is a symbolic as well as real aspect of the services provided the dominant males. In this context, sexual-political relationships are forms of the more general hierarchical principle—dominant men also have men who work for them, and occasionally dominant females have men working for them. It is enough now to suggest that altering the patterns of sexual dominance may have strange effects on the signaling system so deeply embedded in the wiring of the male-female interactions. It has been found consistently that female workers are more likely to be happy with male than with female bosses. No doubt in good measure they have been explicitly taught to respond in this way, as men have. Nonetheless, the ubiquity of the pattern suggests that the instruction is given to willing learners. That the problem is symbolized in the cliché figure of the "office wife" may belie the closeness of the association between the theoretical impersonality of industry and officialdom and the real intensity of the valences between their male and female workers.[53]

Let us summarize the main issues in our discussion of the male-female bond. There are continuities between the human and primate biograms at several points. Sexual behavior cycles with the female cycle, although less spectacularly; the mating sequence—"consort behavior" is very similar, with intense selective attention as the main feature; there is year-round association of males and females, largely having to do with protection of the young.

Human male-female bonding can capitalize on these features in several ways. It can combine the motivations of consort behavior with those of care and protection, to form a "parental bond," and hence a "family." But because of the potential volatility of the consort relationship, it needs to augment the bond with sanctions; it can separate these functions and allow care and protection to fall, for example, to the consanguine bond, while consort behavior remains purely sexual and companionable and never becomes "parental."

Much of the richness and variety of human kinship, marriage, and family systems depends on the possibilities inherent in this separation of "protective" and sexual functions, which we inherit.

This separation and its consequences are possible precisely because human sexual bonding is *not* like animal pair bonding, but essentially a compound of primate materials adapted to human ends.

Sex and dominance, reproduction and power, are so intimately linked that it is hard to disentangle the one from the other when considering sex in its social as opposed to its purely individual and personal setting.

In this chapter the concern has been more with the mechanisms of the bonds—mother-child and male-female—than with the selection pressures that produced them. The focus is the same for human societies as for primate societies—the male control of females for sex and dominance, and the female use of the males for impregnation and protection. But the purposes of this behavior, and hence its direction and content, become radically changed during the transition to humanity that hunting provoked. It is to this that we must now turn.

4.

BOND ISSUE TWO: MAN TO MAN

So FAR THESE primatelike patterns have been seen mostly in terms of their importance for individuals. We must now consider the importance of the bonds for the establishment of community, and focus on the all-important breakthrough from breeding systems to kinship systems.[1] The latter utilize our bonding potential to form unique breeding patterns that build on, but depart from, the basic rules of the primate biogrammar. In this context, male-female and mother-child bonds are not the only ones to be considered. There is the crucial set of male-male bonds that underlie politics, defense, the conduct of war, and a host of other activities vital to the broad self-interest of the community; and the set of female-female bonds important in maintaining social coherence.[2] We hope to show how mother-child and male-female bonds relate to male and female bonds. Humans pay great attention to rules of marriage and authority over children—and this can be seen to tie in with the political interactions of males and the notions of propriety and necessity that males contrive. To put it another way, humans retain many of the basic primate breeding and political patterns, but through kinship they incorporate females directly into the central processes of social life very differently from the way primate females are brought in.

That this happens through the exchange of females from one political group to another, in terms of some agreed scheme of reciprocity and commitment, is the very essence of this human innovation.

Among the terrestrial primates a division of labor among adult males, females, and young males already exists. Mature males control and defend the group; the females take care of the next generation; and the young males at the periphery act as guards and watchdogs. Certain key preoccupations provoke interaction between these "blocks" of the social system. The males are interested in the females for sexual purposes; the females look to the males for sexual encounter and for protection; the young males are attracted both to the females and to the advantages that positions in the central hierarchy can bring. The aim of the primate male is to get to the top of the male hierarchy and so control the females for purposes of sexual satisfaction. This applies to the primate male's *own* females—the females of his own group, who may well be his genetic sisters and daughters (though not usually his mother, for reasons that will be explored later). The philosophy of the human primate male, which seems to be slightly, but is in essence profoundly, different, is to get to the top of the male hierarchy and so control the females of his own group in *order to exchange them for females of another group*—thus achieving sexual satisfaction and political advantage. The evolutionary history of this extraordinary sexual revolution can be usefully reconstructed.

The prehuman division of labor was strongly affected by the radical transition to hunting. (Some primates hunt sporadically and in a rudimentary fashion, but hunting is nowhere a systematic way of life.[3]) The real shift that came with hunting, with its injection of animal protein into the primate diet, was the sharing of food. Primates do not share food. Each animal fends for itself. So of the two essential needs of the mother-child group, protection and provision, only protection is provided by the males. Males and females in the primate group even actively compete for food; and when the males do on the odd occasion indulge themselves in the luxury of the flesh of a newborn gazelle, for example, the alpha male either keeps it for himself or at best allows his nearest male bondmates to take a little. But the females are given nothing.

All this changed when the species changed to a semicarnivorous diet. Biologically, it was simply not possible to have the males taking all the animal protein while the females lived on gathered vegetable matter.

The division of labor was thus extended to the securing of food. Males ventured off into the new and exciting sphere of pursuit and killing of game, while females continued gathering in the ancient tradition of their primate forebears. This, if anything, intensified the differences in function between the two sexes, since very different selection pressures were now being brought to bear on them. But it also required that a new kind of relationship be set up, not only between men and women but also between men and men, older men and younger men, old ladies and young wives, and even between mothers and their children. In short, the whole scheme of social relationships had to be revamped—but only on the basis of what was given in the biogrammar. (It must be remembered that this was *not* a carnivore's biogrammar, which makes comparisons with carnivores interesting but dangerous if taken too literally.)

To put it simply, certain aspects of cooperation in the primate biogram could be capitalized on, while certain aspects of competition had to be rechanneled.[4] These were not bred out or in any way eliminated; they were mitigated or turned to advantage. One result was the women continued to cooperate in many established ways. Another was that the close interest in the young of new mothers that draws primate females together could be worked into the basis for cooperative gathering and food preparation. Also, the bonding of males for competition in the hierarchy and protection against predators could be used as the basis for cooperation, collective hunting, and defense. The hierarchy itself could operate as a selective device in producing good hunters and in the training of the young, as well as establishing candidates for leadership.

But it was absolutely necessary to mitigate the extreme competition in the search for food, where each primate foraged for himself at the possible expense of the others. It is often argued that sexual competition had to be eliminated, too. But sexual competition has never been eliminated—only reworked, and reworked to meet the new needs we have been describing. It was food that mattered, not sex.[5]

Under the new circumstances, each "block" of the social system had to develop strategies to get what it wanted out of the other blocks. The women needed sex, protection, and animal protein from the men; the men likewise needed sex, and the gathering and preparation of vegetable foods from the women. They also wanted two of the other products of female labor—daughters to exchange and sons to incorporate eventually into the male group. And so the adolescent boys were caught in the middle.

In theory, there was no obvious reason why these arrangements should not be made on a group basis, with the men as a whole taking from the women, and vice versa. However, this is neither the primate way, nor was it the best strategy for our emerging humans. As far as female needs are concerned, female primates do show preferences in mating, and the dominant males are more attractive to them as year-round objects of attention than their subordinates are. Besides, this would become doubly true when dominant males were likely to be the best hunters and therefore the best source of animal protein needed by them and their growing offspring. A female, or more likely several, would tend to fasten onto a male who was an excellent and guaranteed source of meat—who literally brought home the bacon. The male who could command the services of these females would in turn have an assured supply of vegetable food for himself and his companions in the hunt; he was also, of course, interested in her as a supplier of males for recruitment to his group, and of females for purposes of exchange.

This is a startling development. It has to do with changed conditions of male bonding. The complexities of human social life in the hunting phase required bonded male groups that were much more complex than those found in the vegetarian primates. For a start, a new phenomenon of *cooperation between groups* came into play for the exploitation of larger hunting territories, or at its most negative, for the establishment of "hands-off" treaties between groups on adjacent hunting grounds. Also, cooperation had to be set up between men previously unrelated—in much the same way as the mating bond set up relationships between men and women previously not bonded. *Allies* became necessary in a way that had not existed before. They were partly an insurance against help in times of difficulty, or again, at the negative end of the scale, partners in an agreement to suspend hostilities. The prototypes of the radically new bonds set up in response to these exigencies are the father-in-law–son-in-law bond and the bond between brothers-in-law. It might even be said that the bond between brothers-in-law is to males what the bond between husband and wife is to males and females. It is a contractual bond formed late in life by two previously unbonded individuals. Man and wife exchange services; brothers-in-law exchange women. That men exchange sisters (or daughters—it amounts to the same thing) is a custom enshrined in many human kinship systems. The brothers-in-law are then bound together by certain obligations, which vary from locale to locale but have the same general aim and object already discussed.

Once this principle is extended across groups, a new basis of integrating larger hunting units is formed. This can be stated as a principle: the men of a group will always take their women from one or more other groups, and yield all their own women in return. This makes the various groups *dependent* on each other for women and hence for offspring, and so binds them into a relationship, even if they are hostile. No one can afford to wipe out the people who supply them with wives. This principle of "out marriage" is technically called "exogamy," and is the basis of all human kinship systems. There are various versions of this basic principle, but it is enough to recognize that a new game is being played: "We will give our women to you if you give yours to us." Successful groups could extend alliances and join in a network of dominance relations between groups. Human kinship systems concern the patterns of relationships between individuals and groups brought about by the exchange of women.[6]

This is not a wild reconstruction of our past, but a description of what humans do all the time. Even in Euro-American society the minimal exogamic prohibition is observed: men do not marry their own mothers, sisters, or daughters. They "unload" them onto the marriage market and take other people's sisters and daughters—and less often mothers—in exchange. This exchange is not "direct," as it is in many other societies. But that is simply one way of playing the game. Too, in our society daughters are not usually the bases for alliances—but parents are often very choosy anyway about whom their children marry; it is not long since marriages were arranged with pecuniary, political, and other interests of the families chiefly in mind, and racial and religious interests are still influential.

Our humanized male primate does not stop competing sexually with other males. Nor does he cease to control and dominate females for purposes of dominance display. But given his changed conditions, he changes the nature of the women with whom these games are played: they are no longer his *own* women, but someone else's. What is more, the competitor is a possible ally. The primate male is playing the eternal game of genetic politics when he consorts with, dominates, and inpregnates his sister. The human male plays this basic game, but with a twist—he dominates, controls, and copulates with someone else's sister. But even copulation is not really the issue—it is control. Marriage is one human institution allocating this control over women and offspring, and making it effective. Copulation can go on inside and outside marriage, and does all the time. In man copulatory and political success are usually coincident, but logically separate. Sultans have been known to have hundreds of wives and never to have copulated with any of them; Shaka Zulu had one hundred wives but only one son,[7] while many men have had great and widespread copulatory success without either becoming demagogues or even marrying.

The "blocks" of the social system involve particular categories of members, with fairly predictable relationships between them. Links between the blocks can be drawn, and arrows seen moving back and forth between adult males and females, between females and young, between adolescent males and adult males, and so on. Social traffic can be plotted between the elements in the overall plan. Now let us imagine that we have diagrammed this on a rubber sheet. If we pull the sheet one way, we lengthen the distance between males and females and bring adolescent and adult males very close. Or we can stretch it another way and create a formidable hiatus between the females and males and bring the adolescent males very close to their mothers, sisters, and aunts. There are many possibilities.

But the different blocks always remain in relationship with one another, and each set of links remains essential to the overall picture. Though this is of course crudely oversimplified, it serves to show that we are dealing with a gestalt, a configuration, which may change its shape and dimensions but not its components and their interrelations. In essence this is an analogy from the branch of mathematics, topology, that concerns itself with this very problem and deals in detail with the regularities in the relationships that continue to exist despite the shape of the figure. The rubber sheet can be twisted, tied in knots, stretched over a steel drum, but the diagram remains the same because the points retain their relationship as long as the diagram remains intact. What human cultures do—to extend this analogy a precarious moment more—is stretch, twist, blow up like a balloon, press together, and influence the distances between the points. Yet the points remain and form the constituents of all cultures.[8]

It is still important to recall that these blocks and their relationships have been selected for, which has consequences for how individuals relate to one another—what they want from one another, what they can give to one another, what they can do together, and what they think of themselves in the presence of others. The women will relate to other women differently from the way men relate to other men. What men as individuals want from women will be very different in emphasis from what women as individuals want from men. Since we are concerned here with social structures rather than with personalities, we will concentrate on the consequences for societies of these outcomes of evolution, rather than on their troubling but often strangely satisfying manifestations in individual lives.

Each individual by definition acts idiosyncratically. But at the same time he is acting in some deep sense as a representative of his age and sex group, just as the speaker of a particular language may never say quite the same things in quite the same way as another speaker, but nevertheless represents that language in speaking it. His speech, however idiosyncratic in style, tone, and delivery, is a valid sample of the language at large and can be used as a basis for analyzing its grammar. So every man, when courting a woman for example, is acting out the evolutionary history of his sex: he is not simply one man approaching one woman, but Man approaching Woman. What he wants from her as an individual is in a broad sense what men have become programmed to want from women in general, and vice versa.

There is not necessarily any symmetry in this system of needs. A good deal of what men want from women has to do directly with what men want from one another and therefore with the processes going on in the male "block" of the system. The collection or conquest of women for dominance display again (even if they are only secretaries, typists, or research assistants), is a comment on relationships between men in their hierarchy. It may well serve a woman's purpose to be so used, insofar as she gets the protection and protein she needs for herself and her offspring. But it is not the congruence of common wants between a woman and her mate that produces their relationship. That women want different things from men than men want from women, or that each wants the same thing but for different purposes, must be related to the topology of the total system. To build a system of marriage, for example, on the assumption that male and female wants are totally coincident and basically the same may be charming, but it is very impractical.[9]

This sounds rather glum, at least; and at the most it can suggest that the relationships between people are crassly exploitative and unthinkingly selfish. However, the point here is just the contrary—that when individuals act in terms of the "interests" we have outlined, they are certainly not just being selfish and manipulative. They are, rather, reflecting their own reality as animals and are members of a larger system adapted to the successful survival of the whole group. Some people speak crudely, some eloquently. Some are careful about the effect of their words, others insult people without care. The same is true about individual behavior in the context of the "blocks" we have described. Some men are bold and frank about their exploitation of women, and some women lack any modesty about their success in depriving males of time, funds, energy, protein, or anything else. One measure of the humanity of a particular society is how well it induces people to be aware of these possibilities, and to be careful and even kind in dealing with other people. In extreme cases, the law will be invoked to remind husbands of alimony and wives of the hazards of adultery. Once upon a time, even breach of promise could be a business of the courts. Though civility comes hard, all communities go through some effort to stimulate its existence.

Against the background of this argument, it is logical that optimists will see these relationships as proof of man's potential for good, and pessimists as vindication of the poverty of their hope for man. The logic is really biological, neither good nor bad in itself. In a jet age, it might be "better" if we had wings, or at least some helicopterish knack of getting to airports. But we do not. In an age of nuclear families, it would be better if there was exact identity between male and female needs and expectations, and those of offspring. But there is not. This is neither proof of human degradation nor denial of human possibility, but a serious feature of the moral realities with which all groups must deal, and in terms of which most individual lives are led.

At the beginning of "Bond Issue One" we caught a brief glimpse of Crow Indian warriors ceremoniously affirming their bonds on the night before a raid. Although this ceremony was obviously intended to promote the solidarity of the group, it recognized the element of sexual competition between the men. It simply eliminated this aspect of male-male behavior in the face of the greater danger to follow, and in face of the even greater competition between the men, not as sexual beings, but as warriors. When the raid is over and, it is hoped, successful, the Crow will return to their camp to celebrate. Then the tally will be taken of enemy slain, horses and weapons captured, number of coups counted, and many other subtleties of status which will result in a rearrangement of the hierarchy, of promotions and demotions in the complex ranking system by which the men relate to one another.

The need of the men to cooperate in order to compete, and to exclude women from the bonding complex, which this involves, is projected spectacularly in another Crow ceremony—the annual wife abductions. The Crow had two major warrior "clubs" or "brigades," the Lump-woods and the Foxes. Each year during a set week the men of these clubs were allowed to abduct the wives of men of the opposite group. The rules were simple: a man could go to the tepee of a member of the other group and take that man's wife (or one of his wives if he was a polygamist) only if the wife had been a former lover. The husband was not allowed to make any move to interfere, and the ab-ductor had to be honest. Crow individuals were not indifferent to this event or unmoved by it. Men and their wives were often very devoted to each other; a man's pride could be deeply offended by an abduc-tion, and a woman's otherwise happy marriage ruined. Men tried some-times to hide their wives—or the wives themselves would go off into the hills. But the abductors were expected to be ruthless. Once the wives had been taken, the warriors, dressed in their finery, would parade around the camp singing and boasting, with the women on the backs of their horses. After this event the first war party of the year would take place, because, as the Crow said, the abductions made the men feel very brave and ready to fight.[10]

This, to us, outrageous ceremony, like its more restrained counter-part in the calling out of mistresses' names, illustrates dramatically a very general point: that when men are called upon to act together in an all-male activity, particularly a dangerous one, they may reaffirm their solidarity partly by degrading the male-female bond at the ex-pense of the male-male bond. Faced with extreme danger, they go to extreme lengths. In a less violent and disturbing way they do it all the time. What they are saying is that, in some circumstances, no woman is as important to any man as men are to one another.

Informal friendship may reflect this same thing as well as traditional wars. In North America a bride-to-be is customarily given a party called a "shower" by her female friends and relatives, in which she is presented with gifts that will help her furnish her home and conduct her domestic ceremonies. Towels, fish forks, sheets, glasses, or money represent her female associates' commitment to the mating bond and in turn enmesh her in a web of female-centered obligations that she will perform in her turn, and that will be renewed when the birth of her child stimulates gifts of the new set of properties babies require and mothers perhaps enjoy.

And what do the males do? Something very different. The roughly analogous ceremony that the men undertake is the stag party. This varies according to ethnic group, class, and region. But the essence of the business is that the groom-to-be is given a party by his male friends at which male camaraderie is stressed and the "antifemale tradition" is often invoked. Pornographic films may be shown, strippers may dance—in any case, the potential tenderness between the man and wife is mocked by his friends' provision of squalid entertainment, perceived by them to be manly. In some American modern groups almost as outrageous as the Crow, the groom will be made to have intercourse with a prostitute in view of his friends. No more clear and demanding claim can be made by the men on the love life of the groom, and no more poignant if disagreeable episode can characterize the difference between the shower and the stag. In one the mating bond is supported and the bride given to her new role with helpful and cementing gifts of property. In the other the principle of woman-sex is scorned and the claim of woman on man—however crassly and episodically stated—is reduced to a man's degradation of women's sex, either on a film or on a table in the center of the room, but nonetheless with the curious mystique that some males at least appear to share.

Examples of this kind of behavior could be multiplied indefinitely for society after society throughout space and time. But beneath the lurid surface differences in custom and conceit, certain general principles stand out. The most obvious is that at all times and in all places men form groups from which they exclude women. The male "block," described in our topology of the social system, asserts its exclusivity, assigns to itself certain privileges, undertakes a number of specific tasks, and both promotes and controls competition among its members. In a small society the entire male block may organize itself as one association, but it is more likely that there will be a number of male associations, each with its emblems and secrets, and that they will compete with one another and cooperate against the males of other societies. The groups may be formal or informal, and they range from the regular Friday-night poker party through the totem lodge to the Athenaeum, the College of Cardinals, and the Pentagon.

As has been seen repeatedly in the discussion of behavioral evolution, the basis for male bonding is deeply involved with the history of the species. The need of primate males to bond is clear and evident. The reasons—hierarchical competition, social stability, and defense—are obvious. If we add to this the exigencies of the hunting life and the burden of provisioning that fell to the males in this formative and prolonged phase, the growing selection pressures become paramount in favor of males who could and would successfully bond with their fellows for hunting and defense. The lone male was probably a dead male—at least a male less likely to contribute effectively to the gene pool.

So we have another very basic and diffuse instruction in the program of human behavior—but one that is sex specific. The male-male bond is to the male block of the system what the mother-child is to the female. It is as important and as emotionally charged for its political/ aggressive purposes as the male-female bond is for its reproductive purposes. It interferes, often traumatically, with these other bonds: the adult males must take the boys away from their mothers, and must, like the Crow Indians, ensure that the mating bond does not undermine male solidarity.

This notion of male bonds can be rather perplexing, because often it does not seem that anything is happening in them that is directly or even remotely biological. Here is where an analogy with the male-female bond is very useful. In the mating situation, a male responds to a female in a particular way; only a small portion of the time they spend in interaction is specifically sexual—that is, erotic. An evening or two or three, or a month's or year's courtship may be consummated in perhaps an hour's physical encounter. But all that precedes and follows is just as sexual as the contact of skin itself. Sex is a critical aspect of systems of behavior, but much of what goes on in its name is social.

In the other primates the fact of being male or female governs not only reproduction, but other things as well—roles in politics, in defense, in socializing the young, the length of time it takes to become adult; all these complex and nonerotic matters are controlled by the biosocial fact of being male or female. Just as they are with other animals. Give a female rat male sex hormones and she will become aggressive, perform mounting and thrusting like a male, abuse her young, and confuse her nesting work. Give a male the female hormones, and he will tend to act accordingly. The fact that it is just a tiny amount of a single substance that is involved underscores its importance in making a massive difference, and suggests how fundamental is the fact of being male or female. The hormones in this sense are like poison; only a little bit has the major effect of killing an otherwise thriving organism. A simple alteration in hormone balance can effect remarkable change in the round of life. So far as one can tell, the higher up the biological scale one goes, the more important, not less, do these regularities become for the infrastructuring of the individual's action.[11]

Healthy human males respond to healthy human females in predictable, biologically determined, and culturally mediated ways. The nature of this response changes dramatically at puberty. If males respond differently to females at this transitional stage, why not to males also? This is more than a rhetorical question, because there is an answer: they do. And they form groups in which to do it.

But what do they actually *do?* In a great many cases it is not obvious that they *do* anything very much in these groups; they just *are* in them. Membership is its own reward, even if the outcome is only a series of bull sessions and a lot of smoke. Often the group is simply an end in itself and seems to exist to satisfy a need to dress up in elaborate insignia of rank; to organize according to a hierarchy of statuses and complex rules; to eat and drink together; to make noise and parade; to outdo one another and other similarly organized groups in ruthlessly unpragmatic activities; to canvass and initiate new members; to preserve secrecy and enforce loyalty; either to exclude women completely or to admit them only on special occasions (which serves to reinforce their exclusion) ; and above all simply to be together, doing things as a group distinct and distinguished from other groups.

Of course, that is only part of the business—the minimal feature of what happens. Usually something else happens too. The group may plot to take over a government, or it may actually be the government, and meet in friendly and confident camaradie in cabinet chambers or the junta's headquarters. It may be their secrets that are a source of the magical power over young boys changing to manhood. The group may be a soccer team, aware of the stars and the aspirants, wary of the management, eager to reward or bilk the fans, but always in connection with their teammates; even stars need a setting; even poor teams of amateurs will enjoy some sense of their skill alongside the physical incompetents who cheer or harass them. The group may be insurance agents working an area with territories divided between them—in competition but also in cooperation under the umbrella of Head Office with its structure of goals and rewards. The process may be represented by a unit of a police force or an army, and even huge groups must be broken down into small face-to-face ones. We may find executives planning a takeover of a smaller company; then two groups may compete for the faith of shareholders and the proxy votes this means. Or it may be the dark and lucrative secrecy of criminals to which the young are inducted by a bond of fear and threat and increasing commitment to the only culture and skill they have. Or a dozen young priests may enjoy one another's support as they venture into a career of a strangely practical and yet theoretical life of juggling ideas, rules, and people in some forcefully benign routine.

Associating with males energizes and gratifies the members of this legion of groups, and the participants in this variety of cooperative enterprises. It is a way of taking up the time and effort of the young by assimilating them into the schemes of the old. It is also a way of deciding which of the young men will be the leaders of the group in the future; it at least delimits the contenders for this opportunity. What happens in the block of the males is common to all societies— this process of tantalizing them with adult power, instructing them, testing them, thwarting carefully their impetuous drive to dominate everything and everyone right away.

This process offers them seniority in return for consent, and privilege in exchange for waiting around. It is not really very sophisticated— though there are many changes to be rung on this standard theme— and it is certainly easily predictable. It is predictable not only because it is so often observed in such a variety of places. As a process, it reflects what we are, and how we evolved as primates uniquely skilled at gluing symbols onto relationships. This should make us as skeptical about the elimination of this bonding tendency as we would be of seriously curtailing heterosexual activity. If one forbids sex among young people, it does not necessarily disappear; it becomes clandestine —as illegitimacy rates testify. Surrealistic as it may seem, the current fashion for decrying and inhibiting male encounter could result in groups of men meeting as conspiratorially as lovers did under regimes marked by a more familiar puritanism.

Whatever may happen in the future, a striking example of male success in managing these bonds so far is the preeminence males as a sex exert over females in the political life of communities. It would be difficult to avoid the conclusion that at least some differences between the sexes—both physiological and behavioral—are biologically based. Consequently, if some universal form of human activity appears to be dominated by one or the other sex, there is at least a prima-facie case for looking at this dominance as a sex-linked characteristic. Men universally dominate the political arena. Women, as all men know, can exert great influence over the course of political events, but formal organization from tribe to empire is predominantly a male activity.[12]

It is also clearly an activity that taps much that is biologically male in behavior. The male primate dominates the troop and keeps order within its boundaries. He protects it against other troops and predators. He plays politics with his fellow males in which he dominates some, ingratiates himself with others, and most importantly, forms strong alliances with still others. In all this he dominates his females. Females definitely exert influence. It is hard for a leader to be successful if he does not have the confidence of the females, who in a real sense may be said to form the most stable core of the group. When new groups are forming among macaque monkeys, for example, the first nucleus is a group of females and young. But the group will persist over time only if a male (and later other males) attaches himself to it and acts as a focus of attention and source of authority.[13] Among humans, male politicians may depend on the female vote, but the politicians are overwhelmingly male. There have of course been female leaders more outstanding than many of their male counterparts—many queens, for example. Here the principle of hereditary succession is so central that failing a male heir, a female is accepted. But no queen has ever surrounded herself with female advisers, female civil servants, female generals, etc. The Amazons exist only in male fantasy. Even in societies where inheritance and succession are through females rather than males, the men ultimately control the situation. There is no such thing as a matriarchy. If succession is through females, then a man's heir is his sister's son, but such a system gives the sister no more power than it gives a wife in the case where a man's heir is his own son.[14]

Why should this male dominance exist? And why should it exist all over the earth, so regularly and so predictably? One favorite explanation is the conspiracy theory.[15] This view holds that men everywhere contrive to keep women everywhere in subservience and in dismayed if baffled ineffectiveness. The notion is that men are as aware of their interests as a sex as bondholders are of their dependence on strong financial structures. This is, of course, possible. But it is very unlikely. We are talking here about so many different cultures, with so many different kinds of religion, economy, ecology, political structure, tradition, and ways of raising children, that it would be statistically inevitable that a fair number of these different systems would throw up a genuinely female-dominated political system. For it is not a question of being technologically primitive—like the aborigines, whose women are not politicians. Or advanced, like the Americans, whose women are only minutely represented in the councils of high power. Or well-meaning, like the Russians—whose women's place in fact is much less exalted than their place in theory. Or in some Arab countries, where the question hardly arises.[16]

Money seems not to be the variable—for then the richest women in the world, the American ones, would be the most powerful. Nor is ideology, nor is religion. It is indeed possible that there is a conspiracy against women, in which case one must slyly ask: if men all over the world have always been able to keep women subdominant all over the world and under all conditions—perhaps they *are* politically superior to women. Perhaps—in the name of sexual equality—we are proposing to admit into political councils already having trouble enough a group of individuals who have proven by their lack of political success over centuries that they are less competent even than men.

This idea must be rejected at once. Division of labor—odious though it may seem to some who see that all people can and should do all things—does not have to mean difference of status. Sexual difference is not the same thing as sexual inequality. Political equality has nothing to do with the facts that women menstruate and bear children and that men die earlier than women and have heart attacks more. Perhaps the political differences between males and females are of the same order as the reproductive differences—politics, evolution, and reproduction have been seen to be so closely linked. One must look at the whole system of reproduction and selection and ask how individual features of our present pattern may result from an old process. The issue here is not female competence and intelligence—these may well be superior to males'—but female political skills and enthusiasms.[17] The business of politics, absurd as much of its posturing, threat, display, cunning, chicanery, bonhomie, and pomposity, with its almost ludicrous tolerance of boredom, must seem to the intelligent or cynical woman, is a business that requires skills and attitudes that are peculiarly male. What is more, women seem to recognize this. For every woman who claims that politics (or war) is as much her game as any man's, there are a thousand women who would feel much more comfortable with a man at the helm. Women vote for men rather than other women. The theory that this male dominance is the result of centuries of brainwashing runs aground again on the argument used before: what kind of creature is it that will allow itself to be so easily brainwashed? The conspiracy theory in fact takes a very low view of female intelligence and ability.

We have seen how sexual differentiation is rooted in primate political-breeding processes: the dominant males are the focus of attention and hence cohesion; they dominate by overt strength and by ritualized threat and display; they protect and keep order; they compete in a never-ceasing test of their ability to dominate; but they also combine in coalitions to exercise more effective dominance or to forage and explore. The course of human evolution added to this basic pattern all the complexities of the hunting life. Man does not live by bread alone, but how he finds his bread is still important, particularly when it is not bread but meat that mattered, and when the hunting way of life persisted for millions of years.

One of the most important effects of hunting was to widen the gap between males and females as far as behavior was concerned. Men hunted, women did not. This was decisive for a very long time. The new knack of killing animals emphasized the sexual differences that existed before. For if males bonded in order to chatter about politics, discipline the young, and defend the troops, it was even more important that they joined together to leave the camp to hunt animals increasingly large and dangerous as time went on, increasingly huntable only by groups, and only by groups of men. When we recall that the brain doubled in size during this initial hunting period—one of the most astonishing of all transformations of all organs in all of nature—we will see that the selective factors that went into this change must have been rigorous indeed. The early primate pattern of bonding became the new and phenomenally significant pattern of cooperative hunting. Out of this grew our ability to attach to the relatively fragile links between men the grand and demanding structures of empire, of moon shots, of corporations, of systems of irrigation, and of the medieval church.

To females, political procedure must seem hopelessly bizarre and almost frighteningly irrelevant to the simple concerns of constituents, children, and anyone else who wants clean air and an agreeable sense of community, among other things. Politicians are very odd, really, with their rotund phrases and meeting-room rotundas; their committees and their extraordinary protocol, their fear of seeming weak and fearful. Yet the peahen, too, must have her doubts about the sanity or at least sense of the male world when she patiently and resignedly waits for the nth display of male grandeur and aggrandizement—for the strutting, the preening, the seemingly overdone intimidation of rivals, the assertion, the condescension—the whole panoply of male vanity. Yes, she is perhaps bored and cynical as yet another silly male begins to do his male thing. But this male thing has been clearly important for the evolutionary story—the story of breeding, nesting, selective mating, territorial defense, protection of young, ritualization of aggression. These mechanics of selection have operated on the behavior of the males of any species to produce the extravagant but effective results that seem so dear to the male ego and so trivial to female good sense.

Boys will indeed be boys, and males will do their male thing with a curious enjoyment in the sensation of being male and doing what men do—without women. Behind many a successful man there stands the proverbial woman—telling him not to make a fool of himself. But the fooling is in deadly earnest. It is the old business of bluff and threat and convoluted rivalry that is part of male being, and it is ridiculous only when seen out of its evolutionary context. The peacock and the fruit fly may seem lunatic in their mating antics, but the selective advantages of their respective rituals can be easily understood. The rituals of male dominance in politics appear to be as necessary and inevitable as the tail of the peacock or the dance of the fruit fly.

The point here is similar to the one, made before, about aristocracies: neither aristocracies nor male dominance as forms of politics are necessarily the "best" forms in terms of human political ideals. But they have a lot going for them that lies deeper than reason and ideology. Any kind of egalitarian system suffers from a disadvantage. Inequality between men and a division of political function between men and women flow naturally from the nature of the primate that we are. Equality and an equal participation of men and women in the political arena are things that must be energetically striven for. Ultimately, they must be imposed. In both cases we must say "no" to nature— our own human nature. To make women equal participants in the political process, we will have to change the very process itself, which means changing a pattern bred into our behavior over the millennia. It may well be possible, but it will not be easy. And it will certainly not be made easier by pretending that all men really want to be equal or that women are simply men who happen occasionally to take time off to have babies.

It is almost impossible to stress this point too much. If we want to change a system, we must understand it first. It did early engineers no good to protest that the law of gravity reduced their most imaginative cathedrals to dust and clutter. They had to know this law, its relationship to rocks and size, its effect on the realities of structure and design. Ideologists may enthuse about the value of creating political systems that involve women fully and with dignity. But what is more necessary and initially more valuable than their admirable enthusiasm is knowledge of just what it is we are trying to change and what kind of success we may expect. Given the current arrangement of politics in nearly all countries—and women have failed to find their places in these so far—it may be statistically unlikely that anything significant will change unless our consciousness changes first. In other words, we must begin to understand the nature of sexual difference and come to terms with it and operate within it, not against it, and to use it constructively and not deny it in the name of equality. Probably equality can be realized only if men become sufficiently understanding of their own peacock enterprises to accept that they have not actually made provision for full female participation in politics. It is hardly enough simply to solicit the votes of females; this is, after all, just another way of keeping power in the hands of candidates who are nearly always male. For men to understand that they are socially different from females, and how, may induce them more effectively to invite women to genuine colleagueship in the places where power is manipulated. On their part, females may more rapidly and happily achieve political goals by asserting the value of specifically female skills and interests rather than by denying the reality of any differences and insisting that all social tasks are performed in the same way by males and females.[18]

This is the place to explore the chief characteristics of the social relations in the "block" of females. Undoubtedly it is women who have borne most of the effects of changes in human technology. Nearly all females for most of their adult lives in nearly all places throughout virtually all of human history have been involved with childbearing and child-rearing. Nothing less than the very survival of the group in which they lived depended upon their successful gestation and raising of a child until it could manage on its own. Because learning and maturation are so important to humans, this is a long process; indeed, it remains the most time-consuming and labor-intensive of all major human tasks. It is also very difficult to mechanize, and even to bureaucratize in some efficient and personal fashion. This has plainly meant that women have had to spend much time with children, one direct consequence of which is that they have also spent much time with other women—their own friends, and mothers of their children's friends.

There are some general questions about the biogrammar of female bonding that must be answered: What patterns may we have inherited from our history as prehumans? What could we do with this inheritance to bend it to our new conditions and to our new ability to impose will between ourselves and nature? And what social relationships among females would fit, influence, and conflict with the patterns among males, and the relations between males and females that we have some reason to believe actually marked our evolution?

Primate females are intensely interested in newborn infants. Mothers have high status among the other females; so do those who are pregnant; childless females will plead to hold an infant, and, as a favor, they will be allowed to.[19] Among humans the situation becomes more complex, though the basic emotional patterns the primates display seem to persist, in however attenuated and modified form. The new complexity stems from the importance of the child as both a measure and as a property of the kinship structure. The matter of what happens to infants is therefore of considerable concern to the males, and the social career of the child is carefully worked out in the context of the overall pattern of social bonds. The net effect of this concern is to bind females into the social structure in a much more demanding, elaborate, and persistent way than is possible among the nonhuman primates where the cycles of estrus rather than the long-term cycle of life govern how males and females interact.

The act of having a child is thus for the human female not only a new event biologically and emotionally but also a contract with her community—a contract perhaps not always formalized but certainly always palpable. The conditions of motherhood are real: mothers must attend to their children, must not leave them alone, must not injure them, and must give them that care and tutelage thought seemly by their fellow citizens. In return females are offered protection, welfare, tax advantages if they have children, and a generalized claim on the resources of time and property of the dominants—both male and female—of the community. (The responsibility of the community to mothers is relatively clear, though with the development in industrial societies of mechanical forms of welfare, women with children but without male supporters are often treated harshly in relation to the difficulty of their task and the scarcity of their resources.)

We have seen how males bond to help one another gain power, defend groups, and acquire animal protein. Females bond too, but in different ways, for significantly different purposes, and with different results for the overall social structure. To put it as economically as possible, males bond for reasons of macrostructure, females for reasons of microstructure—that is, in general, females occupy themselves with interpersonal matters involving face-to-face encounters and focusing upon subjects that have to do with the bearing, nurturing, and training of the young, and with the establishment and management of dwellings and other immediate surroundings. By contrast, males involve themselves with groups and activities that extend directly to the whole community. Here again the primate biogrammar emerges from a variety of possible patterns. The females are at the center of the group; they are concerned chiefly with what happens there and with their relations to the males and young. The males are at the center too, but only after they have served a period of apprenticeship at the periphery, and in some cases only after, in bands of two or three, they have explored some strange terrain and become accustomed to seeing their local place in terms of its wider setting.

This pattern corresponds with a tediously conventional view of the distinction between what men and women do. The important point remains that throughout selection, as we became human, we retained many of the emphases and predispositions of our primate colleagues. We have already noted how significant it was that, alone among the primates, man divided labor between males and females, and that this division depended on males forming effective and cooperative groups for hunting. Females too formed groups, but were best adapted for groups that did different things, and in a different perspective, and with a different set of challenges and satisfactions. This is quite another thing from saying "a woman's place is in the home." If a woman's place is anywhere at all, it is precisely not in the home but in an arena of great interpersonal activity, a place from which brief excursions for purposes of gathering may be undertaken, and a place in which—because of the kinship breakthrough—the lives of individuals are articulated, structured, and blended in concern and competition with the lives of others.

Our concern at this point is with groups, not individuals, because groups of females seem to do different things from groups of males, and have different ways of doing the different things they do. Of course, individual females can perform as well as individual males, and many males can perform tasks usually taken to be the special province of females. But predictably in a gregarious species, male-male bonds differ from male-female bonds, and female-female bonds differ from both.

What are some of these differences? One of the most characteristic and consequential is that the status of females depends on their mates far more than the other way around, and on their reproductive situation. For example, males very rarely take their wives' names at marriage, and this reflects the reality that social placement normally occurs in terms of the occupational and ritual status of the chief male in the female's life.

Females have more to gain and lose by their marriage arrangements than males do. For all males' remarkable concern with status differences, females are capable of even greater interest in the thrust of a snub and the refinement of a pretension. In a real sense this is because females are more committed to the intimate sphere and more dependent on the implications of their personal encounters for their income and satisfaction than males, who may contrive relatively impersonal items of work or group antagonism on which to focus their energy and concern. It is important not to confuse these differences of emphasis and activity with the evaluation of status and importance. To do so is to devalue that intimate sphere in which all people must live, enjoy, and grow, and to glorify activities—often the prerogative of males—that may be destructive, exploitative, crass, and pointless.

We have already noted the significant phenomenon among some primates that although females formed groups of mother-child units (plus interested childless or pregnant females), the groups were totally unstable unless a male joined them as a focus of attention and an agent of social control. This need not seem strange. The female is primarily concerned with the survival of her own little unit—and rightly so. Insofar as other females may help, they are tolerated, but this is at best a tenuous and short-term toleration. Once the child is old enough to fend for itself, the female is interested in getting herself pregnant again and once again is in competition with the other females as she directs her attention toward the mature males.

The human mother is likewise caught in these two intensive activities —looking after her child and maintaining a relationship with a supportive male. In the first instance other women may be useful; in the second, however, they are a direct threat. Coping with the eternal round of birth, copulation, and child-rearing does not leave any primate mother with much time for the great affairs of state, and this has been the lot of the human mother for virtually our whole history as a species. On the other hand, the male, who is not constrained in this way, can exercise these functions and hold the group together—

particularly as the attention of the females becomes fixed on him as a source to which they can turn for protection and sexual satisfaction. The male, then, is concerned with the whole community of mothers, mates, and children, while the female tends to be more narrowly occupied. Thus she cannot act as focus of cohesion, nor can she effectively form the kinds of bonds males form to achieve those male ends that affect the interests of whole communities.

Both females and males enter into sexual competition with others of their sex, and to some extent their status depends on the outcome, but men have always had something over and above this competition for which they must bond and from which they could derive status, while women have rarely had any other source from which to gain a sense of personal worth and social superiority than their position in the reproductive struggle—measured in terms of their mate and their offspring. Women have had little opportunity or reason (in these terms) to bond or form groups for macrostructural purposes. This, then, is the primate situation, and it has been the basic human situation for most of our history. It can be—and is being—mitigated and changed in ways which allow women greater opportunity for involvement in the macrosystem. But these women carry with them a considerable evolutionary burden which may demand more energy and enthusiasm from them than from men to seek these opportunities, and which makes their task more difficult once they become involved in the intricacies of the program they wish to follow.

In one vital and all but unexplored respect the relationships between females differ from those between men. Young males, human and primate, have in a real sense to go to the peripheries of the group before they regain internal status; the distance they go and the length of time it takes them to get back can be considerable. Young females, on the other hand, except in those countries where their education is deliberately fashioned on the male model (but even to some extent in these), are never "peripheralized" to the same extent. Physically they may never move from their mothers until they marry; their base is always "home." Their peripheralization is metaphorical rather than real, in the sense that between puberty and marriage they have a transitional status. But this is usually brief; on marriage the girl automatically joins the ranks of "married women" with all the status implications this carries and often becomes a mother almost immediately. She does not have to win her way back to the center in the same way as a boy; the transition is not so severe; very few will ever fail to make it. She proves herself in a simple biological way—by being fertile; she continues with tasks that she has already been perform- ing anyway in her mother's household. The affluent and technologically advanced nation that peripheralizes females in the same way that it does males may find (and often does find) itself in some difficulty. It reverses the natural trend, breaks the evolutionary continuity which has insisted on a continuing and close bond between older women and young potential wives. Educated young women in particular find the transition to household chores unbearably difficult and uncongenial, not only because they feel they are wasting their education, but be- cause they have suffered a bond disruption and a minor separation trauma. An adolescent female is just not a substitute adolescent male.

Neither is a mother simply a father who has children. But what about the postmenopausal female? In some sense she is a biological anomaly. What use to a species is a female who can no longer re- produce and who is consuming valuable food that might well go to youngsters, mothers, and warriors? In most species the female life span is the reproductive life span, and no more. It occasionally hap- pens that an older female past childbearing will take on some role. The most spectacular example is in the red deer, where an old hind becomes the leader of the group of hinds. She is their focus of atten- tion, and even when the stag has gathered her little group together as a harem during the rutting season, she remains the leader. The stag does not control the movement of the hinds—he simply focuses on the activities of his male rivals. Otherwise he follows the harem about rather ineffectively. Here the experience and sagacity of the older female are called into play very successfully. But this is in a situation where males do not form the focus of the attention structure.

When they do, what role is there for the older female to play? Clearly her usefulness in the human primate society should lie in the area of economic activity. The demands the dependent human infant makes on the young mother inhibit her contribution. But the old woman can make up for this loss in the labor force. Her knowledge of the terrain—of the roots and berries and grains—is incomparably greater, and she can teach all this to her daughters. If they always had to learn it from scratch, it would be an insufferably inefficient system. She is also a store of knowledge and help on the subject of child- rearing. After all, in primitive conditions not that many women live beyond their reproductive period anyway. Certainly in times of food shortage they are often the first to go—along with female infants.

(The death of the one conserves food supplies; the death of the other prevents an increase in future population.)

With the remarkable increase in the life span of recent years, we are faced with the problem of a vast expansion of the numbers of post-reproductive females. These women may not be integrated into the female world of their daughters made independent by machinery and often callous by social mobility or change in generation life style. But the old women are not really making their way into the man's world, either, where they are, logically at least, most likely to fit, since they are through with the essentially female business of child-rearing. For example, from a simple-minded point of view it remains curious that such females do not take a more active role in formal politics, since of all the groups in the population they have probably the most time and the most money with which to support their effort. What in fact do they do?

One important activity, at least in industrialized communities, which they can undertake successfully and with some contentment, is a set of voluntary activities that support other sections of the community. They may be welfare workers, canvassers, fund-raisers for worthwhile causes. The women who tend toward volunteer work are usually well-off; they have none of the need for a job that poor women, even with husbands, have. It is a comment on the impracticality and anti-feminism of most communities that they are more willing to accommodate their otherwise rigid schedules to suit the free time of volunteer workers than of women who need money as well as want to accomplish something outside their home and in their community.

Of course, this varies considerably in many communities. In the Soviet Union many grandmothers live with their daughters or sons; it is the *babushka* who minds the child while the mother is at work. Even in such a committed and self-consciously revolutionary society, there is nothing approaching an adequate number of day-care centers; as usual, it is to old primate bonds that we turn when we want to take part in even postindustrial activity. In a society like ours, the solution is far more complex, because in part the mother-daughter bond is disrupted by education, by mobility, and by the rapidity of social change which makes the mother seem irrelevant to the practices and ideals of the daughter. Indeed, there is often bleak antipathy between mother and daughter, if only because they share households; perhaps one reason for the declining age at which females marry is that girls cannot abide their mothers and must leave their houses and their implicitly supervised bedrooms. And yet, tragically, psychiatric records tell of many girls who bear children earlier than they openly want them or are married or can afford them, in good part because they want to affirm themselves against their mothers.

Once again, then, we see that the fruits of the industrial revolution were most sour for females; it was they who had their important bond earliest threatened and first broken. In school they lost their mothers' philosophy, and in mobility their presence. In the factory they lost the dependence out of which reciprocity is made. With puberty arriving earlier and earlier—four months sooner every ten years—the transitional period described above was extended at the same time as the demand for schooling and for skills increased the time it took the capacities of their bodies to make themselves manifest in their behavior. And it is even possible that the earlier arrival of puberty is in part the result of competition among younger and younger girls to stimulate men to bear them off and away from home.[20] As bodily changes may affect behavior, so different pressures from behavior may (as with psychosomatic diseases) speed up or slow down bodily processes.

Females bond; but in quantity, quality, direction, purpose and even aesthetic, their bonding processes and procedures differ considerably from those of the male block in direct proportion to the difference in life cycle, life style, and life chance of males and females. Their long-lasting bonds are largely kinship bonds. Outside these, their bonding is more tenuous, more episodic, and less productive of groupings that affect the macrostructure than in the case of the male. But the female bonds are as crucial and heroic as the more political male bonds. If they fail, the system collapses, and no amount of male solidarity will be able to hold it together.

If females have difficulties, so do males. In the subhuman primate troop the saddest character is the peripheral male. At a still tender age he has left his mother to go to the edges of the group. For a while he will be indulged by the older males and will form play groups with his peers, where he will sort out his dominance relationships in play-fighting and rough-and-tumble. But with the approach of sexual maturity, he is placed in the impossible position of being driven to compete with males twice his size to whom he has learned to defer and from whom he can expect no charity.

The so-far neglected block of our social system—the block of adolescent boys—is different from the others in that it involves a transitory status. In some societies the adolescent is classified with the females, and can only be "made" into a man. He shares this problem of self-establishment with his primate cousins. Manhood is not achieved simply by maturing, it must be proved. Among the now familiar Crow this was starkly dramatized. A young man was expected to become a warrior—the only other status in the community was that of woman. If he failed to make it as a warrior, then he had no choice but to accept the only other classification. He put on women's clothes, did women's work, got married, and lived as a *berdache*—a man-woman.

For girls it is different. At first menstruation a young girl in a real sense becomes a woman without further effort. She stays with the women, and begins to take part in women's work. In most parts of the world she marries soon after this—if not before. Initiation ceremonies for girls are really puberty ceremonies, to celebrate *menarche*.[21] For boys, however, the ceremonies are correlated only roughly with puberty, and may occur at any age from seven to twenty or may be stretched over a long period.[22] For a man does not just occur—he has to be made. He has to be incorporated into the block of adult males. He will not be measured by secondary sexual characteristics, but by his performance, his behavior, and his success in doing the male thing in a manner that satisfies the already initiated males of his community. The stakes are high, the mortality rate is high, and the demands for achievement are high. For all the disadvantages that females seem to suffer in the political system, they have this one enormous advantage during the treacherous period of adolescence: the community helps them, and it hinders the males. A girl has only to mature physically to be fully accepted as a woman and to contribute to the next generation; a boy has to go beyond mere physical maturity, and here he may or may not succeed.

The other primates, however, resist such sentimentalization. The young males of the troop would kill their older relatives and take over the coveted central position of attention and power—if they could. And when they can, they do. Ethologists speak of the "ritualization of aggression"—but the aggression has to be ritualized because it is so real. And ritual does not always work. The death rate among four-year-old primate males is high during the breeding season. The ritualization helps only when the order has been established, and then it helps to keep it that way.

Freud acutely observed that the primate situation would become much more tricky with the advent of weapons.[23] The older and more dominant baboon is physically bigger and has longer canines than his challenger. But a young man armed with a spear or club may very well be a match for his older opponent. The whole body of young warriors must always appear as much a potential threat to the older males holding power as they appear a delightful prospect to the young girls awaiting marriage. And the whole thing can be, and often is, soured by the fact that the older males have already used their prerogative to take more than their fair share of the young girls. At one stroke this doubles the frustrations of the young males and makes life more difficult for the polygamous elders. Many human societies echo almost directly the primate horde situation: the older males monopolize the females, use various devices to control the young males and their entry into the hierarchy, and spend a great deal of time ensuring that the juniors do not get a chance to copulate with the younger wives.[24]

The traditional way of dealing with the aggression and frustration of the young male is to direct it outward. The peripheral primate is the first to deal with predators, and the young warriors the first to face the enemy and die. The Crow again show how aggression can be turned to advantage by making the war game into a status race. To get into the male hierarchy, the young brave had to perform certain feats of courage and cunning that could be validated before his elders. His energies were directed outward toward the foe rather than upward toward his own superiors. Furthermore, he had to joust with death if he wanted to become an important male. Universally it is the old men who make the rules, own the teams, promote the boxing matches; it is the young men who leap at barbed wire, concuss one another, and devote more physical energy now than at any other time in their lives to attempts to outdo one another. While possessing females is important to the young males, and is in some sense the whole point of the evolutionary process, it is not necessarily the basic motivating factor. The possession of a female or females can be viewed as one more validation of male status, which is an end in itself, because, once achieved, the women follow anyway. Whatever the advocates of student power do want—and it is not always clear—one thing they plainly do *not* want is access to their professors' wives. But then the whole thing might well be different if their professors had managed to monopolize not only decisions about the curriculum, but the majority of the female undergraduates as well. (Although the now declining *in loco parentis* attitude which sought to control where and when female undergraduates should sleep sought to do just that—in a typically blundering and indirect academic way.)

In every human population, the adolescent and postadolescent males are at once a resource and a threat. The platoon of young soldiers is cheered and even idolized; the teen-age gang is feared and hunted down. The resource has to be used; the threat must be handled—and every human society has evolved fairly elaborate methods to handle it. Overwhelmingly, educational systems have focused their attentions on boys; only rich girls were expected to learn some set of practices, and these were more for the management of their domestic lives than for the conduct of communal affairs or the improvement of their own minds. But the boys were sent on mock hunts, enrolled in equivalents of the Boy Scouts, removed to boarding schools, taken on warring parties, set alongside rabbis to learn their bar-mitzvah songs. They have done their vision quests, been apprenticed to carpenters and thatchers, have been unpaid deckhands on the dangerous fish trawlers of Portugal and Hull. The extension of the educational system recently to include females is nothing less than equitable—an extension of human rights. But it means as well that females have joined a system of long-term oppression, one of the functions of which is to induce young males to spend a long time learning particular practices vaguely related to adult statuses, and committing themselves to the structures of the adult males from which all blessings flow.

Validation rather than education is our real concern here. One of the important features of validation for boys is that they must do it in terms of other boys, even if it is the adult males who set the limits and some of the standards. If men form groups, boys form gangs, and swarm kinetically from place to place full of noise and incipient action. These gangs may be scout troops, platoons, slum war machines, musical bands, rowing teams, fraternities, or groups of mechanically minded semisuicidal malcontents keen to race stripped-down cars in some inconvenient arena to show they can do this better than the driver the next car over. Girls are far less likely to do such things, and they are also far less likely to become involved in criminal activity (except for shoplifting—a new-fashioned form of gathering—and sexual crimes, an old-fashioned form of being exploited in the most apt way they know how). But crime spreads among boys as quickly as a new scheme of haircutting or width of trouser leg—ten times as quickly as among girls, in fact, and with far more implication for the eventual relationship which individuals will have with the basic structures of complex societies like those of Europe and America.

The role of these groups in the lives of the boys who are their members is clear. Hours are spent on streetcorners, in clubhouses, and on sportsfields, anywhere they will be tolerated. The activities of sports heroes and other denizens of their imaginations are catalogued, recalled, and analyzed with accuracy and affection. These feats of memory and analysis would baffle a teacher hopelessly confronting their apathetic response to the pleasures of the calculus and American or European history. Boys do best what they are most interested in—with the consequence that they drop out of school more enthusiastically than girls, though there is in one sense much more at stake for them.

This business of gangs may be troublesome to the elders when it becomes disruptive of the social order to whose perpetuation they are committed. But it is essential nonetheless that the gangs exist, because in them boys learn—just before they finally take the plunge into male adulthood—a set of important skills and enthusiasms: How to be loyal to the group and how to get on with it. How to exercise leadership if they can, and how to be helpful if they cannot. How to identify with the totem or symbol of group and see its interest as the same as their own. How to be willing to spend a lot of time not doing anything but keeping the group going. How, in extreme cases, to be wounded for or die for the collective. How to know the limits of their own privacy. How to "walk tall" because they do not walk alone, and how to be helpful to members they do not really like because they are members, and for no other reason. How to do things they hate, and commit cruelties they would privately abhor. In other words, that there is something called morality which is absolute and yet mediated by the local group. In their gangs they learn the enthusiasm and the careful restriction of enthusiasm that will be necessary when they join the men and have to take orders warmly and in the proper spirit.[25]

But these boys do not simply achieve some abstract status of manhood as a result of their trials and exertions: they achieve membership in specific male organizations. Their initiatory struggles are often in the nature of a test whereby the older males select from the candidates those best fitted for the tasks of the group. The cultural elaborateness of all this can easily blind us to its underlying motivation, which is little different, if different at all, from the motivation of the lowly savanna-monkey juveniles and their irascible but cunning elders. There is, however, one big difference: human juveniles are faced not with one hierarchy but, except in the very simplest societies, with many. Dominance patterns established in youth, in the gang or play group, may not persist into adulthood when the gang is dispersed, and the boys then may become members of many different organizations. There is a switch—or several switches—of hierarchy, and this involves selection. For men take their groups, even if they are essentially recreational groups, very seriously. All men—with a few maverick exceptions—will end up in one group or another. But then comes another human twist: some *groups* rank higher than others. This introduces complications, obviously, in that the skills involved in being in one kind of group are not those prized or needed in another. It does mean that in more complex societies there is more room for more and different types of maleness. But in all these cases, any man's personal status will be mediated by one or more immediate groups with which he identifies. The *processes* of induction, acceptance, validation, promotion, and even personal satisfaction are those basic processes of male bonding that characterized the hunting team, and which even the most sophisticated of contemporary male organizations replicate with primitive skill and atavistic energy.

When the pieces of the jigsaw that we have been laboriously constructing over the last three chapters are put together, a scheme of the human social system emerges to place it squarely within the primate biogram and yet to point up its uniquely human attributes. The major division is into three "blocks"—the male block, the female-with-young block, and the adolescent-male block—exactly as with the basic primate system. The dynamics of the system concern on the one hand the processes going on within each block, and on the other the processes that relate them to one another.

The picture is of a very recognizably primate social system, modified by the evolutionary changes introduced by hunting and the consequent division of labor, which give it its species-specific characteristics. Since it is so basic a pattern, societies strain toward it, however much they may bend and twist the rubber sheet. In many rituals, and in times of great crisis, it asserts itself. The mothers of America have very little to say in a system where boards of senior males select those of their sons best fitted to die for causes which may make sense to some powerful men but often not, in the mothers' eyes, worth the life of even one carefully nursed and proudly reared boy. But the mothers may learn to weep with some reluctant dignity and mellow their sorrow with pride if they truly sense that the sacrifice has indeed been for the safety of the greater collective of which their little familial unit is a part. This is one of their basic services—to provide warriors, who in turn will provide protection. Perhaps one moral of this dismal story is that the men had better fight wars that the women can believe in; otherwise, they may shake the confidence of the female block in the credibility of their protective intent and the competence of their plans. And there is another moral to this story of constant and reiterated tragedy. Boys are taken from the women who have devoted the fresh and hopeful years of their lives to raising them to fight against boys similarly hothoused in some enemy tribe, thus expressing in a clear and brutal way the power of the male block over the others and the irrelevance of tender personal histories to the merciless demands some males make and their lackeys enforce.

If we add to these processes the more general political interactions of attention structure, hierarchy, competitiveness, coalition, ritualization, etc., we begin to see the elements into which all societies dissolve and the dynamics on which they all operate—whatever the actual cultural content that their own particular histories and ecologies conspire to infuse into the system.

There remains one brief and general point to make about the bonding process: one good bond does not deserve another. Or, put more accurately, one good bond precludes another. At the beginning of "Bond Issue One" we said that boys and girls in kibbutzim who are raised in the same group do not marry each other. Our point is that they cannot. A teacher and pupil who are well bonded will find it difficult to become colleagues when the pupil becomes a teacher too. A father and son who have a complex history of support and authority will be tried by the equality necessary to run a business together, and a mother and daughter will be hard put to act otherwise after they have for a long time experienced the particular relationship of motherhood and childhood. Though it amuses the fancy of novelists and may be the fantasy of many brothers and sisters, siblings of similar ages never marry and hardly ever court and mate, except where law— such as among the ill-fated Egyptian royal family—says they can or must.

The kibbutz evidence is nothing less than startling. The kibbutz is a communal form devoted to warm camaraderie, the equality of males and females, and growth of population and resource. Everywhere else men and women tend to marry men and women who have been boys and girls with them in the same place—the simple fact of distance keeps them together. But not on the kibbutz; and not only do they not marry, but they do not even court. In the kibbutz, where so-called "free love" is supposed to prevail, they choose to sleep in separate rooms after adolescence. One good bond seems to inhibit another, and this is why so much of the discourse about incest is misplaced and wrong. Hamlet and Oedipus had genuinely difficult problems—mature females are rarely attracted by young and very subdominant males. (Primate males rarely if ever mate with their mothers anyway.)[26] Sexual feeling may mark the encounters of sons and mothers, but that is because sex is part of any human relationship—we are, after all, males and females always. But a full-fledged sexual unit cannot be formed on this basis; it is so difficult to achieve that it is less a problem in fact than a provocation in fantasy.

More tempestuous is the father-daughter bond. A quick look at the reported cases of incest shows that this is the most common of all incestuous encounters. This is understandable enough, because one enhancing spice of some sexual relationships seems to be a touch of that ritual neck-bite dominance the hamadryas baboon or the ambitious sultan appears to show. Fathers dominate daughters, and only the most insensitive father could deny that one claim his daughters make on his time and concern is a wily female one. Of course, the father-daughter bond is nearly always maintained without the courting and mating process interfering, and without sexual intercourse augmenting social intercourse. The whole issue of incest and its fascination and horror may be nothing so lurid as poets and psychoanalysts seem to imagine, but may hinge on the simple fact that to commit incest one has to disrupt an already established bond and substitute another and often antipathetical one. That humans resist this effort on the one hand and are fascinated by its possibilities—because they are sexual, and humans are fascinated by sex—on the other is inherent in the very nature of bonding.[27]

The exclusion principle may well explain why humans experience difficulty in yet another area. The bond between lovers is sexual and a matter for them only; the bond between parents is nurturant and it is mediated by the demands placed on both by, and the affection of both for, the troublesome infant that is the product of their voluntary labors. To some extent, if they are to be successful parents, they must re-create with each other aspects of their own childhood bonds. But this in turn may act to preclude a relationship that is based on sexual encounter. In other words, does the parent-parent bond exclude—or at least make difficult—the lover-lover or courtship bond? The incidence of marital breakdown in our own culture and the ubiquity of marital infidelity in all cultures—including and perhaps especially the polygamous ones—would suggest that this is so. It is not the only ingredient—male aggrandizement and female boredom contribute their share—but the attempt of many people to re-create the sensuousness and irresponsibility of the courtship phase outside the bounds of legal marriage cannot be dismissed as either sin or pathology. If we are searching for universal characteristics of the species, we can safely say that while no one form of marriage is universal, marital infidelity is universal: all cultures may not be monogamous, but they are all certainly adulterous.

There is nothing inevitable about this in the lives of individuals. Some individuals commit incest with their sisters or daughters, others live lives of model sexual constancy with the mothers and fathers of their children. But in terms of central tendency, most people do not commit incest, most men are unfaithful,[28] and most people who have had a long superordinate-subordinate relationship do not easily convert it to a bond of equality. Bonding is too serious for us promiscuously to transmute one tie of great intensity into its opposite, and then run both together. Love and marriage may go together like a horse and carriage, but the horse has to be broken and yoked, and the carriage pulled.

5.

GIVE
AND TAKE

IT REALLY IS better to give than to receive. The very act of giving is perhaps the most basic step on the road to truly human social relationships: it implies an obligation to return the gift.[1] It sets up a relationship of indebtedness unknown in the animal world; it creates networks of indebtedness; vast systems of credit; things offered and things owed; those to whom we have given and those to whom we must give; those from whom we may expect and those who may expect from us in turn. The system of exchange is never in equilibrium; somebody always owes somebody else something. If all debts were canceled, social relationships would scarcely exist; but they are never all canceled. Of all the social bonds that exist, those between debtor and creditor are the most characteristically human, and depart furthest from the basic biogrammar of primate bonding. No monkey was ever in debt to another monkey. While human society is integrated in many of the same ways as primate society, it adds this totally new dimension of exchange and contract—a dimension that cuts across all the bonding processes and creates a strange world of its own. This world is not immediately strange to us, because it is our very own human world of give and take and the sense of obligation. But in evolutionary terms it is very strange indeed, and from our perspective we must look at it for what it is: a remarkable adaptation, a unique adaptive mechanism of one particular species—ours.

The adaptation can be phrased like this: all animal populations have ecologies, only human populations have economies. This has been put another way: humans have a sense of "property."[2] This proposal has been challenged by defenders of animal sagacity on the grounds that animals defend territories—and what is more basically "property" than real estate?[3] The analogy of property and territory has been taken very far and used to explain a great deal about human behavior. But most of this analogizing misses the important point: an animal simply *defends* its territory and would never give it up unless forced; humans use property to *exchange* for other property. In other words, they willingly give up their property, provided they get something equivalent (or better) in return. This an animal would never do. No animal would understand for a moment the elaborate exchanges of pieces of the globe that went on after each European war. Human territories certainly have some of the characteristics of animal territories; they both provide food and living and breeding space, as any nation or tribe under attack will readily demonstrate; but no animal territory can have the characteristic of human property—that it can be exchanged.

Here we want to explore the consequences of this particular change of evolutionary gear from being a primate with a simple ecological relationship to the environment, to being one with a complex economy involving the exchange of property among its members. To do this we will have to look again at our evolutionary history. Once more we will have to be concerned with the hunter's round of life: the hunter dividing his kill with his colleagues, his children, and the needy of his group; the male hunter seeking meat while the females gather vegetables; the hunter gambling—working out the odds against him and against a certain tactic; the hunter exchanging women and arranging feasts. This hunter is not just an affliction of our pages; he is a present reality, he is a feature of contemporary reality: our elaborate cities and their often harsh individualism are closer to the environment in which we were selected and in terms of which we became skilled than is the agricultural or pastoral phase of the human story. Not that there are any real animals left to kill. But there are campaigns to be fought, deals to be made; there is a great possible richness of reciprocity. To be close to nature is not necessarily to be close to human nature. It is what we do that is important, not where we do it. It is with whom and why behavior occurs that matter, not the scenery and the smell of trees that surround the encounters. We are what we do. And now we must look at what we do with our resources and our needs, with our self-concerns and our generosity, and how we run the most exciting and elaborate credit system in nature.

Primates do not share. Neither do they exchange. We have already seen how far-reaching are the effects of that most primitive pattern of exchange that involved the men in providing meat and the women in providing vegetable foods.[4] Again, the human breakthrough involves the evolution of the notion of women as property—perhaps the most primitive form of property. The first debt in the world was probably a woman, and the first blank check was most likely the right to any of his daughters, born and unborn, granted by one man to another. The first economy in the world—and for at least a million years the only economy in the world—was a hunting economy. It was in this context that our behavior as exchanging, distributing, and maximizing creatures evolved. The pitifully short time since we invented agriculture (about ten thousand years ago), and the even shorter time since industrialization began in earnest (perhaps two hundred years ago), should not blind us to the reality of our evolutionary heritage. In our economic behavior, as in so much else, we are still Paleolithic hunters.[5]

Economics reflects evolution just as much as politics and sex do. In some ways the discontinuities between ourselves and our primate ancestors are more pronounced in the area of economics than anyplace else. Certainly our sexuality was changed in our struggle to become human, but for sheer physiological reasons it has a direct continuity with primate ancestry. This holds true for politics, too: we have changed the content but retain the processes and motivations. We effectively radicalized our relationship to resources and their production by introducing property, exchange, and the bond of indebtedness.

But if animals do not have property in the same sense as humans do, how did humans come to need it in the first place? It is not enough to say that hunting was involved; wolves hunt, but they do not have a mania for property. It is not simply hunting, but the manner of hunting that counted. Lacking the natural attributes of the carnivore, human hunters needed tools and weapons for the hunt.[6] Human hunting with its toolbase required also a kind of social organization that had to go beyond that of the pack to be successful.[7] Men had to accommodate to one another and to the varied skills they unequally shared, so they made deals. Tools and deals are the bedrock of human economic behavior, and originally and for a long time the deal was clinched with an exchange of females.[8] The web of indebtedness involved the transfer of women, the exchange of services, and the distribution of meat. The first tools on earth were butchering tools. From the clash of stone and flesh, generosity and economy were born.

The hunting way became successful; from being at first simply a supplementary activity, it rapidly came to dominate the whole course of human evolution. Men became dependent on the hunting way of life and evolved to cope with its ever-increasing complexities. Our whole anatomy reflects this development, from our convoluted brain with its powers of speech and association to our striding walk and upright carriage. From the unpromising beginnings of the little man-ape of south Africa we evolved into a very fine hunting machine geared to the nomadic life of the savannas and the relentless, if not swift, pursuit of game. But at the same time, our emotions, our intelligence, and our social skills were evolving to meet the same exigencies.[9]

But in no hunting group was the distribution of skills exactly even. One man might be an excellent tracker but perhaps useless with a spear; another might be extremely brave at the kill but lack the perspicacity to find the prey; another might be unfit altogether for the hunt but skilled in the manufacture of the necessary tools; another might be useless at anything but taking trips into the world of spirits to bring back messages of health and well-being; another might lack specific abilities but be able to plan large-scale activities with a logistical knack. The old would be stores of knowledge, the young reserves of strength, and the whole machinery must be made to work together for the success and survival of the group. There was also competition, for this was still the competitive primate to whom status mattered as much as meat, and for whom meat might well be the route to status. It was also a world in which groups split up and expanded to exploit wider hunting areas, but did not lose touch and remained in a related but competing bond with the original group and the other groups around. Another major source of differentiation was the division of labor between men and women, and the need of each sex for the products and services of the other.

There was a differentiation of skills, a differentiation of groups, and a differentiation of the sexes with regard to economic activity. The outcome of differentiation and competition was the deal. Men as individuals, and groups of men, set up alliances based on the exchange of property. Obligations were thus assumed by the exchanging parties, whether they were a man and his wife, a young man and an older relative, or two groups of hunting men. No one man could ever ensure his own survival: man was never a lone hunter, and he needed allies as insurance. He needed men who were dependent on him, and men on whom he was dependent. The more dependents he had, the more powerful and successful he would be, and the more likely to be the focus of attention and hence deference in the group. Also he would be most likely to accumulate females and thus disproportionately influence the genetics of future generations.[10]

The economy of hunting, therefore, involved bargaining, calculation, the assessment of odds and the taking of risks, insurance, speculation, the making of deals, the controlling of distribution, investment, capital accumulation, debt and obligation, and a series of similar skills that look different from those we are used to exercising ourselves only because the context is so different to start with. But over millennia we evolved as a creature that derived great emotional satisfaction from having and using such skills. If man is nature's great ward boss and her equally great lover, he is also her supreme wheeler and dealer. The deal is a recognition of one's limited strength, one's frailty in the face of larger problems. It is an assertion of community and a denial of the tiny megalomaniacal center-of-the-world which small children cherish and grown-ups occasionally seek to re-create when they are tired, or have tantrums, or become so pathologically convinced of their special virtue that they can no longer deal but can only command.

And of course it is not only men who deal. Women deal too, be they the lady borrowing a cup of sugar, a Ghanaian mammy-trader selling cans of corned beef to a smaller trader in a suburb, the clever suburban mothers marshaling fleets of station wagons full of children to ballfields, dance classes, birthday parties, and Hebrew schools. The poor mother with an absent or unemployed husband will use a friend or relative to mind her children while she works; girls who are courting will share clothes and cooperate to secure the best dates; childless women will be given babies to hold and feel community with, and not only because this relieves a mother or entertains a child. Women will organize extensive parties for fun or "charity"; they manage businesses, nurse patients, and counsel baffled children. They deal a lot to keep things going.

But the big adventures and the dramatic hunts are male. It appears still to be the case that the uncertainty and particular sensitivity of the hunt and its metaphor galvanizes men more than women, and boys more than girls. It is the band of men who play music like warriors, who worry a melody, turn it around, pass it back and forth, hide from it altogether, pair up, split up, combine to chase it, come crashing or singing around, and then drive to some utterly expert and exhausted point of rest when the improvisation is done and when the millisecond mutual awareness has paid off in a satisfaction only an improvising musician can understand as an essential luxury for his being. There are no bands of women who do this, though women as well as men are made still by the noise of instruments and are entangled in the whole wordless enterprise of solving a problem which need not and does not exist and which to the young particularly is more than entertainment. The music is the hunt; the method is the deal. It is something boys learn themselves, outside of or despite their schools, and then bring to such perfection of time and pitch that their elders almost fail to recognize their offspring for all their skill. They do this because they want to, and because their peers want to hear them. In a relatively free age, this is what some young men choose to do. As they play, they exchange constantly: you take a solo, and then I will; let's all ramify the drummer's statement; let's speed up, though the leader will keep the basic beat in his head; let's play till exhaustion. This is an almost pure emotional analogue of the hunt; music is not only the food of love but of predation too.

Not only is the male body adapted for tropical savanna hunting in groups, but much of his emotional life and many of the skills he most enthusiastically cultivates are also related to huntinglike activities. Our hunting legacy is a male creature evolved for certain work and seeking certain satisfactions. He likes to exchange, to solve, to maximize. Our legatee enjoys speculating, competing, and he loves cooperating and even after work goes out for drinks with his colleagues. Predictably, he enjoys feeling prosperous, but there is a critical ambiguity here, because this prosperity cannot consistently and openly contradict the public interest or what it is thought to be. The reason is simple and very important. High status among males is closely related to being the *center of redistributive activity*. The chief must give gifts as well as receive them.[11] The rich man becomes odious if he remains miserly; he is the moral cousin of the beggar who takes without giving. The miser threatens the whole system of social relationships in the same way as the incestuous man. Each one consumes what he owns and does not give it up in return for something else.

Such behavior carried to its logical conclusion would put an end to social relationships, since it would deny the fundamental importance of exchange and reciprocity. In all human economic systems which involve the accumulation of wealth, and hence the existence of wealthy men, the pressures toward and rewards derived from public generosity are universal and obvious. This is not to say that the rich and powerful always see it this way—miserable exploitation is just as universal but it is a perilous enterprise and usually successful only if backed by force.

No one in the hunting band can afford to exploit or expropriate anyone else too consistently. Individual survival is too fragile. An individual who accumulates and does not redistribute would be doomed if the situation were ever reversed. In any case, the hunting band is a face-to-face economy in which one is locked into a system of personal obligations. Accumulation for a hunter is, after a certain point, useless: he cannot consume more meat than he needs or use more weapons than he can handle. The successful hunter therefore has to convert surplus into prestige. In return he will be deferred to and also will be allowed to accumulate the primeval liquid asset—women. This represents the group's collective investment in him, from which it will reap the reward, it hopes, of fine hunters—the first compound interest. There is a mutuality of goals and indebtedness between the big man and his group. The whole point of being powerful and important is the control of distribution; the whole point of accumulation is the eventual sharing; the outcome of this strategy is, at least theoretically, food for all. Thus, in the ideal economy, accumulation and generosity are two sides of the same coin; getting and sharing are virtually one and the same activity.

But being generous is not purely a voluntary, sunny, and spontaneous act. It is a genuine casting of the bread upon the waters in the expectation of a future return. Our ancestors could not have based their evolutionary success on mere casual generosity. As the great French anthropologist Marcel Mauss put it, there is an *obligation* to give, an *obligation* to receive, and an *obligation* to repay.[12] The belief in these obligations is universal in human society, and the man who fails it is either despised or punished; he is admired only in joke and story, where his very deviousness serves to point up the accepted code. It is a rather tight little system based on the economics of tight little groups working seriously at the business of survival. The topology of its motivations is still with us, but as we shall see, the rubber sheeting has been stretched to breaking point by some of the content we have poured into this mold since the development of cities, civilization, and industry.

The main features of the hunting economy can be succinctly described.[13]

The primate base provides for (a) a rudimentary sexual division of labor, (b) foraging by the males, (c) the cooperation of males in the framework of (d) competition between males.

It is small-scale, face-to-face, and personalized.

It is based on a sexual division of work requiring males to hunt and females to gather.

It is based on tool and weapon manufacture.

It is based on a division of skills and the integration of these skills through networks of exchange (of goods, services, and women).

These are networks of alliances and contracts—deals—among men.

It involves foresight, investment, judgment, risk taking—a strong element of gambling.

It involves social relationships based on a credit system of indebtedness and obligation.

It involves a redistributive system operating through the channels of exchange and generosity; exploitation is constrained in the interest of group survival.[14]

It bases status on accumulative skill married to distributive control—again in the interest of the group as a whole.

It is important to see all these factors as integrated into the hunt. They are social, intellectual, and emotional devices that go to make up an efficient hunting economy, in the same way that muscles, joint articulation, eyesight, intelligence, etc., go to make up the efficient hunting body. They are the anatomy and physiology of the hunting body social. It is a system of the savannas and the hunting range, and it is the context of our social, emotional, and intellectual evolution.

Our economic dilemmas are rooted in recent changes. The anguish is relatively sudden, and what stimulates it is now relatively new. Until about twenty-five thousand years ago the number of hominids in the world was as little as 125,000, as many as two or three million.[15] We hunted with lots of space to range in. Our tools improved, as did our language and our skill for organization. Our brains improved to arrange these stimuli and make them useful for our purposes. We became more prosperous and bred more successfully. By about forty thousand years ago our evolution as a species was substantially at the point where it now hovers. Ten thousand years of agriculture, and the density that results from settling near rivers, deltas, and valleys, allowed us to begin to revise some of our tested procedures for raising the young and keeping the adults alive.[16] We domesticated animals and paid them careful attention as symbols of both prosperity and real wealth.[17] Animals entered our lives in a more intimate way than before.[18] They were no longer there just for us to kill, they now accompanied us on our life cycles, and to this day we attach ourselves tenaciously to expensive and inconvenient creatures we call pets, just as in a supermarket system we grow plants and try to embellish ourselves and our houses with trees and flowers.

We speak glibly and easily of the "agricultural revolution" and see it as the great leap forward in human history.[19] Before it was "prehistory"—the dark ages of the savage hunter. Agriculture gave us, the myth persists, a food surplus, settlement, leisure, and the beginnings of the necessary baseline of civilization.[20] But it also gave us two things calculated to put the severest of strains on the fine-honed hunting animal that we were (and still are): it gave us an uncontrollable and alarmingly increasing population density, and it gave us the daily round, the common task, the drudgery of unremitting year-round agricultural toil. It created the peasant, as inhuman a figure as the bureaucrat, and while it ultimately freed a "creative" class that developed writing and all the other appurtenances of the civilized life, it condemned the overwhelming majority of the mushrooming human population to a sedentary and servile existence.[21]

In a very profound, human sense, the agricultural revolution was the great leap backward. It returned the majority of us to the restrictive food-getting state of our primate past: we spent most of the day in food-getting activity, each day and every day, year in and year out. It condemned us to live and depend on small areas of land, and robbed all but the rich of the pleasures and drama of the chase. It let us continue to wheel and deal and make alliances through our females (the peasant raised all this to a fine if petty art), but it did not connect all this to the macrostructures of economic power.[22] It left us, as individuals, no longer contributing to the destiny of the larger group but insecure and at the mercy of those who were able to maintain the predatory life. Finally it created slaves and serfs who were robbed even of restricted territory and autonomy.[23] And it did this in a breathtakingly brief period, a mere ten thousand years. It did it to an animal that had carefully and beautifully prepared itself through millions of years of natural selection to range and gamble, lounge and play, feast and forage—all in pursuit of four-footed protein over wide and varied areas of the earth.

As if this was not enough, the species had to make a second spectacular leap into a yet more complex and difficult economy and an even more explosive rise in numbers. Two hundred years of industrialization have catapulted the species into a situation as different from the agricultural tradition as this was from the hunting way. The rate of population growth increased, the degradation of the environment begun by the domesticators of plants and animals was brought to near completion, and a new kind of creature—the wage laborer—was created, with no analogue in nature and no place in the evolutionary scheme of things.[24] On top of this the rate of social change was accelerated to a point where any sense of continuity from generation to generation —something deep in the hunter's experience—was lost almost completely.[25]

In one sense it is a great compliment to the hunting brain that it had the reserves and capacity that could cope with, and indeed provoke, these revolutions. But this brain is still the old primate brain with the overlay of gray matter wrinkled into self-consciousness by the hunting transformation.

In the same way, we still have the old primate body molded into a hunting machine by the savanna experience. As we have stressed, there has not been time for an agricultural or an industrial brain or body to evolve. The body was not framed for sitting at a desk or crouching all day in a field—as those who do too much of either usually discover to their cost; our emotional needs and satisfactions were not necessarily framed to these ends either. It is usually assumed that, because we are infinitely adaptable, this does not matter. But does it?

At every stage in these overnight developments we both imposed on ourselves severe costs and allowed ourselves some gains. The question is, did the gains ever outweigh the costs? In a strictly biological sense the species prospered. It multiplied and spread and outmaneuvered other species in the struggle for existence. But the costs to individuals were relatively high. And the distortions of social organization that followed may ultimately prove disastrous. To oversimplify: insofar as any new economic system allowed the participants some of the emotional and intellectual satisfactions of the hunt, it represented at least a holding operation; insofar as it denied a majority of the participants these satisfactions, it represented a definite loss. The frustrations resulting from the repression of the full expression of the hunting syndrome lie behind most of the anger and alienation that have characterized socioeconomic revolt. Marx saw that "alienation" robbed men of their contact with nature.[26] Contemporary workers are alienated not only from the fruits of their labor but also from the roots of their biology. Of course, revolution and revolt are often in the name of equality and take the color of morality. Clearly the demanding indulgences of the rich outrage the poor who must make of frugality a virtue and turn self-denial into self-enhancement. It is plain that the incompetence of generals and commissars oppresses those who are forced to flee their clumsiness. The perception of inequity was the basis of a new dialect for social dialogue—a manner of speaking not commonly heard in many places and often still unclearly understood where it is most often used.

But perhaps we can go beyond this form of deprivation and callousness to another which is rooted more directly in our technological systems and our new customs of working than it is in our selfishness and vested disinterest. Economies must not only provide bread (and even wine), but they must also satisfy the provider: to deny a human enjoyment of work is to a person's behavioral needs as the denial of a vitamin is to his blood, as movement is to his muscles. We have already noted that humans invented work. This was so when we placed new demands on an old creature. We created new milieus to do tasks done otherwise when all managers were also colleagues, and when there were no bosses but rather persons with whom one lived in nice proximity, who had a knack for a task that mattered, and who could be trusted. Not so in agriculture, where the lord might live in Prague or Bath or Alexandria. And certainly not so in industrial places where the lord resides in the system, where the manager will move on elsewhere, and where a shiny head-office building will harbor plans to scatter people as effectively as cavalry, and more tidily. It is a very different matter for a worker to perform a minute task of a small part of a larger construction than it is to prepare a hunting song, to run as swiftly as the others to the scene, to communicate like musicians about the feeling and pace of the business, and to conclude the matter with failure or success but at least in familiar company and with the knowledge that the task was worth the time, and the time was one's own. Punch a time clock, and it punches back. The animal who invented calendars to assist in religious rituals got lumbered with clocks whose intimate tacit tyranny is suspended in the most modern places only in playoff games, murder trials, wars, and such genuine crises where an answer is essential or a resolution the only thing worth waiting for.

The agricultural-pastoral phase, while depriving many of much in the way of behavioral satisfaction, did not entirely undermine psychic economy in the interests of material economy. In tribal agricultural systems there is still the small-scale face-to-face involvement, the immediate satisfaction of food needs through one's own labor, the making and unmaking of alliances and deals through the exchange of women, and the pressure toward redistribution. There is ample evidence that chiefs as such emerged simply as redistributive centers in economic systems that became more complex than the simple hunting band.[27] The chief's granaries, say the Bantu, are always open to the people.[28] The grain, cattle, and even wives that he receives as "tribute" eventually find their way back into the system again through the network of alliances and the generosity of feasts and festivals. Many systems remain "mixed" in the sense that some hunting is still done, or at least its analogue in tribal warfare—often highly ritualized—is carried on. There is continuity from generation to generation, and everyone is a part of the system to which he is responsible and which is responsible to him.[29]

The predominantly pastoral tribes have all these features, to which is added the advantage of movement, of nomadism.[30] The productive unit needed for herding has many analogies with the hunting group, even though the relationship to the animal world is radically altered. Again some hunting or some analogues to the hunt are practiced: at least the whole thing operates out of doors and in a context of movement across the country, passing from place to place, experiencing variety and exercising decision. The gardening and horticultural peoples[31] of the Pacific and Melanesia get their subsistence in peasant fashion from little plots of ground, but their activity in the vegetable gardens is simply the background and prelude to exciting and dangerous overseas trading expeditions by small groups of men in outrigger canoes. These expeditions have less to do with real trade than with the exchange of ceremonial objects among fixed "exchange partners" in various islands along fixed routes traveled in a fixed order. The ceremonial nature of these elaborate voyages was puzzling to anthropologists, until they realized that the exchange was an end in itself— that it simply creates and sustains relationships and that, although this is never stressed, it creates the analogue of the hunting expedition for people who live by growing tubers. This is what exchange is all about anyway, and the "useless" sea voyages of the Melanesians with their exchange of shell necklaces and coral beads are almost pure expressions of the principle: it is done for its own sake, for the intrinsic satisfactions that it brings the creature.[32]

The landlocked relatives of the Melanesians in New Guinea also live by pigs and tubers, and manage to find substitutes for the satisfactions of the sea voyages.[33] Elaborate trading parties formed of groups of related "allies" go off on long overland expeditions; here too the ceremony of aggressive trade is important. Head-hunting parties, largely concerned with vengeance and status validation, are similarly composed, and venture, like the Crow Indian war party, on raids into enemy territory. Warfare is highly stylized entertainment and consists largely of dodging enemy spears and demonstrating bravery. But all these things allow for the free play and elaboration of the tendency to exchange, to range, to face risks and dangers with colleagues, to deal, to ally, to compete, to triumph or mourn in concert, and above all to *participate* on the old hunting pattern. Given all this, those hours in the yam gardens may seem less onerous.

In all these cases the element of hunting-by-analogy rests not only on the expedition and the kill, but on the exercise of certain skills developed in the hunting economy. Of these, the business of ceremonial exchange is perhaps the most elusive and yet the most significant. It is almost akin to what ethologists call a "vacuum activity."[34] Birds that have never had a chance to peck at insects, and yet that in nature feed off them, will indulge in pecking activity on the walls of their cages or ceilings of rooms or wherever they are incarcerated. It is simply what they do, and they will do it even in the absence of the appropriate stimulus. Wind up chickens, and they start to peck: wind up human beings, and they start to exchange things. Exchange is in some ways the prime human skill, and in engaging in "pure" exchange we are simply exercising this skill, much as in running for sport we exercise our capacity to move swiftly through space.

Nothing could be further from the arena of action of our ancestral hunters than the factories emitting smoke and producing metals, than the pristine reasonableness of an automated plastics factory, than the perplexingly detailed massiveness of a large insurance firm. But even in these organizations, bits of the human biogrammar must still be audible and rhythms of its expression still apparent. It is now appropriate to look at industrial and postindustrial economies, to see how they reflect or inhibit what we came to be and are, and to raise that traditionally vexing question: Can economies be contrived better to fit people, instead of people being coerced, or tempted, to fit economies?

The division of labor is nothing new in itself.[35] Those who claim that the only complete human being is the one who does all the work necessary for survival himself are creating an unnecessary and improbable economic saint. The essence of exchange is that it deals with temporary deficits and surpluses of either food or weapons or clothes or time or affection or skill—whatever a community deems valuable, and whatever its members need to survive. Thoreau was an interesting character, and his uncontrolled experiment at Walden Pond a cheerful portrayal of the corrupted Rousseauist fantasy about natural man. But it is no more a metaphor for human potential or reality than a ranting mob. It was an extreme and joyful trick, but no lesson about man and no comment on our economies and our love of commerce and exchange. So unsure are we about our daily reality, and so bemused by the power of our theory of what it could be, that we can take with a straight face an ironic hermit's revenge on what he feared was burgeoning sanctimony about the necessity of industrialization. Thoreau was not only a charming metaphysical jester, he was also wrong. He once asked, tellingly, when a telegraph was installed between Boston and Bangor, "But do the people of Boston have anything to say to the people of Bangor?" The question implied that the answer was, "No, not really." In fact, the answer is, yes, they had, or if they had not, they soon found something to telegraph about. The first reality of industrial community is that it is based on the division of labor, which is an ancient good in itself, and the second is that it permits, even if it also compels, people to communicate with one another.

It is true that the division of labor is pushed further in industrial society than in any other. It is true that it is the basis of industrial efficiency, but it may also be true that it is the basis of industrial misery. Marx hated the division of labor, but his alternative was never clear.[36] Durkheim saw its obvious benefits for producing a more organic society with interdependent parts, but he saw, too, how easily it could lapse into anomie.[37] We can all see the devastating results of overspecialization in the Chaplinesque tragedy of the man whose whole working life is spent in turning nut after nut on car after car on the assembly line.[38] But it is not the division of labor in and of itself that produces this misery. We have to blend this ancient organizing principle with something else before we can produce the explosive mixture Marx rightly saw brewing in the grime of nineteenth-century industrial cities. That men should perform specific and allotted tasks, which, taken together, would produce a finished article or achieve a common goal, was neither new nor terrible in human evolution.

But the primitive division of skills in terms of which we evolved took place in the intimate context of the hunting group with all its characteristics. The contrast is not between the totally self-sufficient individual on the one hand, who never existed anyway, and the overspecialized and depersonalized individual on the other. It is between the depersonalized individual, and the specialized individual who is locked into a small group on equal terms with his fellows—who knows that through his network of alliances he can depend on a return from the group for his specialized effort. He is part of the redistributive network, and from the cumulative effects of his group's activities he can expect some reward. No matter how far down the pecking order he is, he is someone's ally through marriage or ceremonial exchange or partnership, and the group is responsible for him. He is not so much closely connected with the product of his *own* labor as he is with the product of the *joint* labors of his group, in a direct and satisfying way. The unalienated man is not the self-sufficient man at all, but the socially sufficient man—and it is this sense of social sufficiency that modern industrial organization endangers.

It does this by removing the mass of individuals from participation in the predatory process and turning them into "tools"—objects of exchange (to be bought and sold) rather than agents of exchange. The agricultural system did the same thing to peasants, but at least it left them something, some control of their lives and their haggling. Industry, like slavery, robbed men of even that. The arbitrary routines of factories with their callously unwholesome environments and the virtual interchangeability of one jobholder for another were symptoms of a new refinement in the elaboration of anomie. Women lost their womanhood, children lost their childhood, men lost their manhood, because machines demanded their time and small manipulations, and because the virtue of the free-enterprise system was such that higher wages and gentler conditions would quickly put an entrepreneur out of competitive business. One had to work because there was no vegetable garden from which to get food, and no hut to spend the night in. And one had to work in the miserable factories, because the system had few alternatives for the masses forced into cities. One sold one's time and one's unskilled labor the way the modern urban American poor in slums sell bottles of their blood, because it is what—or maybe all—they have to sell. Selling one's labor to the factory was an innovation, a socioeconomic prostitution without even the dubious boon of physical contact with one's buyer and without even the option to charm, bargain, or threaten with guilt. The mercenary soldier also sold his labor. But he saw some fairly immediate results—adventure, the exercise of predatory skills, and not least, booty and women. The factory worker had all the disadvantages of the peasant and none of his advantages. Technically free, he was in effect a wage slave.

What did industry leave, if anything, of the satisfactions inherent in the hunting animal's life-way? It had one advantage over a true slave system: technically, at least, it allowed men and women to provide for their families with their own labor. It permitted them a small feeling of effectiveness, which was, however, so precarious as to rob it of real meaning. The threat of unemployment became a chronic feature of the system, over which the individual had no control, and was a constant reminder of his helplessness.[39] There is no unemployment among hunters. Employment is guaranteed even for slaves.

Like its agriculturally based predecessors, the industrial system easily turned from redistribution to exploitation. Again, this had the effect of concentrating predatory activity in the hands of a few; it condemned the majority to a role more like that of the exploited herds of the pastoralists than that of the participant hunters. Marx's main insight was to see that this exploitation was not the result of human wickedness, but a property of the system itself. The entrepreneur had no choice but to exploit his workers, in the same way that the hunters had no choice but to exploit their particular environment. But the entrepreneur was not locked into any system of redistributive generosity. Individual spontaneous generosity was always present in the form of charity, but the hunter's redistributive system never depended on spontaneity. Even the tribal chief was expected—rather, obliged— to give back that which he received. This was praised in song and tribal legend as generosity, but the praise only underlined the obligatory nature of the giving. There is strong pressure on the wealthy in industrial societies to redistribute their wealth in the form of public and charitable benefactions—with often very beneficial results. But, as Marx clearly saw, no number of gestures of goodwill could alter the nature of the system. His predictions and remedies may have been wrong, but his analysis was accurate enough. Eventually, and despite the opposition of economic theorists, governments had to step in and take over the redistributive functions that the system lacked. Sometimes this change was forced on nations by revolution, sometimes it came gradually as a result of a series of pressures—workers' movements, the spread of joint-stock ownership, the growth of socialist ideologies, etc.—and it is still going on. But, by whatever means, it had to come.

There is no need to chronicle—or even list—the evils of the industrial revolution, or the built-in weaknesses of capitalist economies, or the necessities of responsible social welfare; they are all well enough known. It is enough here to show how any economic system, like any political system, has to take into account the kind of animal we are and the kind of social relationships with which we were evolved to cope. Our adaptation to the hunting economy predisposed us to expect certain satisfactions and to seek certain goals. Economies that fail to provide for these—be they capitalist, socialist, mixed, slave, peasant, or anything else—will founder as much because they fail to deliver the psychosocial as the material goods. The argument here is exactly the same as that for political systems; of course, economic and political systems cannot easily be separated. Any political system has to take into account the political nature of the animal, and no system could really ignore the fundamental satisfactions that the creature needed from its hierarchies, attention structures, coalitions, etc. Therefore, systems that condemn most of their members to places at the peripheries of power have problems similar to those that condemn often the same majority to positions outside the central networks of exchange, production, and distribution. In each case, the system capitalizes on some aspects of the biogram to the often disastrous exclusion of others.

Economic systems are customarily judged by their productivity and by their capacity for generating wealth and economic growth. But that is only one of the criteria for assessing them: our suggestion is that it is both humane and strategical to view such systems as means of providing not only wealth but also a measure of satisfaction for members and some sense of that mutual aid that may be part of the imperial animal's central orientation to his fellow man. We know enough now about wealth to understand that once some basic standard of food and shelter is provided, humans are enormously inventive about immediately creating new wants, which then become needs for some and luxuries for others. Our concern here is with not the "veterinarian" level of satisfying needs but with the behavioral consequences of economic activity. Some economic arrangements generate more wealth than others, but do they necessarily generate more satisfaction?

One of the basic satisfactions, we have argued, is a sense of participation in predatory activity and the consequent exercise of the skills and enjoyment of the rewards associated with it. Another satisfaction lies in the surety of being a participant in the redistributive system. All economies allow some participants these pleasures, but few economies allow them to all participants.[40] In this sense, welfare becomes neither a graceful display of the mercifulness and humanity of an economy nor a technical means of ensuring the health and consent of employed persons. It becomes, instead, as biological a right as the right to shelter, to basic food, to the protection by some agency against the force of others—as biological as the rights of children to the times and resources of adults. What becomes increasingly clear is the foolishness and cruelty of those who claim, in the name of biology, that the so-called strong must not aid the so-called weak.[41] A more accurate claim, in the name of biology, is that the very opposite is more likely the case. The most democratic communities are those based on the commonality of the human gene pool. Sharing resources to sustain those who carry these various genes is nothing more than prudent— and nothing less than a conservative estimate that there is some good for the species in all people. Who can decide at any point which characteristics are more desirable and which more redundant? The narrow-mindedness of eugenicists and all those who quibble about superior and inferior "stocks" represents a crude distortion of the lesson of population genetics.[42]

A person who *receives* nothing from his community loses an important stimulus of his humanity, and so does a person unable to *contribute* to his fellow citizens. This is not to say that a man will be made desperately unhappy if he cannot extend the benefits of his Swiss bank account to Indian peasants. But if he cannot work among his fellows, if he cannot advise, if he cannot offer his experience as a guide to other people's efforts, if he cannot influence the young or satisfy the old, he is deprived of an exchange as meaningful as speech and a basis of commitment more general than patriotism and more energizing than theories of responsibility. The saddest examples of those who lose this aspect of humanness are the unemployed and the unemployables—those deemed unworthy of employment by their fellows and unable to contrive some tasks for themselves which will earn them money and a dignified place in the community. In societies which use it, money is an important index of personal worth, particularly in the basic sense that one either can earn it or cannot. Welfare money is not the same as worked-for money; there is now ample evidence of the effects on personality of receiving welfare for a long time and of being persistently unable to get worthwhile and enhancing work. It is not simply work itself that is at issue here, but the sense an individual may have of being skilled in some way that will allow him some broadly beneficial effect on his community—even as a Buddhist priest who does nothing but encounter the perplexities of his fellow man, or a retired man who stops traffic at a corner for schoolchildren going home, or a girl reading stories to a blind child.

This is not to say that receiving welfare funds is morally bad. It is to say that the right to give, in terms of the kind of active gregarious animal we are, is just as necessary as the right to receive—which progressive legislation has at last reassured with schemes of welfare. And yet this is not progress at all: it is regress to the interdependence of prehistory and to the articulated and assured communality of hunting humans. The dual claims of a "right to work" and "to each according to his need" are not highly developed moral precepts issuing from advanced progressive thought, but some of the most basic demands of the human organism—the political philosopher's elusive "natural rights." In demanding the right to be allowed to give and to receive and to participate, men are simply demanding the right to be human and to indulge in that basic set of exchanges that so defines them.

These are only baseline provisions—like having arms or legs. It is not only the job and the security that count, but the manner in which the job is done. Again, the economy can either maximize the predatory satisfactions or deny them. Usually it gives full rein only to a few of its participants, and the problem is that these then become predators on the rest. Other men become defined as "environment," to be preyed upon and exploited; here, just as in bureaucracy, people are defined as things, tools, objects—as "labor" or "consumer." The satisfactions for the few, however, can be enormous.

In the capitalist, or free-enterprise, economy the entrepreneur is given free play for his predatory tendencies. His small-farmer cousin may be nearer the soil but the urban businessman is nearer his own biology. Outside the teen-age gang, the outlaw band, or the military platoon, that delight of the theoretical economist's dream of perfect competition, the small firm, is the nearest thing we have today to a hunting group. In many ways we can gain by seeing it side by side with its seeming opposite, the illegal, extrasocietal, violent band of outlaws. This is a predatory group par excellence; it is, then, surely not accidental that it is one of the more enduring sacred cows of the entertainment business. From Robin Hood to Jesse James the story has been the same: the band, while often technically democratic, is in fact based on a powerful principle of dominance, with often a latent and intense dominance struggle as part of the plot. It is composed of males joined together by strong bonds. Females play service roles of one kind or another to the males, and often act as catalysts in the plot, either through their provocation of male rivalry, which disrupts the bonds, or through their perfidy, which destroys the group, or through their weakness, which in turn weakens the group. The group preys on the "environment," which in this case is the lawful society. Most of the tension in the group is caused by disputes and haggling over the division of the "kill" and its ultimate disposition. The men make elaborate deals with each other concerning the division of the spoils. In legend, if not in fact, the group is seen as a redistributive agency which takes from the exploiters (barons, bankers, etc.) and gives to the deserving poor, or at least represents the poor in its attacks on the rich. The band, finally, is nomadic, although usually with a home base, and it follows its prey over a fairly extensive range. It is all very familiar and thrilling. The tension involved in the gambling or risk-taking element is essential to good entertainment.

Because of its graphic and violent nature, the outlaw's life is naturally considered better entertainment value than, say, the success story of a business firm. But in essence the same elements are there, even if no one gets killed during the board meeting. At least there the "kill" is not quite so obvious, but the tender, the contract, the take-over, the franchise, and the account all have the attributes of the predatory goal. Gambling and risk are a first principle: even in the abstruse realms of economic theory, profits are the rewards of risk-taking. The business team is most often all-male. Women, usually seen as disruptive to its enterprise, are there only to serve in some way. Establishing and maintaining a hierarchy of command and authority is central to the business organization. The division of profits, the principle on which this will operate, and the control over this redistributive activity—even if it is only the declaration of the dividend—are everywhere in evidence. Haggling, wheeling and dealing, and the making of alliances—not uncommonly by marriage, in some cases—are even more important here than among the outlaws. Ceremonial gift-giving is often rife, and used as a way of cementing or promoting alliances—even if only in the form of elaborate entertainment—from the two-martini business lunch to the long weekend at the hunting lodge. Triumph ceremonies, feasts, and elaborate initiation procedures complete the picture.

Though outlaws and small businessmen differ in what they do and what people think of them, there are similar units in their behavior. The maneuver about position, tactics, and the spoils, the estimation of value—and no creature is vainer and more sensitive to his reputation than an outlaw or entrepreneur—and all the elements of risk and success cut across both enterprises. But groups that cohere and take the right risks with the right resources are bound to grow larger. What happens to this pattern of quasi-hunting action under these new circumstances? What do people do for drama and a sense of easy competence when they are just single units of populous endeavors? When the assistant manager of a shoe section in a mediocre department store returns home, does he carry with him any sense of triumph or even self-regard?

Typically, and here the slang expresses a reality, it is the big wheels who deal; the bosses hunt and calculate, risk and fight, threaten and accommodate, run and pause. In the huge corporation, the very word "executive" implies the facts of the matter. The executive *does* things; he is not a worker, he is a different form of person; he is paid by the year, not the hour, because his scope is so great and his plans so complex. The painful fact is, he *is* different. The executive can take a place in the old hunting program, he can make a difference because of what he does, and he can enjoy the complicated and often hazardous decision-making his job demands. His employees, and the employees of his colleague executives, are a class apart. They are to the executive as bullets, horses, and hardtack are to the outlaw—items to be used in the pursuit of goals. He decides their income and fixes how and with whom they will spend their working hours. He can trade them off by selling a company, or purchase the products of their skills by buying one. He can lay them off, fire them, and insist on eating in a different dining room to preserve the thick sense of power the sleek dominant males at the center of the hierarchy create like some electric current and share like some bequest from an unusually discerning providence. He votes himself stock options and gives himself cars and expense accounts on the basic ground that his very being is so important that all comfort must accompany his mighty efforts. His status is affirmed for all to see and mark. Small wonder he trumpets sober praise of this system which seems so sensible to him; it is no surprise that industrial executives in capitalist and communist countries alike feel properly rewarded only by disproportionate rewards. They, after all, are the ones who do the dramatic and hardy things that we value. They execute, they do not work. They may be tools of the system overall, but their satisfactions are qualitatively different from those of the assembly-line workers, and their options always more momentous.

But they are dispensable too. The jobs they fill are so desirable that there are always hundreds aching to occupy the swivel chairs of power. One need only look at the advertising executive earning a vast sum to know his awareness of his precarious grip on this astonishing boon. He must keep hard to the front line all the time, be beautifully groomed and fit, be as contemporary in all things as decency permits, be the effortlessly effective master of the magic words and pictures he wields in sales campaign after sales compaign. Let him lose a large account, and see the sleekness become tighter, the confidence somewhat urgent, the grasp somewhat cautious or more headstrong. He is part of a benign and splendid group, but he was not born to it. It can be taken away from him, with all the money and the trappings. He has to be at the front line all the time, because the prey is fat and delicious. But it is not his own village that helps him hunt the prey, it is some people whom he must constantly impress and who can turn on him should his work be badly fashioned or should he slip twice or antagonize some statesman from a wealthy advertiser. He can get a lot, but having got it, he is then in the frightening position of perhaps losing as much as that, and more, because the future becomes suddenly gray and the terrain rough.[43]

Let us not ache over the adman teetering on the edge of a thousand dollars a week for pocket money. But his dilemma is in this sense only more glorious and dramatic than the same problem his secretary faces or his chauffeur or barber. He can be splendid and return to his home on the hill bearing cruise tickets and hi-fidelity structures. But he faces the same bleak sense of personal finiteness.

In sum: once the hunting-business-outlaw band turns into the large, impersonal organization, the glories and penalties of the predatory way become the province chiefly of the dominants. The majority, whether of the Mafia or General Motors, are condemned, as "workers," to become tools; again, the opportunity to exercise predatory skills is the province of the few. Even so, there are restrictions. Labor unions intervene to limit the freedom of action of executives. In creating unions, workers became effective predators of a kind themselves.

Unions were at first almost outlaw bands. Secret, continually harassed by police, they demanded of their members high dedication and the ability to assume risk and bear unpleasantness in the face of the larger goal of affecting the division of spoils and control of workers' destinies. Early unions allowed workers a stringent dignity. Later on, the same processes of bureaucratization that affect the entrepreneur affected them too, and union leaders became part of a wider group related to government and business, though with a particular mandate from a clear economic interest group.[44]

If unions were one disruptive subsystem, the government was another. It became patently and painfully clear that free enterprise as a system would not ensure adequate distributive justice just as the communist state would not wither away. Accordingly, through the weapon of taxation and the techniques of economics, capitalist governments sought to make some more acceptable allocation of wealth without inhibiting too much these businessmen presumed to create it. In effect, unionization and government intervention in private economic matters are a close approximation of a pattern of redistributive justice that hunters required. For even very cynical governments are aware of the limits of their options. In any system the relationship between politics and economic activity becomes clear at the point at which the following decisions are made: How much do we redistribute? How much goes for new tools and shrines? How much can the major hunters appropriate? What leeway have individuals in deciding how much of what the community produces should be theirs?

The basic economic propensities of the human animal are compatible with various systems in various degrees. Some systems maximize some potentials and ignore others, offer some satisfactions and deny others. What is important is not only how systems create and distribute wealth but also how they allocate the right to *behave* in certain crucial human ways. A Catholic priest, for example, is given food, clothing, and shelter, but denied sex. Some economies provide these staples for their members but deny all or most of them the right to act in ways that are as basic to the organism's "natural" behavior as sex itself.

In theory at least, laissez-faire capitalist economy gives a very full rein to predatory tendencies and those patterns of behavior associated with them. A large number of small competing firms replicates the hunting situation in many respects. This is in human terms, as well as in economic theory, "perfect competition." This pattern is also easily upset, both by its own dynamics and by its tendencies to monopolistic competition on the one hand and polarization of wealth on the other— as Marx saw. The spread of ownership among thousands of shareholders and the rise of managerial elites and their bureaucratic structures can also alter it beyond recognition. All these tendencies combine to rob the majority of a role in the predatory process and make impossible any equitable system of distribution—either of wealth or of satisfying behavior.

The socialist or communist economy, on the other hand, maximizes the redistributive functions—at least in theory—but plays down or eliminates altogether the predatory patterns of its capitalist counterpart. Indeed, this is its moral object. In social welfare, health, education, housing, and employment, the individual (or family) has a rightful claim on the community's resources—a community to which he is also allowed and encouraged to give his labor, with a sense of important participation and symbolic reward for Stakhanovite effort. But this economy is constantly in danger of stagnation, precisely because competition and predatory infighting have been removed. In removing them, the economy has removed a great deal of initiative and innovation and the keenness that provokes efficiency when profit or even survival are at stake. The cautious experiments at feeding competitive "capitalist" mechanisms into otherwise socialized economies reflect a grudging recognition of the problem.[45]

The mixed economy might seem to be the solution. Predatory free enterprise would be allowed, but the government would own the larger service industries (railways, banks, hospitals, etc.) and act through legislation and taxation as a redistributive center. But this raises the problem of finding a reasonable balance among the subsystems; it could well be that such economies would get the worst, rather than the best, of both worlds. If they really proved inefficient, they would end up by frustrating *all* the behavioral propensities of their members sufficiently to provoke considerable unrest. The problem is the same as for large bureaucratic structures. We were not evolved to cope with organization on this scale, it is almost literally inhuman, however there is no way back; we cannot envisage handling large populations with complex economies in any other way. But we are not here to sit in judgment on economic systems or theories, simply to point out what it is about the evolved behavior of man-the-economizing-animal that such systems and theories have to take into account.

One thing that every system has to take into account is the sexual division of labor. We have maintained elsewhere in this book that the degree and nature of the participation of men and women in the economy is very different. We suggested that this goes back to the evolution of the hunting animal, where male and female were assigned radically different tasks, each essential to the success and survival of the group, and that therefore they were subjected to very different kinds of selection pressure.[46] We can come to the same conclusions about economic as political division of labor, but the details differ insofar as women are of necessity deeply involved in the economy at the same time that they are shut out completely from any political activity. But it can be predicted that in each case men will want to keep them from controlling the system, and women will be unlikely to make effective inroads on any scale into the centers of economic power. The roots of this dilemma are deep in our history. Women did not hunt.

Some of the physical differences between males and females, which are related to different roles during our formative evolution, have already been discussed, but it is necessary here to note some of them briefly in order to root behavior directly in its biological context. These differences are first of all based on clear reproductive distinctions. Female reproductive physiology places simple structural limits on what women can do. They must have wider pelvises than men, because the birth canal must accommodate the infant's large head; therefore they use more energy in locomotion, because their hips swing wider from side to side. In addition, the fat deposits on their buttocks are heavy and use up precious energy. Accordingly, women cannot run as quickly or for as long as men. Of course, there is a normal curve of variation here as elsewhere, and some women will run faster than some men; the curve of variations of the male and female will overlap, but the curves are nonetheless real and significant. This is true also of the ability to throw objects such as balls and spears—a matter obviously relevant to a hunting animal. Furthermore, females adapt less readily than males to changes in temperature—a considerable hazard in hot environments. We now know that there are predictable and disruptive effects on female performance that depend on their menstrual cycles;[47] and it remains an abiding index of male callousness to female realities that rarely are these normal and foreseeable stimuli considered in arranging work and even domestic schedules. (This can become positively inequitable when females are engaged in crucial tests of various kinds. For example, some reports indicate that females achieve some fourteen-percent-lower grades on examination

during the premenstrual days, when they are at a considerable disadvantage. Depending on the nature of the examination in question,
a woman may be affected for her entire career because she could not
demonstrate the ability she normally has. Conversely, if she were to
confront this examination at mid-cycle, her performance might be better than usual. In another milieu, the first female Russian astronaut
has argued that while women could do the tasks men do, it was still
necessary to take the menstrual cycle into account in managing the
routines of space flight.[48])

There is a series of other differences of this kind that could be
described, but it is clearly more relevant today to focus less upon
explicitly physical features of work performance than upon those
involving emotional, intellectual, and social skills and enthusiasm.
There are, after all, relatively few jobs in industrial societies that
demand strength of arm and speed of foot so greedily that females
could not meet the needs. Women can and do drive huge trucks and
airplanes, operate elaborate machines, and physically cope with the
air-conditioned cabins and power-assisted controls of huge cranes and
earth movers. There is very little justification for assuming that any
job that men now do women could not do too. And vice versa: aside
from bearing and suckling children, there is no characteristically
women's work that some husky baritone copilot could not do. Our
ideas about equality and the right to widespread social participation
of men and women all urge us overwhelmingly in the direction of a
society in which male and female roles are more or less interchange-
able and in which no particular cachet or stigma attaches to men
doing what was once women's work, or the other way around.

But the reality falls far short of the ideal. The potentialities are
felt only weakly in what actually still goes on. One of the few general
rules about human cultures that anthropologists can safely affirm is
that in all known societies a distinction is made between "women's
work" and "men's work." The inconsistencies in attitudes are plenti-
ful and comical from one society to another; in one place, men will
carry water and women will plant yams, while ten villages away the
inhabitants will defend with high intensity the obviously correct
proposition that women must carry water and men plant yams. So
the first point is that even where the distinctions are not especially
reasonable or defensible, they are inevitably made. The next general
feature of this division of labor by sex is that some jobs are widely
thought to be the rightful provinces of males, and others of females.
Hunting, the manufacture of weapons, and the construction of boats

are almost universally thought to be male, while such tasks as grinding seeds and gathering nuts are reckoned females' work nearly everywhere. This follows understandably from the hunting past.

But what is not easily understandable is the extraordinary persistence of the division of labor by sex in societies with different forms and levels of industrialization, different climates, different histories, and varying notions about the good man, the good woman, and the good life. This must be explained.

We have already indicated how persistent male-female differences both baffled ideologists and violated the laws of chance. There is no particular reason why females must be part of formal politics. But women must work, and they must be part of the economy, any economy. Of course, in broad terms, they always are, to the extent that they do housework, prepare food, mind and socialize children, and attend to the clothing of their family. That this is not regarded as work in the sense that factory labor is, is a conceit of economic analysis, and part, besides, of a general devaluation of intimate (as opposed to public) activity—a devaluation that applies to the do-it-yourself man who contributes nothing to the Gross National Product when he builds himself a bookshelf but pushes it up two hundred dollars when he buys one from a shop. Women have to be in on the economy. But a basic element of the biogrammar here seems to be that they have to be in on only specially defined terms: there appears to be a tendency to define some work as female and some as male, and to maintain the distinction whatever the content and whatever the cost. This is the same principle of male-bond—female-exclusion that, in politics, so rudely circumscribed the female role. In economic matters, since females cannot be excluded totally, at least they can be segregated into some set of specific activities.

But does it go deeper even than this? We argued that the central arena of politics was male because of differences in male and female potentials for successful large-scale competitive bonding. Insofar as the central arena of economic life demands similar organization, we would expect males to dominate it. Where business and industry, or the organization of production consumption and exchange, generally demand cohort activity, it will be male cohorts who will be in evidence. Where control is involved, men will work together and women will be excluded or allowed in only if they agree to play male roles in a male fashion. Women usually lend themselves to this strategy by agreeing that it is not specific female skills that they bring to their roles as executives, and that in simply filling male positions they are substitute males. This attitude strictly delimits female behavior in business.

It also accounts for the pressures against overt sexuality on the job. Seductive arts are disruptive of male cohesion. The outlaw band or the board of directors assumes that they are not part of its normal routines, and women who want seriously to play the power game must leave their false eyelashes at home.

This may seem a facetious point, but it is a point that underlies a very serious truth. False eyelashes are supplements to female courtship-display behavior. They enhance the "recognition flutter" and coy covering of the dilating pupils in courtship exchanges.[49] As such they are part of the apparatus that aids in promoting and cementing the courtship bond. This is a male-female bond and operates in the arena of sexual competition and eventual mating. It is outside of and inimical to the male-male bond that operates in the politicoeconomic arena for purposes of cohort formation and maintenance in the pursuit of effective defense and predation. This is a point difficult, of course, to prove, yet it seems clear enough: that one serious if tragicomic reason for the difficulty females experience in male work groups is not that males dislike females but rather that the force of their enthusiasm for females can disrupt the work and endanger the integrity of groups of men.

We needn't waste sympathy on men harassed by such enthusiasm for women that they reject them as colleagues and force them into occupational ghettos so the precious male mystique will remain undisturbed. Our suggestion is that it is not malice alone, and not prejudice only, and not just cultural lag and individual fear that stimulate an obvious antifemale inequity. The same pattern emerges both in countries that devalue women and in countries that eagerly support them. The opportunities for women in the economy of the United States have declined over the past sixty years, though the number of women with advanced and technical education has increased enormously.[50] The Israeli experience, both in and out of the kibbutz, is even more discouraging to those who looked to their ideology about sexual equality to produce radical social change. And in Russia itself, the first and most important revolutionary society, the position of women has not been improved in any sense commensurate with either the expressed idealism of the community or its willingness to try relatively egalitarian socioeconomic forms and approaches to the ownership and control of wealth.

So it cannot be a conspiracy of men against women that once swept the world that now—so apparently securely—sets limits to the range of female options to enter the powerful macrostructures of economic life. The evidence against conspiracy comes from too heterogeneous a set of places: females are obviously able to do the tasks men can— that is, when they are given the opportunity; males are unlikely to have deliberately thought up ways of maintaining women in their homes for domestic and sexual convenience and then brainwashed them to accept such an exploitative situation—if exploitative it is. Perhaps, as with some of the other bonds, we are dealing here with a regularity of the biogrammar that has to do with ancient forms of survival that mark us still today. That the thrilling and elaborate innovations of our technology seem to have relatively little effect on the work relationships of men and women attests either to the un-importance of technology—which is foolish—or to the importance of the biogrammar. Though puritans and Calvinists will shrink at the thought, it may be true that social relationships are more important than work encounters, and the apparent rigidity of the sexual division of labor represents both men and women "voting with their feet" for the notion that difference does not necessarily connote inferiority or superiority, and that the division of labor is not necessarily the squalid display of human invidiousness that, for example, racism undoubtedly is. The sexual division of labor has no racial home. The analogy is faulty because sex differences are important biologically and tangible behaviorally, whereas racial ones are unimportant biologically and meaningless behaviorally. The bad analogy confuses policy even more than it confuses people: to avoid the consequences of racism, it is imperative that all people be treated equally, but to avoid the features of the sexual division of labor that many men and women find un-desirable, it may be necessary to treat men and women differently and not deny their real biologies in the name of theoretical equities.

In the same way that sexual intercourse must not only result in offspring but also be enjoyable for its own sake if a mating bond is to "take," so economic activity must not only result in the production of wealth but also provide behavioral satisfactions if people are to realize their humanity. That economies can be dehumanizing is a common-place, but critics of inhuman economic systems have had a hard time locating the truly human element that is at best simply lacking or at worst brutally denied in so many wealth-producing, people-consuming economic machines. The only "psychology" that economists assume is necessary to an understanding of economic man is that he be "rational" —that he can see the difference between the same item at a high price and at a low price, and that he choose the latter as preferable.[51] Economists would undoubtedly hold that the point about economies not providing satisfactions—like Marx's point about their producing alienation—referred to strictly extraeconomic aspects of behavior. But the opposite can be maintained. Economic behavior is as much a part of human nature as sexual behavior: to take away a man's right to exchange, to make deals, to be in debt and to repay, is as damaging as to take away his right to sexual satisfaction. It may even be more damaging, for a man can, after all, relieve his physical sexual tensions himself without help, whereas he cannot make exchanges without a partner. The heart of the argument here is that exchanging is the fundamental human act and that to deny it is indeed to deny humanity.[52]

This is another set of instructions in the wiring of the behavioral repertoire. As with politics and with personal bonds, we can write either compatible or incompatible programs. But we are feeding them not into a void but into an active, demanding organism—an organism demanding to be allowed to behave economically in the way that it has evolved to behave. To revert to the other analogy, certain very specific rules of the human biogrammar can be violated only at the risk of considerable peril. The amount of variety in the spoken language that is possible is very great indeed—as long as the rules are observed. Economic behavioral languages that disobey the rules break down all too blatantly. It seems, in fact, that they are in some ways the most vulnerable. There is considerably greater latitude in the political arrangements we can make without risking gibberish. Perhaps this is because we are still playing primate politics, whereas economies are species-specified—aspects of human behavior deeply implicated in the transition to humanity that took place through the hunting revolution.

The more general points about economic man and human economic systems can be briefly summarized.

The basic and differential feature of human economic systems is property, which differs from animal territory in that it is in its very essence something that can be exchanged.

The exchange of property (real or incorporeal) is the basic act of truly human social relationships.

These social relationships are created through indebtedness as a result of giving (which creates a debt), receiving (which in turn creates an obligation), and of giving back (which fulfills the obligation).

The socioeconomic system is therefore a credit system in which everyone always owes something to someone else. The importance of the giver-receiver, creditor-debtor relationship is often expressed in acts of ceremonial or "pure" exchange.

This basic pattern evolved in a hunting context that molded its content and direction. The basic economic group is the hunting group or its analogue, and basic economic activity is on the predatory model.

In consequence, all the following features figured prominently in the evolution of human economic behavior: cooperation for competition; division of labor; exchange and alliance; participation in risk-taking; a sexual division of function; and a redistributive system. That this begins to apply—however incipiently and inadequately—not only between individuals but also between nations suggests the strength of the pattern of giving, taking, and sharing.

6.

THE
BENIGN
OPPRESSION

EDUCATION HAS ONLY a little to do with the transfer of objective information. Its purpose—and it starts at birth and continues into old age—is to produce acceptable members of the community. It substitutes for instinct the inculcation of fixed habits of thought and action. It is the end product of the trend in mammalian evolution toward a greater use of learning and a longer learning period. It is another illustration of the refractory truth that our uniqueness lies in being more mammalian than the other mammals, not qualitatively different from them. Among all the social mammals, learning becomes very important, since instinct cannot cope with the complexities of social life. The instructions in the genes become more general and open-ended; they consist more and more of instructions to *learn* rather than simply instructions to *perform*.[1] In this evolution the growing cortex has two crucial functions: it provides for greater memory storage, and it promotes ease of self-control or inhibition.[2] Thus impulses come under the control of thought, of hindsight and foresight, of knowledge, of the process of deferred gratification—the knowledge that giving up immediate pleasure may lead to greater pleasure in the future. The advantage in flexibility of such a system is obvious, but it has its costs. If the learning is ineffective, there is no instinct to take over automatically. The more prolonged and complicated the learning process, the more likely things are to go wrong, because there are more choice points and thus more opportunity for wrong choices. To compensate, the learning process has to do something very curious: it has to instill into the organism patterns of behavior that are, in their effects, the same as instincts. They must be general in the population, relatively unmodifiable, and relatively automatic in their functioning. Loosely we call these patterns habits, and inculcating them is what most education is about.[3]

This transfer from instinct to learning—a transfer to a different kind of wiring system—has gone further in man than in any other mammal. In primate socialization there is little in the way of teaching. Most primate learning consists of picking up behavior patterns and information through play, observation, and imitation. Among some carnivores it seems that the deliberate inculcation of behavior is at work when the young are "taught" hunting.[4] This may be an interesting clue in examining the shift of emphasis, not only from instinct to learning, but within the process of learning itself, from learning to teaching. Onto the primate learning patterns were grafted the new urgencies resulting from the transition to hunting. Society became more complex: knowledge was accumulated, and social control began to involve processes more subtle than gestures of threat and appeasement.

Ultimately, a thing unheard of in nature was invented to take care of the programming of the human young—the teacher. The amount of information that the young human has to store in order to deal with the complexities and absurdities of civilized society is such that the species can no longer depend on simply picking it up during the normal processes of living. Nor is the average adult able to carry enough of this information to pass it on to his own children.

A specialist class of teachers is needed. Children are taken away from their "natural" learning environments and put into specially constructed, highly artificial environments. These are devoted solely to the instilling of knowledge and habits more or less related to the children's futures as members of the community.

But even where there are no formal schools, no paid teachers, and no packs of students, there is still education.[5] A broad notion of education must be used here, not just one that rests on printed curricula and fifteen minutes for recess. Every human gets educated, though not all go to school. A baby whose parent dangles a mobile in front of its eyes is learning coordination and delight in objects. The small child jumping, at first timidly, from a medium-high fence, is learning something about gravity and his skill in dealing with his falling body. The young fisherman sharing a beer with his elders in a seashore bar is learning, if indirectly, how to heed the tides. A middle-aged man talking with an old man can apprehend what the state of being old is, how it represents itself in experience, and how it can be sensibly encountered. Every time we see a movie, stare at a new cut of coat, fiddle with the parts of a simple gadget, try to cook a favorite food in a novel way, we are learning, educating ourselves, and being educated. For most of us the limits on what we can learn, if we have the time and will, are so far away from our present skills and knowledge that we need have no fear of running out of subjects. We are not just plastic animals, we are also porous. Not only do we try to learn about what we already know, but we also try to find out what we do not know. We have recently come to honor scientists who prove to us how imperfect our grasp is of where we live and why we do what we do. If we are imperial animals, part of the empire we claim and adorn is in our own heads. Whether we are having fun with making riddles and doing crosswords for no other reason than just doing them, or puzzling about the architecture of Assyria and the structure of the gene, we are probing and handling our environment.

We are all active participants in the learning process, and not simply the passive learning machines of the behaviorists that can be "trained" only by processes of reward and punishment. Education involves our whole beings, not just our intellectual forebrain processes. These latter provide for rational learning in the same way that they provide for rationality in economic decision-making. The argument here is the same as for economics: to concentrate solely on these rational processes is to ignore the satisfactions and conditions under which either educational or economic rationality operates effectively. The forebrain can certainly handle the formalities of learning mathematics, but if the teaching of mathematics is done in a way that obstructs the normal motivations of curiosity in the young human primate, then no amount of formal rationality can repair this deprivation. It is an unbalanced diet lacking in vital behavioral vitamins; only too often we see the results in "learning failures," "behavioral problems," "learning blocks," and "dropouts."[6] The process of creating a desirable "whole man" and "whole woman"—one ideal of most formal educational systems—itself involves the whole person. To ignore this is as foolish as to ignore the health of a dancer in allocating ballet roles, or to assume that only the fingers and the feet constitute the pianist. The tedious and traditional conflict between "instinct" and "learning" is fruitless and beside the point. If anything, we have a propensity to learn, as higher animals do. And we also have a propensity to teach. These combine to make the teacher-student relationship a potentially very satisfying one. That it often is not may very well mean that the context is wrong, that the rewards are too removed from the encounter, and that what is primarily a social relationship has become a technical transaction between organisms insufficiently comparable to make exchange agreeable or even possible.

Criticism of formal educational systems is commonplace, and there is no need to add to the catalog of complaints.[7] Everyone knows that the patient is sick, but the diagnoses are as numerous as the doctors, and some of the proposed cures more disturbing than the illness. Here we want to locate, if we can, the basic biogrammar of the system of education. Then we can look at educative processes in human society to see how they either conform to or distort this grammar, and if they conform to it, whether they put it to eloquent or clumsy use.

What are the basic instructions of the educational biogrammar for the human primate? Like all other behavior systems, it has two layers—the underlying primate layer, and the additions and modifications that hunting brought in its wake.

Primates want to live as much as humans do, and living involves them in many of the complications it presents to us. Yet primates learn how to get on, what to eat and where, with whom to fight and to whom to show respect, how to play and how to threaten. They learn the social prelude to mating. Primate mothers are more skilled with their second infant than with their first. It requires no particular imagination to see how many of their simple underlying forms of social life are cousins to our own; it is clear now that they learn this social formality, and that *they want to do so*. That young monkeys learn things and want to learn things is just as predictable as that they get hungry and that after they eat, they digest. They are fortunate in that they have solved the problem of relevance in education: monkey see, monkey do—and what he does do is pertinent to surviving and to being sociable. Not for a monkey the puzzling business of deciding the relevance of algebra to being a good field-hockey player, and the importance of the names of presidents and kings for decorating the gymnasium for a dance. Monkeys are spared the cynical gap between sanctimonious visions of how our societies are supposed to work and the ghetto children's emergent understanding that the numbers man and the cop both violate the version of truth so confidently asserted by teachers and elders and by official spokesmen of mythic culture. This violation recurs in human community after human community; cynicism is an extra dimension of human educational systems. For primates there is no such highly evolved feature of growing up. All the dimensions are plain, and all the characters are there in front of the face. Learning is an emotionally rich enterprise, part of a lively network of encounters and retreats. It may now be useful to spell out what and how our cousins learn at "school."

It is too simple to say that they learn by imitation. Of course they do, but their imitating is embedded in a network of social relationships. In the earliest part of its life the young primate learns primarily about its relationship to its mother. It literally clings to her. As long as the mother-child bond is firmly established, the young animal will begin to explore in ever-widening circles, always returning when frightened in any way. Once it has learned the basic lesson that its mother is there at all times to be turned to, it will begin to unleash its curiosity on the social and physical environment. What it learns at this stage is a basic security and confidence, without which its motivation to explore is severely impaired.[8] This underscores the importance of the mother-child bond. It is not only emotional maturity that is affected by the bond, but the capacity to learn in general. Bold exploration and mischievous curiosity,[9] the desire to manipulate and investigate the environment—none of these will successfully mature if the young animal lacks a sense of security. It will go out into the world—physically and intellectually—only if it has somewhere to come back to in case of emergency, or just plain fright.[10]

This sense of security is a kind of overdrive, a facilitating mechanism that stimulates a wide range of activities necessary to the learning process. The lack of it at best inhibits, and at worst cripples, the whole range of learning behaviors. It may very well, for example, inhibit the animal's capacity to play and thus cut it off from the most important of all learning experiences.

Play: schooltime is divided into work and play periods; our lives are divided unhappily and unevenly between work and play. We speak of "schoolwork," but the compound word "schoolplay" would appear simply ridiculous. Learning has become identified with working, and children plow through the assigned pages in their "workbooks" with the same glum persistance as the peasant behind his oxen. No other primate would make or understand this distinction. The first transition the young primate makes is from his mother to his peers. But before this he has started to become playful.[11] He romps around his mother and possibly his older siblings, and he bothers the big males, who tolerate him in a way that would never be tolerated from his older brothers. After he has found his feet, his playfulness with his peers increases, and becomes intense. Playing becomes a full-time activity. Games of hide-and-seek and follow-the-leader teach the young animal to use the terrain, to maneuver through the trees, to develop skills in discriminating between objects, and above all to relate to his fellows through a knowledge of his own strengths and weaknesses. In all this "play" he is learning through active participation. No one teaches him anything; at best, adults will chastise and sometimes divert or control in a mild way, but they do not instruct. If he is bothering the big males too much, the mother chimpanzee will grab him and lead him away. In a savanna baboon troop the group of playmates is always watched by a big male, to provide protection (and unintentionally a sense of security), but also to break up quarrels if they become too rough. A mother chimpanzee will "termite" (use prepared twigs to pick ants out of anthills) while her infant climbs all over her, watches at ridiculously close quarters, and hinders her efforts with his clowning. She takes little or no notice. But he will taste the ants and observe the performance and imitate it many times until he is himself an expert with the peeled twigs.[12]

But mostly he is learning role-playing. He is learning what dominance and submission mean, when and whom to groom, when and how to try his strength and exercise restraint. He is storing up incredible amounts of information, but not as a passive learner. Perhaps the most important thing of all is that he is *moving about*. The pleasure he has learned to take in the widening range of things he can do well with his body is wedded to the social actions that are features of his particular and unique "personality" and place him in his community. His high-energy output is matched by a high-information input; he constantly trades energy for information. He is not a receptor only, but a seeker-out, a seemingly inexhaustible investigator. He actively solicits and provokes stimuli. And, most significantly, this play-learning gives him enjoyment, pleasure in doing and risking within the framework of security provided by his mother in the first instance, and by the social organization of his troop under the control of the big males in the second.

For the growing primate, learning is inseparable not only from playing but also from living—from what he himself can see as relevant to what he does. No little primate has to sit down and relate the bad deeds of Henry VIII to the realities of his own existence. There is an immediate feedback from what he learns to what he does, since he learns through doing, and doing is the same as being, as existing in society and through society and for society. Thus in his rough-and-tumble play with the originally democratic play group, he gradually learns to sort out those he can beat from those he cannot; he learns how to appease those stronger than himself whom he has provoked too much; he learns how to threaten those less tough than himself who assert themselves too much; he learns the limits of his own capacity to control and to cajole; he learns how to associate with peers to achieve joint ends. All this learning is of immediate and continuing relevance, since it is with these peers that he may spend his whole life.[13]

It is in the context of the whole life cycle that learning has to be seen. We have already discussed the importance of the mother-infant bond. From the Harlows' experiments with isolated and badly mothered infants, we know that once a rhesus macaque has been deprived of affection and even physical contact, no amount of subsequent experience can totally reverse the traumatic effects.[14] Not only does learning take place all the time, but it appears to be rather predictably phased; there may be "critical periods" as relevant to other activities as early mothering is to adult sexuality.[15]

We gain a graphic sense of this phasing process by focusing on the differences between males and females. Though, among the other primates, this varies between species, broadly speaking, males take almost twice as long to assume adult roles as females do. For one thing, they must grow more, because they may end up twice the size of females. And for another, there is the possibility that the skills that they must learn take longer to acquire and that the selection process in which they find themselves is more drawn out than among females. This is a sociological feature of the same order as differences in rates of maturation. Among savanna baboons, for example, by the age of three and one-half the females are already involved in the estrous cycle and may bear their first infant shortly thereafter. At that time the males are still part of subadult male groups, playing increasingly rough games (though from the start males play more roughly and aggressively than females), and—most significantly—moving to the outskirts of the group. Now, at this roughly adolescent stage, they become unsettling to the dominant males, who attack them if they approach too closely. The annoyance expressed by the dominants at their very existence seems as uncritical and self-righteous as that of some suburban principals commenting on the preposterous hair and habits of some of their young men. These young baboon males then circle the troop; their next task is somehow to work their way back in by maintaining their useful truculence and energy while at the same time slowly making themselves acceptable enough to the dominant males to be able to join a coalition and take over the breeding and the power.

But this takes a long time and is dangerous. We have noted that mortality rates in primate groups are far higher among young males than females; one estimate is that as many as eighty percent are killed before adulthood. But if the task of the male is more difficult to learn than the task of the female, the individual male is less important than the individual female. Only a few males are necessary to breed with a large number of females and even to defend the group. While they are in the vulnerable stage, they also serve as the sentries for the group and its unwitting first line of defense against predators and other dangers. They serve their time as the draftees of their group. If they are clever and lucky, they return to take advantage of what they have learned and what they have endured, and of their now more formidable appearance and demeanor.

It is quicker and easier for the females. They do not have to leave the central area at all, and they do not. It is the males who form the roving bands moving from troop to troop; the females lose their infancy, gain their childhood, and pass through their adolescence all within the same physical space. This may be because the adult males do not resent them as they do the young males, but it may also be that there is less need for them to learn outside the area where the infants and the senior females are. For this is where their life contingencies will be worked out—in their encounter with the dominant males, who will fertilize them; with the other females, who will help them with their infants; and with the infants themselves, whose behavior they can mark and with whom they can themselves learn the skills and confidence a successful mother requires.

Why we think this is also true for the human primate will become clearer when we consider the transition to a hunting economy in these terms. For the moment it is essential to remember that we retain some primate characteristics in our bodies and central nervous systems. Before moving on to humans once more, let us very quickly summarize these characteristics.

The potential for efficiency and efficacy is maximized when the animal is secure and confident. This security enables it to explore and exploit its natural curiosity.

Playfulness is the basis of successful learning. Participation and sheer movement are important, and the animal learns best when it is actively seeking stimulation rather than receiving it passively.

Guidance and tolerance rather than positive instruction characterize the role of the adult in the learning process.

The learning is immediately relevant to the social existence of the learner.

The most important skill learned is how to play social roles.

There is a marked difference between the learning histories of males and those of females. The male pattern is more complex and demanding, and the female more circumscribed spacially.

Most of a young animal's learning is done with its peers, which, in the male case at least, introduces tension and competitiveness even if the animals are playful.

There are critical periods in the learning process when certain kinds of information should be acquired; failure to do so may impair future performance.

This or something very like it was the educational system we had to work with when we made the leap into hunting. What did we have to add to or subtract from the scheme to adapt our learning patterns to the hunting way? A number of specific things; for example, with the advent of home bases and camps we had to teach our young not to foul their nests, which is their natural inclination. Toilet training, as every psychoanalyst and every baby will testify, is a traumatic imposition on the organism. But this is too specific, here, where we want to explore some of the more general consequences.

We must recapitulate a little. The hunting transition coincided, and not accidentally, with the rapid growth of the neocortex. This is itself related to the need for greater storage of information and greater inhibition. The consequence for education was that sheer instruction became more important. It was a long time before this became specialized instruction, but the careful chipping of flint arrowheads, the preparation of poisons to smear on the points, the dressing of hides, and many other skills obviously required something other

than trial-and-error learning. The same was true of social skills.
The "manners and customs" that accumulated after the development
of language, the values and traditions by which the early humans
lived, their rules of descent, marriage, property, and exchange, all
had to be learned and stored as a result of fairly direct instruction. In
some areas, such as the learning of spells, myths, shamanistic techniques, art, etc., the instruction definitely took on the character of
"teaching" as we understand it. Even so, the greater part of the
process of learning continued to be through play—hunting play, house
play, sex play, and through active participation in the life of the
band.[16]

The greatest responsibility to be instructed fell on the postpubescent
males during their initiation into adulthood. They were still, despite
their languages and decorations, the same young primates who were
bucking for the central hierarchy. The same motives were—and are—
present in both the young men and their elders, but they had to be
handled differently if the young men were to be channeled into the
tribe as useful members. We have already examined the bonding
aspects; here we must look at the consequences for education. The
elders could no longer rely on their physical weight to keep the
young men in check, but they could rely on the weight of tradition.
Without a knowledge of the traditions of the group, a man was as
helpless as a lower animal that by some genetic quirk had failed to
acquire its proper instincts. Without a knowledge of male secrets
and male rituals and taboos, a boy could not be a man. This was the
trick. One could not simply *become* a man, one had to *know how* to
become a man. The first schools, in the technical sense, were initiation
schools. Their overt function was to pass on knowledge and to "make
men"; their covert function was to preserve the ascendancy of the
elders. These functions allied knowledge and power in the process
of ensuring safety and seeking food. Without this contribution, the
hunting primate stood in danger of losing his characteristic knack, and
was in danger of having to poke at ants and grub for roots once more.

Initiation procedures vary, but there are some standard elements.
The initiates are separated from the women and kept in seclusion.
They are hazed and humiliated by their elders. They undergo ordeals of
endurance and tests of manly skills. They are often physically
mutilated, and quite commonly and significantly the mutilation is
of the genitals—circumcision, superincision, subincision (the slitting of
the urethra), or all three. They are compelled to learn masses of

arcane wisdom, as well as the proper conduct of ritual and the proper cherishing of myths and traditions of the group. They often indulge in homosexual practices. Finally, they are sometimes ritually slain and brought back to life as "men." Isolation, endurance, testing, mutilation, and the internalization of tribal wisdom in some form or other crop up in society after society as each in its peculiar way copes with the problem of tapping and controlling the ambivalent energy of the initiate.[17]

While all this may seem to the civilized reader a little excessive, one has to remember that at this period these young men are secreting some ten to thirty times more testosterone than they did as boys.[18] (Girls only double their level, and from a lower base to begin with.) This hormone is what changes boys into men. It is closely connected with heightened levels of aggression as well as of sexuality. Very suddenly, yesterday's boys receive massive doses of this powerful stimulant. Suddenly they are the most energetic and aggressive members of the community. But they have not had time to learn how to cope with this infusion of novel and stormy information from the ancient areas of the brain. One strategy involves forcing them to exercise the inhibiting functions of the newer brain by learning restraint on the one hand and by storing large amounts of information on the other. That the information may well be largely "useless" in some objective sense is neither here nor there; many of the "physical" things they learn are not very useful either. What it does is to make them use their forebrains rather than act out the more devastating instructions from the lower brain. These latter can then be controlled and channeled to the advantage of the community.

Female initiation is of relatively minor importance,[19] which illustrates another consequence of the great shift: the differences already present in primates between male and female socialization are accentuated by adaptation to the hunting pattern. While it appears that physical differences between males and females diminished—such as in size, teeth formation, and coloring—there was a critically important increase in the distinction between what men had to do and what women had to do, and hence in what they had to learn. There is much evidence from an enormous range of human societies that female initiations, compared with male, are gentle, often focused on mating, less likely to require long and difficult isolation, and less caught up with the business of acquiring and producing bits of information and sets of cultural lore. We can conclude also that the female ceremonies were far less oppressive and less provocative of consternation, hysteria, and simple excitement. With the females, the old primate program is quite reliable: they will first come to maturity, and perhaps indulge in some premarital sex play with what appears to be a "programmed" adolescent sterility that protects them against having infants when they are themselves too inexperienced as persons. Then they will marry, or take part in whatever organization of breeding their community has. Once they have an infant, they will assume full adult status and be rewarded accordingly.

Of course, there is a great deal they must learn—how to deal with themselves, with other females, with males, with infants and children. They learn skills involved with the management of households, and in many places with the conduct of some public business such as trading. But they do not have to be *controlled* in the same way as males. They appear to get less from the process of maturation, but they also give less insofar as they run less risk of death or mutilation, are less prone to attacks of anxiety and neurosis, and by and large, are assured that they will be able to achieve a fit and proper adult role by producing a child. They will compete for males—compete certainly in the exercise of the skills they know and the arts of decoration they employ. But unless there is a great preponderance of females—and there may be in warlike communities that do not also practice female infanticide—they are assured on purely statistical grounds that they will become the powerful females they observed as children, and continued to observe in the intimate arena of their adolescence. For the males, though, the statistics are unpropitious; there are not that many splendid posts; there are too many young men for the elders to select from. And finally, in the grimmest and most important context of all, in only six countries of one hundred and twenty-one do contemporary males live longer than females.

What children find easy to learn and enjoy learning reflects the biogrammar with which we are concerned. It is the starting point for any efforts at assimilating what (and how) we teach children with what they are and need.

Let us take two simple and contrasting examples. One cannot stop children from learning language. They assimilate language as they breathe air. Child language, as we now know, is not simply a poor imitation of adult speech; the child takes the raw material of the adult language as it is presented to him and uses it in consistent ways based on a simple grammatical scheme to make two- and three-word sentences.[20] He does this eagerly and easily unless he is actively prevented. He does not need to be taught; indeed, he demands and provokes the stimuli he needs for fresh information with which to work. His skill grows in a measurable way as his "language-acquisition device" takes in and puts out more complex structures. And in all this the child delights. Grammar is not for him the crabbed misery that ruins warm summer afternoons, but a thing to be reveled in and played with, to show off and romp about in. It is the pleasurable exercise of a skill that is essential to his survival. All he needs are encouragement, security, and input. He will do the rest. But at the same time as he is putting forth his first two-word sentences, the adult world is trying to "train" him to control his bladder and sphincter. While his speech is allowed to pour forth, his feces and urine are being ruthlessly held back. This is something for which the biogrammar, as we have seen, has no inbuilt rule; it must, in consequence, be culturally imposed.

The child will learn to control his excretory activity, but not without resistance, pain, and possible psychic damage. It is clear that much less damage is done if he is not "trained" early but left, as is the case in many so-called primitive cultures, until he can walk about.[21] Then he can easily imitate adult defecation postures and habits. Among many hunting tribes, for example, the infant is allowed to do as he pleases until such time as he can toddle. At this point an older sister will simply take him to the edge of the camp, gently and without fuss. Since our early ancestors lived out in the open and were actively nomadic, this was less of a problem for them than for later dwellers in permanent sites. There was no selection, obviously, for easy learning of early sphincter control, as there was for easy learning of early word control. The one is pleasurable, the other traumatic; the one emanates from the biogram, the other is an imposition on it. (There is one very important instruction in the wiring as far as excretion is concerned: when men are mortally afraid, their bodies automatically react in various ways, one of the more important being defecation and urination. Colloquial language recognizes this: a man is "scared shitless." This instruction is very ancient and is found in all mammals. Its explanation is very simple: the animal is preparing for flight and so gets rid of unwanted body weight, just as a fleeing bomber drops its unused load. This impulse is phylogenetically so deep that no learning is needed; its role in survival is too important to be left to that.)

To deal with the need for education in huge populations organized

on a national scale is to confront the same dilemma posed by
political and economic organization: whatever the evolutionary
demands and needs of the organism, the demands of the social system require bureaucratic organization, which of its very nature must
thwart the evolutionary thrust of the creature it controls. It may be
that the animal has been wired in terms of particular principles—
to learn certain things at certain times in certain ways. But because
of its sheer numbers of students and the complexity of the demands
made upon it, the educational system cannot be predicated on these
principles. It may also be, of course, that the system is organized in
ignorance of these facts and could be modified to meet them in some
degree. Perhaps this is the best we can hope for.

It is easy enough to blame school systems for rampant short-
comings, but we should first ask ourselves whether or not we are
asking too much of the schools in the first place. Young primates and
young hunters alike undertake their learning in the intimate surroundings of the kinship group into which they were born. They
learn things that are directly relevant to them and their relatives.
They have, throughout their evolution, learned to learn from role
models essentially parental and siblinglike. The transfer of knowledge
is only a part of this learning and cannot be separated as a process
from the context of learning in general. What we do with the institution of schools is to split off the inculcation of knowledge and hand
it over to specialists. This is curious enough. But even more curiously,
we proceed to hand more and more of the "familial" or "kinship"
functions—but not all of them—over to the schools as well. Then, when
the school, presented with this uneven package of demands, neither
educates the children well nor socializes them to our satisfaction, we
grumble and blame the teachers, the system, the government, or
anyone but ourselves. Parents who demand that sex education should
not be taught in schools may well have a point—if only we could
be confident that these same parents would not also treat it as a
taboo subject at home. We regard the teacher as *in loco parentis*
when it suits us to load him with responsibilities we do not want.
But we are quick to remind him that he is not a parent when he tries
to take this responsibility seriously in areas we consider "parental"
rather than purely "instructional." That this confuses a little hunting
primate trying precariously to speak his behavioral language to
people who talk different kinds of language themselves should not
surprise us. How could he ever learn his spoken language if only

nouns were spoken at home and verbs somewhere else, while the proper place to learn adjectives and adverbs was constantly in dispute?

We have already indicated the importance of security in stimulating and encouraging learning. What effect has it upon a child to move out of the home environment into one which—with the trend to larger and larger schools in the name of some (probably spurious) efficiency—may well be relatively far from his home, and will be composed of large numbers of unfamiliar persons? Of course, children survive such situations, and many even thrive on precisely that separation that we are questioning. But for the culture as a whole, the effects upon children's views of reality and of learning may be substantial, and even stimulate the constant rhetorical barrage erected to discuss the concept of "relevance" and its implication for school activities. The political and moral bases of the decision are clear: what is less clear is what, for example, "busing"—which is an exacerbation of this trend—does to the child's expectation of school and his attitude to home. Such a plan seems topsy-turvy; to overcome inequalities determined by affluent adults' unwillingness to share their resources and their sense of well-being with the poor and disadvantaged, the children of all these groups are urged at school into alliances of aliens to their own homes and to their own patterns of life. Cunning zoning regulations—in 1971 declared constitutional by the United States Supreme Court—enforce de-facto apartheid in various communities with racially and economically heterogeneous groups. The well-meaning assumption is that what parents cannot solve with equity and providence, children must solve by propinquity and by learning ways of relating to others which their parents are afraid to try, and which—if the children learn them well, as many no doubt do—will make them moral strangers to their parents. The question "What did you learn in school today?" comes to imply an answer tinged with rebuke at the strange antipathies of one's most familiar people, one's parents.

It would be foolish to emphasize this point at the cost of denying validity to all efforts to achieve equality of spirit and option in communities. But when educational systems are assumed to be the critical levers for changing morally and socially abhorred situations, children become condemned to soldiering in a war they never made and that they themselves cannot win. That the world they enter as adults may have the appearance or reality of improvement over the one they joined as children is a related but also another question. It is related, because educational systems are closely linked to all others in the society. But precisely because they become tools of social change, they are forced to perform very different functions from those that are demanded of them by their clients—the children. The basic biogrammar of instruction and initiation was not set up by natural selection to effect political changes in complex societies, but to let children know *how things are* in the world around them. This knowledge begins in the most intimate sphere and then allows them to apprehend first how they must behave in social situations, and then in those involving technical skills. Put another way: educational action has always been intensely conservative, concerned with integrating the child into the group. Our proposition is that it works best when it is conservative, because this is how the animal is geared. This is not political conservatism that we are talking about—a child can be socialized into a radical group—but, rather, temperamental conservatism, the conservatism of a system geared to the child's understanding of the continuities between the events of his life rather than their discontinuity of frank and conscious opposition. An educational system that teaches a child to survive in, and cope with, the ghetto where he lives is more successful *as an educational system* than one that fails to teach him to live securely and successfully in the disintegrated society of white suburbia with which he has no identification and to which he may not even aspire. The argument becomes immensely precarious if it is interpreted to mean that residents of ghettos should be trained like the slaves of yore to live happily and easily in their slums. Our point is exactly the reverse. The answer to the problems posed by the existence of ghettos is the abolition of ghettos. The answer to the difficulties placed in the way of ghetto residents' achievement of professional competence, economic integrity, and social pleasure is not to shift the children of ghettos into established environments where they must compete in an intense and irremediably stressful way. The answer is to revise notions of what constitutes competence, who decides who shall be accepted and advanced, who is allowed to set the community's standards, and finally, why it should be taken for granted that a child skilled at living in a complex and demanding ghetto should be held to require contact with the suburbs of Princeton and Burnt Oak in order to improve his talents and advance his prospects. Driving little children around in buses from place to place to permit them some contact with people different from their parents is a measure only of adult despair and communal disarray. This may be the only way poor schools can get more tax money—by having the children of the rich and powerful compelled to go to them. In such a case—and if the simple strategy of private schooling were unavailable—a mixture of children for socially desirable purposes is defensible as an expedient of transition. Education and directed social change are not the same thing, given the creatures children are and the problems they face. The social direction may "take," and future assistant professors, "apparatchniks," cadre leaders, and managers of debt-collection agencies will pop smoothly from the system like biscuits. But it may not take; the discontinuity between what children were promised was reality and what they see around them when the awkward chrysalis of school colors is shed may lead to cynicism and dismay.

We are pointing here to an unprimate and unhunter separation of home, school, and community. We have instanced a case in which the noneducational needs of the community have dictated the location and nature of schooling. We do not need to document the conflict between school and home; the problem is multiplied in our multi-community society, where a child may go through a very successful education (in the strictly adaptational sense of the term) in a restricted community, only to find that he has to apply this painfully won success in a totally different setting. Our child has been trained as a hunter and then rudely presented with a plow. Any educational system that, like our own, is essentially a system of selection rather than instruction, is faced with this problem. Whether schools are used as melting pots for immigrants or as an escalator for the socially mobile, they are promoting discontinuity and widening the gaps between themselves, home, and society; and this is the root of the problem.[22] Learning, like life, has ceased to be all of a piece and all of a purpose. The creature has been wired to learn in security, in familiar surroundings, from peers who will be lifelong companions and from elders who must be followed first and cared for later. He is wired to learn with an expectation of continuity in personnel and relevance of what is learned to what is done. It is hard to see anywhere in modern society where this wholistic, basic, biological process is operating. Perhaps it cannot, but we should at least be aware of how near to behavioral gibberish we are, and reserve our wonder for the courage of the young who tolerate as well as they do the uncouth grammar of their elders.

The fragmentation of the educational process puts considerable burdens on that figure of fun and awe, the teacher. His role deserves some consideration, since his specialized function is a truly human innovation. His function seems obvious to us, but it is not in any sense "given" in nature. His emergence is related, of course, to the growth of specialized knowledge; the first teachers, as such, were probably shamans who taught their successors; the first apprentice was probably the sorcerer's apprentice.[23] These magicians were specialists in traditional knowledge for its own sake—the myths of the tribe, and "useful arts" such as healing and divination: all things outside the normal primate repertoire. His modern successor is still expected to be something of a magician, and while in one sense he is unnatural, in another, at least as far as human life is concerned, he is inevitable. In his role as instructor he is an extension of the forebrain. In his role as controller he amplifies its functions just as the spear-thrower lengthens the hunter's arm. In his twin duties of instructing the child and molding his behavior, the good teacher can be very effective in the right setting.

Two utterly simple biological characteristics are in his favor: he is old and he is big. (If he is very big he has a good chance of becoming a principal.[24]) From at least the younger and smaller pupils he, or she, can therefore expect deference and attention. But to get these, he must naturally fulfill the conditions for them that lie in the old primate biogram waiting to be tapped. Given that set instruction is the pattern, the teacher can command the attention of the pupils if he combines the qualities of a successful dominant primate—authority with protection and credibility. The play group of young baboons always had with it an older male who did not interfere unless there was danger from outside the group or the threat of violence from within. But the moment he interfered, he was deferred to. The young animals liked to be near the dominant males, especially in times of danger. If the teacher can exhibit the right qualities, he should also be able to spark off the right reactions of deference and attention. A combination of impressive manner (however this is culturally defined), firmness, justice, and kindness will do the trick. But it is hard work, as every teacher knows. "Keeping the attention of the class" and "keeping them still" constitute two of the teacher's most difficult problems. Which raises a basic question about the whole pattern of "set instruction" and perhaps explains why, even with so much in his favor, the teacher often finds his job tiring and unrewarding.

The crux of the matter is very simple: dominance and attention are political devices, not instructional ones.[25] Children learn best when their attention is wholly on what they are doing rather than on the teacher. Attention to the teacher and all the neural and emotional processes that this involves may even interfere quite directly with learning. Dominance and attention are aspects of control rather than instruction, and while teachers must control as well as instruct, they run into trouble if they confuse the two. Good teachers know this very well, but they are often as constricted by the system as the children are. "Keeping still" is exactly what the young primate does not want to do. It cannot even learn very well by "keeping still." The teacher can use to advantage all the curiosity and exploratory urges of the child, but these are at their best when the child can move about to explore and manipulate—always in complete security and knowing that the adult is present to ensure justice. In forcing children to be still, the teacher may well abuse the energy that would be of most help to him in helping children to learn. He will get attention at the cost of curiosity, political control at the cost of instructional efficiency. And it is efficiency, not morals, that we are concerned with here. We are not asking whether the system is good or bad, but whether or not it can possibly do, given the methods it adopts, what it sets out to do. Schools always have to balance uneasily between discipline and learning; because they are bureaucratic institutions, they often decide in favor of discipline at the expense of learning. This may make them good political units, but it also makes them unfit teaching ones. Children who drop out are dropping out from the political, not the instructional system, although by the time they make this decision they may well be as confused as their teachers about the difference between the two.[26]

The teacher also has going for him both the child's delight in play and his propensity to learn through play. Again, the good teacher knows this. But again the system demands that work and play be segregated, and often denies play to punish a failure to work. Time segregated into work and play periods, and learning used as a vehicle of punishment, maximize control, but always at the expense of curiosity. It is like driving the car slowly with the brake firmly on: there is less danger of an accident, but one will not get very far—and do the car a lot of damage if one continues.

This is not to say that pure uninhibited play *for human children* is the only and best way for them to learn. We have to remember the forebrain and the hunting heritage. The teacher can utilize the incredible memory of the child and his long period of eager learning. He must instruct. The only question is what is the best way to instruct effectively. The answer, given the biogrammar, is that to guide the child's movement and curiosity toward whatever must be learned, to provide him with a model of learning activity oneself, and above all to provide him with the security to explore and find out, are infinitely more likely to work, since they tie in with the motives and propensities of the child himself, than dependence on dominance and attention structure. To make a simple equation, *guidance is to intellect what dominance is to initiation.* Education should be, at least in some respects, the expression of man's highest faculty—the free play of the intellect. Initiation is part of the political process and has to do with bringing restless youngsters into the hierarchical attention structure of the wider group. What is appropriate to the one process may be inimical to the other. But schools have always had to do both. Educational crises are often simply the outcome of the cross-cutting demands of the two pressures. Socrates was killed by the state because he saw the demands of intellect as superior to the claims of initiation.

Socrates' martyrdom symbolizes an important shift in formal attitudes to education. We know that educational systems perform both functions—teaching techniques and facts, and inspiring students with reverence for the community's ideology and attentive respect for the dictates of its leaders. Report cards, perhaps in most schools still may have two pages, one for "achievement in school" and the other for "Citizenship" or "Character" or even (in a stunning abuse of the English language) for "Behavior." The effect of "behavioral" failure in making "academic" failure more likely in school is known; it is hard to estimate how much this has to do with the assault on children's intellectual self-confidence. But a minimal prediction is that among primary-school children at least, the puzzling distinction upon which grown-ups insist between having skill and having "character," can lead only to progressive deterioration of the integrated skills, shared by all children in some measure and some way, for learning and for becoming more complexly sociable.

These are all old statements in an old battle about educational practice and ideals. Our concern here is with placing particular procedures in the context of what a relatively generous view of primate patterns of learning may help us see about the behavior of students and teachers. The amount of contention and the extent of the protestations of failure and alarm that surround the subject must encourage even an apparently oblique approach to what in many countries is one of the largest industries. It is now clear that there is a drastic relationship between early environment and experience, and what children can subsequently achieve in schools. One major study yielded that up to eighty percent of a child's ability to learn and perform was determined by the age of about four.[27] In other words, a tedious and oppressive four years at home will fix even a bright and energetic child at a level of performance that even a superior education can improve by little more than a margin of twenty percent. If his mother and father are themselves uninspired by the adventure of spending time with a child, if his house is unstimulating because it is poorly lit, because there are few objects with which he can play, because the emotional setup of the place denies him security or offers him no sense that what he can do himself and with friends is valuable and charming; if he is without effective role models and harassed by frightened or abused adults, the child will be very substantially set for life in a mold less generous than he might otherwise encompass and less demanding than he might otherwise crave. Yet this is very low-level human learning—and very high-level primate learning—that is involved; if so much is determined so early, it is not only necessary but urgent to attend to the biological infrastructure of even such a sophisticated and cerebral business as educating the young and allowing the old some confidence and pleasure in what they pass on to their offspring.

A prime example of how biological reality has been replaced by educational and political theory may be seen in how schools and teachers treat the chief biological difference—the sexual difference. Sex differences are also social differences. They are real, not just fictions of malevolent planners and bigoted patriarchs (though such types are nonetheless sprightly and active in this regard). The same point can be made with dual relevance for the educational system. Marion Levy, Jr., has noted that for the past two or three generations North Americans have been doing something very fundamental that no other community has ever done—using women teachers to discipline and instruct boys.[28] Historically and typically, where girls were educated at all, males and females were separated. We have already noted the major differences in the learning problems, options, and experiences of male and female primates. It is prudent to consider the possibility that similar distinctions apply—again with variation and convergence—to the human form of primate life.

To begin with, we can restate Patricia Sexton's argument about the feminized male—that creature who is successful in, and a product of, a school system largely staffed by females and in which female rather than male characteristics are rewarded.[29] For one thing, girls mature earlier than boys, who are thus at a constant disadvantage, since all statistical weighting is based on age, and since, in the name of equality, sex differences are not regarded as suitable to take into account in giving reward and threatening sanction.[30] In general boys are more physically active and wider-ranging than girls, yet much is made in schools of the strange virtue of keeping still, sitting in proper rows, moving about in orderly fashion, going like nuns to lunch and prisoners to games. Boys are more aggressive than girls, yet schools reward those who listen carefully, are obedient to rules, do not disturb either their teachers or their classes, and who cause minimal disruption of the other students. Boys who act more like girls than like other boys are more likely than their rambunctious and headstrong friends to succeed in the system.

The point of the educational system is to prepare people to assume adult roles in whatever community they inhabit. Historically, programs of formal education were geared to produce skilled adult males to fill the dominant roles. When coeducation developed, it was reasonably enough thought invidious and discriminatory for girls to learn different things from boys just because they were girls, and so, in many places an identity between male and female educational patterns became the rule rather than the exception. As a consequence, in many schools and colleges, certainly in Euro-America, there are only minor differences between what boys and girls learn. However, the crux of the dilemma is that, after the expensive and demanding exercise of learning things that males traditionally learned—but in ways more "feminized" than before—we find that female participation in those groups and activities for which they have in theory been trained is extremely low. Again, the sexual structure of occupations has changed very little over sixty years, despite extraordinary increases in the absolute and relative numbers of educated females.[31]

What does this mean? And why does it happen? The fact that education has made surprisingly little difference does not constitute a recommendation that females should learn only typing, baby care, and airline-hostessing. Why, then, this major discontinuity, which is financially expensive on one hand—because so much of the community's wealth is devoted to education, and perhaps one-third to one-half of this is used by females; and psychologically expensive on the other— because so relatively few women get to use or at least do use those skills that they patiently and hopefully acquired.

Perhaps the most obvious feature of what happened to educational systems under coeducation was that girls learned what boys had always learned, but boys did not also learn what girls had learned— however informally and casually. Also, school systems increased in size, and this required more taxes and more teachers. From having been a largely male occupation, teaching became largely female, at the lower levels particularly.[32] A woman is far more likely to be a third-grade teacher than a high-school and a college and university instructor. Female help is usually cheaper than male, though there is no evidence that it is worth less; this was clearly a reason for the sexual shift in the teaching corps. But there may have been another and possibly more interesting ethological basis for this change: grown men have nothing helpful to say to little girls in the context of the school. Or, rather, what they do have to tell little girls, both the men themselves and their communities at large may regard with less than enthusiasm.

In one sense this is a spurious argument, since teachers can in theory teach anyone equally well. But education is not just about knowledge and technical skill; it is also about initiation. What may be involved in much of the confusion and urgency surrounding educational thinking is a blurring of the lines, not only between education and initiation in general, but between male and female initiation and education. Among the other primates and among most humans still, female learning is especially relevant to childbearing and domestic roles, male learning to the groups in which they will one day find themselves as politicians, defenders, monitors, hunters, thinkers, etc. What was taught and by whom, and what was learned and by whom, were related to these clear visions of the future which the young could have and which the old could portray.

But once again, as with busing schoolchildren, we have pressured the educational system to make some changes that remain maladapted to the communities in which the schools exist. So parents will send a daughter to college and rebuke her silently or openly if she does not marry, or if her notion of her sexual experience does not include the proper summary—in their view—of the female pattern: husband, children, home, and local sacred perfection. Girls will do well in school and yet be mocked if they are or feel or want to be plain and not very active with the opposite sex. There remains the widespread folk myth that beautiful females must be stupid or that brilliant ones must be cheerless, bluestocking quasi-males. One need not append more details to the unhappy catalog. But its upshot is: that the system is predicated on the notion that what males do is superior to what females do, because that is how it once was, and still is, in terms of prestige and payment, and that at the same time males and females— throughout the educational life cycle—are the same. Our suggestion is that this becomes a fraudulent imposition on females, because their primate and sexual realities are denied as they seek mature participation in the major system of social opportunity in their community. And because in any breeding system, what one sex loses, the other loses too: directly and indirectly, the males with whom they have to spend this educational time are equally deprived. It is worth exploring what males also lose in a system purporting to be for their advantage and edification.

It would be too simple, but not untrue, to say that the boy loses early in the game because he is expected to behave like a girl, while the girl loses later in the game because she is expected to behave like a boy. In any case, whatever might be glossed over in the stages of sexual immaturity cannot be overlooked when puberty makes boys and girls more sharply diverge. In evolutionary terms, this is the period when girls enter almost immediately into motherhood and the female tasks of the division of labor, and when boys begin the intensive period of testing and proving their newfound manhood. Whether among primates or hunters, this is a period when the boys are in close and ambivalent contact with men, and when the men are testing the boys, and when both have little use for women, and even sex is often banned.

Perhaps it makes no difference that boys and girls are at school together before puberty; latency seems to be a period when sexual differences are suspended so that the child can learn skills. This may be the whole point of the much-discussed latency period. If Oedipal hostilities were not suspended for a while, no one would learn multiplication tables. But in the postlatency phase the whole thing erupts again. This is when the boys begin their physical or at least symbolic peripheralization. They may, like our Crow Indians, have to go off alone to the edges of their known world to suffer alone and mutilate themselves until they receive a vision of manhood. They may, like young BaVenda in southern Africa, go into lengthy initiation schools where they will be generously helped along by their elders.[33] It may be that they will simply be drafted into military service and trained in esoteric or useful knowledge, and what used to be known in less squeamish days as "manly arts" or even "male sympathies." Whatever the method, the males go through their apprenticeship at this period and learn the delicate and often painful—but presumably, their community hopes, rewarding—art of identifying with the society of the men. This is an ancient system of behavior—not in its specific forms, but in the underlying necessities. All this we know. And yet, in the name of sexual equality, we make girls behave as if they too were creatures of the transitory periphery, of the staggeringly increased testosterone, of the hostility and truculence to the older male, of the keen, impatient desire to be men.

Of course, even though girls' boarding schools are usually direct imitations of boys', and sororities of fraternities, girls' team sports modeled on boys', and even girls' clothing based on a ludicrously boyish pattern, it is hard even for imperceptive adults to push the analogy too far. Coeducation, particularly at the college level, means that both sides give something up in the quest for a common way of living. The end result is that many of the sheer initiatory functions of education get blurred. College—and the same is true of high school —becomes more and more an arena of courtship and less and less gladiatorial. Thus, while girls are trying, at a period of their lives when courtship is uppermost in their repertoire, to master knowledge in a way meant for boys, boys, who should be mastering the arts of maleness, are more and more pulled into a female pattern of behavior.

This may very well be a good thing, according to some standards of values held by those who would like to see differences between the sexes in behavior, life style, work, and even clothing and personal appearance reduced to nothing. The old joe-college type, with his sports, fraternities, panty raids, beer drinking, stag movies, and dirty jokes, is certainly now altogether a figure of fun. Nor is the Vassar beauty who cannot wait to pack her suitcase to get to Princeton for the weekend less ludicrous. But it may not be that simple: educational practice, if it is to achieve truly equal treatment, may well have to realize again that equality does not mean sameness. To pretend that boys and girls between fifteen and twenty-one-plus are really substitutable the one for the other is to deny not only obvious biological realities but the whole course of evolution. At least, if we are to tamper with the set of instructions that determine critically different paths for males and females, we should be aware of what we are doing. The case for allowing girls access to the means of higher education is certainly unarguable. The question is how and when, not why.

This raises the whole question of the phasing of education. One of the problems of "set instruction" for grade-schoolers was that the infant computers were being fed adult programs. We were putting in the wrong information in the wrong way—or, at best, the right information in the wrong way. We insist on trying to program the turbulent organisms of young adults of both sexes as if they were rational middle-aged scholars. This is the same mistake that was made with the grade-school children, and should be explored a little further.

We have seen the pressure in various kind of communities for the initiation of young males, and the apparently clear compliance of the initiates. They must feel that they are being initiated into something worthwhile, and if only because they do not know any other, into a company of worthwhile men. What happens, though, when it is no longer clear (a) that males are being initiated at all, (b) what they are being initiated into and with whom, and (c) that initiation is a real certification and the recognizable beginning of adult life? Young males in many cultures dominated by occupational choice, political and ethnic diversity, and a socially secular ideology can no longer enjoy the clarity that would allow them to aspire without ambiguity to an honorable place in their groups. High-school graduation? University graduation? Bar mitzvah? A driver's license? Being able to drink legally in public? Some of these involve tests, and some just becoming old enough. Our notion is that the drama, dedication, belief in their elders, and certainty about the value of their hard experience are considerably diminished by the feminized system within which many males are raised, and in terms of which their commitments to their community must be expressed. Much of the change results quite plainly from the fact that we are no longer hunters, and that many if not most jobs lack any evident majesty, any clear mandate and autonomy, even any opportunity to exercise those physical skills so important to adolescent males. In some communities the issues are more sharply drawn. Among the Iroquois near Montreal, the culture of the warrior found an apt and profitable translation into the dangerous and demanding work of rigging steel on skyscrapers. To this day Iroquois Indians create the structures within which admen and bookkeepers puzzle away over bits of paper.[34] Or among the boys of Hull and Newfoundland, where the male role is deep-sea fishing, the choice is easy: the only real thing men do is fish, so the boys fish too.[35] Even though trawler fishing is highly risky and not especially munificent, the recruits to the trade continue to come from among the sons of those who know it best—with all its dangers and inequities.

This is not to recommend some stunning ceremony which will cap the program of self-improvement, deferred gratification, and growing social commitment implied in many initiatory schemes. If anything, it is the mindless and parochial certainty of well-initiated politicians and generals in most countries of the world that threaten the peace of neighbors and the affable routines of those who pay for politicians' schemes and for generals' tools for the serious games of war. Nonetheless, the absence of such markers of initiation has its effect. Being male means essentially doing male things. If males are prevented from doing these things—some of which are deep in the wiring system—there remains the grim possibility that they will be unable to perform effectively their functions of protection, provision, and even procreation.

The problem becomes more acute when we appreciate that both males and females mature sexually earlier and earlier, but are compelled to stay in schools longer and longer to achieve that measure of certification that will permit them contact with whatever hopeful national myth about life style they seek to have. It may take a highly trained physicist or geographer thirty years to nab the doctorate, and then perhaps seven or eight more while he is scrutinized by calculating superiors who will decide at last whether he can join their little tribe, permanently, with tenure. In many communities a man is born, initiated, becomes a warrior, adviser, father, leader, and is dead by thirty-eight. In more "advanced" societies it may even happen that at thirty-eight a man has his first job giving him the security and sense of place that his age-mate in a poorer place has enjoyed from the time his voice was fully low and his beard marked him as a boy no longer. Small wonder that as the young become better informed about the acts of their elders, they insist on some symmetry between the ideals they have been taught for almost two decades of their lives and the realities they see around them that deny these ideals and make the managers of reality seem utterly crass and empty. Perhaps the managers are fools, thieves, incompetents, and liars— even to themselves. Perhaps not. But the ire of the young and the outrage of the old are perhaps more sanely seen to result from the lack of any acceptable contact between them.

Our life cycles have a predictable and rhythmical pattern that cause us on the one hand to put forth energy of a particular kind in a particular way and on the other hand to seek information and interaction of a certain kind in certain ways. The energy, interaction, and information that we both express and desire change over time in shape and substance; what is appropriate for one phase is inappropriate, or even detrimental, for another. The optimal conditions for learning when we are very young are astonishingly different from optimal learning conditions when we are young adults. The one phase demands security, the other risk. But what we want to learn and how we want to learn differ as much as the means whereby we learn. As we move into adulthood, we again change in both input and output; perhaps we forget the stresses of our youth as we mold the world of the young in our adult image. The behavioral rhythm of this life cycle, like the body which literally embodies it, is the end product of many millions of years of primate evolution, and several million of hominid hunting. The whole series of behavioral changes is as careful an adaptation to savanna life as the ankle bone and the buttocks are. Working from the general primate base, nature has produced a creature whose learning patterns, over its lifetime, have been mapped as carefully as the instincts of lower animals. We cannot assume that the demands of technology, bureaucracy, or ideology can go on redrawing this map without the risk of our losing our way completely.

7.

GOOD
GROOMING

ATTENTION TO RELATIVELY sophisticated forms of social life may deny
us insight into deep structures of community life that are so important
to us we can hardly perceive them. Here we want to indicate how the
despair, pain, and anxiety of our concerns about health and death are
closely tied in to our social performances, to our recreations and
our gossip, to our play and our jovial use of spans of time. The people
bending over an operating table are performing a stringent special act
that is nonetheless as embedded in the same deep-structural system as
the act of circling a roulette wheel in the community of gamblers. The
husband and wife exposing their privacies and the particular dilemma
of their marriage to a psychiatrist have just taken one step further
in a process that began at a dinner party of close friends where they
spoke for the first time of the circumstances which vexed them. The
doctor's manner beside the bed and the lover's on it both affirm efforts
to bestow some gift on another person; both intimacies are possible
only in the context of some etiquette about permissible forms of giving
and taking. The patient family doctor, the Sinhalese monk, and the
sinewy lifeguard at a plush Riviera hotel are all part of the free-
masonry of intervention in other people's lives—through the use of
what we call medical skill, the invocation of what we call the supernatural, or the encouragement of what we call pleasure.

177

These various activities and processes look different to us largely because our category systems insist that they are. In the same way that we separate play from work and insist that all activity be categorized in either/or fashion, we segregate recreation from medication (the one is play and the other work, of course) without ever seeing the continuity of motive and activity between them. The bridge lies in "grooming." But not grooming in the narrow sense of simply picking parasites from the fur and skin of another animal. Man certainly performs this useful function. But he also trades in symbolic parasites and grooms symbolic fur. Grooming for him is the whole range of social activities that have to do with the well-being and being well of the community. This includes a great deal of seemingly nonpragmatic recreational activity and the whole body of charitable, caretaking, medicinal, and social-welfare services that communities erect for the sustenance of the weak and the insurance of the strong.

We are the only animal with hospitals, the only animal with psychiatrists, the only animal with an extremely complex way of feeding skillfully the experience of the past into managing the health and mortality of the animals of the present and the future. We are our own veterinarians.

Yet these patterns build on some generalized primate processes that can be identified. What primatologists barbarously call "epimiletic" behavior is a common feature of higher mammalian existence. It is care-giving and caretaking activity—a specialized form of reciprocity and a generalized way of building and maintaining links to the body social. All cultures have ways of relating private needs for health and psychological security to the apparatus of the community, to its resources of time, compassion, and skill. In Europe and North America—which are ambivalent indeed about the luxury of personal grooming behavior—the medical profession is able to perform grooming acts and ceremonies in the careful privacy of its offices and the bizarre hotel-hospitals in which the distraught are placed under the care of the inept. The medical profession nonetheless must remain our final spongy buffer against the animal fact of mortality. For to whom else can individuals turn when the tissue of expectations of further and better life is clearly rotting like the skin and bones on which these expectations are so elaborately based? In many other cultures medicine refers to magic; "medicine," the word, even means magic the process. But in our culture it has become confused with efficacious science. Science or not, it is a system to which we make pleas and demands when the programmed ways of preserving the body against the intrusions of the world fail. They fail either because the world has created new intrusions and hazards quite unanticipated by evolution— for example, silicosis and other pollutions—or because the expectations of any further life the symbol-making animal can contrive painfully outrun his ability to repair his own disease without the knowledgeable intervention of others.

As our evolution did not prepare us for some of the afflictions we have awarded ourselves, it may also have given us varieties of shape and action that once were useful but that now we reject. We tend to assume that mental illness is the result of the pressures of civilization on our "instinctive" life. It is probably the reverse. Most so-called mental illnesses are adaptive behaviors very useful to a hunting animal. But they are simply out of place in civilization, and so they are called crazy. And yet some mental attitudes—such as chronic and blinkered acquisitiveness—*are* products of civilization and are not called pathological.[1]

Caretaking as a general activity occurs in many forms among primates. We have seen it in operation between mother and child, between the young and the older females of the troop, between the young of the play group and the guardian older males, and between any two animals—mates, consorts, siblings, parents and children, bonded males —that groom each other for mutual comfort and cleanliness. The greatest amount of caretaking goes on between mother and child, but at the same time, the whole troop spends many hours in mutual grooming.[2] The overt purpose of this careful picking over of the fur of other animals is the removal of lice and ticks and other foreign matter. Animals that spend a lot of time alone are often in bad condition with unhealed wounds and patchy fur, apparently from lack of grooming. The "well-groomed" animal is usually a superior one. Good health means high status, because of the amount of grooming available as much as the high intake of favorable foods. Young infants also are greatly in demand for grooming, which is clearly to their advantage. Consort pairs groom each other incessantly, males groom one another as long as they belong to the exclusive central club, while peripherals perform their own mutual grooming—usually not as extensive. Caretaking is a social activity of a very integrative kind, and even though its overt function is the health of the community, a measure of who grooms who, when, where, and how much would almost be a measure of the structure of the whole social system. Outside of eating and sleeping, grooming takes up more time than any primate activity—far more than sex, for example.

But this social, reciprocal, health-promoting, caretaking behavior stops short of real medicine. We can consider it more useful in some ways than our own medical notions, since it is essentially preventive in its function: it is concerned with keeping up the general level of community health. But what it does not do is to care for the animal that is sick or wounded, except indirectly. A wound will heal faster if parasites are removed through grooming and the wound consequently kept clean. But an animal that is persistently sick and handicapped becomes a liability to the group, as there is no skill or even motivation to preserve it. Eventually it drops behind and dies or is picked off by predators. If it is a dominant animal it is rapidly and ruthlessly usurped. Healthy animals will help keep one another healthy, but the truly disabled animals will go to the wall.

Nevertheless, the fairly constant level of careful attention that these animals are paying to the welfare of others in a host of different ways is impressive. The basic caretaking program is there, embedded in social signals and social relations; it took humans to turn it into clinics and charities, into shamans and surgeons, into schemes for public welfare and private recuperation. Just as we specialized to develop the teacher, we created the specialist in grooming. Surrounding this specialism is an enormous complicated body of myth, truth, expectation, and resentment. The process and what accompanies it invite further examination.

Medicine, like economics, is a human creation cradled in a primate program. Like economics, it is dependent on the basal idea of reciprocity, of giving and receiving. In the small early human hunting community, membership was its own insurance policy. In return for contributing one's life and efforts to the group, one expected protection and care in times of trouble. The group in turn had nothing to gain by losing a member, and would bend its efforts to keep him alive. It thus actively intervened in the selective process—hence the genetic composition of the group—by refusing to let nature take its course. This intervention is a remarkable breakthrough in evolutionary history— as remarkable as the breakthrough from breeding systems to kinship systems or from ecologies to economies, and perhaps more far-reaching than either in its consequences. The old primate caretaking pattern moved from a system of preventive medicine to curative medicine: the group did not give up the ghost, or the body, once it was in disrepair, but turned all the caretaking attention at its primate disposal onto the sick member. It must be remembered that primate caretaking is embedded in social relationships—indeed, it is both a cause and an expression of them. In small human groups it was the same, and is the same today: the health and recovery of the members who are sick is a function of the whole network of social relationships. The sick person is not just restored to health, but to a place in society, a place jeopardized by his sickness in the first place, reconfirmed by his re-entry in the second. And in reconfirming him in his physical and social health, the group reconfirms its own social and spiritual health.

That this group concern with the sick member came about as a result of the transition to hunting should be obvious. Hunters were precious, as were women, who were the mothers of future hunters. In the same way that a man ensured his economic position by culturally patterned "generosity," he ensured his health by standing by sick relatives and affines. When he was sick they would stand by him in turn. It was part of the network of obligations and counterobligations in which kin were enmeshed. But it was not simply ruthless self-interest that promoted this caretaking activity. Man had foresight. He knew he was going to die.

Despite tales of the happy hunting ground in the sky, most hunting peoples essentially see the next world as rather gray and colorless. Happiness and reward are in this life, and no one wants to end it prematurely.[3] In another man's potential death one sees one's own; in confirming the power to spare and lengthen an individual life, members of a group confirm their power to extend their own. In the hunting group more than any other, no man is an island, and every man's death diminishes the survivors in a real as well as a symbolic sense.

But the symbolism is real. A case of sickness and death is a reminder of the fragility not only of the individual but also of the group, and each individual knows that he cannot exist without the group. Even in other species, sheer natural selection has operated to produce what has been dubbed the "genetics of altruism": one can calculate when it pays, genetically, for any one animal in a population to sacrifice itself for the others—and patterns of behavior have evolved that ensure that the appropriate animal will do so.[4] Humans go further: not only do members sacrifice themselves, but they cooperate to give time and effort in restoring sick members to health. Genetically this is enormously important, since it means that selection for sheer physical health is not uppermost in the selective process. Individuals with brain power but weak bodies, for example, could be succored and preserved, and could eventually breed. Variation in the gene pool (other than that to do with physical abilities) could be preserved and passed on. This was definitive in an animal that was to depend more on brains than on brawn to survive. The intervention of medicine has often been cited as an example of man "going against" natural selection by cultural means. But, as usual, it is nothing of the sort. What it does is to preserve a greater range of variation in the species and help those to survive who are needed by the species in its growing dependence on intelligence, inquisitiveness, and social invention. True, it does this at the cost of preserving some deleterious specimens, but there is a gain and a cost in all genetic balance. It is not clear always, in any case, that congenital "illnesses" are deleterious, except to the people who suffer them. Epileptics may be great leaders, and someone with leukemia may be a genius. Social groups may need these, as they need people with certain emotional and artistic skills, capacities for love and poetry, entertainment and clowning, or anything to enrich and expand the life of the animal that put its money on the cerebral cortex rather than on fangs and speed in the struggle for survival. In other words, it was a biological necessity, not an intrusion into biology, that every effort be made to preserve every member.[5] If emotions of aggression are easy to arouse in man, so are emotions of pity, mercy, charity, self-sacrifice, empathy, and the desire to help those in need—to preserve the lives of allies as much as to take the lives of enemies. The pleasure we take in ministering to the sick is as much part of our biogram as the pleasure we take in the destruction of those who seek to destroy us.

All this is at the physical level, but the group and the individual are faced also with the *knowledge* of their potential extinction and so have to handle not only the problem of mortality but also the problem of immortality. The symbolizing animal has to guard against the fact of death not only on the physical but also on the spiritual level. In its earliest manifestations, medical practice cared about the soul as much as the body; indeed, it did not see a distinction between the two. Sickness and soul loss are often equated; to restore a man's health is to restore his soul.[6] Our ancestors, and their contemporary analogues, would be baffled by the concept of psychosomatic medicine.[7] This can be a concept only for people who began by making a distinction between mind and body, between a person and a disease that is something alien. The doctrine "cure the patient, not the disease" would not be a revolutionary medical slogan to a hunter, but a statement of normal practice. The medicine man dealt with the patient as a whole person in a familiar social setting, a person with spiritual problems expressing themselves in bodily discomfort, a person who needed restoring to wholeness and to a place in a society jeopardized by his disequilibrium.[8]

Medicine arose as a biological necessity, and with it a set of emotions and responses that are still with us. It arose as a group response to threats to group existence and to equilibrium within the group. It arose as an attempt to restore the whole patient to health and proper social functioning in society. Many so-called "primitive" healing systems retain these features but lack the technology to make their practices effective in a wide range of illnesses; our own system has perfected medical technology but in the process has lost touch with the behavioral setting in which medicine evolved and in which it is most satisfying to patient and practitioner alike. In the same way that our economies have produced material wealth but alienated men, our medical systems offer physical health but create strangely disturbed and dissatisfied people whose resentment of doctors and the medical professions in general seem to increase almost in accord with the advances, not to say cost, of technical skill.

It may be instructive to review some ways in which contemporary medical practice may reflect and inhibit the caretaking enthusiasms we do have. Bureaucracy forced people to relate to one another as instruments of a higher purpose, and not as individuals. The bureaucratization of mercy is even more difficult for the creature to tolerate. Particularly so when the individual is ill, fearful, and confused about the pains in his body or the distortions in his understanding of his social world. It is unnecessary to talk about the large, poorly staffed, and overworked urban hospitals in which individuals are treated with minimal effectiveness, humor, and affection. Of course, arms get bandaged, legs set, babies born, and ulcers cut away. It would be irresponsible to claim that these services are less than adequate because they are unaccompanied by the intimate contacts between patient and nurses and doctors that help locate the patient in a structure of dignity and feeling.

But this can be set beside the Greek ideal of the hospital as the place with the best food, the finest furnishings and paintings, and the most skilled musicians and comedians. It is not the healthy, but the sick who most vitally needed such agreeable and re-creative stimuli; and the resources the community had were most beneficially and sanely used in helping them ease their personal disarray and feel encouraged by this display of their community's careful concern.

In a labor-intensive activity such as medical care, people's time becomes valuable indeed, and thus attractive to economizing administrators. Nonetheless—as judicious and sensitive doctors and administrators know—such economies may be false, particularly in light of the fact that roughly half of all patients suffer from psychological rather than clearly defined physiological or structural difficulties. There is now a wealth of detail and analysis of the subjugation of individual patterns and autonomies to the demands of "total institutions," of which hospitals are perhaps the most obviously self-defeating kind. How many patients have been sent to the hospital for rest and removal from daily stresses only to be awakened routinely at six A.M. because that is when the departing night-shift nurses traditionally take the temperatures of patients whose breakfasts will not arrive for two hours? How many patients, resentful because they are weak, are treated as idiotic incompetents by members of hospital staffs who see personal and intellectual ineptitude as necessary accompaniments to illness? How many patients—even in as socially committed a scheme as the National Health Service of England—will not know, when they anticipate an operation, who the human being will be who will cut into their bodies, perhaps save them, or perhaps be the final agent of a death from which their consciousness will be hidden by drugs? How many patients must wait for half-days and whole days on clinic benches because there is no system for saving the time of ill people? In how many hospitals can patients make an even limited choice of foods they wish to eat, even though it is clear how important a link food is to the sense of well-being?[9]

Such a list could go on and on and still avoid discussing those cruelties and that outright cynicism which characterizes so many treatment centers that questions must be raised about the overall suitability of formalized places for recovery from illness. These are symptoms of the larger situation. Like a car being garaged for servicing, a patient is removed from a community and from a pattern of life, and forbidden explicitly and by implication to engage in the web of contacts that could reassure him and hearten his kin and friends with the prospect of his return to health. At a time when he most needs his community's support (whatever the community may be), he is taken away from it. This is only an example of the point that what is most efficient technically may be most unsound biologically. There is a double loss here, a loss to the patient and to the community to which he belongs. Curing is no longer a concern of the community for the member, and through its concern for the member, a statement of its faith in itself.

Consider an alternative approach to healing: the Negritos of northern Luzon in the Philippines live in small bands where the members all know one another intimately. When a Negrito is sick for any reason, he is put into a trance and observed and encouraged by the whole group. In the trance he overcomes the demon causing the illness, and demands a song and dance of it. Once out of the trance, he sings the song and performs the dance for the rest of his people. They learn these from him and sing and dance with him. His song and dance become part of the repertoire of the band—part of their recreational, religious, and aesthetic life. Through his illness he contributes to his culture, which he has made a participant in his illness.[10] The whole thing is therefore a community affair, public and ceremonial. Or take a healing ceremony of the Cochiti Indians in New Mexico. If a person has a persistent illness, the Cochiti put him through an adoption ceremony whereby he becomes a member of the clans of ceremonial mother and father—a man and wife chosen for the occasion. They wash his head and give him food and gifts and new names in the presence of his own clanspeople. He is then welcomed into the new clans by his adopted relatives, and when these clans in turn cure other people, he will go along and participate.[11]

In both these cases—and many like them could be cited from tribes around the world—the cure is *built into* the culture. In the case of the Negritos there is total participation, and the patient is made to contribute to the tribal repertoire; in the case of the Cochiti the patient is strengthened in his social allegiances: the clans—key elements in the social structure—become the means of restoring health by restoring the patient to a fuller role in the society and demanding his continued participation in the sociomedicinal system. Nothing less than the combined social and technical-supernatural resources of the community are brought to bear on this vital issue; and no possible source of comfort, encouragement, and knowledge of the patient's needs and style is overlooked in this enterprise of improvement.[12]

Of course, all this energy may not cure broken bones and perforated appendixes. And, most importantly, as far as the danger of unexpected death is concerned, the blandishments of rich cultures will be lost on infants in the first year. It is a plain fact that the life expectancy is higher in just those communities whose medical schemes we have seemed to see in such a gloomy light. Nonetheless, even members of poor cultures, once they reach puberty, stand almost as good a chance of a sixty-year life span as an American or Swede. The average is weighted heavily by the many infants who cannot survive; given their relative poverty of modern medical goods and savvy, the longevity of adult Bushmen, Australian aborigines, and Congolese raises some provocative questions.

The point is not the focus of our argument for nothing: a great discovery of so-called modern medicine was that a very considerable proportion—some physicians estimate anywhere from one-third to two-thirds, though these figures are mercurial—of the illness which they are asked to treat is significantly related, on the one hand, to social and economic stresses, and, on the other, to private anxieties and circumstances. Psychosomatic medicine is simply a reencounter of what technologically primitive people—and possibly even primates—know when they see bodily afflictions as expressions of spiritual distress or of malignancy in the web of social contacts. The perversion of supernatural power—essentially a social power—to individual and antisocial ends is called witchcraft. This implies that the normal functioning of the social network has broken down, that mistrust and suspicion, deceit and accusation, have taken over from reciprocity and mutuality. Accusations of witchcraft, as social anthropologists have shown so admirably, always reflect breakdowns in social relationships and in turn cause further breakdowns.[13] That the fear of witchcraft can also cause actual illness and even death is well enough known; that is why "cures" for witchcraft are often as concerned with restoring the whole community to health as they are with responding to the needs of the allegedly bewitched individual.[14]

This may seem strange to us. But the principle is the same here as in much of our own socially generated stress-disease. In some way or other the society ceases to be satisfying to the participant; he feels it as a series of pressures and unworkable demands rather than as a source of pleasure in participation. His body responds physiologically like an animal afraid and about to flee; this feeling, without release in actual flight, leads to physical breakdown.[15] The web of social contacts becomes not a home but a trap, and there are no longer any witches to blame. The harried executive with his ulcer and the nervous housewife with her migraine are as much victims of social breakdown as their counterparts in Congolese compounds or Haitian villages dying from the fear of the conspiracy of evil at work against them.

Illness is a social, not an individual, fact. Sickness in the body social and sickness in the individual body are closely related. The primitive tribe that sees an increase in illnesses as a signal that something is wrong with the society is going directly to the heart of the matter. When it musters the community to restore the social structure to a healthy state and the sick individual to his former social participation, it is showing an unconscious insight into an evolutionary truth now more than half-forgotten. Communal grooming and communal health are inseparably intertwined.

This point can be crystallized by looking no further than at the various manifestations of the role of the doctor—a creature as critical to the medical breakthrough as the teacher was to the educational revolution. Very small hunting and gathering bands often do not have any kind of medical specialization. As with the Negritos, the whole band musters to help a sick person, unless his near kin have a special responsibility for him. At a slightly higher level of sophistication the world's first specialist appears—the medicine man. Medicine, despite the alluring claims of other specialisms, is undoubtedly the oldest profession in the world. But since at this stage we had not begun to make inviolable categorical distinctions between the individual and society and between soul and body, the doctor had to have much more in his repertoire than first-aid skills. He was the preserver of esoteric knowledge about the supernatural, the repository of practical skills in healing, the diviner of personal fortune, and the prognosticator of social misfortune. He was often the only contact with the other world and the only guarantee, over and above the strength and skill of the warriors themselves, of victory in war. In his diagnosis of personal and social ills he started with an expert knowledge of the patient and of the social relationships of his little world. He was the world's first sociologist, and in his exploration of dreams and the significance of small events, the world's first psychiatrist. His custody of the supernatural made him the world's first priest, master of ceremonies, and even manager of the weather and the timing of the hunt. For his services he often received very considerable gifts.[16]

All these items in his "primitive" doctor's bag were seen as connected the one with the other, and all tied in with the health and happiness of the people in his care. He was the first professional groomer.

Discussions of the crisis in modern medicine are probably equaled in frequency and intensity by worried examinations of the crisis of the modern family, whatever that is. The crisis of medicine is far more clear-cut, however. The problems the doctor faces are definable. We are not primarily concerned here with what is known in the trade as the "delivery system" of medicine (as if medicine were like letters or bread) and the various public and private devices for paying for medical service. Nor do we question the right of all members of the community to enjoy a standard of medical care commensurate with that community's wealth and skill. Nor do we wish to assign blame to participants in the medical interaction, but rather to try to define what is happening in this interaction.

And what is not happening. We have suggested that the doctor has traditionally been a person concerned with relating his technical knowledge about the body and its processes to his knowledge of the patient and the patient's psychosocial reality. For nearly all the time there have been human doctors this has been the pattern that substantially prevailed. But because of our astonishing technological increments and an even more astonishing set of metaphysical beliefs based on the mind-body distinction, we have come to separate the treatment of the disease from the broad understanding of its host; we have come to see doctors as experts in the servicing of subsections of bodies. This shift is neatly revealed in the word that now describes where the doctor meets his patient—"office"; it used to be "surgery." Like many university professors, whose traditional "studies" have now become "offices" too, the doctor is part of the bureaucratization of human encounter. He gains status among his colleagues by specializing, not generalizing. From his patients he gets money for doing one thing quickly and well.

But while he gains control over time in a new way, and certainly control over a vast amount of specialized information and technique, it is possible that he loses much of what the doctor has always had going for him—a place in a deeply rooted pattern of mutual grooming in which information and social commitment were virtually inextricable, and in which the willingness of the patient to yield to the skill and magic of the doctor was balanced by the doctor's own participation in a system of meaning beyond the pragmatic. Just as the teacher, if he or she is lucky, can tap "programs" for teaching and for learning that must be deep in an animal that needs so much knowledge and understanding, so the doctor can make use of the urge to groom and be groomed that marks all the primates and that in some human forms is the symptom of our greatest artistry and wisdom. But as the teacher is often prevented from using the resource that is rightfully his by overorganized, overpopulated, and underenjoyable school bureaucracies, so the doctor is forced by the notions of status that modern doctors have, by the methods of his payment, and by the trend to the special and the particular, to lose the vital ingredient of the patient's will to recover and his confidence in the higher meaning of the doctor's life and ethic.[17]

Efforts are always being made to overcome the formal rigidity of the system and to return to the warmth and equability of the traditional scheme. Even when a patient is sent to a specialist, it is customary for the specialist to take a rather lengthy and elaborate case history, which he may never consult. He is making a grooming gesture; he is seeking to assert an interest in the patient's whole being, not just his ear or femur or liver or episodic acne. Even the most imperiously esoteric practitioner cannot retain patients without some chitchat, some exchange of feeling, and some assertion of his personal commitment to the special version of the patient's problem. But if the patient is cunning or suspicious, he may test his doctor out next visit, to see what he recalls, to probe the doctor's memory of the poignant moment of revelation of the crisis and its meaning. Good doctors remember. The point is simply that a successful doctor has too many patients with too many statuses, indecisions, social relations, and private complexities ever to remember even a portion of these.

Competent doctors should treat just as many people as need them. The logic of our argument in its simplest form is that there should be more of them. Our concern is with the effectiveness of many contemporary medical arrangements for solving the broader problems of social affiliation and personal welfare; as primates and humans we have in other times and places solved them in ways far simpler and—so we propose—more likely to enhance the group's welfare as well as the patient's health.

This problem of social affiliation is not unknown to those concerned with broader aspects of health care, and a variety of practitioners and techniques have been developed to try to cope with this and other problems outlined here. Public health workers, nurses, psychiatric case workers, social workers, recreation directors, school nurses, and so on all augment the basic medical role of restoring the health of damaged organisms. (Psychiatry is a special matter and will be discussed shortly.) Obviously there are many possible approaches to managing communal health. But two trying problems have emerged, the first sociological, the second ethological. One of the characteristics of occupational groups in virtually any society is that they try to improve the standing they have in public esteem and the amount of control they exercise over their work and who is eligible to do it. The proof of the change from "occupation" to "profession" is that the state licenses only members of a profession to perform the services it claims it alone can provide—such as doctors, dentists, and lawyers—and that these services are so clear-cut that they permit an exact decision about the mandate to offer them. This same process is visible in the medical field, where customarily it takes longer and longer to become a more and more specialized member of the "grooming team"; this naturally affects the commitment of practitioners as well as their income and status. The net effect is a proliferation of precisely the problems that the creation of these additional specialties was meant to solve—to overcome the loss of the small-scale family-doctored community, and to provide compassion over the life cycle instead of a technique of the moment.[18]

This leads directly to the second, the ethological, difficulty, that a person in distress can be sent on a Kafkaesque adventure within a bureaucracy founded, ironically, on the belief in mercy. Yet he may find that in the interests of professional integrity and organizational efficiency, his special personal crisis becomes routine. His problems become the work load of a functionary and not the ardent business of someone whose commitment to a solution is as intense as his own anxiety.

We have fragmented the doctor's role, split it up among a host of specialists, not all of whom are medical: the priest, the troubleshooter, the teacher, the psychiatrist, and many others all have little pieces of the doctor's role in their repertoire. Yet we still demand all these things of the physician himself. The old small-town family doctor in many ways embodied them: he was the wise man of his community who knew its troubles and its weak spots, who was there to listen and advise, to patch up lives as well as limbs. As any such practitioner would be the first to assert—although not perhaps in so many words— he spends most of his time in nonmedical grooming activity. But this is perhaps the basic issue: in our perspective it *is* medical grooming that he is doing. He is close to his evolutionary roots and is satisfying a need that comes directly from the evolutionary demands of the community he serves as a genuinely concerned participant.

In the crowded urban communities with which we have so many difficulties, and increasingly in many entire countries, this no longer holds. A devoutly personal activity becomes more and more impersonal as the cross-currents of demands increase. The high status accorded specialization and the feeling that general practice is "amateurish," the increasing pressures on the time of doctors, the complexities of modern medicine, and the relatively low monetary rewards of the twenty-four-hour-on-call, house-visiting family physician, all combine to push even doctors otherwise inclined in the direction of emulating business "efficiency." A doctor wants to be like any other businessman, to have appointments and business hours, to go home from "work" and not have to worry about patients, but have his "life" to himself, and to draw the appropriate rewards. He is responding to a system overload with a form of withdrawal. Undoubtedly this is a natural strategy for the individual doctor, but it leaves the mass of anxious patients without the kind of shamanistic support that they need and now have to shop for, literally, in a dozen different places.

The shaman often had to have a vision to be "called" to the life of a doctor. We ourselves echo this in referring to medicine, teaching, and the priesthood as "callings" or vocations—the giving of a whole life to something because of an inner feeling or need. Now, in all these spheres the sense of vocation is being lost. They are all becoming "jobs." The practitioners increasingly resist the emotional demands for nurture that are made on them, and ask that they have the same privileges as other people in other jobs. In this context it becomes more understandable why so many pills are prescribed to patients to pep them up, tranquilize them, put them to sleep, make them indifferent to pain, make them lose weight or gain it. On one level these gifts of pills are sensible enough and overt in what they do. On another, they represent a continuation of the grooming process, even though the groomer is not physically near; a month's supply of pills begins to compensate for the ten-minute interview, which was all the practitioner could give. Of course, this is one reason why placebos work effectively as often as they do. Perhaps it is less the power of suggestion than the memory of encounter that gives pills of sugar such efficacy. And it is also understandable why doctor and patient are together forced to enter into a conspiracy based on the taking of drugs—to create even by artificial means the continued contact that their relationship may really need but can only symbolically achieve.

Again, an evolutionary perspective might alter our view of the nature of mental as well as physical illness. Already we have established that the psychosomatic approach—as well as notions of community care of the mentally ill—is compatible with an evolutionary perspective.[19] But what of mental illness itself? Let us not beg the question of what is normal and abnormal in behavior; in fact, let us avoid absolutist definitions of psychic health and ill health.[20] When behavior is looked at objectively, all that is obvious is a range of variation. Like all other natural features of natural populations, this variation will fall along a normal curve. Take aggressivity: at one extreme there will be people who revel in violence and enjoy killing and bloodshed, at the other people of immense timidity and passivity who could not under any circumstances be provoked to violence. In the middle there is the vast bulk of people who are capable of some violence but most of the time not particularly aroused to it. Take compulsiveness: at one end there are the "compulsive neurotics" who are meticulous to a fault and to whom orderliness is an end in itself; at the other there are the happy-go-lucky, totally unorganized folk; and in the middle, again, the vast majority, who have some compulsions, some degree of disorder, and, all in all, a working mixture of the two. Clearly societies are geared in their general day-to-day operations to the inclinations and abilities of the many; they have to be. But social circumstances will determine whether any of the extremes on any dimension are stigmatized as useless or rewarded as valuable. It is the same with natural selection itself: most of the time the extremes will be wiped out, but there will come times when selective pressures favor the odd-men-out, and these survive to change the structure of the gene pool and eventually the characteristics of the species. All we can say as good zoologists is that in all spheres of behavior variation exists, and that the same kinds of variation occur in all human populations. It is improper, therefore, to take moral positions and label any behavior good or bad; the proper procedure is to ask what the range of variation seems to be *for*.[21] What contingencies does nature have in mind in producing the particular kinds of variations that she does? (Whether these are learned or innate is beside the point, both because the dichotomy is unreal and because, as we have argued, if variations occur so regularly, there must be a statistically predictable propensity for learning them.)

In assuming that mental "illnesses" might have adaptive functions, we are not so far from Freud, to whom neuroses were essentially adaptive pieces of behavior. He, however, saw them only as adaptive in the life of the individual, not the species. The problem with neuroses was that while they might have been useful at their inception, they certainly were not in future years. The proposition here is to put behavior that falls at either end of the curve into social perspective by seeing it as part of the normal variation in a population—as normal as variations in height, speed, strength, intelligence, or any other feature. Extremely high intelligence, for example, is "abnormal," and people so endowed often cannot function very well in society. But they can solve chess problems faster than computers, and so society eventually finds a use for them. When people occur for whom we can find no use at all, we call them lunatics and lock them away. But their seemingly abnormal behavior may have once had a function that we can no longer recognize because our circumstances have changed. Conversely, chronic acquisitiveness would have been positively harmful in hunting societies, and chronically acquisitive people would have been ostracized. In our own society it is considered a "healthy" motive, and the man who gives away all he earns is promptly suspected to be a nut. Thus, the end of the curve that is favored has shifted.

Let us take an obvious example of how this process can work even over short spans of time. Our maximum-security prisons and prison hospitals are full of homicidal maniacs—compulsive killers. Many of them have multiple and "senseless" killings to their credit. Some we kill in turn, others we declare insane and lock up for life. These are men who enjoy killing for its own sake, who are fascinated by the business of death, who get a strange fulfillment from the act of murder. Loose in society, they are a menace, and we are right to put them away. But in every society the dedicated killer crops up, and it takes no great imagination to see how useful he would be in times of trouble. A man who will give himself wholly over to the killing life with dedication and even pleasure is just the man to send against the enemy on raids—which are essentially murder expeditions. In our own time he is the perfect commando, marine, green beret, or whatever. Among the Crow Indians there was a society called the Crazy Dogs, or Those-born-to-die. These were young men dedicated to fight to the death and never move away from the enemy. To this end they would stake themselves into the ground with thongs tied through their back muscles and face the enemy. They were reckless and lawless and were allowed all kinds of privilege and indulgence. On the night before a battle or raid, the Crazy Dogs would wreck the camp and rape the women—with impunity, because the next day some of them would surely die. They were among the most honored men of their community. The same is true of our own commandos, who receive medals and honors for acts that, performed on their own people in peacetime, would land them in the security wings of mental hospitals. These killers are always with us, but whether or not they become our greatest heroes or our criminal lunatics depends on which end of the curve we decide to reward. They are always with us, because if there is a curve of aggressivity, there must be someone at the violent end of it. A society of such men is clearly impossible, but a proportion of them is clearly useful, as is a proportion of cunning cowards.

The example of compulsion neuroses is much the same. The overly compulsive person can be useful in certain tasks requiring superfine ordering and routine repetitiveness. He is, for example, an excellent ritualist; Freud in fact noted the similarity of religious ritual to the compulsive acts of the neurotic patient.[22] Insofar as compulsion is a part of most religious ritual, and insofar as such ritual became a growing part of the hunter's adaptive repertoire, the relationship may be more than simply analogous. Once, we may have even needed our compulsive neurotics to keep the universe turning over in a proper and orderly fashion.

We mentioned that epilepsy is a very ancient and subtle form of behavior, probably deriving from mammalian escape techniques. Epileptics have two valuable traits: they go easily into trances, and they have to exercise great self-control.[23] On the one hand their trance behavior could well have been important in ritual and healing; on the other, their excessive self-control often makes them tough and effective leaders—with the added advantage that their occasional seizures are viewed by many peoples as cases of possession by God or the gods, and hence enhance the spiritual authority of leadership.

But what of true states of schizophrenia? What of delusions, paranoia, manic-depression, catatonia? Again, they crop up everywhere, and again they often serve very important functions. Christ would no doubt be diagnosed today as suffering from paranoid delusions (talking to God, destroying the world, etc.),[24] while Joan of Arc with her voices would not be burned, but bureaucratically incarcerated for life for her own good. But their "delusions" helped them to complete almost impossibly difficult tasks requiring more than the usual quota of heroism and dedication. In our hunting past, such requirements cannot have been uncommon, and a proportion of people with such "delusions"— with immediate and confident contact with the other world, for example—would have been more than useful and well worth the minor costs. We ourselves do not seem to mind paranoid delusions of grandeur in our leaders; it is only when they occur in "inappropriate" people— like assistant professors and busboys—that we send for the strait-jackets.

The roots of these mental-behavioral adaptations may go very deep. The origins of grandiose delusions, for example, may lie in the comportment of dominant animals under stress; a form of megalomania would have helped to make a convincing show of really dominant be-havior. On the other hand, deep withdrawal symptoms may have characterized chronically subservient animals trying to stay out of trouble. Similarly, manic phases may have coincided with sudden rises in the hierarchy and the energy necessary to complete and maintain these, and depressive phases with equally sudden changes downward.[25] Sociologists have noted how sudden changes in status (in either direc-tion) affect mental illness and especially suicide in contemporary human society.[26] In fairly small hunting groups it must have been much easier to find roles for all variant forms of behavior exhibited by the mem-bers. In our own huge societies the lack of fit between an individual's behavior and the roles available to him is often glaring, and so we have to put out of the way those whose behavior is "inappropriate" to their station. Our own failure to allow any honorable role to the homosexual contrasts miserably with the place he was accorded in the most manly of human cultures, the Plains Indians. That we have nothing to equal their *berdache* is a constant reproach to the tyranny of our norm.

And not content with harassing homosexuals and otherwise insisting on production norms of "adjustment," "personality," and "citizenship" from young and old alike, we are now employing our skill in making drugs to normalize the behavior of those who are found to be different. Some educators decry the growth of drug use among students yet also give drugs such as dexedrine and other stimulants to so-called slow learners. Persons who are nervy and abrupt are tranquilized because their sharpness impedes their smoothness. Truck drivers and business-men gulp pep pills to maintain a pace of output set by the hardiest in their groups. Athletes stung by fear of competing poorly stimulate their central nervous systems before games, and shy people are encour-aged to take a formidable martini before a social meeting to ease the transition from privacy to extroversion. Whole societies become cor-rupted by the tyranny of the normal curve, especially in sexual activity, and by the psychologists and other engineers of life who buy their single-minded theory of social value in the narrow marketplace of high competitiveness. In the name of demos, the focal democratic principle of the preciousness of human variation becomes a coercive principle of exploitation of those whose most grievous error was to have been born in a less populous segment of the normal curve than someone else.

The essential point here is that natural groups are systems. The fast need the slow, the brilliant require the context of the steady, the big are burly only among the small. The "central tendency" in biological patterns still depends on what or who is *not* moderate or modish. Nothing is gained by laughing at midgets.

If humans are clever and provident enough to take care of one another when they are clearly ill, they are also sufficiently subtle and foresightful to amuse one another when they are well. The other side of the currency of grooming is play, recreation, social work, much of psychiatry, and the host of informal actions that all humans everywhere daily undertake to come into contact with friends, colleagues, and various arts and insights. In England when an automobile has an engine running because it will begin moving shortly, it is said to be "ticking over." Much of what Americans call "hanging around" is ticking-over behavior—that activity which keeps the body social in trim, cements social bonds, informs people about the character, strengths, and weaknesses of their friends and co-workers; provides artistic and dramatic rendition of forms of social life; and, in general, permits the community to be in shape to cope with crises and to celebrate triumph.

Medical grooming ensures that physical bodies are healthy so that when called upon they can go into action on behalf of the community. What we can loosely call "social grooming" keeps the members in psychological trim, keeps their engines ticking over in readiness for activity. Sometimes this is obvious. A good deal of competitive sport is indulged in not only for physical fitness, which is a by-product, but for the avowedly spiritual qualities it promotes—team spirit, loyalty, subservience of the individual to the team, strict observance of rules, fair play, etc. The first sociologist to give this overt recognition was the Duke of Wellington, who observed that the battle of Waterloo was won on the playing fields of Eton—it was a commonplace of imperialistic English rhetoric that the Union Jack flew over every Rugby scrum. But perhaps it is not so obvious that gossip and gambling may well play equally important roles and that the seriousness with which these are pursued may be as justifiable as the training regime of an Olympic sprinter.

All of this is intensely social. The isolated animal of any gregarious species—and in particular the higher mammalian species—even if well fed and healthy, soon becomes morose and miserable if he lacks the contact with his kind for very long. We are attuned to interaction with our fellows. They keep us ticking over and alive. Symbolic human interchange has little to do with the passage of information, except in the very broadest sense. It has to do with *keeping up the interaction,* and with subtleties such as asserting or discovering status differences and maintaining in-group/out-group distinctions.

Play and learning are closely related, and the relationship promotes both general competence and social cohesion. As anyone who observes children at play will know, they take their efforts very seriously indeed. As they should, because there is much they must learn about the world, themselves, and about one another. Adult play is part of a more general grooming pattern, with functions for whole communities, comparable to child's play for the individual children. We know that children *must* play, and even the most unscintillating puritan schoolmaster will allot some miserable bit of time to his charges, if only to permit him a break in his own routine. But what does adult play mean, and why do we play? Why *do* we play poker and bridge, and bet on which horse runs faster than some other? Why do we scream our heads off when the hero scores a goal and pull our breath in sharply when the dancer takes a leap as beautiful as it is improbable? Why do we spend hours curling our hair and determining lapel shapes and producing overmuch overrich food for guests at feasts? Why do we believe that "talking things over" helps solve problems? Why is gossip so important?

All these seemingly unpragmatic pieces of behavior help to keep up the psychological tone of the community so that it is ready for really pragmatic action. They seek as well to reaffirm the psychological health of the members and of the social relationships in which they participate. Let us take some apparently unrelated areas of behavior. Gambling is a universal male activity.[27] Females indulge in it less, and usually imitate male forms when they do. In many hunting groups gambling is the most common leisure-time activity. Sometimes these are games of pure chance, sometimes they involve skill. Whatever their form, they involve a fascination with doing chance one better, with beating the odds. The more they become games of skill, the more

analogous they become to true hunting situations, in which the calculation of odds is always important. Among the Hadza of East Africa a
man or a group of men will go into the bush with poisoned arrows and
perhaps hit an animal at a distance. The poison works slowly; the
animal has to be tracked, killed, and then carried home. The men
return to the base camp and try to persuade other men to join them
in the tracking, which needs at least half a dozen hands to be successful. The men in the camp have to assess the odds: Will the expedition
be worth it? How reliable are the original hunters? How good are their
arrows? How long will it take to get the animal? Would they be better
employed going off and looking for an animal of their own? What are
the conditions in that part of the country where the animal was hit?
What, in sum, are the odds for and against success?[28] This is only
one kind of assessment of odds that hunters face. In the actual hunt
itself they must be calculating all the time. The experienced hunter,
like the experienced gambler, begins to see regularities and patterns;
he learns how to play for all it is worth whatever hand nature and his
own skill deal to him. A younger player is more reckless, but he learns
by experience when it is not worth making a large bet on a long shot,
and how to play shrewdly from a poor position.

It should not surprise us that men are fascinated by gambling. They
are always trying to reduce risk, to make a chancy experience more
certain, to beat the long odds. All over the world, in cultures otherwise
almost totally diverse, men gamble and engage one another in mara-
thon games of skill and chance. Along with pornography and drinking, it is the most nearly universal form of male ticking-over behavior.
It is just as important to the modern businessman as it was to his
hunting ancestor, since chance and odds are the order of the day in
the stock market as much as in the veld. A group of businessmen discussing whether or not to make a tricky deal are directly analogous to
the Hadza and their problem with the wounded animal in the bush.
Even men who no longer face the uncertainties of the universe in quite
the same way as their Paleolithic ancestors still find in gambling a
re-creation of that truly primitive thrill in pitting oneself against
opponents and trying to beat the laws of chance in order to make a
"killing."[29] Gambling is one of the more spectacular pieces of ticking-
over behavior.

There is a social gamble too in gambling. One also assesses one's
partners and fellow gamblers in the process. One becomes familiar with
their idiosyncrasies and weaknesses, their strengths and occasional
strokes of brilliance and stupidity. A great deal about a man comes

out when he gambles, as does a great deal about his colleagues. In the sharing of time, tension, and the remarkably repetitive and (to outsiders) tedious banter, there develops also a commitment to the little group, its unique patterns, and its role in the histories of its members. This is predictable, of course. But if we see such gambling as a ritual way of intensifying the bonds that must come into play, we can understand why people who could be otherwise occupied sit about grunting about cards, dice, and pebbles, groaning about their misfortune and the luck of others, whooping about their skill in anticipating the laws of chance and the error of an opponent—but also making more coherent a group that will have to act soon, and act well and with mutual ease.

Now, in cultures such as Europe and North America, this may not apply at all, because the people may be different from the people they gamble with. An Italian accountant may work with Jews and Puerto Ricans but play poker with Italians. A doctor may play cards with his friends from high school who are not now of his social class. An Ashanti civil servant will seek Ashanti kin rather than Ewe bureaucrats for his game. But the fact remains that an overall orientation is being expressed and stimulated by this exposure to significant males. Though the gambling may have no overt function, the implicit grooming is reward enough even for men who do not work together but who may nonetheless turn to one another in times of personal crisis—for brief loans, for advice about a wife or child, for evaluation of the merits of changing jobs or selling a house and moving to an apartment instead. Or, just for company, just to "hang around," to feel a warmth and support and some assurance that the five people or two or three all share commitment to the destiny of any troubled member and are happy to stand by, express opinion, and offer skill. Such ideas may appear strange within the context of cultures in which friendship between males is often awkward unless formalized, and suspicious unless clearly and aggressively "masculine." The exchange of tenderness and the assertion of rich commitment between men are problems often solved by participating as spectators at sports and occasionally as drinking comrades at bars and pubs.[30]

Male primates groom one another as a function of their dominance relations, and to maintain the overall tone of their essentially political relationships. The same applies to human male bonding, and to the forms of grooming such as games, conversation, and hanging around. When businessmen take each other to lunches, when construction workers share the task of buying a sixpack of beer, or when English

telephone repairmen heat water for a communal tea, they are all performing inessential actions—apparently inessential, that is—that elaborate the bonds between them, and put into richer and more humane
context the work they have to do together.

If gambling and other forms of emotional and skillful interaction
keep the men in trim for male activities, what happens among females?
Of course, females gamble sometimes, and men gossip a lot, but each
sex seems to have specialized in bringing its own particular grooming
activity to the status of a high art. Few would dispute that women
excel at gossiping. This area of intense interaction has been relatively
neglected by sociologists and left to the brilliance of some social
novelists. But recently social anthropologists have produced a variety
of theories about the ritual functions of gossip in delineating in-group
from out-group ("if we gossip with you, you are 'in' ") and passing
out information.[31] Gossip does these things and more, but there are
more general, underlying characteristics. The incessant attempts by
female primates, for example, to groom newborn babies and infants
not their own, and the constant interest shown in these young, is
matched in the symbolic animal by the intensity of interest and talk
that surrounds babies, new babies especially, and the whole absorbing
task of raising children. In the seemingly endless, and to male ears
repetitive, chatter that goes on among women regarding their offspring,
not only is information passed, and not only are in-group practices
confirmed, but a massive and encyclopedic confidence is built up in
the gossipers. Deviants are mulled over and condemned, excellence is
praised; but again, above all, there is sheer interaction between those
currently concerned with this crucial task, those who have been concerned and are eager to pass on knowledge and retain some place
around the infantile focus of attention, and those who will be concerned
and who will almost unconsciously pick up attitudes and information
that they will trade and use in turn.

Gossip is not only about babies, it is about morals. Gossip in the
popular sense refers to accounts of scandalous behavior, to what the
English charmingly call "goings-on." It preserves a rather tight
morality among the female block of any local social system by sub-
jecting the minutiae of behavior to exacting, horrified, and fascinated
scrutiny. It is often thought of as a divisive force in society, but it is
probably just the opposite, since it serves to unite the women into a
common system of values and then maintain these. Gossip differs from
simple conversation in that it deals essentially with standards and
values, and their maintenance and abrogation. Through gossip the

gossipers constantly reassure one another of their own worth and contrast this with the wickedness of those gossiped about. Again, this could scarcely be called a pragmatic activity; men who would cheerfully spend an evening playing poker would likely condemn it as a silly waste of time. But gossip serves exactly the same grooming functions for the women as poker for the men. All concerned are servicing one another in highly symbolic ways: they are keeping their morale in trim, they are preserving and reinforcing the system of social relationships to which they are committed, and above all they are ticking over—maintaining their emotional engines in states of readiness for action by the constant tune-up of social interaction with their fellows.

What applies to males with males, and females with females of course extends to the two together. As gossip is to ladies and gambling to gentlemen, flirting is to both together. This is the great erotic tune-up, the encounter that keeps active the enthusiasm for sex and the confidence to engage in it.[32] We are not concerned here with the strategic man or woman who exploits sexual skill for deliberate gain of money or clear advancement, but with the pair next to each other at a dinner party or opposite each other on a train or at coffee after work. Flirting goes on all the time—whenever a male and female of suitable age, style, habit, etc., happen to be in proximity. There are gestures of courtliness or strategic avoidance, there are ploys; we know even that when males see attractive females their pupils dilate on a purely automatic basis (this suggests the depth of the responses involved). Flirting is the first stage of the courtship pattern, which can lead in its complex turn to sexual intercourse and to what follows or does not follow that. Flirting may embarrass some people, outrage wives and husbands, cause disruption in the routines of men and women, lend intrigue to parties and danger to rendezvous. There can be little doubt that the presence of attractive males and females in an office or factory or hospital or anywhere will have an effect on the overall level of intensity and sense of pleasure of the people involved. A handsome electrician or a beautiful laboratory analyst may indeed interfere with patterns of work; but the switchboard operator will enjoy the contact with the man who repairs the board, and the doctor will find it entertaining and vitalizing to fetch a report from the lab. Some media industries—television and advertising, for example—deliberately employ pretty girls in preference to others. These industries depend on a constant level of creative productivity from the males—on keeping up their level of creative tension—and the pretty girls, far from distracting the men, act as a spur to their pride and a source of

excitement to their imaginations. All cultures flirt; indeed, there seem
to be universal patterns of flirting associated with eye contact, lower-
ing of the eyes, averting the head, glancing sideways, giggling, raising
the eyebrows, etc. Again, this is not the real thing, but it is a constant
state of readiness for the real thing, and perhaps the most obvious of
all ticking-over mechanisms.

There is much in common between the covey of males on the street-
corner watching girls pass by, the adolescent girls' screeching like some
novel beasts when a pop star makes an appearance, and the suddenly
enraptured wife and someone else's husband conferring elaborately at
a party. What they all share is a commitment to the pleasure of a
special form of grooming that, in turn, is tied to an always urgent
pattern of sexual exchange, intrigue, and blandishment.

Psychiatry has been mentioned here as a symbolic grooming phenomenon. It is also an example of one of the many junctions between
"medical" and "social" grooming. Psychiatry involves a subtle combination of flirting, gambling, and gossip with overtones of the supernatural. The old medicine man knew this very well when he threw
bones to divine the "illness," but based much of his diagnosis of witchcraft on what he knew from gossip about the patient. With the
fragmentation of the doctor's role and the abdication of communal involvement in curing, the old business of "hearing out" the patient's
complaints about his abuses and troubles has passed over to these
specialists in "mental" events. Even the boldest psychiatrists, however, do not claim to "cure" many people, but they do "help" them by
enabling them to understand themselves better. One extreme school of
"nondirective" therapists claims that it is best to do this by letting
the patient reach his own understanding through talk, with a minimum of interference.[33] The cynical critics of this method ask why,
then, a psychiatrist is any more use than a best friend. Perhaps this
is the point. The psychiatrist is a very skilled best friend, one trained
in a very special kind of friendship. In primates, friendship is, as we
know, expressed by grooming. When in our species the symbolic mental
equipment becomes tangled, infected, and painful, it needs grooming
just as much as the fur of a baboon. The psychiatrist helps us to pick
over the messy details of our confused and unhappy lives and to
reorder them in some more satisfactory way. But he is only a more re-
fined version of talking-it-over-with-a-friend. In this world of specialists he replaces some of the functions of the medicine men, of the
elders of the tribe, of kin and companions, of confessors, of people who
are there to listen with sympathy and to guide from experience. He

concentrates in himself a whole range of caretaking and even caring activities that were once more diffuse. This may explain both his relative success and his elusive sense of failure, for like the hospital and the specialty clinic, he treats the patient outside of his milieu. Unlike the medicine man, he does not belong to the intimate society in which the patient finds both the source and the cure of his trouble.

Psychiatric skills and their derivatives can, however, be applied in social contexts, as they have been in family therapy, encounter sessions, and in a wide variety of enterprises of psychiatric social workers, recreationists, and others concerned with assimilating the confusions and fears of lonely individuals into the resilience and interest that come from groups. This can become bizarre, as with commercial encounter groups in which strangers off a street come together to experience some contact with other people, the spontaneity of which is equaled only by its spuriousness as a real factor in their lives. And it becomes dangerous when such superficial contacts come to replace the more trying and involving links between people that long-term contacts based on gossip, fun, religion, and games may stimulate.

There are many other modes of solution to these problems of keeping the body social in trim. Perhaps the most influential theory about the functions of religion, Émile Durkheim's, comes to precisely this conclusion about the social meaning of religion and what it does: it is a highly ritualized, repetitive, and satisfyingly communal rendition of man-nature, man-god, and man-man relationships.[34] Since there are no gods and no supernatural, the business of coping with these nonexistent matters must relate to some real earthly human problems. So must drama, opera, and works of artistic fantasy—all so clearly important to the understanding of man's extensions of himself and his delicate use of these extensions to reach other people either in truth or in fact. If poets are the unacknowledged legislators of mankind, it is because they greet people at this level of supersocial encounter— encounters extrapolated from those around us, and attuned more acutely to beauties and miseries a jump too far away for aldermen and merchants, princes and physicians. This is grooming radically far away from the stroking of faces and quiet muttering of contented creatures. And yet the acts of reading and writing, of hearing music and humming it to someone, of planting an interesting garden, and wandering contentedly around it, are gestures of persons to persons. They are gestures made and received to serve needs as focal and primitive as the form these gestures take is remarkable and colorfully unexpected.

8.

THE
NOBLE
SAVAGE

FOR CENTURIES—PROBABLY for the whole of its existence—the species has deplored violence and taken steps to protect itself from the worst ravages of violence. But it has accepted it as part of the natural world in the way that it has accepted sex. Both urges have been at once glorified and vilified, and yet both the urge to kill and the urge to copulate have been accepted as inevitable. The question has been how to utilize or contain them according to one's aims. However, both were part of the package of original sin and therefore of human nature. Properly used, both were virtuous; improperly used, both were noxious. Legal fornication for the production of legitimate offspring was good, while inconsequential sexual pleasure outside marriage was bad; violence in the service of a legitimate cause such as religion or national defense was good, violence in the service of individual gain was bad—and so on. But no one doubted that sex and violence were "natural." For that reason, it was argued, we had to have stern religious and moral codes backed up by authority, even force to make sure that both these propensities were used legitimately. If individuals, or communities, or nations were sufficiently pious and strict, they might just be able to keep these dangerous propensities under control—and even end up "good." But the goodness thus achieved would proceed from their conquest of a natural tendency to be violent and promiscuous. And

204

the goodness would not consist in being nonsexual or nonviolent, but in being sexual and violent in socially approved ways. Beasts, this philosophy maintained, could not achieve goodness, since they lacked souls. They could simply act out their sex and aggression without restraint. Only man, with his divine moral sense, could overcome his animal nature and perfect himself.

This essentially "medieval" view is interesting, since it accepts that there is a "beastly" part of man that makes him one with the rest of animal nature. In this respect he does not differ from the beasts. Where he differs is in his capacity to manipulate this animality in the service of symbols. His soul—or later his reason—could work on the animal part of him, tame it, and put it to uses determined by human will and conscious intention. About the time of the Romantic Movement in Europe, a new view of man arose that proposed a radical departure from this conception of human nature.[1] Man became different from the animals not only in that he had a mind and consciousness but also in that he lacked the basic animal nature that, in the medieval view, linked him to the rest of the mammalian universe. In this new view man was born without evil propensities. These were learned as a result of living in evil and corrupt societies. It therefore became possible, this philosophy went on to maintain, not just to contain and manipulate the animal wickedness of man (since this did not exist), but to eliminate all human violence by not teaching evil to people in the first place—by getting rid of the corrupt societies that spawned violence, terror, and subjection. (The same argument was not applied to sex, but then no one wanted to be rid of sex altogether, so the problem did not arise.)

Two world wars, hundreds of local wars, and millions upon millions of deaths by violence later,[2] many of us stubbornly cling to this view: that we can end violence by changing circumstances. Since violence is learned, we can simply stop teaching it—remove all the provocations to it—and men will then be the good and peaceful beings that they are by nature. Those who still cling to the medieval notion are likely to find themselves condemned as evil men who argue that violence is inevitable and thus encourage it.

At the risk of joining the ranks of the condemned, we argue that the medieval view is intellectually more satisfactory, scientifically more accurate, and pragmatically more sensible. It is also more humane, and in the long run less likely to push the species to the verge of annihilation than appealing delusions about human perfectibility.

It is easy to see how the view of man as basically good but corruptible could be transformed into the view of man as basically blank but teachable. The culturalists vary in their estimation of man's innate goodness, but mostly they are opposed to anything that suggests innateness at all and therefore see man as faced with two alternatives: either he can teach goodness, cooperation, etc., or he can teach wickedness, violence, etc. Since all human behavior is, in this view, learned, violence as well as love must be learned; it must be impressed upon the tabula rasa.

There is no question that both violence and love are indeed learned. But they are learned as language is learned—easily. In our own terms, violence and love are learned easily because we are wired to learn them; because they have both been essential to survival, and so mutation and natural selection have produced a creature which will readily learn both in the same way as it will readily learn languages and rules. The potential for all this is there in the animal, and its large forebrain gives it the ability to shape and discipline these propensities to its own symbolically determined uses. This is both our problem and our opportunity: we are easily turned on by violence, but we can in consequence do something about the switches; we can try to turn ourselves on less. To rid ourselves of violent potential altogether, however, while it may seem superficially attractive, is possibly dangerous. There are times when men need violence to do right.

This is really very embarrassing. No one, except a few psychopaths and some strange adventurers in other people's suffering, wants to create violence and damage other people. It is embarrassing simply because we return to violence again and again. Which is less dignified: To be a cultural animal and yet consistently produce such appalling cultures that they inevitably lead us to war? Or to be a violent animal and disrupt our otherwise congenial and helpful cultures because we have a taste for blood and a zest for mayhem?

We are both; we do both; we must fear both. A punch-up at a bar can wreck a nose, a friendship, and leave a wide wake of gossip and regret. A lovers' quarrel or a family feud can lead to pain and even death; most homicides are between people who know each other well. Intimacy, not distance, stimulates the murderer. These are always desperate rips in the social fabric. We are rightly intrigued by the trials of murderers and the circumstances of their awful dramas. But these are little tragedies for modern communities. The big ones are precisely those in which our cultural skills and our organizational structures are most directly involved—when we make up gangs and rumble one another; when we give wealth to policemen to oppress ghettos and discipline the poor; and most spectacularly when we use our vast techniques with machinery and with people to conduct wars and to kill the others, whomever we culturally decide these evil others are.

It is a relatively modern conceit to assert that man is peaceful until he proves otherwise. In our enthusiasm for progress and our success in achieving forms of wealth and welfare, we have become committed to perfectibility and aspire to its wellsprings as ardently as at least one of our ancestors sailed after the fountain of youth. And yet we do fight; we always have fought, though most of the time we do not fight but tend our fields and flocks. Kings have always had barons to marshal foot soldiers; parliaments have always sought the power to raise armies; Russian communists came to power through violence; to protect their people and interests a state that was to wither away supported a vast militia that was in theory unnecessary. In constitutional terms, Americans were to be free to pursue liberty and happiness—even equality—and to carry guns and raise armies in small states. This grievously benign self-image has led to Guatemalas, Vietnams, and a stack of pious treaties. Switzerland is a neutral country whose male citizens train in the military three weeks each year. A thoughtless general ordering his troops toward Zurich and the Matterhorn would find the country a costly conquest. Neutral Sweden, the tough mecca of skilled optimists, has airplane factories carved into mountains, and troops who (with well-schooled Irish forces too) spent months in effortful schemes to bring peace to the Congo. The very day the French surrendered, in 1940, the Resistance became the official violent opposition, and some years later collaborators were shot and only their families grieved—if they did. In 1945 Japanese were fried like smelts by atomic rays, and just a generation later, some Japanese argued seriously for a proper military force again. Alleged to have a racial memory, a gene for war, the conquered Germans are urged by their allies to pull their warlike weight; the German army is once again the largest in Western Europe. The peaceful Indians swoop on Goa and contend with Pakistanis and Chinese for bits of remote territory. Boiling oil is dropped from parapets, and then napalm from airplanes. Women and children are still lined up and shot and pushed into graves. Only their names—if they have any—differ from the people who have died in the same way before; the insignia on the uniforms of their slaughterers are the only things that have changed.

The claim that we would live at peace if only there were no causes for war is a legitimate claim, but as pungent and provident a comment about reality as the affirmation that without disease there need be no hospitals. There is disease, there are hospitals; there is violence, and there are wars. We have saved millions because we accept that disease is real. We kill millions because we decide that we are good and the enemy is evil. In our rage at warriors we too easily fail to recall that they are human too.

Humanity has not changed; it goes on doing with more ruthless efficiency what it has been doing for the whole of its existence. But perhaps because of this, and because we now face the prospect of complete destruction for the species, we desperately maintain that this cannot be inevitable, that men are not in some deep way irrevocably committed to violence. If we accept that they are, and given the instruments of violence at their command, there is no hope for us. Indeed, it does seem to many that there is no longer hope of restraining or containing violence. The Pax Britannica and the Pax Romana are things of the past. We cannot depend on superpowers using their instruments of violence to keep the peace of the world—if this is ever what they really did. Nor can we depend on "rules of war," for in atomic wars there are no rules, only unequivocal results.

Many of our intellectuals rush to quell our fears by telling us that *theoretically* none of this has to happen, that violence is not part of human nature, that it occurs only because of evil intentions and circumstances that we can eradicate.[3] They are the Christian Scientists of sociology; and they have not as yet solved the paradox: if we are not by nature violent creatures, why do we seem inevitably to create situations that lead to violence? If it is in our natures constantly to provoke violence in what is an essentially nonviolent organism, then we cannot win, however we play the game. The preliminary answer is clear: we are creatures who are by nature easily aroused to violence, we easily learn it, and we are wired to create situations in which the arousal and learning readily take place and in which violence becomes a necessity.

We have not talked about the "problem of aggression." This is because there is no problem of aggression, despite the gallons of printer's ink that have been used in discussing it.[4] Aggression in the human species is the same as aggression in any other animal species.[5] It springs from the same causes and subserves the same functions. It is a necessary force in the evolutionary processes taking place in any sexually reproducing species. There has to be competition in order for natural selection to occur. One animal has to strive to outdo another for nest sites, territory, food, mates, dominance, so that selection can take place. Selection can of course favor timidity where a species is oriented toward camouflage or hiding and fleeing behavior; only inspection of the behavior of a species can tell us which way the pendulum has swung. In the successful and gregarious higher mammals (among others) it has swung decidedly in favor of aggression, and there is no warrant, and above all no evidence, to suggest that the human species is an exception. That a species is characterized by aggression does not mean that its members do not cooperate and are never helpful or loyal or loving—quite the contrary. Aggression is an essential component of these virtues, and ethologists have argued very cogently that we should view it as a constructive motive, a positive force acting for the benefit of a species.[6] Only when this positive force spills over into violence does it threaten internal order and survival. Even then, violence against predators can be seen as another constructive device. There is a delicate balance to be achieved here; ethological studies have brought out brilliantly how various animal populations manage it. There must be sufficient aggression between members of the same species in the same population to ensure that selection takes place and various subfunctions are served; this must be contained—usually by the process of "ritualization"—so that it does not develop into internal violence and destroy the population; violent opposition to threats from without the population must nevertheless be fostered.[7] Nonviolent aggression within, and violent opposition on the outside, have constantly to be balanced in any human society: members must be capable of violence in order to preserve its integrity, but toward one another they should be nonviolently competitive.

Even this nonviolent competition will work only once it has become clear to the participants that violence will *not* work, or, alternatively, once violence *has* worked. Take our cousins the baboons: their intricate social system, with its hierarchies and coalitions, etc., is maintained by "ritualized" activities of threat and submission that rarely break out into open violence. But they do break out on occasion, and savage injuries can be inflicted. The savagery is contained because they know it will not work; that is, the subdominants will not risk open violence against their superiors because they know they would lose. The showing of the canines will lead the subdominant to turn and present. But this same subordinate animal is one that survived because *he did not provoke the alpha males to savagery in the first place.* When the young males come to maturity and start to challenge the older males, many end up dead or badly wounded. There is no question that if they could they would indeed kill their elders and take over the leadership and the females. Equally, their elders and betters would cheerfully dispose of them if they really became a menace. But the balance is struck somewhere between these two extremes. Some old males disappear through natural death, or as a result of an ouster by coalitions of other-wise subdominant males. Some young males die or leave the band. Those that remain settle down to an "understanding," in which a reminder of the real facts of the situation—through threats and appeasements—is enough to preserve a stable structure. But the violence is there, and it is real. When leopards or lions or Ethiopian village dogs attack the troop, the violence is directed outward with spectacular success. The young males will be the first to turn their violent attention to the predator, while the alpha males come out from the center of the troop to tackle him.[8]

It is very important to bear these facts in mind in any discussion about the "ritualization" of aggression among animals, and to com-pare them gloomily with our own failures. In some ways, our own attempts at ritualization are just as impressive in view of the greater potential for destruction that we have evolved. Therein lies the crux of the issue. If the baboons were equipped with hand grenades (which they could probably learn to use quite easily), then there would not be many baboons left in Africa. The reason the baboons survive and flourish is that it is really very difficult for them to kill one another. Given the means, they would undoubtedly use them. The average young baboon, driven by primal urges to dominate and copulate, does not have the long-term interests of his species at the forefront of his imagination, and would not hesitate to try anything at his disposal to subdue his unwanted and tyrannical elders. With their territorial rivalries and competition for ranges, troops of baboons or prides of lions can be easily imagined wiping one another out—*if they had the means.* As George Schaller has remarked, if a lion strays onto the territory of another lion pride, then the only ritualization at its dis-posal is to run like hell.

Aggression and violence occur in animal societies and do not differ in kind from their human counterpart. Man has no *special* killer instinct that makes him different from the baboon.[9] Nor has he lost his powers of ritualization. He has simply handed himself a whole heap of problems for those by now familiar reasons: his forebrain and his artifacts. It was these that turned his primate power struggles into human politics, his primate ecologies into human economies, and his primate violence into human wars. Wars and organized killing, with the imperial component of conquest, arrive on the scene when the tool was perfected into the weapon, and the expanding and convoluting brain was able to cope with organization on the one hand, and with categories of friend and foe on the other. The latter is the most important leap after the advent of weapons. For animals these categories are fixed by nature, but for men they are capable of everchanging definition and redefinition. The human peril is only specifically human for the same reason that human politics and art and economics and religion are human. Man added no new genetic qualities and lost no old ones in the areas of aggression and violence. He is still the angry and conciliatory primate; he still strives to dominate and outdo rivals; he still resorts to bloody combat to gain his ends—in all this he is no different. But he adds the human dimension—tools and language; if you like, weapons and concepts. This is his problem here as in any other sphere, since it gives him the opportunity either to use his primate violence to his advantage or to work it to his own pain and destruction. About the violence he has no choice, any more than his ancestors and relatives had; about the use of the violence and its constraint he has all the possibilities of choice laid at his feet by his peculiar evolution.

Since we are primates and do have hand grenades, it is amazing that we molest one another so little and kill so rarely. One baboon troop cannot destroy another, because most of the losers will solve the problem with that ancient ritual, flight, in aid of which adrenalin like some super-overdrive is instantly brought into the system.[10] We secrete adrenalin too, but have other ways of coping with fights that build on animal rituals and become human artifacts. Just as the young baboon knows better than to step right up to the dominant male and demand he resign, so most humans have contrived ways of managing the antipathies they feel within their own communities. Though we are constantly in a state of aggression against at least some persons, we are rarely in a state of real violence against even one or two for long enough to harm them physically. When we do such harm, commonly there is some remand for this, some policeman-person to stop it, and some judge-person to ponder its implication for the people involved and for their community. There is no community so convinced of the normality and perhaps healthfulness of human violence that it permits murderers to wander about unmarked and unguarded.

But there are few communities without soldiers—without a group of people trained to kill. When they return from battle with blood in their histories, they are given honors and rewards—the very opposite of the isolation, bitterness, and often death incurred by the local strangler.

Why? What in the human biogrammar allows us this inconsistency? How indeed can we manage this special symbolic enterprise of defining enemies and friends and judging murder and heroism accordingly? A brief glance back at the biogrammar helps explain. We have seen that in the basic system of the human animal, young males are always in the situation of expressing enough energy, initiative, and skill to win the approval of their more powerful elders, but not so much that these same supportive elders will turn against them out of fear or out of custom and propriety masking fear. The male career involves sexual skill with females and social skill with males, and in both these areas a measure of tact and consent is always part of the mix along with zest and competence. An important way in which young males have related traditionally—and in many places still relate— to the dominant males in their communities is reflected in one simple, crude fact: war is not a human action but a male action; war is not a human problem but a male problem.[11]

Only males governed, only males hunted, and out of this lopsided sexual fact emerged another: only males cooperated to fight. The relentless and harassing initiations that young males received, and receive, stimulated loyalty to the group and willingness to defend it. When to this strong structure was added the heavy refinement of what the new cerebral cortex could do, we acquired war. Only an animal with brain enough to think of empires and try to manage them could conceive of war. Only an animal so wedded to the truths inside his skull could travel many miles and expend endless, precious calories and hours and artifacts to destroy others. Only an animal smart enough to build laboratories could be skilled enough to build bombs. Only a hunting primate could want to as much as the arsenals of the world suggest they do.

Perhaps the argument can be sketched more boldly with a simple prediction. So long as the use of nuclear weapons could be banned for one year, if all the menial and mighty military posts in the world were taken over by women, there would be no war. Of course, this is an unrealistic surmise, because for this to happen politics would have to change markedly, along with the control of force. But were we to continue this unfortunately frivolous proposition, we could well find that all the elaborately pious ritual, all the quietly insane military rigmaroles, all the puzzling hauteur of admirals huffing about their autonomy and their advancement, and finally all the energetic killing of the troops at the front would be radically changed. An army of women would be more intimate, less presumptuous about the outside world, more realistic, occasionally more vicious in small doses, but never initiating the vast episodes of poisoning that the wars of men are now and have been.

The very improbability of this ever happening is a measure of its foreignness to the biogrammar. It is the young males who practice throwing balls and spears endlessly, who play mock warfare in their games, who are excited by the rituals of military performance from which females are normally exempted (even where they are not, such as in Israel and Vietnam, they are never used on the front lines). Women may fight bitterly and with effect when their homes or homeland is being attacked. But they do not leave the home territory to fight on someone else's. They do not fly the fighter planes and steer the submarines (though of course they can). They do not become steeled marines or legionnaires lusty for agonized encounter. They do not huddle with the other generals and commanders in the headquarters tent. They are the military sex of last resort.

However, *organized predatory violence* has always been a male monopoly, whether practiced against game animals or those enemy humans defined as "not-men" (and hence also a kind of prey animal). This is the important step in the move toward human warfare. It is not that man (or rather *men*) in the course of his evolution either learned to be a killer or lost his capacity to ritualize. He always was a killer—he still ritualizes. What he learned was the use of weapons, the predatory skill, and above all the organization of predation in male bands. He built into his biogram a whole set of satisfactions that did not have to do with killing as such, but with enjoying dangerous and status-enhancing activity in the company of other males.

Our armed and belligerent young primates in the evolving hunting groups were as status-conscious as their primate ancestors. The evolving human society solved this potentially dangerous situation by making status within the community of males dependent on success in conflict with males of other communities. The bands of young initiates, having forged their bonds, turn their status striving outward, to achieve success in war and/or hunting: a young Masai must kill a lion; a New Guinea Highlander must bring back a human head; a young Crow had to kill a buffalo and bring home a scalp.[12]

At this very primitive level there is not—nor was there ever—much of what we would recognize as "war." The history of our international violence has been, for more than ninety percent of the time, a history of raid and skirmish.[13] The actual violence took up much less time than the elaborate male rituals of violence, of preparation and celebration. In many cases there was nothing obvious to fight about. Men did not need justifications for their activities beyond the activities themselves. Sometimes "real" causes could be assumed—disputes over territory, hunting rights, water holes, women, real or imagined insults to tribal honor. But for the most part, enemies were what were traditionally defined as such. No Shoshone needed any "real" cause for fighting the Sioux: they existed to be fought. A great deal of this fighting was highly ritualized so that the men could get the maximum satisfaction from their sense of danger and exercise of courage, while neither side lost too many lives. Of course, this could all get out of hand, but so could the ritualization of animal fighting. The showing of courage and skill and the braving of dangers were more important than the wholesale slaughter of the enemy. The evolution of our fighting skills and motivations has been in this small-scale context, closely linked to male-group activities and needs. Hunters do not conquer one another, although they may occasionally displace one another. What they do is prey upon one another in a way controlled, or "ritualized," by customary modes of small-scale fighting. It was the recent agricultural leap backward that gave rise to that markedly human institution, the war of conquest.[14]

There is no advantage in conquest for hunters. There is a limit to the amount of territory any hunting band can exploit, and hunters have little use for slaves, who would simply be more mouths to feed.[15] But our agriculturist with his burgeoning populations and his toilsome work in the fields is open to temptation. He carries over into his radically altered and potentially large-scale operation all the motives and satisfactions of the warrior-hunter. He adds to these the possibilities of conquest and enslavement, simply because these are to his obvious advantage if he can pull them off. The combination of the ancient traits embedded in male hunting and male vanity with the new advantages so obvious in conquest and material gain was, and remains, explosive.[16]

As societies grew and became more complex, local and sectional interests came into conflict, and internal violence became common. Man had little precedent for dealing with communities above fifty or sixty people. Within these small communities, order was a face-to-face matter; violence would have been directed against one's kin and friends and intimate allies and acquaintances. It was relatively easily controlled at this level. The only precedent for larger-scale organization was the "treaty"—a relationship with other bands of the same language group, or other bands of a common territory. These treaties were usually sealed with marriages. They were relationships between equals, as with nations. Once classes, estates, castes, professions, baronies, and satrapies came into existence, all technically within one national framework, even this old precedent could not operate, since these were not equals and were engaged in exploitative relationships the one with the other. The possibility therefore was opened that one section of a technically united society would come to define another as essentially a different tribe—a group of "not-men," or a kind of game animal to be preyed upon.[17] And between such groups it was harder to "ritualize" violence, since real issues were at stake. Peasant rebels were not interested in counting coups on their oppressors in order to prove their manhood and improve their status with their fellows; they wanted bread for their children. Thus sectionalism within societies and conquest and booty between them became the issues into which all the male energy of the warrior-hunter heritage was poured. This has been our history, and there is nothing remarkable or strange about it. It needs no *special* explanation in terms of our innate wickedness and desire to kill and torture, or our innate goodness and fall from grace through the inability to give ourselves a better deal. It is an inevitable outcome of our primate heritage and our weapon-bearing, hunting past, with the addition to these of dense settlement and huge numbers.[18]

Why a pattern should continue to emerge even though conditions for it are unpromising is related to the simple fact that males will still be males. The intervening variable between individual interest in violence and the actual violence of a group is the male bond. The reason we could confidently assert that female warriors would be remarkably less dangerous to the species in general is that females do not bond in a warlike way. They do not create the structures, they do not maintain the continuities, and they do not stimulate the emotions and loyalties among each other that are essential for the sustained conduct of stressful violent enterprise. But males do. Put a bunch of males together long enough, and once they establish some hierarchy and etiquette they will begin to seek some external focus for their interest—something to change, to master, to construct, to destroy—to leave a mark of the special existence of this special group of men. They do this to relate to one another—looking together outside the group focuses the loyalties inside. As any cheap politician knows, shake a bayonet at the outside threat and reap immediate political advantage. In the more local context, under most circumstances the best proof or symptom of the internal strength of a group of males is its keenness to affirm its own reality against the resistances of the outside. Its failure to do so, and repel attack, will be seen widely as a proof of weakness and hence of unimportance.

They do this not because they are evil (though they may become so), nor because they are insecure (though they may be), nor because they are greedy and rapacious (though they may be), but because they are stone-age hunters with stone-age emotions and ways of interacting. They have all the enthusiasms of the hunting primate, but with few of the circumstances in which this reality can be reflected. So they create their own realities: they make up teams; they set up businesses and political parties; they form secret societies and cabals for and against the government; they set up regiments; they make up fantasies about honor and dignity; they turn their enemies into "not-men"—into prey. They generate forms of automatic loyalty and complete dedication that can spread the Jesuitical message of the Church Militant and also send screaming jets to a foreign country. All a country needs is a couple of dozen males who take their fantasies about their own omnipotence so seriously that they spend money, kill people, and even commit Abraham's presumptuous conceit of sacrificing their sons to voices of grandeur they think they hear.

We have immodestly elected to discuss the world's two most severe problems, overpopulation and war. One problem results from the urgency of male-female bonding, and we will come to that shortly. The other is the consequence of male bonding, and is just about as biological, just about as cultural, as elaborately real and yet fantasy-filled as thoughts of love and acts of sex. Once upon a time an animal developed battle skills, ways of controlling interpersonal and inter-group hostility on a small scale. War was part of the quintessential male career. It allowed men to do the things many apparently love: dress up in glorious garb festooned with primitive indices of rank; exercise physical skills and a talent for ordering and for obeying; protect the community by sharpening their toughness and their talents at comprehending their enemy; seek out and kill and ritually praise the animals that gave them meat and part of their spiritual estate.

War was controlled ritually. It was controlled also because to kill meant to look clearly at the whites of their eyes and to smell the fear of a man being beaten. Killing was done in small groups, and—as they do still—warriors fought in terms of their clan, their fraternity, their platoon. Battle cries could be heard and drums banged and war dances jumped. There were no memos from abroad and no ridiculous flying generals and ward bosses pouncing down to pronounce on matters of which they could have only indirect knowledge. But it is precisely symbolic knowledge that makes our world go around. It stimulates our yarns about overkills, endless missile or other gaps, and encourages us to distrust those who talk of peace and disarmament because we know our own imaginative capacity to prepare destruction well enough to fear them. At the same time, symbolic knowledge is, and can be, the instrument for peace and reciprocity. Meanwhile, the most dangerous weapon the soldier has is the cerebral cortex under his hat.[19]

The imperial tendency had its roots in the devices that were used to hold together groups of early humans that would have otherwise drifted apart. Baboon troops split up when they are too large, and become wholly separate entities, potentially in conflict with one another. Human hunting groups can split, but because they speak the same language, worship the same ancestors, claim descent from the same mythical animal, reckon to have come from the same hole in the ground, they remain attached. The attachment is not necessarily to other people as individuals, but to other people as sharers of the same symbols. I do not owe hospitality and loyalty and protection to you because you are my neighbor and always have been, but because we are both attached to a common symbol, because we are both members of the Emu totem, or speakers of the Sioux language, or serve the same flag, or owe allegiance to the same constitution, or acknowledge the same God.

This great evolutionary change of gear—from attachment to people to attachment to symbols—was necessary to take the species over the

crucial divide between horde-living primate and tribe-living man. But
what was a useful device for integration at the tribal level became a
source of monstrous divisiveness for the species as a whole. In pre-
symbolic days, conflict was by definition realistic, but now we can
create our own conflicts out of any material at hand.

By the very nature of this process, groups are defined as in conflict.
Systems of ideas, attitudes, beliefs, and values can differ profoundly,
and if *our* system is to be legitimate, then *yours* must be illegitimate
and very easily seen as a threat. In this conflict of symbols, be they
nationalistic, religious, linguistic, class, ethnic, or whatever, the truly
human skills evolved for local-level person-to-person living can play
little part, although we constantly attempt to utilize them. But the
controls that we must institute—the ritualizations that we must invent
—to deal with gargantuan clashes of arms between coalitions of nations,
or Christians and Muslims, or the proletariat and the forces of capitalist oppression, or the third world and imperialism, etc., are something
of a different order from the ritualizations and controls that constrained
our evolving warrior ancestors for all those millions of years. The
new controls have to be, like the causes of the conflicts, highly symbolic. What this means is that controls on large-scale violence in large-
scale society are dependent on the fragile reed of human inventiveness.
The conduct of modern war is not at all the same as the conduct of war
as we have been evolved to pursue and control it. It has become part
of the apparatus of the bureaucratically organized market economy, in
which decisions are made in arbitrary and technocratic ways. At the
same time, it is still being fought and organized by groups of males
acting under all the commands of an ancient aesthetic of battle which
has little to do with the rhetorical issues politicians mouth in justification.

The human animal is hoist on its own cerebral petard. The brain
that was good enough to produce the skilled hunter who excelled and
found satisfaction in his male-group predatory activities was also
good enough to produce huge empires, noble causes to die for, vast
armies, and megadeath. With all these at his disposal, he goes on behaving as if he were still a hunter-warrior, in a war party, on a raid
for scalps, glory, and honor among equals. It is obvious to anyone
that all the pomp and panoply of war, which may have served splen-
didly to boost the morale of a war party, is completely ridiculous when
the outcome is not a few scalps and a feather in the war bonnet, but
the annihilation of the species. Yet men do not seem to know what

else to do except go through these archaic paces. The aesthetic of the male war ritual is self-perpetuating. When it becomes associated with immensely powerful industrial and financial forces whose prosperity depend upon a high level of military expenditure, the temptations for the more fantasy-ridden and more inflated leaders to spend public money on "defense" become, apparently, unbearable. It comes to seem crass weakness and patriotic indecency to refuse requests from militarists whose schemes are limitless and whose ability to create immediate and ever-present dangers would challenge a corps of gifted poets. It is rather as if a group of attractive and aggressively alluring young females were suddenly put to room and board in a seminary. The mere fact of their existence would disturb the young seminarians carefully intent on their devotion and the moral craft they want to have. Have soldiers around, and they will quickly bond with entrepreneurs and politicians. They will make smooth and plausible speeches to a public impressed by their willingness to serve and even die, and by their eagerness to withstand those forces of the untrustworthy enemy they have so prudently understood. If you have a Pentagon, you will use it, and it you.[20]

Nonetheless, there *are* military machines, and it is a plain fact that weak countries have been invaded by others that have cultivated warfare and paid the cost of guns. Whoever started the escalation, whatever the original or recurrent causes of any potential conflict are, why communities decide to spend astonishing sums of money and life cycles of energy on the military—all this is in a deep sense beside the biological point, which is that a more or less large group of male organisms is primed and equipped to fight some other group, and will receive honor and benefit from so doing.

This remains an agonized question for all persons whose disposition is to peace and to the gentle resolution of human differences. What does one do or think to do about the reality of the use of force and the stubborn recurrence of episodes of violence? How can a reply be framed to the proposal that only powerful countries are proof against attack; that to rely on the goodwill of powerful neighbors is charming but hopeless and indeed perilous? Is it in fact possible any longer for a community to be without serious means of self-protection—which must by definition involve people who can hit and hurt, and some apparatus for destruction?

The evidence is discouraging for pacifists. There is no need to go once again into the dismal war record of the species even in its ad-

vanced state of allegedly reasoned modernity. That warlikeness seems
to bear little relationship to the forms of society must dismay those
who see in internal changes the basis for external affability. Peace-
loving Communist Russia? Peace-loving Capitalist United States?
Peace-loving Maoist China? Peace-loving Peru? Peace-loving Israel? Peace-loving Lebanon? Peace-loving France? Peace-loving Ni-
geria? Peace-lovers all, and all adulterous with a soldier. From the
melancholy, slovenly cruelty of the South American general torturing
his opponents, to the glow-eyed, self-declared emancipators in Washington, to the compactly cunning guerrillas in Southeast Asia, there is
some pact with force, some decision of first or last resort about the
need for specialists in hostility. Of course, after the war there will
certainly be peace, and it is often best to declare war to make peace.
Yes, goes the familiar wretched promise, this is a limited action, a bit
of healthy surgery, a maneuver, really. Do not become alarmed, we are
your leaders, prudent, aware, deep, men of peace whom our generals
salute with gratitude and respect. The peasants may mass at monu-
ments, may demonstrate, even the barons may grumble because there
is a shortage of good harness and their hunting fields are used for
training. The young may rebel against the press gang or the draft
board, and fathers and mothers may connive to buy their sons out of the
danger of having to serve. In international organizations, yards of
words will be spun out in the air. And yet the hopeless logic regularly
wins out, of warriors caught in structures built like corporations to
expand indefinitely, appropriating as much wealth as possible.

We are not concerned with the causes of armed conflict. It has as
many causes and justifications as it has instances. To those who fight
them, all wars are just wars. We are concerned with the weight of
evidence that indicates that groups of men banded together in some
interest will readily resort to violence against other groups of men who
are seen as opposed to that interest. The interest itself does not seem
to matter: violence can serve any master. The answer seems to be, in
our evolutionary perspective, that we are a naturally aggressive species
easily aroused to violence; that we have invented the means to practice
violence effectively on a large scale; that our cultural systems constantly provoke us to violence; that these systems always contain
groups of males whose proclivity is violent; that within the last few
thousand years of human history, violence has been taken out of its
small-scale evolutionary context; that there are few evolutionary pre-
cedents for the control of violence on the scale on which it now occurs.
The atavistic stimuli to violence still exist, but the means of ritualizing

violence that evolved in the small-scale skirmishing days of our ancestors simply cannot operate in the huge, complex, and heavily armed international society of today.

The answer, if there is an answer, lies in the medieval attitude to violence. Left to their own devices, people will fight—or, rather, men will fight. They will make love *and* war. This may not stem from a basic killer instinct, but the end product is certainly the same. That it is not a basic drive seeking expression gives us some slender hope. We may not be able to get rid of violence by refusing to teach it, but we can contain and constrain it by ritualization, by agreement, by threat of greater violence, or by supernatural sanction. We cannot depend on any "natural" controls to operate here: they work only on that small scale we have irrevocably abandoned. And even they do not get rid of violence; they utilize and contain it. And that is what we must do. We must recognize our proclivity for it, our readiness to use it, our excitement in its exercise, our sense of its possible rewards. Given this recognition, we must seek to control it—without any very sanguine notions about getting rid of it altogether—by creating circumstances in which it will not be learned. The circumstances in which it is learned are our human circumstances, and these are a million times amplified by the events of the recent past—the past few thousand years, that is.

There is no great mystery about all this. The facts are clear. The problem is practical, not intellectual. The challenge is to deal with the literal, the obvious, by actually dealing with it, not by wishing it away. It would indeed be better if it were not so, but it is so, and we must try to make it better.

If war is the most public activity, lovemaking is the most private. What was once universally acclaimed for its long-run usefulness for the human group—that it gave us another member and established yet more firmly our hold on our earth and on our future—has now in some places at least become an ardor fraught with ambiguity and a form of creativity increasingly maligned by those who claim to speak for the species' future. What is essentially at issue is the extraordinary burgeoning of human population in this century, and the inevitable problems of housing, feeding, organizing, educating, healing, and living together that accompany this quantitative prosperity. The noble savage constrains his freedom and distorts his experience as much in enthusiastic sexual congress as in bitter acrimony and war.

Just as with hunting-become-war, population-expansion-become-explosion results from old urgencies and from strong and explicit programs. At puberty the human male and female change radically; they are now physically able to reproduce. The source of the population crisis is that people enjoy sexual intercourse and what precedes it. Copulation control is as much the issue as population control. It is surprising that so much of the emphasis in the search for solutions to this problem has been on the chemical and technical tools of contraception and not on the pattern of behavior that makes these necessary. For though means of contraception are now rather widely available (few women in North America of whatever class and education need become pregnant if that is not their clear intention), reproductive rates remain sufficiently high to make us wonder why once again human will fails while physical process perfectly succeeds. It is laughable to claim that those same women accused of wanton and rococo patronage of drugstore makeup counters are incapable of crossing over the aisle to the section where contraceptives are readily available. And males who concern themselves with moon rocketry, tubeless tires, and the horsepower of Fords are in a strong position to understand the nature of the condom, and of *coitus interruptus.*

The same people who say that man has no biological patterns of consequence, no innate propensities, no behavioral relationship to the other primates, are also realistically exercised about the growth of population—clearly a biological matter that must have some connection to our lives as animals. The facts, any way they are looked at, are all too clear. The human species cannot go on reproducing itself at the present rate, because soon there will not be enough food, or air, or room to maneuver. Finally the simple bodily heat our expanded masses will produce will literally cook us like some horribly superior nuclear device.[21] Because the expansion is geometric, not arithmetic, and because our medical skill keeps us alive longer and longer, and because for both nutritional and ethological reasons puberty widely occurs earlier and earlier, we are faced with a genuine and frontally personal crisis to which everyone who makes a child contributes. To have to think of the birth of a baby as an aspect of the pollution problem is gruesome, but realistic. Yet, so far, few of the warnings given and few of the predictions of dire consequences have very much affected how men and women comport themselves. As with violence, to which we are easily stimulated, however miserable the outcome, so we are intrigued and cajoled by the quiet private encounters an animal once learned to find agreeable and essential, but which now become an antisocial act. How private sexual acts can be antisocial in the animal world—where reproductive success is the criterion of fitness in the struggle for survival—repays our scrutiny.

We are perhaps back in the medieval situation: we see violence and sex as dangerous to us, and rightly, and we seek to control them without thinking that we can or should eliminate them. While we may, with some justification, toy with the idea of eliminating violence, we do not think of eliminating sex. Yet these are closely associated functions in human physiology, and the arousal and control of sex and aggression are intimately linked in the brain and in the glandular and nervous systems.[22] It may well be, therefore, that they are equally intimately linked as social phenomena. It is not simply that men fight over women (in fact, they fight much less over women than over property, for instance), but that the consequences of sex—more and more people—may in themselves be potent stimuli to violence. Not only may they stimulate violence, but, more importantly, they may change the condition of violence so that controls break down. If the species is living in dispersed bands with plenty of room for maneuvers, violence will occur. But it will itself be dispersed and sporadic, and related rather to the internal status structure of the band than to conquest or genocide. This we have established. But begin to fill in the intervening spaces with more and more people, and violence spills over onto them and envelops them. Hunters need space and will fight for it. Those who take up the valuable hunting territory will be destroyed. This rarely happens with hunters, because they manage, and managed for all that tediously familiar ninety-nine percent of our history, to keep their populations down to sizes that were in keeping with their hunting ecologies.[23] There was, besides, always somewhere else to go. And, like Schaller's lions, in the face of implacable and unbeatable harassment, one could always run like hell. Little hunting bands on the move from Siberia—perhaps about six of them—eventually populated the whole American continent.[24] Small crews of brown-skinned people from Southeast Asia filled up the islands of the Pacific. And so on. But once areas were filled, they proceeded, with the advent of agriculture and settlement, to become fuller and fuller, and soon there was nowhere else to go. Violence in these complex new circumstances continued, but it was now more difficult to contain. Dispersed rivals clash at intervals, then go away to lick wounds, celebrate or mourn, and prepare to try again. It all has a nice rhythm, a predictability, a control. But when potential rivals are living on top of one another all the time, they cannot play these games. The provocations to violence are constant, and the enemy is always there. He will go away only if he is killed, and there is often a great deal of killing to be done. Even if he is killed, he will be quickly replaced as human population continues to grow. It is endless.

It is often argued that sheer numbers, that density itself, is a cause or even *the* cause of constant armed violence in man.[25] This is only a half-truth. Man was violent *before* he had dense populations. What the dense populations do is to make the ancient means of organizing violence impossible—to change the stakes completely. We no longer wish to score off our enemies, but either to get rid of them to make way for ourselves or to conquer them so that we can use them for our purposes.

Density is not a basic *cause* of violence, but it remains a possibility —some would say a distinct probability—that density has its own pathological consequences, which, benignly enough, reduce the very density that causes them. For animal populations one can work out a "critical population density"—a figure above which it is dangerous for the population to rise without risk of social breakdown and subsequent drastic loss of numbers.[26] This ultimately has the effect of keeping the population in balance with its resources, but resources themselves do not seem the prime cause of the breakdowns. Populations with ample food, shelter, light, etc., will nevertheless crack up if the numbers rise above a certain point. This is because animals have space needs, social needs. They need a certain amount of space in which to perform their natural functions, and without this space these functions cannot be performed. If they are crowded, their sociospatial system breaks down, with the result that many die or remain unborn. Mothers will kill their young or neglect them until they starve to death. Animals low in the hierarchy will be arrested in constant submission and starve. Strong animals will kill one another in frantic fights. Pregnant females will abort or absorb the eggs back into the uterus. Disease will spread easily, and some animals will die "spontaneously," apparently from stress.[27]

The likenesses of animal to human breakdown in dense conditions are obvious and do not have to be challenged. But with humans the matter is more complex. Again, it does not seem to be sheer density— not density as such—that causes the pathologies. It is the conditions of density. There may be some features of density that inevitably give rise to stress, but it seems that it is not large numbers but the way the large numbers live and are organized that counts. We may have psychological difficulties dealing with large numbers, but we can deal with them more easily if they are crowded into luxury apartments than if they are herded into tenements. The inhabitants of the luxury apartments in overcrowded Manhattan can get out, move around a lot, and take long holidays in the Bahamas or on yachts. The apartment is simply a home base for a ranging life that can be quite satisfactory. The tenement dweller in Harlem is trapped physically and socially. There is nowhere for him to go. His adaptability is remarkable, but not infinite. Physically, socially, mentally, at some point he will crack, or withdraw, or revolt. And his revolt will often seem to the luxury-apartment dweller or the suburbanite to be of that random, destructive kind that afflicts the overtaxed society of animals. Density, plus social and physical constraint, seems to be the condition for social pathology in human communities. This follows from the failures of political and economic systems. It is not so much that slum dwellers are denied space, although this is important, as that they are denied participation. The denial of space is only a symptom of the denial of the right to participate. Given all the space in the world, men will revolt and resort to violence if they are too severely peripheralized for too long by too few.[28]

If we cannot use population pressure as an alibi for our violent propensities, there is still the dreadful truth that this very pressure increases the incidence and extent of violence and multiplies its consequences so that it embraces women and children and the old and innocent. While congregation may not be a novel and root cause of violence, dispersion would certainly help in the process of containing it.

The dispersed hunters are plugged into nature in a very profound and direct way. What the naturalist Wynne-Edwards has called "conventionalized competition" seems to be a prerequisite for population control in animal societies.[29] Uncontrolled violence would be damaging and would ultimately wipe the species out. But if the violence is "conventionalized"—or "ritualized"—it has the effect of spreading animals over a wide area. The animals so dispersed will guard and maintain territories on which they will breed. Those that do not obtain territories will not breed. This is one way of helping to keep numbers and resources in balance. It has been argued that social life in the world of animate things has its origin in the conventionalizing of competition for space. Human hunters are really only rather efficient predatory animals. They do what the lion and the panther do, only they do it with better brains and with tools and cultural adaptation. Thus they were able to spread to many more ecological niches than any of their predatory competitors—but they stayed within the scheme. They were hunting animals engaged in conventionalized competition, and they were consequently dispersed, and their numbers were never out of balance with their resources.[30] Exactly how this operates is not the concern here; it is still a matter of academic dispute. What is important is that at this level we were still part of the natural scheme of things, of which ritualized violence was a necessary part. It is *this* that changed with the advent of agriculture, pastoralism, and settlement, and the successive explosions of numbers that now threaten to double the population of the globe every thirty years. About ten thousand years ago we cut adrift from nature with a vengeance; if our violence now seems unnatural, it is not because it is alien to us but because we have drastically changed the scenario.

This raises the whole issue of the role of "territoriality" in human violence, about which so much has been written. That territoriality is closely connected with population control on the one hand, and with the conventionalizing of violence on the other, is obvious enough. Whether or not the defense of territory depends on an "instinct" common to man and animals is another point. In some species there seems to be a deeply programmed quality; in others there seems to be a contingency on circumstances. Many primates do not become "territorial" unless they are literally pushed for space. Hunting animals often do not defend specific areas, but have overlapping "ranges." There are many variations on this theme, and it does not really need a uniform instinct to explain what happens; the fact is obvious that no two animals can occupy the same space. Where space has a value for the animals, they will compete for it as for anything else. In this sense man is a territorial animal as much as any other, and he will accordingly fight over territory. But he will fight over so many other things as well. A piece of the earth's surface can become one of the things to which a group of humans express deep emotional commitment, but so can a language, a religion, a flag, or a way of life. It is hard to disentangle these things. When a people seem to be fighting for territory—in driving off an invader, for example—what they are probably really fighting is the prospect of domination. If an animal loses its territory, it loses its place in the breeding system, and perhaps even its life. A conquered people do not in the same sense "lose" their territory, but they do lose control over their own lives. Nevertheless, a man's defense of his home, and a people's of their homeland, are acts of the same order as an animal's defense of its piece of ground. Many of the same basic animal processes are brought into play. The analogy breaks down in the identification of human *property* with animal territory. The animal's defense of its space is absolute in the sense that if it loses this, it is finished. The same is sometimes true of human territory in the strict sense, and people will fight tenaciously for their farms, hunting grounds, and sacred places. But human property in general, including real estate and even parts of national entities, has the other essential feature that makes it truly human: it can be exchanged. Men will fight to defend and expand their property. Fights over women in primitive societies are mostly fights over women as property. They have nothing to do with fights over territory as such.[31]

While humans do have fights over territory that are equivalent to animal conflicts, their fights over property and over other focuses of symbolic attachment such as nationality or religion are not so readily equatable. These have much more to do with the preservation of autonomy and control over one's own life, both personal and national, than with the defense of a patch of earth.

What overcrowding and overpopulation do is to restrict this autonomy more and more—this sense of having some control over a personal life and fate. One is literally and metaphorically restricted. Huge populations require ever more efficient and impersonal bureaucracies, and the number of positions of dominance open to males does not increase in proportion. The cabinet in America is not much bigger now in a country of two hundred million than it was at the time of the Revolution, when there were only four million. And there is still only one President. Males live longer—one cause of population increase, of course—and continue to occupy positions of power, while generations turn over beneath them in increasing impotence.[32] What is lost in all this is the hunter's sense of his own power and responsibility and his immediate participation in the society on which he depends and which in a real sense depends on him. It is *autonomy* that is threatened by numbers and that results in frustration and an ever-ready tendency to resort to violent solutions: one thing that easily turns this animal on to violence is to cramp its style.

Here, once again, we encounter a gross and tragic paradox. One of the most direct and real ways people have to gain an outright sense of their own significance, and of their elaborate connection with their community and its future, is by having children. The widespread difficulty the species encounters in limiting population by conscious and technical means reflects an underlying unit of the biogrammar that is immensely persuasive, highly energized, and a source of special, long-term satisfactions. It is more than sentimentality to assert that the pleasures and provocations of motherhood and fatherhood are everywhere known by most adult men and women. That there may be disillusion and hardship for some from having children underlines the force of the pattern that urges people to undertake the responsibility, nonetheless. From an innocent perspective, it is altogether astonishing that so many people will either consciously or with less clear intention embark on the expensive and demanding career of parenthood. Why should members of even materialist cultures agree to devote their future and comfort to unborn organisms that will give little of formal value in return, except—what? Pleasure? A sense of personal continuity? An offering to one's parents? A re-creation of youth? Insurance of continued control of one's property? To cement a marriage or stimulate an as yet uncontracted one?

All such reasons may apply. But the simplest one is that the program is there, from puberty. All communities offer a sense of joy and accomplishment to parents of newborns. Infants and children themselves are extremely attractive organisms most of the time (as they are throughout the primate species). Having babies confirms adulthood in a strangely conclusive way. And finally—until this generation—conceiving and bearing a child was a deeply constructive affirmation of social ties and the continuity of the species. Even where contraceptive information is widespread, many babies are born. It may be claimed that the techniques are too complex and expensive and that men and women do not understand their meaning. Undoubtedly this is partly true, but the reduction in birth rates resulting from the pill is sufficiently small to force us to conclude that, for whatever reasons they do so, humans want to have children, enjoy having them, and seem intent on having them, despite options and blandishments to the contrary. For example, it is estimated that between a quarter and a third of North American babies are conceived out of wedlock—against law, against custom, against economic self-interest of many of the persons involved, and with little "going for" the pregnancy apart from its role in uniting a couple and its effective meaning for the life cycles of the parents.

This is not to overlook the effect of contraception and particularly abortion on reducing populations, particularly in Eastern Europe and

Japan. Where it is crowded, people have fewer children than where there is ample space for movement and play. Safe and easy legal abortion permits a conscious decision about having a child at a time when there are relatively disturbing and unpleasant hormonal changes reaching their peak in the female's body, and when the full consequences of having a first or another child become more pronounced.

Ever since Malthus, the clear consciousness of overpopulation as a problem has haunted human beings. The problem has burgeoned, until it is now staggering and beginning to approach a point of no return. The nub of the matter is that reproduction is private. For all intents and purposes, it is the consequence of an uncontrollable behavior. To have few children, people will have to decide to; and so far, the outlook for such voluntary restriction on the global scale which is necessary is unpromising. For one thing, it is not only individuals who will make their decisions in their own terms, but also governments.[33] Many governments currently support high birth rates by tax advantages and other perquisites because they are committed to a pattern of economic growth to some extent dependent on an expanding population. For another, governments always concern themselves with supplying their economies with labor—preferably native-born. For example, curious as it may seem to those who find that country already crowded enough, the Japanese government has been contemplating ways of encouraging births to fill its long-term manpower needs, since the effects of contraceptive and abortion practices have been so marked.[34] For decades France has sought to stimulate higher birth rates, and so have some Eastern European countries.[35] A worldwide birth-rate policy will be no easier to achieve than a worldwide policy of governing violence, or pollution, or the equitable distribution of wealth.

We can appreciate the problems on the international scale. What about the national? How can governments disinduce people from taking part in an enjoyable and fulfilling procedure? One answer lies in levying taxes with advantages for those who do not have children instead of for those who do. But as children are already expensive enough to parents, it is not clear that this will work. Must societies wait until the lives of adults are so cramped and ugly that it will seem merciless to bring children into the world? This may happen too late—the reproductive pattern is that uncritical and that strong.

The grimmest alternative unites population growth and violence. Faced with the mounting problems of controlling ever-greater numbers, states will have to exercise more and more rigid control over behavior. They have done this before with less justification, but as numbers lead us toward chaos and anarchy, unflinching control of even the most intimate details of lives will become more and more commonplace. The techniques exist; they need only to be applied.[36] The techniques will be applied in the name of saving humanity from itself, but we all know what happens when men achieve the kind of absolute power that such altruistic ends confer. It is too much part of the political biogrammar that power is an end in itself for us ever to trust the mandarins to act indefinitely as unselfish trustees of the public good. To control us for our own sakes, to save us from ourselves, is simply in the long run to control us for the sake of controlling us. It is only another means of putting power into the hands of a few. And when the ranks of the peripheralized become inordinately swollen, the fangs of the dominants will be lengthened and sharpened in proportion. They will not abandon violence—it is not their way; they will seek to monopolize it. And should we therefore seek to abandon violence in our turn? It is a hard question to answer for all who deplore armed and bloody conflict of any kind, and yet who are not willing to abandon human dignity.[37]

Such is the stark focus that must inevitably expose the two biological facts central to all natural process: living and dying. Who gets born and why, and who loses life and why, must preoccupy anyone interested in the species as a whole and not only in its local versions. In one way or another it seems likely that some human beings will have to try to urge many others to have only some children, or fewer children, or even none. Can this be done? Infanticide is miserable to contemplate. It is not even clear which would involve more administrative chicanery and simple human inequity—enforced celibacy, or celibacy stimulated by education. It is possible that people will accept the sanity of requiring licenses to conceive, just as there commonly are certificates of marriage. Yet this runs directly opposite to widespread feelings of all peripheralized persons that there is already too much adjudication by others of people's lives.

It is not likely that the conditions under which people now live will tend toward greater autonomy, more participation, and more provident encounter with cooperative, not antagonistic, fellow humans. It is also unlikely, given our experience so far, that administrative and political managers will yield any of their power to their clients. Precisely here the threat or reality of violence may have some meaning—when it is directed against a power structure by those who claim a more generous mandate for power and a more attractive structure with which to use this power in a wider interest. This was the bet the followers of George Washington, Padraig Pearse, Lenin, Castro, Bolívar, and Tito made. Communities may win or lose this often desperate and seemingly quixotic bet on energy and will against structure and the certainty of power. But it may be idle to ignore the forces potentially generated by the human wish to maintain at least some of the major conditions of being human in a situation in which these conditions threaten to become so scarce as to force some members of our species to live in ways that render them very much less than human.

In "Political Nature" we related the political system and the breeding system in primates and explored their role in the control of violence. We saw how in man these two systems became separated. In this chapter we have come around again to looking at the direct and potentially disastrous relationship between the political and reproductive systems of contemporary man. It would be a joyless anticlimax if man's extraordinary trajectory through the scheme of nature should come full circle to the principle that only the elite may breed.

9.

THE
CITY
OF MAN

OUR AIM HAS been to put a lot of well-known facts into a new focus—or a not-so-new focus if our claim to be in the Darwinian tradition is correct. We have tried to look at fairly general features of social structure and process that are true for all human societies as end products of the evolution of social behavior in our species. Building on those general features that we hold in common with our nearest relatives (and some more distant, for that matter), we have examined the consequences for the biology of behavior that followed from the hunting revolution and the transition to humanity. What we have examined is the transition from the simple life to the symbol life. But in progressing to those vast structures of symbol and fantasy that we call human cultures, man retained much of his primate heritage. The old primate brain was not lost, it was augmented. The old primate behavior was not abandoned but rechanneled, amplified, and supplemented by the rapidly expanding hunting forebrain. The end result is a creature that actively demands certain inputs and actively puts out certain energies involving the other creatures in its social universe. What we have tried to do is to locate these various basic inputs and outputs, for they form the skeleton of the human social biogrammar. This presents a very different picture of human social behavior from the one offered by cultural anthropology, behaviorist psychology, or instinct theory.

We neither posit specific instincts in man, nor do we see the human infant as a tabula rasa. We see certain human institutions as inevitable, since they follow from the interactions between creatures who are wired to learn certain things, to expend certain energies, and to respond to certain stimuli in ways that have been built into them by the peculiar evolutionary history of the species. If our perspective has any merit, it is that it focuses on these basic grammatical processes that unite mankind into a body of people all speaking the same behavioral language. Social science heretofore has tended to be obsessed with dialect differences, and has even denied that the dialects are linked into one language. While it is perfectly true that the speakers of different dialects often have great difficulty in communicating, it is also true that they are in some very profound way speaking the *same* language. It is this basic unity that we are interested in, and it is the basic categories and processes of the universal behavioral grammar of the species that we have been exploring. An important philosophical outcome of this kind of inquiry is a reassertion of the fundamental unity of mankind, and a natural basis for a theory of "natural" rights. The rights of man are not cultural inventions but statements about the nature of the creature. Men are not simply the creatures of culture, they are the creatures that create culture, because that is the kind of creature they are. But this is jumping ahead.

What are the limits of our approach? On the one hand it appears grandiose to seem to be mapping out huge schemes for the total understanding of human behavior; on the other, it appears simple to reduce human behavior to a few economical principles. Again, the grammatical analogy might help. Any outline of the grammar of a language is at one and the same time more comprehensive and more simple than any actual lengthy expression of the language in prose or poetry. The outline goes beyond any particular expression of the language by providing the rules it is necessary to observe in order to produce more expressions; but on the other hand it cannot, in and of itself, produce the expression nor predict any future expressions. This is precisely the limitation of our approach. We can point out the very general rules that must be observed if behavior is to be "human." We can also point out what will happen if these rules are abrogated or distorted. We cannot predict how the rules will be applied or distorted in any particular case, or how eloquently or clumsily their expression in actual behavior will emerge. No grammar can predict what people will actually say; only a close attention to their literary and oral traditions, their style and manner of speech, and the ethnography of their speech habits will allow us anywhere near our goal. Even if our aim is not prediction but "understanding," a grammar is of limited help. One must know French grammar in order to read Balzac, but this knowledge alone does not guarantee that one will "understand" Balzac in the fullest and widest sense. Thus, detailed analyses of historical events and cultural patterns are very necessary to a full understanding of human social behavior. Our approach does not mean to usurp these at all. All we would argue is that if one wants to learn a language one had better start by knowing the grammar.

Our problem as analysts of our own behavior is like that of speakers who deal with their own language. Students of English literature who speak English anyway do not need to learn English grammar in order to understand the symbolism of Ulysses or the unconscious origins of Shakespeare's Hamlet. If they wanted to follow out the philosophical development of Goethe's ideas, however, they would have to master German grammar. Our own social scientists take the grammar of human behavior very much for granted, since they are humans and they behave. When they come to deal with other species, it is a different matter: the grammar becomes important and cannot be taken for granted. We have treated our own behavior as if it were that of another species, as if it were an alien grammar whose code has to be cracked. At the moment, researchers move uncomfortably close to the Japanese scholar who is interested in the role of word rhythms and symbols in Nabokov but who does not know English. Or even to the serious Nabokov student who does not understand Nabokov's native language. Our concern is with the point of departure and not the meaning of the exploration and its consequence. Anyway, much of the work on human behavior now uses some notion of biogrammar, but it is an inadequate one that harshly separates man from the natural circumstances that envelop him, and from the specifically human portion of his primate history.

It would be stupid and cheerless to demand a unanimous approach and an affection for a new orthodoxy. The form of this biosociological explanatory exercise is relatively underdeveloped; what we have tried to do is create an opportunity for more precise and organized analysis of propositions that appear to flow legitimately and helpfully from well-tested work in the natural sciences. Finally, it is evident that facts can be interpreted in a variety of ways, and while we are willing to stand by the structure of our argument and the components with which we have made it, we are and must be strategically skeptical of any closure of these matters and of a set of *dicta* so self-supporting that critique of one invalidates all and evaluation of the set condemns the components.

More than one grammar can account for the actual speech of any linguistic community. Grammars based too heavily on Latin models, it has been shown, often turn out to be totally inadequate to describe economically the facts of very unlatinate languages. Alternative kinds of grammar exist for describing the actual speech of English speakers. We have suggested that the grammars of behavior based on learning theory or enculturation are not as adequate, not as comprehensive, not as economical as a grammar based on the biological nature of man. The proof of the pudding lies in its eating. The better the grammar, the easier it is to understand the language. The adequacy of a biobehavioral grammar should, once it gets beyond the sketchy stage it is in at the moment, enable people to understand their own social behavior better and hence to become better speakers, or at least to understand the limits of their capacity: they may well be trying to say too much too quickly. There is ample material for both optimists and pessimists. For the former a better knowledge of human nature may lead us to become better and more sensitive humans; for the latter this knowledge can only confirm that in some areas at least people have lapsed into irreversible behavioral gibberish.

There is also room for maneuver for both conservatives and radicals. Our perspective justifies neither one nor the other, but it can provide material for both. No attempt at a scientific assessment of human possibilities and limits justifies any moral position, since ideologies select from among the range of these possibilities those they wish to conserve or those they wish to change. Conservatives may be very foolish in trying to retain certain features on the grounds that they are part of "human nature" when they are clearly nothing of the kind. This was the fault of Social Darwinism and laissez-faire. Unbridled competition with no mitigating redistributive and communal grooming system is not an expression of human nature. But on the other hand radicals may be just as foolish in trying to make drastic alterations in something that should be rechanneled or molded gently because it does indeed reflect a basic propensity. It may even be that radicals are not radical enough, since their grasp of reality is colored by the traditional visions of the future they so ardently espouse. If our analysis of male-female differences is at all correct, then the greater participation of women in national life will not come about within the framework of the system as it stands. The realities of male-female interaction will simply get in the way. It may need something much more drastic like laws that compel boards of directors to have female members, or female quotas in legislatures, before the greater participation that would obviously be to everyone's benefit could be effected. On the other hand, radicals are undoubtedly right to suggest that war machines are a primary cause of wars, and that by dismantling these we would go a long way toward cutting down on warfare. They are right, but for reasons they may not be aware of.

We could proceed to list an elaborate series of policy proposals that could follow from the analyses we have made. But we do not regard this as either our responsibility or our particular competence. To state the matter as citizens, we see our function as part of the preliminary process of diagnosis and analysis. In this sense we are biological Fabians—committed to understanding biological infrastructure as a basis for social change, just as English Fabians were devoted to comprehending the factual realities of English society. Only such introductory social-scientific work, they knew, would permit social reforms to be undertaken with information in hand, and with some confidence that desirable innovations would have a predictable effect on social circumstances that had been clearly described.

This is not a particularly glamorous position to adopt, nor is it immediately exciting to those who would seek instant alteration of social conditions and rapid redress of obvious historical wrongs and inefficiencies. Some of these may be possible indeed. But our own confrontation with the data and theory of natural science in conjunction with what is known about human social life and how humans behave urges us to insist on the need for a tutored and probing knowledge of the range of options available to ambitious reformers. Paradoxically, the experience of researching and writing this book has committed us to the position that radical social changes will be within our grasp only if we first know the shape of the conservatism of the species and build on this with more than hope and ardor.

For humans alone among all the species on earth are able to organize themselves consciously against their own extinction. We are our own conservationists as well as our own veterinarians. And this should push home the point that what is proposed here is not a kind of determinism, any more than the law of gravity is a kind of determinism. To those who think that the law of gravity interferes with their freedom, there is nothing to say. To most sensible people this law is simply something that has to be taken into account in dealing with the world, like the second law of thermodynamics. If we ignore the famous second law, we will waste a lot of time trying to make perpetual-motion machines and other useless devices. In the behavioral sphere we may be ignoring laws just as fundamental. Our ability to ignore them illustrates the lack of determinism involved. We are not here proposing that man *must* behave in certain ways, but only that he is programmed *to* behave in certain ways. If he chooses to behave otherwise, then he must do so with as much hope of success as those who ignore the basic physical laws. Man conquered the physical world not by insisting that he could *outdo* nature but by finding out exactly what it was he could *do with* nature. Our modest suggestion is that the same demanding principle should be applied to our attempts at social transformations.

At this point we must consciously cross the boundary between scientific analysis and moral judgment. We can begin with another animal's situation—the chicken. Much of the world's chicken population lives in batteries—in highly mechanized assembly lines in which the sole concern is for the production of eggs and edible chickens. The creatures are bred to suit some market need or other—for more breast meat, smaller beaks and legs, faster laying cycles, and so on. But the behavior of the chicken is of no concern to anyone except insofar as it abets or hinders the process of production and of making profits. The unfortunate animals remain chickens, of course, but their behavior is not chicken behavior in the broad sense, and their view of the entire matter is perhaps reflected in the precautions necessary to prevent their flight from the specialized conditions under which they live.

The analogy with humans is all too clear. Humans can be made to live in battery-farm conditions, and to some observers either prison life or city life or Hong Kong life or the rat race or what have you are merely disguised versions of the miserable chickens' circumstance. Whatever one's response to this lament, the point remains that the limiting conditions of what can be done to human beings in the name of some theory or some power structure or some experiment are not settled; there are always innovators and tyrants with exotic mandates who claim some special view of what life should be like. The whole argument has been that while human potential for change and for being coerced by power and symbol is enormous, nonetheless there remain certain regularities in our needs: even astronauts have to defecate, and even blind children smile at people.

Perhaps our most profound confusion is that in precivilized conditions what were simply human needs, in postcivilized conditions became human rights. In dealing with our hunting evolution, we have documented at length what these needs are: needs for space to move about in; for a share of the communal kill; for participation in the predatory activity of the whole group; for a chance to rise in status through merit; for an opportunity to take risks; for the means to make deals and alliances; for exploration and novelty when young; for a sense of security derived from close association with the mother; for education geared to the realities of the life cycle; for accurate knowledge of the environment; for a chance to be brave and prove oneself; for a place at the triumph feast; for an acknowledgment of individual worth; for children and the caring for them and the protection and security that accompany this; for recreation and free use of the imagination; for support in times of stress; and above all the intense need to contribute with dignity to the community of which one is part.

These and more are the basic behavioral needs of the creature. They should not be things it has to claim and justify, any more than it has to claim and justify its right to breathe, or the chicken has to justify its right to peck, the hawk to swoop. We do not ask whether the cock has a right to crow; we accept that crowing is what the cock does. To prevent it from crowing is to take away something that is intrinsic to being a cock. The same is true, for example, of the so-called "right to work" in human societies, or the "right to vote." It is heartless to claim that these are abstract symbolic things that must be justified on the basis of divine intent or rational political theory; they are statements about what it is to be a human being: that a human being is the kind of animal that, of its very nature, contributes its labor to the group and participates in the conduct of the group's affairs. The "right" to a minimum wage, for example, or to adequate and inexpensive medical care, or to an education, or to a free and creative use of the intellect, is simply a "right" to behave in a way that is intrinsic to being human; it needs no more justification than the crowing of the cock.

By the same token, however, we cannot expect Utopias. It is as natural to man to create hierarchies, to attach himself to symbolic causes, to attempt to dominate and coerce others, to resort to violence either systematic or lunatic, to assert, to connive, to seduce, to exploit. The only possible Utopia, in our perspective, would lie in a return to a simple hunting existence. But this is impossible. We have crossed the divide in terms of population alone. Our societies of the future will be places that will have to deal with the continuing tension between the needs of a hunting primate on the one hand, and the conditions it has created for itself on the other—conditions that often work to negate the very needs that move it in the first place. Neither the state nor bureaucracy will wither away, and we are not evolved to cope with either. Nor were we evolved to cope with violence in the context in which it now manifests itself. But this new context is one with which we are stuck, and it is this with which we have to deal. Utopian idealism can only help to make the misery more unbearable by deluding us into thinking that we can, by simple acts of will and rational activity, make either a different creature out of man, or wish away the tensions that emanate from his premature leap into civilization. The reality is difficult enough to cope with, but we cannot begin to cope with it until we accept it as real. Utopias may be as careless in their treatment of the basic needs of the species as the real societies they implicitly or explicitly reproach and reject. It is difficult to envisage the possibility of human society without violence, disease, selfishness, oppression, and injustice. These are as much a part of human life as their opposites— love, health, altruism, and fair dealing. Many different social systems and sets of cultural beliefs are compatible in some degree with the range of human needs—even systems that may be repulsive to the tender-minded or obnoxious to the tough.

The insights gained from the evolutionary, species-wide perspective do not lead to Utopia or any very sanguine and comforting forecasts about the future of mankind. But it is our belief that they leave us less helpless in the long run. Without this perspective we are not tackling reality but only our own cultural versions of reality—and often just our conceit about what reality should be. With this perspective we should be in a position to assess what the problems really are, and to tackle them with a knowledge of how they came to be problems in the first place. Most of our problems with crime, economics, political unrest, the revolt of youth, the disaffection of women, the clash of races, are behavioral problems. They have to do with the constraints and distortions of behavior that we create, or, to be kind, that are created by the almost impossibly difficult context into which we are trying to fit our evolved human behavior. The behavior is in many cases clearly wrong for the context, and in other cases the context can only twist, fragment, and frustrate the behavior. We hear ourselves speak our own behavioral language through a set of amplifiers and loudspeakers that deafen us to our own words and garble our grammar. As long as we know the grammar, we can at least try to retune the instruments.

If there is any hope or confidence in the future of man, it resides in the lie this perspective gives to the dismal theories of culturalists of whatever school. If man were indeed a blank slate for his culture to write on at will whatever perverse message it chose, we would be in even greater peril than we appear to be. Our capacity to produce hideous cultures is immense, and we indulge it with a grotesque fondness. But time and time again men stand up and say no to their cultures in the name of humanity. And even if their versions of this humanity may differ the one from the other, there are enough common elements to suggest that enough men have an inkling of the grammar to demand that we speak properly. If the culturalists were correct, men would be wholly brainwashed by their cultures. Nevertheless, men keep asserting, by violence if necessary, those very basic needs that are part of the evolved repertoire of our behavior. Men do not need to learn or to be taught that slavery and exploitation are inhuman. They know they are. And they know this because they are human themselves, and they understand what it is to be dehumanized.

The Renaissance was a time of splendid and delicate contortion that we now admire and praise as the beginning of personality, of perspective, of a devotion to the protection an individual must have from the maelstrom of community. But it robbed humans of something to which some quick mention has already been made in this book— a sense of the ordered likelihood of evil and connivance and the absolute requirement for a special supervisory abstraction to assimilate the diverse human energies and turbulences in any place. God commanded, and in their lights kings, doges, princes, popes, cardinals, and sundry chiefs interpreted this improbable scheme first to support their palaces and even finally to ensure the persistence of their Genevans, Kumasians, Bangkokians, or Pekingese. At least in Europe, God could rule, and a host of squalid well-placed entrepreneurs tax-farm in his name. Out of the intimacy of empires no bigger than a Paris *arrondissement* or Philadelphia ward they established some theory of feudal order—almost primate in its certainty—of the necessity of human variation and the community of all those who served the God nobody had seen.

No such generous God interested in our welfare and interpreted by understandably enthusiastic divine-right kings and cardinals can help a species driven to distraction by its success in breeding, holding its nose against the rot of the mounds of products it tastes and drops away, and warmly expending millions of dollars every year on supersonic shields and spears and date-line-crossing missiles. Spaceship earth is on its own; so are its humans. Like hereditary shareholders in some golden corporation, we all have a piece of the remarkable genetic action, a touch of the wealth that the ages of testing, evolution, and defeat have laid by against good times and hard times. It may be stupid to assert these are especially bad times and that our credit with the natural order must be more carefully used than ever. This was the alarm of Greeks and Romans; Jeremiah gave the passion a name; Luther, Napoleon, and Hitler all threatened the old and good order with remarkable catastrophe. But these were parochial radicals—all believers in some preposterous charmless pomp about superior religions, superior classes, superior races, superior nations, even superior individuals. It is not the extermination of a class, religion, race, or nation that we face, but the possible extermination of the species. If the universal megalopolis that we are building for ourselves can no longer find its unity as the City of God, then it must find it as the City of Man. That in this city there may not be room or enthusiasm for a crying baby or an uncertain senile man is a violation of the glory of the prince and a rebuking disharmony for the melody of the poet. No one can make city walls out of paper theory, or even metal spikes, and no one can utterly destroy with ease the intimate affections and thoughtful providence of mothers and fathers and friends and children, even of pet dogs, even for familiar streets and places. No suave formula can entertain the citizens and ensure survival, and no special machine can proof us against disrepair. A stubborn million-year-old animal pushes its big-brained head above the litter of pieces and contrivances and stares with some new confusion at the other bigbrains across the way, in the other dump. Once before they joined to make a little empire. Again that stamina for encounter and that tenderness about the movements in the tribe are necessary, if only that swollen brain can contrive a method to harmonize all the massive schemes and affirm the absolute value of intimacies no more extensive than the reach of an unarmed arm.

NOTES

Books and articles are referred to by name of author and date of publication. Thus, Hull 1943 refers to the bibliography entry: Hull, C. L. 1943. *Principles of Behavior*. New York: Appleton, Century. References to books are to the edition actually consulted.

1. BEGINNING BIOGRAMMAR

1. Works by Darwin: Darwin 1859; 1871; 1873. For modern reviews: De Beer 1968; Roberts and Harrison 1959. General views of Darwinism: Barnett 1958; Eiseley 1958. Darwinism and the social sciences: Banton 1961. An anthropological approach: Alland 1967.
2. On adaptation: Williams 1966.
3. Striding walk: Napier 1967.
4. On concept of "species specific" behavior: Hinde and Tinbergen 1958; Tinbergen 1963.
5. Animal communication systems: Critchley 1958; Haldane 1955; Marler 1967; Sebeok 1965; Tinbergen 1962. On animal communication and human languages: Hockett 1958; 1959.
6. On primate threat gestures: Wickler 1967.
7. Herring gulls: Tinbergen 1953b.
8. Hamadryas: Kummer 1967; 1968.
9. Human gift giving: Mauss 1925.
10. Chimpanzees: Goodall 1968.

11. "Biogram" coined by: Count 1958-1959. Developed further in: Count 1958; 1967.
12. For a development of this argument (on which the chapter is partly based): Fox 1970a. *See also:* Dillon ed. 1971.
13. On physical continuity: Clark 1950.
14. Behavior and speciation: Romer 1958.
15. Bipedalism: Napier 1964.
16. Evolution of brain and behavior: Hassler and Stephen 1966; MacLean 1964; Roe and Simpson 1958, part II. *See also:* Penfield and Rasmussen 1950.
17. Anatomical evolution generally: Campbell 1966; Napier 1970; Pfeiffer 1969. For a comparative social ethological perspective: Crook 1970.
18. The "culturalist" position (attacked by Ardrey 1970 as "environmental-ism") is echoed in most of the official pronouncements and textbooks of cultural anthropology and sociology. For examples from anthropology: Boas 1948; Bock 1969; Kaplan 1965; Kroeber 1917; 1952 (a partial re-traction); Murdock 1945; White 1948; 1949; 1959. For criticism: Opler 1964. For an extended and perceptive review: Bidney 1953. For review of political aspects: Bressler 1968; Tiger 1970c. For a sociologist's view of the innate: Ginsburg 1964 (1921). Definitions of culture: Kroeber and Kluck-hohn 1952. The nature-culture distinction: Lévi-Strauss 1949; Malinow-ski 1944. Conditioning, reinforcement, behaviorism: Hull 1943; Pavlov 1927; Skinner 1953; Watson 1930.
19. Chomsky 1965; 1966; 1968. Lenneberg 1967.
20. On instinct: Barnett 1967; Bowlby 1969, vol. 1, part II; Lorenz 1965; Schiller 1957; Thorpe 1956; Tinbergen 1951. On human instincts: Crombie 1965; Fletcher 1957. An elaboration of instinct theory regarding man: McDougall 1908. On the demise of instinct theory: Beach 1950; 1955. On the ideological aspects: Pastore 1949.
21. Needs and functional prerequisites: Aberle *et al.* 1950; Malinowski 1944.
22. Relations between older and younger males: Nissen 1961. Initiation: Tiger 1969, chap. 6.
23. Evolution and natural selection: Fisher 1958; Huxley 1963; Simpson 1950; 1953; Smith 1958; Tax 1960.
24. Evolution of behavior: Fox 1967b; Freedman 1968; Gavan 1955; Lorenz 1950; 1958; 1965; Roe and Simpson 1958; Simons 1962; Tinbergen 1960a; 1960b; 1964; 1965. Classic paper: Huxley 1914. On "ethology" as the science of the evolution of behavior: Eibl-Eibesfeldt 1968; 1970; Eibl-Eibesfeldt and Kramer 1958; Freedman 1965; Hess 1962; Hinde 1959; 1966; Huxley 1963; Roeder 1963; Thorpe 1956; Tinbergen 1953a; 1955; 1963. For criticism: Lehrman 1953; Schneirla 1956. For a defense: Lorenz 1965; 1969. *See also:* Hebb and Thompson 1954; Klopfer and Hailman 1967; Scott 1958.
25. Genetic code: Crick 1962.
26. Life cycle: Bonner 1965.
27. Brains producing culture: Keith 1948; Kroeber 1948 (1923), chap. 2.

28. Criticisms of this position: Geertz 1965; Howell 1964; Washburn and Howell 1960.
29. Toolmaking and use by early man: Dart 1957; 1959; Lancaster 1968; Napier 1962; Oakley 1950; 1957; 1961.
30. Tool use in chimpanzees: Goodall 1964.
31. Tools and brain evolution: Washburn 1959; 1960. For a critique of brain size as a criterion of advance: Holloway 1966. For another view: Caspari 1963. For evolution of specific areas of brain: Kotchetkova 1960.
32. On hunting as a selection pressure: Ardrey 1961; Dart 1953; 1958; 1959; Read 1920. For another view: Jolly 1970.
33. Speech and evolution: Hockett and Ascher 1964; Lancaster 1968.
34. Speculations on selection pressures affecting the evolution of primate and early human behavior: Bartholomew and Birdsell 1953; Crook and Gartlan 1966; Etkin 1954; Kortland and Kooij 1963; Shultz 1961.
35. Evolution of rule-obeying behavior: Waddington 1961.
36. Habits and instincts: Russell and Russell 1961.
37. Culture as selection pressure: Garn 1964.
38. Culture as aspect of human biology: Dobzhansky 1962; Simpson 1966.
39. For a bold and prophetic statement of a similar viewpoint to the one argued here, and one that contradicted the prevalent culturalist stand: Wissler 1916; 1923. For some relevant modern statements: Chapple 1970; Freedman 1967; Freeman 1966; Haldane 1956; Hallowell 1950; 1956; 1960; 1962. For a review of some of the issues: Callan 1970.
40. On possible antiquity of hominid line: Leakey 1967: Pilbeam 1967; Simons 1964; 1965. For another view setting a later date: Sarich 1968; Wilson and Sarich 1969.
41. On antiquity of known hominids: Clark 1970; Howell 1969; Rheinhold 1971. On *Australopithecinae:* Broom 1949; Broom and Schepers 1946; Clark 1967; Robinson 1964.
42. *Homo erectus:* Howells 1966.
43. For good general reviews: Washburn 1965; 1968; Washburn and Jay 1968.
44. On "newer" and "older" parts of brain: MacLean 1962; 1964; 1967.
45. Selection for immunity to epidemics: Livingstone 1960.
46. On conflicts between older and newer parts: Koestler 1967.

2. POLITICAL NATURE

1. Ant and insect societies: Kettlewell 1965; Richard 1953; Schneirla 1941.
2. Social organization of animals generally: Allee 1958; Eisenberg 1966; Etkin 1964.
3. Competition, pair-formation, territory, and breeding: Wynne-Edwards 1962.
4. Formation of systems through persisting dominance relationships: Chance and Jolly 1970; Tiger 1970a.

5. Major sources on primate social behavior: Altmann 1965; 1967; Carpenter 1964; DeVore 1965b; Hall 1965b; Imanishi 1960; 1963; Jay 1968; Morris 1967; Southwick 1963. General information on primates: Napier and Napier 1967.
6. Savanna primates and human evolution: DeVore and Washburn 1963; Jay 1968; Washburn and DeVore 1961. An alternative view: Reynolds 1966a; 1968.
7. Sex as basic bond: Sahlins 1959; 1960. Based on: Zuckerman 1932. Critique: Lancaster and Lee 1965.
8. Red deer: Darling 1937.
9. Effect of high-ranking mothers on rank of offspring: Kaufman 1966; 1967; Kawai 1965; Kawamura 1965; Koford 1963b; Koyama 1967; Sade 1965; 1967.
10. Care of infants by males: Itani 1963.
11. Watchfulness and attention: Chance 1967.
12. Dominance and breeding: Chance 1962b; Chance and Mead 1953; DeVore 1965; Ginsburg 1968.
13. Hunting transition: Lee and DeVore 1968. *See also:* note 32 in Chapter 1.
14. Fission in primate groups: Furuya 1969; Koford 1963a.
15. Size of hunting populations: Birdsell 1953; 1957; 1958.
16. On King Ismail: Barbour 1965.
17. Types of political domination: Weber 1947. Discussion of Weber: Bendix 1960.
18. On despotism: Wittfogel 1957.
19. Disraeli on aristocracy: Blake 1966.
20. Rebellion and feudalism: Gluckman 1954; 1955; 1963.
21. On badges of rank, etc.: Spencer 1876.
22. Stability of constitutional monarchies: Lipset 1959.
23. Visibility and democratic politics: Canetti 1962; Wallas 1948.
24. Political society as the integration of unequal organisms: Ardrey 1970; Masters 1968.
25. On prophets: Emmett 1956.
26. Weber on charisma: Gerth and Mills 1948.
27. Weber on charisma and biology: Weber 1947, p. 107. *See also:* Tiger 1966.
28. Critique of bureaucracy: Merton 1957.
29. Weber on bureaucracy: Gerth and Mills 1948.
30. On days of misrule, role reversal, etc.: Gluckman 1955; Leach 1961, chap. 6; Turner 1969.
31. Loyalty and orderliness in packs: Read 1920.
32. Breeding for different behavioral strains: Fuller and Thomson 1960; Hirsch 1967; Spuhler 1968.
33. "Trainability" and nervous system: Eysenck 1951. This is an extension of Pavlov's distinction between "hysterics" and "dysthymics," *see* Pavlov 1927; 1928.
34. Devonian lung fishes and conservatism of innovation: Romer 1958; 1959.
35. For a biological view of politics as a science: Somit 1968; Somit, Davies, and Schwartz (forthcoming).

3. BOND ISSUE ONE

1. Crow Indians: Lowie 1956.
2. On Kibbutz socialization: Spiro 1956; 1958. Kibbutz exogamy: Shepher 1971.
3. Bonding, aggression, and territory: Lorenz 1966.
4. Mother-child bond in mammals: Eisenberg 1966; Rheingold 1963.
5. Suckling and mother-child bond: Count 1967.
6. Mammalian nature of man: Hill 1957; LaBarre 1954.
7. On imprinting: Bateson 1966; Fabricius 1962; Hess 1958; 1964; Lorenz 1935; Moltz 1960; Salzen 1967. Critique: Klopfer 1965. Imprinting in humans: Ambrose 1969; Gray 1958; Hinde 1963. General discussion: Bowlby 1969, vol. 1, chap. 10.
8. Adverse effects of malnutrition on growth: Glass 1968b, part II; Zeman and Stamborough 1969.
9. Myelin and malnutrition: Chase, Dorsey, and McKhann 1967; Stock and Smythe 1963.
10. Effects of institutionalization on children: Bowlby 1951; Provence and Lipton 1962.
11. Psychoanalytic interpretations, see e.g.: Freud 1949; Horney 1945; Klein 1949.
12. For general treatments of separation: Ainsworth 1962; Bowlby 1953; 1958; 1960; 1961a; 1961b; 1963; 1969; Cassler 1961; Mead 1962.
13. On texture: Harlow 1958; 1959. On smell: Brill 1932; Kalogerakis 1963.
14. Social development in monkeys and apes: Hinde, Rowell, and Spencer-Booth 1964; Hinde and Spencer-Booth 1967; Mason 1965a; 1965b. Primate mothers and young: DeVore 1963; Harlow 1962a; Harlow, Harlow, and Hansen 1963; Harlow and Zimmerman 1959; Lawick-Goodall 1967a.
15. Effects of deprivation on sexual behavior: Harlow 1962b; Harlow and Harlow 1965.
16. Effects of deprivation on maternal behavior: Hansen 1966; Seay, Alexander, and Harlow 1964.
17. Effects of deprivation on primates generally: Griffin and Harlow 1966; Harlow and Harlow 1962; Kaufman and Rosenblum 1967a; Mason and Sponholz 1963; Nissen 1956; Seay, Hansen, and Harlow 1962. Critique: Meier 1965.
18. Mammalian mothers at parturition: Count 1967; Hediger 1955, chap. 7.
19. Exploration and curiosity in infants: Rheingold 1961; 1963.
20. Termination of bond: Kaufman and Rosenblum 1969.
21. Deer: Darling 1937.
22. Wolves: Mowat 1963; Murie 1944.
23. Hamadryas: Kummer 1968.
24. Gibbons: Carpenter 1940.
25. On family as a "natural" unit, see e.g.: Bell and Vogel 1960; Goode 1964; Murdock 1949; Westermarck 1903. On "pairing instinct": Morris 1967a; 1970.

26. For similar dissident views: Adams 1960; Bohannan 1963; Goodenough 1970; Linton 1936; Spiro 1954.
27. For a survey of patterns of attachment of males to mother-child units in man: Fox 1967a; 1970.
28. Examples of activation of brother-sister bond: deMoubray 1931; Gough 1959; 1961; Nakane 1963; Williamson 1962.
29. Examples of "sharing" between brother-sister and husband-wife ties: Eggan 1950; Malinowski 1929.
30. Examples of cooperative female households: Smith 1962; Smith 1956.
31. Kama sutra: Burton and Arbuthnot 1962 (1883). *See also:* Burton 1963 (1886).
32. On reproductive cycles in mammals and primates: Amoroso and Marshall 1960; Bullough 1961; Erickson 1967; Everett 1961; Harlow 1965b; Zuckerman 1930.
33. Savanna primate breeding systems: DeVore 1965a.
34. Smell as a sexual signal: Michael 1968; Michael and Keverne 1968.
35. Consort relationships: Reynolds 1970.
36. Desert baboons: Crook 1968; Kummer 1968.
37. Chimpanzees: Goodall 1965; Lawick-Goodall 1968; Reynolds 1965.
38. Gibbons: Carpenter 1940.
39. Carnivores and human evolution: Schaller and Lowther 1969.
40. Decline of hormonal control: Beach 1947; 1965; Ford and Beach 1952; Spuhler 1959.
41. *See* note 34.
42. On copulatory success in human and primate females: Michael 1970; Michael and Zumpe 1970; Udry and Morris 1968.
43. Female cycle generally: Dalton 1964; Moos 1969.
44. Smell sensitivity and cycle: LeMagnen 1950; 1953.
45. Hamburg 1968; Kopell 1969; Parker 1960.
46. Kopell 1969.
47. Dalton 1960b; 1964.
48. Dalton 1959; Janowsky *et al.* 1969.
49. Dalton 1960a; 1960c.
50. Pair bond and marriage: Morris 1970.
51. On courtship: Bastock 1967; Morris 1956.
52. Based on a personal communication from Dr. Kurt Freund.
53. For a development of the general argument: Fox 1967d; 1968.

4. BOND ISSUE TWO

1. Breeding systems and kinship systems: Fox 1971. *See also:* Darlington 1969.
2. Male-male bonds in general: Tiger 1969. Significance of male bonds in primates: Chance 1962a.
3. Hunting in primates: Dart 1963; Lawick-Goodall 1967b.
4. Cooperation in primates: Crook 1966. On male-female division of labor in hunters: Lee 1968. A recent general treatment of sex roles: Holter 1970.

5. Elimination of sexual competition: Sahlins 1960.
6. On exogamy and exchange of women: Chagnon 1968; Fox 1967a, chaps. 7 and 8; Lévi-Strauss 1949a; McLennan 1865; Needham 1962; Tylor 1888.
7. Shaka: Ritter 1955.
8. On topology and anthropology: Leach 1961, chap. 1. Topology as a science: Kuratowski 1962.
9. For an extended development of this argument: Fox 1971.
10. Crow wife abductions: Lowie 1956.
11. Hormones and sex behavior: Ball 1940; Beaman 1947; Harris 1964; Harris and Levine 1965; Levine 1966; Michael 1968; Money 1965; Witalen 1967; Young 1961; Young, Gay, and Phoenix 1964.
12. Sex-linked dominance: Duverger 1955; Goldberg 1968; Greenstein 1961; Murphy 1959; Royal Commission on the Status of Women 1970; Tiger 1970a; 1970b.
13. Formation of macaque groups: Vandenberg 1967.
14. Succession and control in matrilineal systems: Fox 1967a, chap. 4; Schneider and Gough 1961.
15. On the male conspiracy: Millett 1970.
16. On limited female participation in public life: Dahlstrom 1967; Evans-Pritchard 1965; Mead and Kaplan 1965; Paulme 1964.
17. Female intellect: Maccoby 1970.
18. Political goals of feminist movements: Friedan 1963; Morgan 1970. Historical account of feminism: O'Neill 1967. *See also:* Bird 1968. For a complementary statement of male difficulties: Bednarik 1970. For a review of sex differences as reflected in reading matter: White 1970.
19. Primate females and newborn infants: Hinde 1965; Rowell, Hinde, and Spencer-Booth 1964.
20. Decrease of age at puberty: Tanner 1960.
21. Initiation for girls: Brown 1963.
22. Initiation for boys: Cohen 1964; Whiting *et al.* 1958.
23. Freud: Fox 1966; 1967b; Freud 1952.
24. On gerontocratic monopoly of females: Hart and Pilling 1960; Hiatt 1967; Goodale 1962; Nissen 1961.
25. Gangs: Thrasher 1936; Whyte 1943; Yablonsky 1964. Gangs and evolution: Davis 1962.
26. Inhibition of son-mother mating in primates: Sade 1968.
27. The literature on incest is vast. For some reviews: Aberle *et al.* 1959; Fox 1962; 1967a, chap. 2; Slater 1959.
28. As evidenced, for example, in the research of Kinsey and his associates: Kinsey, Pomeroy, and Martin 1948.

5. GIVE AND TAKE

1. On gifts and counter gifts—the basic insight on which this chapter is based: Mauss 1925.

2. On property: Engels 1905; based on Morgan 1877. Evolution of private property: Hobhouse 1913.
3. Territory and real estate: Ardrey 1966. Critique: Montagu 1968, especially Crook 1968. On territory generally: Carpenter 1958; Hediger 1962; Klopfer 1969.
4. Significance of food sharing: Laughlin 1968; Sahlins 1960. Hunting and food-sharing in carnivores: Kühme 1965; Shaller and Lowther 1969.
5. Paleolithic hunters: Howell and Clark 1963; Pericot 1962; Sollas 1924. Survey of hunting societies: Lee and DeVore 1968; Service 1966. On hunting and evolution *see* note 32 in Chapter 1.
6. On significance of tools *see* notes 29–31 in Chapter 1.
7. Social organization and evolution of hunting: Washburn and Lancaster 1968.
8. On exchange of females: Lévi-Strauss 1949. *See* note 6 in Chapter 4.
9. Emotions and evolution: Hamburg 1963; 1968.
10. Polygyny of hunting leaders: Laughlin 1968; Rose 1960; 1968.
11. Sanctions against "ungenerous" chiefs: Lévi-Strauss 1944.
12. Mauss 1925.
13. General characteristics of hunting economies: Lee 1966; 1968; Woodburn 1964.
14. Redistribution and reciprocity as basic principles: Polanyi 1967; Sahlins 1963a.
15. Deevey 1960a.
16. Origins of agriculture: Childe 1946. Critique: Binford and Binford 1968.
17. Domestication: Ucko and Dimbleby 1969.
18. Animals and man: Leeds and Vayda 1965.
19. Agricultural revolution: Braidwood 1960.
20. Agriculture and civilization: Adams 1966; Flannery 1965; MacNeish 1964.
21. Peasants generally: Redfield 1956; Wolf 1966.
22. Peasant marriages, *see* e.g.: Arensberg and Kimball 1968. Peasant economies: Firth and Yamey 1964.
23. Slavery: Nieboer 1900. Serfdom: Bloch 1961. Precapitalist economies generally: Marx 1964b.
24. Industrialization and its consequences: Disraeli 1845; Engels 1958.
25. Rapid social change and its consequences: Bock 1970; Leach 1967; Mead 1970. Also, on "hot" and "cold" societies: Lévi-Strauss 1966.
26. Marx on alienation: Marx 1964a; 1967; Marx and Engels 1948 (1888). Commentaries: Aron 1969; Axelos 1961; Wilson 1940. Alienation as a concept: Josephson and Josephson 1962; Kahler 1967; Pappenheim 1968.
27. Emergence of chiefs as redistributive centers: Fried 1967; Sahlins 1963b; Service 1965. Example of tribal system as redistributive: Maquet 1961.
28. Bantu: Schapera 1937.
29. Tribal economies generally: Dalton 1962; Forde and Douglas 1956; Nash 1966.
30. Pastoral economies: Darling 1955; Gulliver 1955.
31. Gardening and horticultural economies: Forde 1952.
32. Melanesian overseas "trading": Malinowski 1922; Uberoi 1962.

33. On New Guinea: Gardner and Heider 1968; Rappoport 1967; Salisbury 1962.
34. Lorenz 1956b.
35. Division of labor—classic work: Smith 1904 (1776).
36. Marx 1887.
37. Durkheim 1893.
38. Dehumanizing effects: Mayo 1945; Mumford 1934.
39. Effects of unemployment: Lebergott 1964.
40. On participation and its effects: Roethlesberger and Dixon 1939. On participation in industry: Blumberg 1968.
41. For "survival of fittest" arguments: Hofstadter 1944.
42. On eugenics: Pickens 1968.
43. On executives generally: Barnard 1954.
44. Early unions: Webb and Webb 1894.
45. Comparative economic systems: Schumpeter 1942.
46. Pervasiveness of division of labor by sex: Murdock 1937. On some causes: Brown 1970. Other aspects of sex differences: D'Andrade 1966.
47. On physiology of menstruation and behavioral effects *see* notes 43–49 in Chapter 3.
48. Astronauts: Tereshkova-Nikolayova 1970.
49. Female courtship behavior: Eibl-Eibesfeldt 1970. On pupil dilation and sexual interest: Hess 1965.
50. Sexual structure of occupations over time: Gross 1968; Wilensky 1968.
51. Economic rationality: Diesing 1950. Economic man: Chalk 1964; Gide 1930. General discussion: Parsons and Smelser 1956; Robbins 1932.
52. Exchange as fundamental: Blau 1964; Homans 1961.

6. THE BENIGN OPPRESSION

1. On the biology of learning: Harlow 1958b; Pribram 1969.
2. On brain and memory: Young 1965. On cortex and inhibition: Chance and Mead 1953; Fox 1967b; 1971.
3. Habits and instincts: Russell and Russell 1961.
4. Carnivore teaching: Mowat 1963.
5. For an example of learning without schooling: Opie and Opie 1961.
6. Learning failures: Holt 1964.
7. Criticism of formal education, *see* e.g.: Bruner 1966; Leonard 1968; Silberman 1970.
8. Security: Harlow 1959; 1962; Menzel 1963.
9. Curiosity: Butler 1954.
10. Fright: Freedman 1961.
11. On play in mammals: Beach 1945; Hediger 1955; Jewell and Loizos 1966; Welker 1961. Play in primates: Hinde and Spencer-Booth 1967; Loizos 1967; Welker 1956a; 1956b.
12. Goodall 1963.
13. Importance of peers: Hinde 1969.
14. Deprivation in macaques: Harlow 1965a.

15. Concept of "critical periods": Ambrose 1963; Caldwell 1962; Scott 1962.
16. General characteristics of education in primitive societies: Fortes 1938; Henry 1960; Levine 1963; Mayer 1970; Middleton 1970; Raum 1940; Read 1959.
17. Reviews of male initiation procedures: Cohen 1964; Eisenstadt 1955; Garfinkle 1956; Gluckman 1962; van Gennep 1909; Whiting 1958; Young 1965.
18. Testosterone at puberty: Hamburg 1970; Hamburg and Lunde 1966.
19. Female initiation: Brown 1963; Richards 1956.
20. Child language: Bellugi and Brown 1964; Braine 1963; Lenneberg 1967; Miller and Erwin 1964; Weir 1962.
21. Varieties of toilet training: Whiting and Child 1953.
22. Education and social mobility: Young 1958.
23. Education of sorcerers, *see* e.g.: Evans-Pritchard 1937.
24. Size and principals: Gross 1958.
25. Attention: Chance 1967.
26. Educational philosophies and schemes reflecting the nonformal approach: Becker 1967; Dewey 1916; Holt 1967; Kohl 1969; Montessori 1964; Neill 1960; Pettitt 1970.
27. Bloom *et al.* 1965.
28. Levy 1969.
29. Sexton 1969.
30. Sex differences in maturity: Tanner 1955.
31. Sex and occupation: Gross 1968; Wilensky 1968.
32. Teaching as a profession: Tropp 1957.
33. BaVenda: Stayt 1931.
34. Iroquois: Wilson 1960.
35. Hull: Tunstall 1962; Newfoundland: Faris 1966.

7. GOOD GROOMING

1. Acquisitiveness: Tawney 1921.
2. Grooming in primates: Sade 1965; Sparks 1967; Yerkes 1933.
3. Other world of hunters: Fox 1971.
4. Genetics of altruism: Hamilton 1963.
5. A precursor of this view: Kropotkin 1902.
6. Souls: Tylor 1870, vol. 2. Soul loss: Tax 1952.
7. Psychosomatic medicine: Grinker 1953; MacLean 1949.
8. Primitive medicine generally: Ackerknecht 1942.
9. On social organization of hospitals generally: Bachmayer and Hartman 1943; Belknap 1956; Caudill 1958; Goffman 1961. On authority and power in hospitals: Cumming and Cumming 1956; Henry 1954; Parsons 1957; Rapoport and Rapoport 1957.
10. Negritos: Stewart 1954.
11. Cochiti: Fox 1964.
12. Primitive psychotherapy: Benedict and Jacks 1954; Kaplan and Johnson

1964; Kiev 1964; Leighton and Leighton 1941; Messing 1958; Wallace 1958.

13. Witchcraft accusations/confessions and social structure: Douglas 1970; Erstein 1959; Evans-Pritchard 1937; Gluckman 1955; Kitteridge 1929; Marwick 1965; Middleton and Winter 1963; Nash 1961; Turner 1957.
14. Death from witchcraft: Cannon 1942; Gillin 1948.
15. Physiology of flight and illness: Simeons 1960.
16. On medicine men, shamans, and divining: Evans-Pritchard 1937; Lévi-Strauss 1949a; Murphy 1964; Nadel 1946; Park 1938; Park 1963; Rasmussen 1929; Reichard 1939; Turner 1964.
17. Role of doctor: Henderson 1935; Parsons 1951b. In primitive society: Berndt 1964.
18. On professionalization: Abel-Smith 1964; Devereux and Weiner 1950.
19. Community care: Jones 1953.
20. On defining "health" and "normality": Devereux 1956; Foucault 1961. *See also:* Freeman 1965.
21. Psychiatric diagnosis as a "moral" judgment: Laing 1959; 1967. For a sociologist's view: Naegele 1970.
22. Religion and compulsion: Freud 1948–1950; 1952.
23. Trances: Bogorás 1904–1909; Lee 1967; 1968a.
24. Christ and paranoia: Schweitzer 1948.
25. Mental states and hierarchy: Price 1967.
26. Change of status and suicide: Durkheim 1951 (1897).
27. Gambling: Thomas 1906. Gambling and play: Huizinga 1949.
28. Hadza: Woodburn 1964.
29. On pitting oneself against environmental odds: Gould 1963.
30. Men in bars: Cavan 1966.
31. On gossip: Colson 1953; Gluckman 1963b; 1968; Paine 1967.
32. On flirting *see* note 49 in Chapter 5.
33. Nondirective therapy: Sullivan 1953; 1954.
34. Durkheim 1915.

8. THE NOBLE SAVAGE

1. Romantic view: Masters 1968; Russell 1945, Bk. III, part II.
2. Numbers of deaths by violence: Richardson 1960.
3. Nonviolent nature of man, *see* e.g.: Montagu 1968; Russell and Russell 1968—among many others.
4. On aggression: Bass 1961; Berkowitz 1962; Carthy and Ebling 1964; Scott 1958; Storr 1968. Frustration and aggression: Dollard *et al.* 1944. Critique: Berkowitz 1969; Tiger 1971.
5. Functions of aggression for animals: Collias 1944; Crook 1968; Eibl-Eibesfeldt 1961; Tinbergen 1936.
6. Aggression and bonds: Lorenz 1966.
7. Ritualization of aggression: Huxley 1966; Lorenz 1964; Tinbergen 1968.
8. On "real" aggression in baboons and other animals: Fisher 1964; Hall

1962; 1964; Matthews 1964; Washburn 1966; Washburn and Hamburg 1958.

9. On killer instincts: Ardrey 1961; Freeman 1964. Related arguments: Leakey 1967b; Trotter 1916.
10. Adrenalin and "fight and flight" response: Klopper 1964.
11. On war as male activity: Tiger 1969, chap. 7. Relation of individual to group aggression: Durbin and Bowlby 1939.
12. Status and war: Mishkin 1940.
13. Primitive warfare: Bohannan 1967; Gardner and Heider 1968; Newcomb 1950; Secoy 1953; Turney-High 1949; Vayda 1960; 1961.
14. Conquest and its consequences: Spencer 1896.
15. Slavery—lack of in hunters and expansion in agriculturalists: Hobhouse, Wheeler, and Ginsberg 1915.
16. Conquest and expansion among agriculturalists: Cook 1946; Otterbein 1967; Sahlins 1961; Vayda 1961.
17. Out-groups as "pseudo-species": Erikson 1966.
18. History and sociology of war generally: Andreski 1954; 1964; Davie 1929; Fried, Murphy, and Harris 1968; Wright 1942.
19. Psychology of men at war: Gray 1959.
20. Pentagon and economy: Rubinoff 1967.
21. Fremlin 1964.
22. Links between sex and aggression in brain: MacLean 1958; 1962; 1968— the latter a specific discussion of brain and violence. *See also:* Mark and Ervin 1970.
23. Population size and dispersion in hunters: Birdsell 1957; Carr-Saunders 1922.
24. Peopling of north America: Griffin 1960; Hopkins 1959.
25. Density as cause of violence, *see* e.g.: Russell and Russell 1968.
26. Density and social breakdown in animals: Calhoun 1962a; 1962b; Deevey 1960; Green and Evans 1940. In man: Leyhausen 1965.
27. Effects of stress: Barnett 1958; Barnett *et al.* 1960; Green and Larsen 1938.
28. Density and slums: Schorr 1966.
29. Wynne-Edwards 1962.
30. Population-resources balance: Christian 1970; Cragg and Pirie 1955; Lack 1954; Stott 1962; Wynne-Edwards 1964. In human populations: Thompson 1970. Critique: Douglas 1966.
31. On territory and property *see* note 3 in Chapter 5.
32. Restriction of top positions: Bednarik 1970. Constancy of numbers in cabinets: Parkinson 1957.
33. Population policy and its effectiveness: Davis 1967.
34. Japanese policy and abortion: Coyle 1959.
35. European policy: Class 1940.
36. Techniques of terror: Lowenthal 1946; Kogon 1950.
37. Numbers and power: Davis 1954.

BIBLIOGRAPHY

ABEL-SMITH, B.
1964 *The Hospitals, 1800–1948; A Study in Social Administration in England and Wales*. Cambridge, Mass.: Harvard Univ. Press.
ABERLE, D.F.; COHEN, A.K.; DAVIS, A.K.; LEVY, M.J.; SUTTON, F.X.
1950 The Functional Prerequisites of a Society. *Ethics* 60: 100–111.
ABERLE, D.F., *et al.*
1963 The Incest Taboo and the Mating Patterns of Animals. *Amer. Anthrop.* 65: 253–265.
ACKERKNECHT, E.H.
1942 Problems of Primitive Medicine. *Bulletin of the Hist. of Med.* XI: 503–521.
ADAMS, R.
1966 *The Evolution of Urban Society: Early Mesopotamia and Pre-Hispanic Mexico*. Chicago: Aldine.
ADAMS, R.N.
1960 An Inquiry into the Nature of the Family. Dole, G.E., and Carneiro, R.L. (eds.), *Essays in the Science of Society in Honor of Leslie A. White*. N.Y.: Thomas Y. Crowell.
AINSWORTH, M.D.
1962 The Effects of Maternal Deprivation: A Review of Findings and Controversy in the Context of Research Strategy. *Deprivation of Maternal Care: A Reassessment of its Effects*. Public Health Papers (14), Geneva: W.H.O.

ALLAND, A.
1967 *Evolution and Human Behavior.* N.Y.: Natural History Press.
ALLEE, W.C.
1958 *The Social Life of Animals.* Boston: Beacon Press.
ALTMANN, S.A. (ed.)
1965 *Japanese Monkeys: A Collection of Translations.* Atlanta: Altmann.
1967 *Social Communication Among Primates.* Chicago: Univ. of Chicago Press.
AMBROSE, J.A.
1963 The Concept of a Critical Period for the Development of Social Responsiveness. Foss, B. (ed.), *Determinants of Infant Behavior* 2. London: Methuen. N.Y.: John Wiley & Sons.
1969 *Stimulation in Early Infancy.* N.Y.: Academic Press.
AMOROSO, E.C., and MARSHALL, F.H.A.
1960 External Factors in Sexual Periodicity. Parkes, A.S. (ed.), *Marshall's Physiology of Reproduction* (3rd ed., vol. 1, part 2). London: Longmans.
ANDRESKI, S.
1954 *Military Organization and Society.* London: Routledge and Kegan Paul.
1964 Origins of War. Carthy, J.D., and Ebling, F.J. (eds.), *The Natural History of Aggression.* London: Academic Press.
ARDREY, R.
1961 *African Genesis.* London: Collins.
1966 *The Territorial Imperative.* N.Y.: Atheneum.
1970 *The Social Contract.* N.Y.: Atheneum.
ARENSBERG, C., and KIMBALL, S.T.
1968 (1940) *Family and Community in Ireland.* Cambridge, Mass.: Harvard Univ. Press.
ARON, R.
1969 *Marxism and the Existentialists.* N.Y.: Harper & Row.
AXELOS, K.
1961 *Marx, penseur de la technique de l'aliénation de l'homme à la conquete du monde.* Paris: Editions de Minuit.
BACHMEYER, A.C., and HARTMAN, G. (eds.)
1943 *The Hospital in Modern Society.* N.Y.: The Commonwealth Fund.
BALL, J.
1940 The Effects of Testosterone on Sexual Behavior of Female Rats. *J. Comp. Psychol.* 29: 151–165.
BANTON, M. (ed.)
1961 *Darwin and the Study of Society.* Chicago: Quadrangle Books.
BARBOUR, N.
1965 *Morocco.* London: Thames and Hudson.
BARNARD, C.I.
1954 *The Functions of the Executive.* Cambridge, Mass.: Harvard Univ. Press.
BARNETT, S.A.
1958 (ed.) *A Century of Darwin.* London: Heinemann.

1958 Physiological Effects of "Social Stress" in Wild Rats. The Adrenal Cortex. *J. Psychosomatic Res.* 3: 1–11.

1967 *"Instinct" and "Intelligence."* London: Macgibbon and Kee.

BARNETT, S.A., EATON, J.C., and McCALLUM, H.M.

1960 Physiological Effects of "Social Stress" in Wild Rats, 2: Liver Glycogen and Blood Glucose. *J. Psychosomatic Res.* 4: 251–260.

BARTHOLOMEW, G.A., JR., and BIRDSELL, J.B.

1953 Ecology and the Protohominids. *Amer. Anthrop.* 55: 481–498.

BASTOCK, M.

1967 *Courtship: An Ethological Study.* London: Heinemann.

BATESON, P.P.G.

1966 The Characteristics and Context of Imprinting. *Biol. Rev.* 41: 177–220.

BEACH, F.A.

1945 Current Concepts of Play in Animals. *Amer. Nat.* 79: 523–541.

1947 Evolutionary Changes in the Physiological Control of Mating Behavior in Mammals. *Psychol. Rev.* 54: 297–315.

1950 The Snark was a Boojum. *Amer. Psychol.* 5: 115–124.

1955 The Descent of Instinct. *Psych. Rev.* 62: 401–410.

BEACH, F.A. (ed.)

1965 *Sex and Behavior.* N.Y.: John Wiley & Sons.

BEAMAN, E.A.

1947 The Effect of the Male Hormone on Aggressive Behavior in Male Mice. *Physiol. Zool.* 20: 373–405.

BECKER, E.

1967 *Beyond Alienation.* N.Y.: George Braziller.

BEDNARIK, K.

1970 *The Male in Crisis.* N.Y.: Alfred A. Knopf.

BELKNAP, I.

1956 *Human Problems of a State Mental Hospital.* N.Y.: Blakiston Division, McGraw-Hill.

BELL, N.W., and VOGEL, E.F. (eds.)

1960 *A Modern Introduction to the Family.* N.Y.: Free Press.

BELLUGI, U., and BROWN, R.

1964 The Acquisition of Language. *Monog. Soc. Res. Child Devel.* 29 (1).

BENDIX, R.

1960 *Max Weber: An Intellectual Portrait.* London: Heinemann.

BENEDICT, P.K., and JACKS, I.

1954 Mental Illness in Primitive Societies. *Psychiatry* 17: 377–389.

BERKOWITZ, L.

1962 *Aggression: A Social Psychological Analysis.* N.Y.: McGraw-Hill.

BERKOWITZ, L. (ed.)

1969 *Roots of Aggression.* N.Y.: Atherton Press.

BERNDT, C.H.

1964 The Role of Native Doctors in Aboriginal Australia. Kiev, A. (ed.), *Magic, Faith, and Healing.* Glencoe, Ill.: Free Press.

BIDNEY, D.

1953 *Theoretical Anthropology.* N.Y.: Columbia Univ. Press.

BINFORD, S.R., and BINFORD, L.R.
  1968   *New Perspectives in Archeology.* Chicago: Aldine.
BIRD, C.
  1968   *Born Female: The High Cost of Keeping Women Down.* N.Y.:
          David McKay.
BIRDSELL, J.B.
  1953   Some Environmental and Cultural Factors Influencing the Structuring
          of Australian Aboriginal Populations. *Amer. Nat.* (Supplement, May–
          June).
  1957   Some Population Problems Involving Pleistocene Man. *Cold Spring
          Harbor Symposia on Quantitative Biology* XXII.
  1958   On Population Structure in Generalized Hunting and Collecting
          Populations. *Evolution* (June).
BLAKE, R.
  1966   *Disraeli.* London: Eyre and Spottiswoode.
BLAU, P.M.
  1964   *Exchange and Power in Social Life.* N.Y.: John Wiley & Sons.
BLISS, E.L. (ed.)
  1962   *Roots of Behavior.* N.Y.: Harper and Bros.
BLOCH, M.
  1961   *Feudal Society.* London: Routledge and Kegan Paul.
BLOOM, B.S.; DAVIS, A.; and HESS, R.D.
  1965   *Compensatory Education for Cultural Deprivation.* N.Y.: Holt, Rine-
          hart and Winston
BLUMBERG, P.
  1968   *Industrial Democracy: The Sociology of Participation.* London:
          Constable.
BOAS, F.
  1948   *Race, Language, and Culture.* N.Y.: Macmillan.
BOCK, P.K.
  1969   *Modern Cultural Anthropology.* N.Y.: Alfred A. Knopf.
BOGORAS, W.
  1904–1909 *The Chukchee.* Franz Boas (ed.), *The Jesup North Pacific
          Expedition* VII. Leyden: E.J. Brill.
BOHANNAN, P.
  1963   *Social Anthropology.* N.Y.: Holt, Rinehart and Winston.
BOHANNAN, P. (ed.)
  1967   *Law and Warfare: Studies in the Anthropology of Conflict.* N.Y.:
          Natural History Press.
BONNER, J.T.
  1965   *Size and Cycle.* Princeton: Princeton Univ. Press.
BOWLBY, J.
  1951   *Maternal Care and Mental Health.* Geneva: W.H.O.
  1953   Some Pathological Processes Set in Train by Early Mother-Child
          Separation. *J. Mental Sci.* 99: 265–272.
  1958   The Nature of the Child's Tie to His Mother. *Int. J. Psycho-Anal.* 41:
          89–113.

1960   Grief and Mourning in Infancy and Early Childhood. *Psychoanalytic Study of the Child* 7: 82–94.

1961a   Separation Anxiety. *Int. J. Psycho-Anal.* 41: 89–113.

1961b   Separation Anxiety: A Critical Review of the Literature. *J. Child. Psychol. Psychiat.* 1: 251–269.

1963   Pathological Mourning and Childhood Mourning. *J. Amer. Psychoanal. Ass.* 11: 500–541.

1969   *Attachment and Loss: Volume 1 Attachment.* (International Psycho-Analytical Library no. 79). London: Hogarth Press and the Institute of Psycho-Analysis.

BRAIDWOOD, R.

1960   The Agricultural Revolution. *Scientific American* (Sept.).

BRAINE, M.D.S.

1963   The Ontogeny of English Phrase Structure: The First Phase. *Language* 39: 1–13.

BRESSLER, M.

1968   Sociology, Biology and Ideology. Glass, D. (ed.), *Genetics.* N.Y.: Rockefeller Univ. Press and Russell Sage Foundation.

BRILL, A.A.

1932   The Sense of Smell in the Neuroses and Psychoses. *Psychoanalytic Quarterly* 1: 7.

BROOM, R.

1949   The Ape-Men. *Scientific American* (Nov.).

BROOM R., and SCHEPERS, G.W.H.

1946   *The South African Fossil Ape-man: The Australopithecine.* Transvaal Museum Memoirs No. 2.

BROWN, J.

1963   A Cross-Cultural Study of Female Initiation Rites. *Amer. Anthrop.* 65: 837–853.

1970   A Note on the Division of Labor by Sex. *Amer. Anthrop.* 72: 1073–1078.

BRUNER, J.

1966   *Toward a Theory of Instruction.* N.Y.: W.W. Norton.

BULLOUGH, W.S.

1961   *Vertebrate Reproductive Cycles* (2nd ed.). London: Methuen.

BURTON, R.F., and ARBUTHNOT, F.F. (trans.)

1962 (orig. 1883)   *The Kama Sutra of Vatsyayana.* N.Y.: E.P. Dutton.

BURTON, R.F. (trans.)

1963 (orig. 1886)   *The Perfumed Garden of the Shaykh Nefzawa.* London: Spearman.

BUSS, A.

1961   *The Psychology of Aggression.* N.Y. and London: John Wiley & Sons.

BUTLER, R.A.

1954   Curiosity in Monkeys. *Scientific American* (Feb.).

CALDWELL, B.M.

1962   The Usefulness of the Critical Period Hypothesis in the Study of Filiative Behavior. *Merrill-Palmer Quarterly* 8: 229–242.

CALHOUN, J.B.
1952 Social Aspects of Population Dynamics. *J. Mammalogy* 33: 139–59.
1962a Population Density and Social Pathology. *Scientific American* (Feb.).
1962b A "Behavioral Sink." Bliss, E.L. (ed.), *Roots of Behavior*. N.Y.: Harper and Bros.

CALLAN, H.
1970 *Ethology and Society: Towards an Anthropological View*. Oxford: Clarendon Press.

CAMPBELL, B.G.
1966 *Human Evolution: An Introduction to Man's Adaptations*. Chicago: Aldine.

CANETTI, E.
1962 *Crowds and Power*. London: Gollancz.

CANNON, W.B.
1942 Voodoo Death. *Amer. Anthrop.* XLIV: 169–181.

CARPENTER, C.R.
1940 A Field Study in Siam of the Behavior and Social Relations of the Gibbon (*Hylobates Lar.*) *Comp. Psychol. Monog.* 16.
1958 Territoriality: A Review of Concepts and Problems. Roe, A., and Simpson, G.G. (eds.), *Behavior and Evolution*. New Haven, Conn.: Yale Univ. Press.
1964 *Naturalistic Behavior of Nonhuman Primates*. University Park: Penn. State Univ. Press.

CARR-SAUNDERS, A.M.
1922 *The Population Problem: A Study in Human Evolution*. Oxford: Oxford Univ. Press.

CARTHY, J.D., and EBLING, F.J. (eds.)
1964 *The Natural History of Aggression*. London: Academic Press.

CASLER, L.
1961 Maternal Deprivation: A Critical Review of the Literature. *Monog. Soc. Res. Child Devel.* 26: 1–64.

CASPARI, E.
1963 Selective Forces in the Evolution of Man. *Amer. Nat.* XCVII (892): 5–14.

CAUDILL, W.
1958 *The Psychiatric Hospital as a Small Society*. Cambridge, Mass.: Harvard Univ. Press.

CAVAN, S.
1966 *Liquor License: An Ethnography of Bar Behavior*. Chicago: Aldine.

CHAGNON, N.A.
1968 *Yanomamo—The Fierce People*. N.Y.: Holt, Rinehart and Winston.

CHALK, A.F.
1964 Economic Man. Gould, J., and Kolf, W. (eds.), *Dictionary of the Social Sciences*. N.Y.: Free Press.

CHANCE, M.R.A.
1962a Nature and Special Features of the Instinctive Social Bond of Primates. Washburn, S.L. (ed.), *Social Life of Early Man*. London: Methuen.

1962b   Social Behaviour and Primate Evolution. Ashley Montagu, M.F. (ed.), *Culture and the Evolution of Man*. N.Y.: Oxford Univ. Press.

1967   Attention Structure as the Basis of Primate Rank Orders. *Man: The J.R.A.I.* 2 (4): 503–518.

CHANCE, M.R.A., and JOLLY, C.J.

1970   *Social Groups of Monkeys, Apes, and Men*. N.Y.: E.P. Dutton.

CHANCE, M.R.A., and MEAD, A.P.

1953   Social Behaviour and Primate Evolution. *Evolution: Symposium of the Society for Experimental Biology* 7. N.Y.: Jonathan Cape.

CHAPPLE, E.D.

1970   *Culture and Biological Man*. N.Y.: Holt, Rinehart and Winston.

CHASE, H.P.; DORSEY, J.; and McKHANN, G.M.

1967   The Effect of Malnutrition on the Synthesis of a Myelin Lipid. *Pediatrics* 40: 551–559.

CHILDE, V.G.

1946 (orig. 1942)   *What Happened in History?* N.Y.: Penguin.

CHOMSKY, N.

1965   *Aspects of the Theory of Syntax*. Cambridge, Mass.: MIT Press.

1966   *Cartesian Linguistics: A Chapter in the History of Rationalist Thought*. N.Y. and London: Harper & Row.

1968   *Language and Mind*. N.Y.: Harcourt, Brace and World.

CHRISTIAN, J.J.

1970   Social Subordination, Population Density and Mammalian Evolution. *Science* 168: 84–90.

CLARK, J.D.

1970   *The Prehistory of Africa*. N.Y. and Washington: Praeger.

CLARK, W.E. LE G.

1950   *History of the Primates: An Introduction to the Study of Fossil Man*. London: British Museum.

1955   *The Fossil Evidence for Human Evolution: An Introduction to the Study of Paleoanthropology*. Chicago: Univ. of Chicago Press.

1960   *The Antecedents of Man: An Introduction to the Evolution of the Primates*. Chicago: Quadrangle Books.

1967   *Man-Ape or Ape-Man?* N.Y.: Holt, Rinehart and Winston.

COHEN, Y.A.

1964   *The Transition from Childhood to Adolescence*. Chicago: Aldine.

COLLIAS, N.E.

1944   Aggressive Behavior Among Vertebrate Animals. *Physiol. Zool.* 17: 83–123.

COLSON, E.

1953   *The Makah Indians*. Manchester: Manchester Univ. Press.

COOK, S.F.

1946   Human Sacrifice and Warfare as Factors in the Demography of Pre-Colonial Mexico. *Human Biology* 18: 81–102.

COUNT, E.W.

1958   The Biological Basis of Human Sociality. *Amer. Anthrop.* 60: 1049–1085.

1958–1959 Eine Biologische Entwicklungsgeschichte der Menschlichen So-
zialität. *Homo* 9: 129–146; 10: 1–35, 65–92.
1967 The Lactation Complex: A Phylogenetic Consideration of the Mammalian Mother-Child Symbiosis, with Special Reference to Man. *Homo*
18 (1): 38–54.
COYLE, D.C.
1959 Japan's Population. *Population Bulletin* 15 (7): 119–136.
CRAGG, J.B., and PIRIE, N.W. (eds.)
1955 *The Numbers of Man and Animals.* Edinburgh: Oliver and Boyd.
CRICK, F.H.C.
1962 The Genetic Code. *Scientific American* (Oct.).
CRITCHLEY, M.
1958 Animal Communication. *Transactions of the Hunterian Society of
London* 16: 90–111.
CROMBIE, D.L.
1965 An Evolutionary Approach to Human Behavior. *J. Coll. Gen. Pract.*
12 (133).
CROOK, J.H.
1966 Cooperation in Primates. *Eugenics Review* 58 (2).
1968 Gelada Baboon Herd Structure and Movement. *Symp. Zool. Soc.
Lond.* 18: 237–258.
1968 The Nature and Function of Territorial Aggression. Montagu, A.
(ed.), *Man and Aggression.* N.Y.: Oxford Univ. Press.
1970 Social Organization and the Environment: Aspects of Contemporary
Social Ethology. *Animal Behavior* 18.
CROOK, J.H., and GARTLAN, J.S.
1966 Evolution of Primate Societies. *Nature,* London 210 (5042): 1200–
1203.
CUMMING, E., and CUMMING, J.
1956 The Locus of Power in a Large Mental Hospital. *Psychiatry* 19:
361–369.
DAHLSTROM, E. (ed.)
1967 *The Changing Roles of Men and Women.* London: Duckworth.
DALTON, G.
1962 Traditional Production in Primitive African Economies. *The Quarterly J. Economics* 76: 360–378.
DALTON, K.
1959 Menstruation and Acute Psychiatric Illness. *British Medical Journal*
1: 148–149.
1960a The Effect of Menstruation on Schoolgirls' Weekly Work. *Brit.
Med. J.* (Jan).
1960b Menstruation and Accidents. *Brit. Med. J.* 2.
1960c Schoolgirls' Behaviour and Menstruation. *Brit. Med. J.* (Dec.).
1964a The Influence of Menstruation on Health and Disease. *Proc. Royal
Soc. Med.* (57).
1964b *The Pre-Menstrual Syndrome.* Springfield, Ill.: Charles Thomas.
D'ANDRADE, R.G.
1966 Sex Differences and Cultural Institutions. Maccoby, E. (ed.),

The Development of Sex Differences. Stanford: Stanford Univ. Press.

DARLING, F.
1937   *A Herd of Red Deer.* London: Oxford Univ. Press.
1955   Pastoralism in Relation to Populations of Men and Animals. Cragg, J.B., and Pirie, N.W. (eds.), *The Numbers of Man and Animals.* Edinburgh: Oliver and Boyd.

DARLINGTON, C.D.
1969   *The Evolution of Man and Society.* London: George Allen and Unwin.

DART, R.A.
1953   The Predatory Transition from Ape to Man. *International Anthropological and Linguistic Review* 1 (4).
1957   The Osteodontokeratic Culture of Australopithecus Prometheus. *Memoir Transvaal Museum.*
1958   The Minimal Bone-Breccia Content of Makapansgat and the Australopithecine Predatory Habit. *Amer. Anthrop.* 60 (5).
1959   *Adventures with the Missing Link.* N.Y.: Harper and Bros.
1963   Carnivorous Propensity of Baboons. *Symp. Zool. Soc. Lond.* 10: 49–56.

DARWIN, C.
1859   *The Origin of Species by Means of Natural Selection.* N.Y.: New American Library (1958 edition).
1871   *The Descent of Man.* London: Murray.
1873   *The Expression of the Emotions in Man and Animals.* N.Y. Appleton-Century-Crofts. (New edition—N.Y.: Philosophical Library, 1956; preface by Margaret Mead.)

DAVIE, M.R.
1929   *The Evolution of War.* New Haven, Conn.: Yale Univ. Press.

DAVIS, D.E.
1962   An Inquiry into the Phylogeny of Gangs. Bliss, E.L. (ed.), *Roots of Behavior.* N.Y.: Harper and Bros.

DAVIS, K.
1954   The Demographic Foundations of National Power. Berger, M.; Abel, T.; and Page, C.H. (eds.), *Freedom and Control in Modern Soc.* N.Y.: Van Nostrand.
1967   Population Policy: Will Current Programs Succeed? *Science* 158: 730–739.

DEBEER, G.
1968   Evolution by Natural Selection. Freed, M. (ed.), *Readings in Anthropology* 1. N.Y.: Thomas Y. Crowell.

DEEVEY, E.S.
1960a   The Human Population. *Scientific American* (Sept. 1960).
1960b   The Hare and the Haruspex: A Cautionary Tale. *The Yale Review* (Winter 1960).

DEMOUBRAY, G.A. DE C.
1931   *Matriarchy in the Malay Peninsula and Neighboring Countries.* London: George Routledge and Sons.

DEVEREUX, G.
1956   Normal and Abnormal: The Key Problem of Psychiatric Anthro-

pology. *Some Uses of Anthropology: Theoretical and Applied*. Washington, D.C.: Anthrop. Soc. of Wash.

DEVEREUX, G., and WEINER, F.R.
1950   The Occupational Status of Nurses. *Amer. Sociolog. Rev.* 15: 628–634.

DEVORE, I.
1963   Mother-Infant Relations in Free-Ranging Baboons. Rheingold, H.L. (ed.), *Maternal Behavior in Mammals*. N.Y.: John Wiley & Sons.
1964   The Evolution of Social Life. Tax, S. (ed.), *Horizons of Anthropology*. Chicago: Aldine.
1965a   Male Dominance and Mating Behavior in Baboons. Beach, F.A. (ed.), *Sex and Behavior*. N.Y.: John Wiley & Sons.

DEVORE, I. (ed.)
1965b   *Primate Behavior: Field Studies of Monkeys and Apes*. N.Y.: Holt, Rinehart and Winston.

DEVORE, I., and WASHBURN, S.L.
1963   Baboon Ecology and Human Evolution. Howell, F.C., and Bourlière, F. (eds.), *African Ecology and Human Evolution*. N.Y.: Viking Fund Publications in Anthropology No. 33.

DEWEY, J.
1916   *Democracy and Education*. N.Y.: Macmillan.

DIESING, P.
1950   The Nature and Limitations of Economic Rationality. *Ethics* 61: 12–26.

DILLON, W. (ed.)
1971   *Man and Beast*. Washington, D.C.: Smithsonian Institution Press.

DISRAELI, B.
1845   *Sybil, or, The Two Nations* (3 vols.). Philadelphia: Colburn.

DOBZHANSKY, T.
1962   *Mankind Evolving; The Evolution of the Human Species*. New Haven, Conn.: Yale Univ. Press.

DOLLARD, J. et al.
1944   *Frustration and Aggression*. London: Routledge and Kegan Paul.

DOUGLAS, M.
1966   Population Control in Primitive Groups. *Brit. J. Sociol.*, p. 263.

DOUGLAS, M. (ed.)
1970   *Witchcraft Confessions and Accusations*. A.S.A. Monograph 9. London: Tavistock.

DuBos, R.
1968   *So Human an Animal*. N.Y.: Charles Scribner's Sons.

DURBIN, E.F.M., and BOWLBY, J.
1939   *Personal Aggressiveness and War*. N.Y.: Columbia Univ. Press.

DURKHEIM, E.
1893   *De la Division du Travail Social*. Simpson, G. (trans.), *The Division of Labor in Society*. Glencoe, Ill.: Free Press. 1933.
1951 (orig. 1897)   *Suicide*. Spaulding, J., and Simpson, G. (trans.), Glencoe, Ill.: Free Press.

1915 *The Elementary Forms of the Religious Life.* Swain, J.W. (trans.). London: Allen and Unwin.

DUVERGER, M.
1955 *The Political Role of Women.* Paris: UNESCO.

EGGAN, F.
1950 *The Social Organization of the Western Pueblos.* Chicago: Univ. of Chicago Press.

EIBL-EIBESFELDT, I.
1961 The Fighting Behavior of Animals. *Scientific American* (Dec.).
1968 Ethological Perspectives on Primate Studies. Jay, P.C. (ed.), *Primates: Studies in Adaptation and Variability.* N.Y.: Holt, Rinehart and Winston.
1970 *Ethology.* N.Y.: Holt, Rinehart and Winston.

EIBL-EIBESFELDT, I., and KRAMER, S.
1958 Ethology, the Comparative Study of Animal Behavior. *Quart. Rev. Biol.* 33: 181–211.

EISELEY, L.C.
1958 *Darwin's Century: Evolution and the Men Who Discovered it.* Garden City, N.Y.: Doubleday.

EISENBERG, J.F.
1966 *The Social Organization of Mammals.* Handbuch der Zoologie 8: 1–92.

EISENSTADT, S.M.
1955 *From Generation to Generation.* Glencoe, Ill.: Free Press.

ELLIOTT, K.
1970 *The Family and Its Future.* London: J. and A. Churchill.

EMMETT, D.
1956 Prophets and Their Societies. *J. Royal Anthrop. Inst.* 86 (part 1): 13–24 (Jan.–June).

ENGELS, F.
1905 *Origins of the Family, Private Property, and the State.* Chicago: C.H. Kerr.
1958 (1892) *Condition of the Working Class in England.* Oxford: Blackwell.

EPSTEIN, S.
1959 A Sociological Analysis of Witch Beliefs in a Mysore Village. *The Eastern Anthropologist* 12 (4): 234–251.

ERIKSON, E.H.
1966 Ontogeny of Ritualization in Man. *Philosophical Transactions of the Royal Society of London B* 251: 337–349.

ERIKSON, L.B.
1967 Relationship of Sexual Receptivity to Menstrual Cycle in Adult Rhesus Monkeys. *Nature* 216: 299–301.

ETKIN, W.
1954 Social Behavior and the Evolution of Man's Mental Capacities. *Amer. Nat.* 88: 129–142.

ETKIN, W. (ed.)
1964 *Social Behavior and Organization Vertebrates.* Chicago and London: Univ. of Chicago Press.

EVANS-PRITCHARD, E.E.
  1937 *Witchcraft, Oracles, and Magic Among the Azande.* Oxford: Clarendon Press.
  1965 *The Position of Women in Primitive Societies.* N.Y.: Free Press.
EVERETT, J.W.
  1961 The Mammalian Female Reproductive Cycle and Its Controlling Mechanisms. Young, W.C. (ed.), *Sex and Internal Secretion.* Baltimore: Williams and Wilkens Co.
EYSENCK, H.J.
  1957 *Sense and Nonsense in Psychology.* Harmondsworth: Penguin.
FABRICIUS, E.
  1962 Some Aspects of Imprinting in Birds. *Symp. Zool. Soc. Lond.* 8: 139–148.
FARIS, J.C.
  1966 *Cat Harbour: A Newfoundland Fishing Settlement.* St. Johns, N.F.: Instit. of Social and Economic Research.
FIRTH, R.W., and YAMEY, B.S.
  1964 *Capital, Saving, and Credit in Peasant Society.* Chicago: Aldine.
FISHER, J.
  1964 Interspecific Aggression. Carthy, J.D., and Ebling, F.J. (eds.), *The Natural History of Aggression.* London: Academic Press.
FISHER, R.A.
  1958 *The Genetical Theory of Natural Selection.* N.Y.: Dover.
FLANNERY, K.
  1965 Ecology of Early Food Production in Mesopotamia. *Science* 147.
FLETCHER, R.
  1957 *Instinct in Man.* London: Allen and Unwin.
FORD, C.S., and BEACH, F.A.
  1952 *Patterns of Sexual Behaviour.* London: Eyre and Spottiswoode.
FORDE, D.
  1952 *Habitat, Economy and Society.* London: Methuen.
FORDE, D., and DOUGLAS, MARY
  1956 Primitive Economics. Shapiro, H.L. (ed.), *Man, Culture, and Society.* N.Y.: Oxford Univ. Press.
FORTES, M.
  1938 *Social and Psychological Aspects of Education in Taleland* (Supplement to *Africa* 11:4) London: Oxford Univ. Press.
FOSS, B.M. (ed.)
  1961–1969 *Determinants of Infant Behavior* I–IV. N.Y.: John Wiley & Sons.
FOUCAULT, M.
  1961 *L'Histoire de la Folie.* Paris: Plon [*Madness and Civilization*, Howard, R. (trans.), N.Y.: Pantheon 1965].
FOX, R.
  1962 Sibling Incest. *Brit. J. Sociol.* 13: 128–150.
  1964 Witchcraft and Clanship in Cochiti Therapy. Kiev, A. (ed.), *Magic, Faith, and Healing.* Glencoe, Ill.: Free Press.

1966   *Totem and Taboo* Reconsidered. Leach, E.R. (ed.), *The Structural Study of Myth and Totemism.* (A.S.A. Monograph No. 5) London: Tavistock.

1967a *Kinship and Marriage: An Anthropological Perspective.* London and Baltimore: Penguin.

1967b In the Beginning: Aspects of Hominid Behavioural Evolution. *Man: The J.R.A.I.* 2 (3): 415–433.

1967c Human Mating Patterns in Ethological Perspective. *Animals* (July).

1968   The Evolution of Human Sexual Behavior. *The New York Times Magazine* (March 24), pp. 32–33, 79–97.

1970a Comparative Family Patterns. Elliott, K. (ed.), *The Family and Its Future.* London: J. and A. Churchill.

1970b The Cultural Animal. *Information Sur Les Sciences Sociales* (UNESCO) 9 (1): 7–25. Also in: Dillon, W. (ed.), *Man and Beast.* Smithsonian Inst. Press, 1971.

1971   North America. Bleeker, C.J., and Widengren, G. (eds.), *Historia Religionum* II. Leiden: E.J. Brill.

1972   Alliance and Constraint: Sexual Selection in the Evolution of Human Kinship Systems. Campbell, B. (ed.), *Sexual Selection and the Descent of Man.* Chicago: Aldine.

FREEDMAN, D.G.

1961   The Infant's Fear of Strangers and the Flight Response. *J. Child. Psychol. Psychiat.* 1: 242–248.

1964   Smiling in Blind Infants and the Issue of Innate Versus Acquired. *J. Child. Psychol. Psychiat.* 5: 171–184.

1965   An Ethological Approach to the Genetic Study of Human Behavior. Vandenberg, S.G. (ed.), *Method and Goals in Human Behavior Genetics.* N.Y.: Academic Press.

1967   A Biological View of Man's Social Behavior. Etkin, W. (ed.), *Social Behavior From Fish To Man.* Chicago: Univ. of Chicago Press.

1968   An Evolutionary Framework for Behavioral Research. Vandenberg, S.G. (ed.), *Progress in Human Behavior Genetics.* Baltimore: Johns Hopkins Press.

FREEMAN, D.

1964   Human Aggression in Anthropological Perspective. Carthy, J.D., and Ebling, F.J. (eds.), *The Natural History of Aggression.* London and N.Y.: Academic Press.

1965   Anthropology, Psychiatry and the Doctrine of Cultural Relativism. *Man* 65: 59.

1966   Social Anthropology and the Scientific Study of Human Behavior. *Man: The J.R.A.I.* 1 (2): 330–342.

FREMLIN, J.H.

1964   How Many People Can The World Support? *New Scientist* 415: 285–287.

FREUD, A.

1949   Certain Types and Stages of Social Maladjustment. Eissler, K.R. (ed.), *Searchlights on Delinquency.* N.Y.: International Universities Press.

FREUD, S.
1948–1950 Obsessive Acts and Religious Practices. *Collected Papers* II. London: Hogarth Press and the Institute of Psychoanalysis.
1952 *Totem and Taboo.* Strachey, J. (trans.). N.Y.: W.W. Norton.
FRIED, M.
1967 *The Evolution of Political Society.* N.Y.: Random House.
FRIED, M.; HARRIS, M.; and MURPHY, R. (eds.)
1968 *War: The Anthropology of Armed Conflict and Aggression.* Garden City, N.Y.: Natural History Press.
FRIEDAN, B.
1963 *The Feminine Mystique.* N.Y.: W.W. Norton.
FULLER, J.L., and THOMPSON, W.R.
1960 *Behavior Genetics.* N.Y.: John Wiley & Sons.
FURUYA, Y.
1969 On The Fission of Troops of Japanese Monkeys: II. General View of Troop Fission of Japanese Monkeys. *Primates* 10 (1): 47–69.
GARDNER, R., and HEIDER, K.G.
1968 *Gardens of War.* N.Y.: Random House.
GARFINKLE, H.
1956 Conditions of Successful Degradation Ceremonies. *Amer. J. Sociol.* 61 (5).
GARN, S.M. (ed.)
1964 *Culture and the Direction of Human Evolution.* Detroit, Mich.: Wayne State Univ.
GAVAN, J.A. (ed.)
1955 *The Non-Human Primates and Human Evolution.* Detroit, Mich.: Wayne State Univ.
GEERTZ, C.
1965 The Transition to Humanity. Tax, S. (ed.), *Horizons of Anthropology.* London: Allen and Unwin.
GENNEP, A. VAN
1909 *Les Rites de Passage.* Paris: Nourry. [*Rites of Passage.* Vizedom, M.B., and Caffee, G.L. (trans.); Univ. of Chicago Press.]
GERTH, H.H., and MILLS, C.W. (eds.)
1948 *From Max Weber: Essays on Sociology.* London: Routledge and Kegan Paul.
GIDE, C.
1930 Economic Man. *Encyclopedia of the Social Sciences.* N.Y.: Macmillan.
GILLIN, J.
1948 Magical Fright. *Psychiatry* XI: 387–400.
GINSBURG, B.E.
1968 Breeding Structure and Social Behavior of Mammals: A Servo-Mechanism for Avoidance of Panmixia. Glass, D.C. (ed.), *Genetics.* N.Y.: Rockefeller Univ. Press and Russell Sage Foundation.
GINSBURG, M.
1964 (orig. 1921) *The Psychology of Society.* London: Methuen.

GLASS, D.
1940   *Population Policies and Movements in Europe.* Oxford: Clarendon Press.

GLASS, D.G. (ed.)
1968a   *Biology and Behavior: Genetics.* N.Y.: Rockefeller Univ. Press and Russell Sage Foundation.
1968b   *Biology and Behavior: Environmental Influences.* N.Y.: Rockefeller Univ. Press and Russell Sage Foundation.

GLUCKMAN, M.
1954   *Rituals of Rebellion in South-East Africa.* Manchester: Manchester Univ. Press.
1955   *Custom and Conflict in Africa.* Oxford: Basil Blackwell.
1963a   *Order and Rebellion in Tribal Africa.* N.Y.: Free Press.
1963b   Gossip and Scandal. *Current Anthrop.* 4: 307–315.
1968   Psychological, Sociological and Anthropological Explanations of Witchcraft and Gossip: A Clarification. *Man: The J.R.A.I.* 3 (1): 20–34.

GLUCKMAN, M. (ed.)
1962   *Essays on the Ritual of Social Relations.* Manchester: Manchester Univ. Press.

GOFFMAN, E.
1961   *Asylums.* Garden City, N.Y.: Anchor.

GOLDBERG, P.
1968   Are Women Prejudiced Against Women? *Transaction* (April).

GOODALE, J.
1962   Marriage Contracts Among the Tiwi. *Ethnology* 1 (4): 452–465.

GOODALL, J.
1963   Feeding Behavior of Wild Chimpanzees: A Preliminary Report. *Symp. Zool. Soc. Lond.* 10: 39–48.
1964   Tool-Using and Aimed Throwing in a Community of Free-Living Chimpanzees. *Nature* 201: 1264–1266.
1965   Chimpanzees of the Gombe Stream Reserve. DeVore, I. (ed.), *Primate Behavior.* N.Y.: Holt, Rinehart and Winston.

GOODE, W.J.
1964   *The Family.* Englewood Cliffs, N.J.: Prentice-Hall.

GOODENOUGH, W.H.
1970   *Description and Comparison in Cultural Anthropology.* Chicago: Aldine.

GOUGH, K.
1959   The Nayars and the Definition of Marriage. *J. Royal Anthrop. Inst.* 89: 23–34.
1961   Nayar: Central Kerala. Schneider, D.M., and Gough, K. (eds.), *Matrilineal Kinship.* Berkeley and L.A.: Univ. of California Press.

GOULD, P.R.
1963   Man Against His Environment: A Game Theoretic Framework. *Annals of the Assoc. of Amer. Geographers* 53: 290–297.

GRASSÉ, P. (ed.)
1956   *L'Instinct dans le Comportement des Animaux et de l'Homme.* Paris: Massero et Cie.

GRAY, J.G.
   1959   *The Warriors.* N.Y.: Harcourt, Brace.
GRAY, P.H.
   1958   Theory and Evidence of Imprinting in Human Infants. *J. Psychol.*
          46: 155–166.
GREEN, R.G., and LARSEN, C.L.
   1938   A Description of Shock Disease in the Snowshoe Hare. *Amer. J. of
          Hygiene* 28: 1087–1093.
GREEN, R.G., and EVANS, C.A.
   1940   Studies on a Population Cycle of Snowshoe Hares on Lake Alexander
          Area. *J. of Wildlife Management* 4: 220–238, 267–278, 347–358.
GREENSTEIN, F.
   1961   Sex-Related Political Differences in Childhood. *J. Polit.* 23: 2.
GRIFFIN, J.B.
   1960   Some Prehistoric Connections Between Siberia and America. *Science,*
          pp. 801–812.
GRIFFIN, G.A., and HARLOW, H.F.
   1966   Effects of Three Months of Total Social Deprivation on Social Adjust-
          ment and Learning in the Rhesus Monkey. *Child Development* 37:
          533–548.
GRINKER, R.R.
   1953   *Psychosomatic Research.* N.Y.: W.W. Norton.
GROSS, E.
   1968   Plus ça Change. . . . ? The Sexual Structure of Occupations Over
          Time. *Social Problems* 16: 198–208.
GROSS, N. *et al.*
   1958   *Explorations in Role Analysis: Studies of the School Superintendency
          Role.* N.Y.: John Wiley & Sons.
GULLIVER, P.
   1955   *The Family Herds: A Study of Two Pastoral Tribes in East Africa,
          the Jie and Turkana.* London: Routledge and Kegan Paul.
HALDANE, J.B.S.
   1955   Animal Communication and the Origin of Human Language. *Sci.
          Progr.* 40: 385–401.
   1956   The Argument from Animals to Men: An Examination of its Validity
          for Anthropology. *J. Royal Anthrop. Inst.* 86: 1–14.
HALL, K.R.L.
   1962   Sexual, Derived Social, and Agonistic Behavior Patterns in the Wild
          Chacma Baboon, *Papio Ursinus. Proc. Zool. Soc. Lond.* 139: 284–327.
   1964   Aggression in Monkey and Ape Societies. Carthy, J.D., and Ebling,
          F.J. (eds.), *The Natural History of Aggression.* N.Y.: Academic Press.
   1965   Social Organization of the Old-World Monkey and Apes. *Symp. Zool.
          Soc. Lond.* 14: 265–289.
HALLOWELL, A.I.
   1950   Personality Structure and the Evolution of Man. *Amer. Anthrop.* 52.
   1956   The Structural and Functional Dimensions of a Human Existence.
          Quart. Rev. Biol. 31: 88–101.

1960   Self, Society and Culture in Phylogenetic Perspective. Tax, S. (ed.), *Evolution of Man: Evolution After Darwin* II. Chicago: Univ. of Chicago Press.
1962   The Protocultural Foundations of Human Adaptation. Washburn, S.L. (ed.), *Social Life of Early Man.* London: Methuen.
HAMBURG, D.A.
1963   Emotions in Perspective of Human Evolution. Knapp, P. (ed.), *Expression of the Emotions in Man.* N.Y.: International Universities Press.
1968   Evolution of Emotional Responses: Evidence From Recent Research on Non-Human Primates. *Science and Psychoanalysis* 12.
1970   Recent Research on Hormonal Regulations of Aggressive Behavior. Paper presented at: UNESCO Expert meetings on the implications of recent scientific research for the understanding of human aggressiveness. Paris, May 1970.
HAMBURG, D.A., and LUNDE, D.
1966   Sex Hormones and the Development of Sex Differences in Human Behavior. Maccoby, E. (ed.), *The Development of Sex Differences.* Stanford: Stanford Univ. Press.
HAMBURG, D.A. *et al.*
1968   Studies of Distress in the Menstrual Cycle and the Postpartum Period. Michael, R.P. (ed.), *Endocrinology and Human Behaviour.* London: Oxford.
HAMILTON, W.D.
1963   The Evolution of Altruistic Behavior. *Amer. Nat.* 97: 354–356.
HANSEN, E.W.
1966   The Development of Maternal and Infant Behavior in the Rhesus Monkey. *Behavior* 27: 107–149.
HARLOW, H.F.
1958a   The Nature of Love. *Amer. Psychol.* 13: 673–685.
1958b   The Evolution of Learning. Roe, A., and Simpson, G.G. (eds.), *Behavior and Evolution.* New Haven, Conn.: Yale Univ. Press.
1959a   Basic Social Capacity of Primates. Spuhler, J.N. (ed.), *The Evolution of Man's Capacity for Culture.* Detroit, Mich.: Wayne State Univ. Press.
1959b   Love in Infant Monkeys. *Scientific American* (June).
1962a   Development of Affection in Primates. Bliss, E.L. (ed.), *Roots of Behavior.* N.Y.: Harper and Bros.
1962b   The Heterosexual Affectional System in Monkeys. *Amer. Psychol.* 17 (1): 1–9.
1965a   Total Social Isolation: Effects on Macaque Monkey Behavior. *Science* 148: 666.
1965b   Sexual Behavior in the Rhesus Monkey. Beach, F.A. (ed.), *Sex and Behavior.* N.Y.: John Wiley & Sons.
HARLOW, H.F., and HARLOW, M.K.
1962   Social Deprivation in Monkeys. *Scientific American* (Nov.).
HARLOW, H.F., and HARLOW, M.K.
1965   The Affectional Systems. Schrier. A.M.; Harlow, H.F.; and Stollnitz,

F. (eds.), *Behavior of Non-Human Primates* II. N.Y.: Academic Press.

HARLOW, H.F., HARLOW, M.K., and HANSEN, E.W.
1963 The Maternal Affectional System of Rhesus Monkeys. Rheingold, H.L. (ed.), *Maternal Behavior in Mammals.* N.Y.: John Wiley & Sons

HARLOW, H.F., and ZIMMERMAN, R.R.
1959 Affectional Responses in the Infant Monkey. *Science* 130: 421.

HARRIS, G.W.
1964 Sex Hormones, Brain Development, and Brain Function. *Endocrinology* 74: 627–651.

HARRIS, G.W., and LEVINE, S.
1965 Sexual Differentiation of the Brain and its Experimental Control. *J. Physiol.* 181: 379–400.

HART, C.W.M., and PILLING, A.R.
1960 *The Tiwi of Northern Australia.* N.Y.: Holt, Rinehart and Winston

HASSLER, R. and STEPHAN, H.
1966 *Evolution of the Forebrain.* Stuttgart: Georg Thieme Verlag.

HEBB, D.O., and THOMPSON, W.N.
1954 The Social Significance of Animal Studies. Lindzey, G. (ed.), *Handbook of Social Psychology* I. Reading, Mass.: Addison-Wesley.

HEDIGER, H.P.
1955 *Studies of the Psychology and Behavior of Captive Animals in Zoos and Circuses.* London: Butterworths.
1962 The Evolution of Territorial Behavior. Washburn, S.L. (ed.), *Social Life of Early Man.* London: Methuen.

HENDERSON, L.J.
1935 The Patient and Physician as a Social System. *New England J. Med.* 212: 819–823.

HENRY, J.
1954 The Formal Structure of a Psychiatric Hospital. *Psychiatry* 17: 139–151.
1960 A Cross-Cultural Outline of Education. *Current Anthrop.* I (4): 267–304.

HESS, E.H.
1958 Imprinting in Animals. *Scientific American* (March).
1962 Ethology: An Approach Toward the Complete Analysis of Behavior. Brown, R. (ed.), *New Directions in Psychology.* N.Y.: Holt, Rinehart and Winston.
1964 Imprinting in Birds. *Science* 146: 1128–1139.
1965 Attitude and Pupil Size. *Scientific American* 212: 46–54.

HIATT, L.R.
1967 Authority and Reciprocity in Australian Aboriginal Marriage Arrangements. *Mankind* 6 (10): 468–475.

HILL, O.W.C.
1957 *Man as an Animal.* London: Hutchinson.

HINDE, R.A.
1959 Some Recent Trends in Ethology. Koch, S. (ed.), *Psychology: A Study of a Science* 2. N.Y.: McGraw-Hill.

1963   The Nature of Imprinting. Foss, B.M. (ed.), *Determinants of Infant Behavior* 2. London: Methuen and N.Y.: John Wiley & Sons.

1965   Rhesus Monkey Aunts. Foss, B.M. (ed.), *Determinants of Infant Behavior* 3. London: Methuen and N.Y.: John Wiley & Sons.

1966   *Animal Behavior*. N.Y.: McGraw-Hill.

1969   Influence of Social Companions and of Temporary Separation on Mother-Infant Relations in Rhesus Monkeys. Foss, B.M. (ed.), *Determinants of Infant Behavior* IV.

HINDE, R.A.; ROWELL, T.E.; and SPENCER-BOOTH, Y.

1964   Behavior of Socially Living Rhesus Monkeys in Their First Six Months. *Proc. Zool. Soc. Lond.* 143: 609–649.

HINDE, R.A., and SPENCER-BOOTH, Y.

1967   The Behavior of Socially Living Rhesus Monkeys in Their First Two and a Half Years. *Anim. Behav.* 15: 169–196.

HINDE, R.A., and TINBERGEN, N.

1958   The Comparative Study of Species Specific Behavior. Roe, A., and Simpson, G.G. (eds.), *Behavior and Evolution*. New Haven, Conn.: Yale Univ. Press.

HIRSCH, J. (ed.)

1967   *Behavior-Genetic Analysis*. N.Y.: McGraw-Hill.

HOBHOUSE, L.T.

1913   The Historical Evolution of Property in Fact and in Idea. Hobhouse, L.T. (ed.), *Property: Its Duties and Rights*. London: Macmillan.

HOBHOUSE, L.T.; WHEELER, G.C.; and GINSBERG, M.

1915   *The Material Culture and Social Institutions of the Simpler Peoples*. London: Chapman and Hall.

HOCKETT, C.F.

1958   *A Modern Course in Linguistics*. N.Y.: Macmillan.

1959   Animal "Language" and Human Languages. Spuhler, J.N. (ed.), *The Evolution of Man's Capacity for Culture*. Detroit, Mich.: Wayne State Univ. Press.

HOCKETT, C.P., and ASCHER, R.

1964   The Human Revolution. *Current Anthrop.* 5: 135–147.

HOFSTADTER, R.

1944   *Social Darwinism in America*. Philadelphia, Penn.: Univ. of Penn. Press.

HOLLOWAY, R.

1966   Cranial Capacity, Neural Reorganization, and Hominid Evolution: A Search for more Suitable Parameters. *Amer. Anthrop.* 68: 103–121.

HOLT, J.

1964   *How Children Fail*. N.Y.: Pitman.

1967   *How Children Learn*. N.Y.: Pitman.

HOLTER, H.

1970   *Sex Roles and Social Structure*. Oslo: Universitetsforlaset.

HOMANS, G.C.

1961   *Social Behavior: Its Elementary Forms*. N.Y.: Harcourt, Brace and World.

HOPKINS, D.M.
1959 The Bering Land Bridge. Stanford: Stanford Univ. Press.
HORNEY, K.
1945 The Neurotic Personality of our Time. N.Y.: W.W. Norton.
HOWELL, F.C.
1964 The Hominization Process. Tax, S. (ed.), Horizons of Anthropology. Chicago: Aldine.
1969 Remains of Hominidae from Pliocene/Pleistocene Formations in The Lower Omo Basin, Ethiopia. Nature, London 223 (5212): 1234–1239.
HOWELL, F.C., and BOURLIÈRE, F. (eds.)
1964 African Ecology and Human Evolution. London: Methuen.
HOWELL, F.C., and CLARK, J.D.
1963 Acheulean Hunter-Gatherers of Sub-Saharan Africa. Howell, F.C., and Bourlière, F. (eds.), African Ecology and Human Evolution. Chicago: Aldine.
HOWELLS, W.W.
1966 Homo Erectus. Scientific American (Nov.).
HUIZINGA, J.
1949 Homo Ludens: A Study of the Play-Element in Culture. (Int'l Library of Sociology and Social Reconstruction) London: Routledge & Kegan Paul.
HULL, C.L.
1943 Principles of Behavior. N.Y.: Appleton, Century.
HUXLEY, J.S.
1914 The Courtship Habits of the Great Crested Grebe (Podiceps cristatus); with an addition to the Theory of Sexual Selection. Proc. Zool. Soc. Lond. (1914), 491–562.
1963a Evolution: The Modern Synthesis (2nd ed.). London: Allen and Unwin.
1963b Lorenzian Ethology. Zeitschrift fur Tierpsychologie 20: 402–409.
HUXLEY, J. (ed.)
1966 Ritualization in Man and Animals. Philosophical Transactions of the Royal Society of London B, 251.
IMANISHI, K.
1960 Social Organization of Sub-Human Primates in Their Natural Habitat. Current Anthrop. 1: 393–407.
1963 Social Behavior in Japanese Monkeys, Macaca fuscata. Southwick, C.H. (ed.), Primate Social Behavior. Princeton: Van Nostrand.
ITANI, J.
1963 Paternal Care in the Wild Japanese Monkey, Macaca fuscata. Southwick, C.H. (ed.), Primate Social Behavior. Princeton: Van Nostrand.
JANOWSKY, D.S.; GORNEY, R.; CASTELNUOVO-TEDESCO, P.; and STONE, C.B.
1969 Pre-Menstrual Increases in Psychiatric Hospital Admission Rates. Amer. J. of Obstetrics and Gynecology 103: 189–191.
JAY, P.
1968a Primate Field Studies and Human Evolution. Jay, P. (ed.), Primates. N.Y.: Holt, Rinehart and Winston.

1968b *Primates: Studies in Adaptation and Variability.* N.Y.: Holt, Rinehart and Winston.

JEWELL, P.A., and LOIZOS, C.
1966 *Play, Exploration and Territory in Mammals.* (Symp. Zool. Soc. Lond. No. 18) London: Academic Press.

JOLLY, C.J.
1970 The Seed-Eaters: A New Model of Hominid Differentiation Based on a Baboon Analogy. *Man: The J.R.A.I.* 5 (1): 5–26.

JONES, M.
1953 *The Therapeutic Community.* N.Y.: Basic Books.

JOSEPHSON, E., and JOSEPHSON, M.
1962 *Man Alone: Alienation in Modern Society.* N.Y.: Dell.

KAHLER, E.
1967 (orig. 1957) *The Tower and the Abyss.* N.Y.: Viking.

KALOGERAKIS, M.G.
1963 The Role of Olfaction in Sexual Development. *Psychosomatic Medicine* XXV (5).

KAPLAN, B., and JOHNSON, D.
1964 The Social Meaning of Navaho Psychopathology and Psychotherapy. Kiev, A. (ed.), *Magic, Faith, and Healing.* Glencoe, Ill.: Free Press.

KAPLAN, D.
1965 The Superorganic: Science or Metaphysics. *Amer. Anthrop.* 67 (4): 958–974.

KAUFMAN, I.C., and ROSENBLUM, L.A.
1967a Depression in Infant Monkeys Separated From Their Mothers. *Science* 155: 1030–1031.
1969 The Waning of the Mother-Infant Bond in Two Species of Macaque. Foss, P.M. (ed.), *Determinants of Infant Behavior* IV. London: Methuen.

KAUFMANN, J.H.
1967 Social Relations of Adult Males in a Free-Ranging Band of Rhesus Monkeys. Altmann, S.A. (ed.), *Social Communication Among Primates.* Chicago: Univ. of Chicago Press.
1966 Social Relations of Infant Rhesus Monkeys and Their Mothers in a Free-Ranging Band. *Zoologica* 51: 17–28.

KAWAI, M.
1965 On the System of Social Ranks in a Natural Troop of Japanese Monkeys: (1) Basic Rank and Dependent Rank. Altmann, S.A. (ed.), *Japanese Monkeys.* Atlanta, Ga.: Altmann.

KAWAMURA, S.
1965 Matriarchal Social Ranks in the Minoo-B Troop: A Study of the Rank System of Japanese Monkeys. Altmann, S.A. (ed.), *Japanese Monkeys.* Atlanta, Ga.: Altmann.

KEITH, A.
1948 *A New Theory of Human Evolution.* London: Watts.

KETTLEWELL, H.B.D.
1965 Insect Survival and Selection for Pattern. *Science* 148: 1290–1296.

KIEV, A.
1964 *Magic, Faith, and Healing.* Glencoe, Ill.: Free Press.

KINSEY, A.C.; POMEROY, W.B.; and MARTIN, C.E.
1948 *Sexual Behavior in the Human Male*. Philadelphia, Penn: W.B. Saunders.

KITTREDGE, G.L.
1929 *Witchcraft in Old and New England*. Cambridge, Mass.: Harvard Univ.

KLEIN, M.
1949 *The Psycho-Analysis of Children*. London: Hogarth Press.

KLOPFER, P.H.
1965 Imprinting: A Reassessment. *Science* 147: 302–303.
1969 *Habitats and Territories: A Study of the Use of Space by Animals*. N.Y.: Basic Books.

KLOPFER, P.H., and HAILMAN, J.P.
1967 *An Introduction to Animal Behavior*. Englewood Cliffs, N.J.: Prentice-Hall.

KLOPPER, A.
1964 Physiological Background to Aggression. Carthy, J.D., and Ebling, F.J. (eds.), *The Natural History of Aggression*. London: Academic Press.

KNAPP, P.H. (ed.)
1963 *Expression of the Emotions in Man*. N.Y.: International Universities Press.

KOESTLER, A.
1967 *The Ghost in the Machine*. London: Hutchinson.

KOFORD, C.B.
1963a Group Relations in an Island Colony of Rhesus Monkeys. Southwick, C.H. (ed.), 1963. *Primate Social Behavior*. Princeton: Van Nostrand.
1963b Rank of Mothers and Sons in Bands of Rhesus Monkeys. *Science* 141: 356–357.

KOGON, E.
1950 *The Theory and Practice of Hell*. N.Y.: Farrar.

KOHL, H.
1969 *The Open Classroom*. N.Y.: Vintage.

KOPELL, B.S. *et al.*
1969 Variations in Some Measures of Arousal During the Menstrual Cycle. *J. Nervous and Mental Disease* 148 (2): 180–187.

KORTLANDT, A., and KOOIJ, M.
1963 Protohominid Behaviour in Primates. *Symp. Zool. Soc. Lond.* 10: 61–88.

KOTCHETKOVA, V.I.
1960 L'evolution des regions specifiquement humaines de l'écorce cerebrale chez les Hominides. *Proc. 6th Int. Cong. Anthrop. and Ethnol. Sci. Paris* 1: 623–630.

KOYAMA, N.
1967 On Dominance Rank and Kinship of a Wild Japanese Monkey Troop in Arashiyama. *Primates* 8 (3): 189–216.

KROEBER, A.L.
1917 The Superorganic. *Amer. Anthrop.* 19: 163–213. Also in: *The Nature of Culture*. Chicago: Univ. of Chicago Press, 1952.

1948 (1923) *Anthropology*. N.Y.: Harcourt, Brace.
KROEBER, A.L., and KLUCKHOHN, C.
  1952 Culture: A Critical Review of Concepts and Definitions. *Papers of the Peabody Museum of American Archeology and Ethnology* 47 (1). Cambridge, Mass.: Harvard Univ. Press.
KROPOTKIN, P.
  1902 *Mutual Aid*. London: Heinemann.
KUHME, W.
  1965 Communal Food Distribution and Division of Labor in African Hunting Dogs. *Nature, London* 205: 443–444.
KUMMER, H.
  1967 Tripartite Relations in Hamadryas Baboons. Altmann, S.A. (ed.), *Social Communication Among Primates*. Chicago and London: Univ. of Chicago Press.
  1968 *Social Organization of Hamadryas Baboons*. Chicago: Univ. of Chicago Press.
KURATOWSKI, K.
  1962 *Introduction to Set Theory and Topology*. London: Pergamon and Reading, Mass.: Addison-Wesley.
LABARRE, W.
  1954 *The Human Animal*. Chicago: Univ. of Chicago Press.
LACK, D.
  1954 *The Natural Regulation of Animal Numbers*. Oxford: Clarendon Press.
LAING, R.D.
  1959 *The Divided Self*. London: Tavistock.
  1967 *The Politics of Experience*. N.Y.: Ballantine.
LANCASTER, J.
  1968a Primate Communication Systems and the Emergence of Human Language. Jay, P. (ed.), *Primates: Studies in Adaptation and Variability*. N.Y.: Holt, Rinehart and Winston.
  1968b On the Evolution of Tool-Using Behavior. *Amer. Anthrop.* 70: 56–66.
LANCASTER, J.B., and LEE, R.B.
  1965 The Annual Reproductive Cycle in Monkeys and Apes. DeVore, I. (ed.), *Primate Behavior*. N.Y.: Holt, Rinehart and Winston.
LAUGHLIN, W.S.
  1968 Hunting: An Integrating Biobehavior System and Its Evolutionary Importance. Lee, R.B., and DeVore, I. (eds.), *Man the Hunter*. Chicago: Aldine.
LAWICK-GOODALL, J. VAN
  1967a Mother-Offspring Relationships in Free-Ranging Chimpanzees. Morris, D. (ed.), *Primate Ethology*. London: Weidenfelt and Nicolson.
  1967b *My Friends, The Wild Chimpanzees*. National Geographic Society.
  1968 The Behavior of Free-Living Chimpanzees in the Gombe Stream Reserve. *Anim. Behav. Monog.*, vol. 1, part 3.
LEACH, E.R.
  1961 *Rethinking Anthropology*. London School of Economics Monographs

on Social Anthropology (22). London: Athlone Press.

1967　*A Runaway World?* London: B.B.C.

LEAKEY, L.S.B.

1967a　An Early Miocene Member of Hominidae. *Nature* (Jan. 14).

1967b　Development of Aggression as a Factor in Early Human and Pre-Human Evolution. Clemente, C.D., and Lindsley, D.B. (eds.), *Aggression and Defense.* Berkeley and L.A.:
Univ. of California Press.

LEBERGOTT, S. (ed.)

1964　*Men Without Work.* Englewood Cliffs, N.J.: Prentice-Hall.

LEE, R.B.

1966　! Kung Bushman Subsistence: An Input-Output Analysis. Damas, D. (ed.), *Ecological Essays: Proceedings of the Conference on Cultural Ecology, National Museum of Canada.*

1967　Trance Cure of the ! Kung Bushmen. *Natural History* (Nov.), pp. 30–37.

1968a　Sociology of the ! Kung Bushman Trance Performances. Prince, R.H. (ed.), *Trance and Possession States.* Montreal: R.M. Bucke Memorial Soc.

1968b　What Hunters Do For a Living, or How To Make Out in Scarce Resources. Lee, R.B., and DeVore, I. (eds.), *Man The Hunter.* Chicago: Aldine.

LEE, R.B., and DeVORE, I. (eds.)

1968　*Man The Hunter.* Chicago: Aldine.

LEEDS, A., and VAYDA, A.P. (eds.)

1965　*Man, Culture, and Animals: The Role of Animals in Human Ecological Adjustments.* Amer. Assoc. for the Advancement of Science (78).

LEHRMANN, D.S.

1953　A Critique of Konrad Lorenz's Theory of Instinctive Behavior. *Quart. Rev. Biol.* 28: 337–363.

LEIGHTON, A.H., and LEIGHTON, D.C.

1941　Elements of Psychotherapy in Navaho Religion. *Psychiatry* IV: 515–524.

LeMAGNEN, J.

1950　Physiologie des sensations: Nouvelles données sur la Phénomène de l'Exaltolide. *Compt. Rend.* 230: 1103.

1953　L'olfaction: le fonctionnement olfactif et son intervention dans les régulations psychophysiologiques. *J. Physiol.* (Paris) 45: 285.

LENNEBERG, E.H.

1967　*Biological Foundations of Language.* N.Y.: John Wiley & Sons.

LEONARD, G.B.

1968　*Education and Ecstasy.* N.Y.: Delta.

LEVINE, R.A.

1963　Child Rearing in Sub-Saharan Africa: An Interim Report. *Bulletin of the Menninger Clinic* 27 (5): 245–256.

LEVINE, S.

1966　Sex Differences in the Brain. *Scientific American* (April).

LÉVI-STRAUSS, C.

1944　The Social and Psychological Aspects of Chieftainship in a Primitive

Tribe: The Nambikwara. *Trans. of the New York Acad. of Sciences* (series 2, vol. VII, no. 1).
1949a Le Sorcier et sa Magie. *Les Temps Modernes*, 4 annee, No. 41. (Reprinted in *Anthropologie Structurale*. Paris: Plon.)
1949b *Les Structures Elémentaires de la Parenté*. Paris: Presses Universitaires de France.
1966 The Scope of Anthropology. *Current Anthrop*. (April).
1969 *The Elementary Structures of Kinship*. Bell, J.H., and Von Sturmer, J.R. (trans.); Needham, R. (trans. and ed.), Boston: Beacon Press.

LEVY, M.J.
1969 Kinship Contexts and Some Human Universals, Past and Future: A Set of Hypotheses. *Amer. Sociol.* 4 (1).

LEYHAUSEN, P.
1965 The Sane Community: A Density Problem? *Discovery* (Sept.).

LINTON, R.
1936 *The Study of Man*. N.Y.: Appleton, Century.

LIPSET, S.
1959 *Political Man*. London. Heinemann.

LIVINGSTONE, F.B.
1960 Natural Selection, Disease, and Ongoing Evolution, as Illustrated by the ABO Blood Groups. Lasker, G.W. (ed.), *The Processes of Ongoing Evolution*. Detroit, Mich.: Wayne State Univ. Press.

LOIZOS, C.
1967 Play Behavior in Higher Primates: A Review. Morris, D. (ed.), *Primate Ethology*. Chicago: Aldine.

LORENZ, K.
1935 Companionship in Bird Life: Fellow Members of the Species as Releasers of Social Behavior. Schiller, C. (ed.), *Instinctive Behavior*. N.Y.: International Universities Press (1957).
1950 The Comparative Method in Studying Innate Behavior Patterns. *Physiological Mechanisms in Animal Behavior*. (Sympos. Soc. Exp. Biol. No. 4) N.Y.: Academic Press.
1956a The Objectivistic Theory of Instinct. Grassé, P. (ed.), *L'Instinct dans le Comportement des Animaux et de l'Homme*. Paris: Masson et Cie.
1956b Plays and Vacuum Activities. Grassé, P. (ed.), *L'Instinct dans le Comportement des Animaux et de l'Homme*. Paris: Masson et Cie.
1958 The Evolution of Behavior. *Scientific American* (Dec.).
1964 Ritualized Fighting. Carthy, J.D., and Ebling, F.J. (eds.), *The Natural History of Aggression*. London and N.Y.: Academic Press.
1965 *Evolution and Modification of Behavior*. Chicago: Univ. of Chicago Press.
1966 *On Aggression*. London: Methuen.
1969 Innate Bases of Learning. Pribram, K.H. (ed.), *On the Biology of Learning*. N.Y.: Harcourt, Brace and World.

LOWENTHAL, L.
1946 Terror's Atomization of Man. *Commentary* 1 (3).

LOWIE, R.H.
1956 *The Crow Indians*. N.Y.: Holt, Rinehart and Winston.

MACCOBY, E. (ed.)
1966   *The Development of Sex Differences.* Stanford: Stanford Univ. Press.
1970   Feminine Intellect and the Demands of Science. *Impact of Science on Society* 20: 1. U.N.E.S.C.O.
MACLEAN, P.D.
1949   Psychosomatic Disease and the "Visceral Brain." *Psychosom. Med.* 11: 338–353.
1958   The Limbic System with Respect to Self-Preservation and the Preservation of the Species. *J. Nervous and Mental Disease* 127: 1–11.
1962   New Findings Relevant to the Evolution of Psychosexual Functions of the Brain. *J. Nervous and Mental Disease* 135 (4): 289–301.
1964   Man and His Animal Brains. *Modern Medicine* (Feb. 3).
1967   The Brain in Relation to Empathy and Medical Education. *J. Nervous and Mental Disease* 144 (5).
1968   Alternative Neural Pathways to Violence. Ng, L. (ed.), *Alternatives to Violence.* N.Y.: Time-Life Books.
MACNEISH, R.S.
1964   The Origins of New World Civilization. *Scientific American* (Nov.).
MALINOWSKI, B.
1922   *Argonauts of the Western Pacific.* London: Geo. Routledge and Sons.
1929   *The Sexual Life of Savages.* London: Geo. Routledge and Sons.
1944   *A Scientific Theory of Culture and other Essays.* Chapel Hill, N.C.: Univ. of North Carolina Press.
MALTHUS, T.R.
1798   *An Essay on the Principle of Population.* London: J. Johnson.
MANDEL, J.
1967   The Menstrual Cycle and Suicide. *J. Amer. Med. Ass.* (May).
MAQUET, J.
1961   *The Premise of Inequality in Ruanda.* London: Oxford Univ. Press.
MARK, V.H., and ERVIN, F.R.
1970   *Violence and the Brain.* N.Y.: Harper & Row.
MARLER, P.
1967   Animal Communication Signals. *Science* 157: 769–773.
MARWICK, M.G.
1965   *Sorcery in its Social Setting.* Manchester: Manchester Univ. Press.
MARX, K.
1887   *Capital: A Critical Analysis of Capitalist Production.* [3rd German ed., trans. by Moore, S., and Aveling, E.] London: S. Sonnenschein, Lowrey and Co.
1964a   *Early Writings.* N.Y.: McGraw-Hill.
1964b   *Pre-Capitalist Economic Formations.* Hobsbawm, E.J. (ed.). London: Lawrence and Wishart.
1967   *Writings of the Young Marx on Philosophy and Society.* Easton, L.D., and Gaddat, K.H. (eds.). Garden City, N.Y.: Doubleday
MARX, K., and ENGELS, F.
1948   (orig. 1888)   *Communist Manifesto, Socialist Landmark.* (Original text plus a new appreciation written for the Labour Party by H.J. Laski) London: Allen and Unwin.

Mason, W.A.
1965a   Determinants of Social Behavior in Young Chimpanzees. Schrier, A.M.; Harlow, H.; and Stollnitz, F. (eds.), *Behavior of Nonhuman Primates*. N.Y. and London: Academic Press.
1965b   The Social Development of Monkeys and Apes. DeVore, I. (ed.), *Primate Behavior*. N.Y. and London: Holt, Rinehart and Winston.

Mason, W.A., and Sponholz, R.R.
1963   Behavior of Rhesus Monkeys Raised in Isolation. *J. Psychiat. Res.* 1: 299–306.

Masters, R.D.
1968   *The Political Philosophy of Rousseau*. Princeton: Princeton Univ. Press.

Matthews, H.L.
1964   Overt Fighting in Mammals. Carthy, J.D., and Ebling, F.J. (eds.), *The Natural History of Aggression*. London: Academic Press.

Mauss, M.
1925   Essai sur le don. *Année Sociologique* N.S.1 [*The Gift*, Cunnison, I.G. (trans.), London: Cohen and West 1954].

Mayer, P. (ed.)
1970   *Socialization: The Approach From Social Anthropology*. (A.S.A. Monographs in Social Anthropology 8) London: Tavistock.

Mayo, E.
1945   *The Social Problems of an Industrial Civilization*. Cambridge, Mass.: Harvard Univ. Press.

Mayr, E.
1963   *Animal Species and Evolution*. Cambridge, Mass.: Harvard Univ. Press.

McDougall, W.
1908   *Social Psychology*. London: Methuen.

McLennan, J.F.
1865   *Primitive Marriage*. London: Black.

Mead, M.
1962   A Cultural Anthropologist's Approach to Maternal Deprivation. *Deprivation of Maternal Care: A Reassessment of its Effects*. Public Health Papers (14). Geneva: W.H.O.
1970   *Culture and Commitment*. Garden City, N.Y.: Natural History Press.

Mead, M., and Kaplan, F.B. (eds.)
1965   *American Women: The Report of the President's Commission on the Status of Women*. N.Y.: Charles Scribner's Sons.

Meier, G.W.
1965   Other Data on the Effects of Social Isolation During Rearing Upon Adult Reproductive Behavior in the Rhesus Monkey (*Macaca mulatta*). *Anim. Behav.* 13: 228–231.

Menzel, E.W., Jr.
1963   The Effects of Cumulative Experience on Responses to Novel Objects in Young Isolation-Reared Chimpanzees. *Behavior* 21: 1–12.

MERTON, R.K.
  1957 Bureaucratic Structure and Personality. *Social Theory and Social Structure*. Glencoe, Ill.: Free Press.
MESSING, S.D.
  1958 Group Therapy and Social Status in the Zar Cult of Ethiopia. *Amer. Anthrop.* 60 (6): 1120–1126.
MICHAEL, R.P.
  1968 *Endocrinology and Human Behavior*. London: Oxford Univ. Press.
MICHAEL, R.P., and KEVERNE, E.B.
  1968 Pheromones in the Communication of Sexual Status in Primates. *Nature, London* 218: 746–749.
MICHAEL, R.P., and ZUMPE, D.
  1970 Rhythmic Changes in the Copulatory Frequency of Rhesus Monkeys (*Macaca mulatta*) in Relation to the Menstrual Cycle and a Comparison with the Human Cycle. *J. Reproduction and Fertility* 21: 199–201.
MIDDLETON, J. (ed.)
  1970 *From Child to Adult; Studies in the Anthropology of Education*. N.Y.: Natural History Press.
MIDDLETON, J., and WINTER, E.H. (eds.)
  1963 *Witchcraft and Sorcery in East Africa*. London: Routledge and Kegan Paul.
MILLER, W., and ERVIN, S.
  1964 The Development of Grammar in Child Language. *Monog. Soc. Res. Child Devel.* 29: 9–33.
MILLET, K.
  1970 *Sexual Politics*. Garden City, N.Y.: Doubleday.
MISHKIN, B.
  1940 Rank and Warfare Among the Plains Indians. *American Ethnological Society Monograph*.
MOLTZ, H.
  1960 Imprinting: Empirical Basis and Theoretical Significance. *Psychology Bulletin* 57: 291–314.
MONEY, J.
  1965 Psychosexual Differentiation. *Sex Research: New Developments*. N.Y.: Holt, Rinehart and Winston.
  1965 *Sex Research: New Developments*. N.Y.: Holt, Rinehart and Winston.
MONTAGU, M.F.A.
  1957 *The Reproductive Development of the Female*. N.Y.: Julian Press.
MONTAGU, A. (ed.)
  1962 *Culture and the Evolution of Man*. Oxford Univ. Press.
  1968 *Man and Aggression*. N.Y.: Oxford Univ. Press.
MONTESSORI, M.
  1964 *The Montessori Method*. N.Y.: Schocken.
MOOS, R.R.H.
  1969 Typology of Menstrual Cycle Symptoms. *Amer. J. of Obstetrics and Gynecology* 103 (3): 390–402.
MORGAN, L.H.
  1877 *Ancient Society*. N.Y.: H. Holt.

Morgan, R. (ed.)
1970 *Sisterhood is Powerful.* N.Y.: Random House.
Morris, D.
1956 The Function and Causation of Courtship Ceremonies. Grassé, P. (ed.), *L'Instinct dans le Comportement des Animaux et de l'Homme.* Paris: Masson et Cie.
1967 *The Naked Ape.* London: Constable.
1970 *The Human Zoo.* N.Y.: McGraw-Hill.
Morris, D. (ed.)
1967 *Primate Ethology.* London: Weidenfeld and Nicolson.
Mowat, F.
1963 *Never Cry Wolf.* Boston: Little, Brown.
Mumford, L.
1934 *Technics and Civilization.* N.Y.: Harcourt, Brace and World.
Murdock, G.P.
1937 Comparative Data on the Division of Labor by Sex. *Social Forces* 15 (4): 551–553.
1945 The Common Denominator of Cultures. Linton, R. (ed.), *The Science of Man in the World Crisis.* N.Y.: Columbia Univ. Press.
1949 *Social Structure.* N.Y.: Macmillan Press.
Murie, A.
1944 The Wolves of Mount McKinley. *U.S. Department of Interior, Fauna Series* (5): 1–238.
Murphy, J.M.
1964 Psychotherapeutic Aspects of Shamanism on St. Lawrence Island, Alaska. Kiev, A. (ed.), *Magic, Faith, and Healing.* Glencoe, Ill.: Free Press.
Murphy, R.F.
1959 Social Structure and Sex Antagonism. *Southwest. J. Anthrop.* 15 (1).
Nadel, S.F.
1946 A Study of Shamanism in the Nuba Mountains. *J. Royal Anthrop. Inst.* LXXVI: 25–37.
Naegele, K.D.
1970 *Health and Healing.* San Francisco: Jossey-Bass.
Nakane, C.
1963 The Nayar Family in a Disintegrating Matrilineal System. Mogey, J. (ed.), *Family and Marriage.* International Studies in Sociol. and Soc. Anthrop. 1. Leiden: E.J. Brill.
Napier, J.
1962 The Evolution of the Hand. *Scientific American* (Dec.).
1964 The Evolution of Bipedal Walking in the Hominids. *Arch. Biol.* 75. Suppl., pp. 673–708.
1967 The Antiquity of Human Walking. *Scientific American* (April).
1970 *The Roots of Mankind.* Washington, D.C.: Smithsonian Institution Press.
Napier, J.R., and Napier, P.H.
1967 *A Handbook of Living Primates.* London and N.Y.: Academic Press.

NASH, M.
1961   Witchcraft as Social Process in a Tzeltal Community. *America Indigena* 20: 121–126.
1966   *Primitive and Peasant Economic Systems.* San Francisco: Chandler Publ.

NEEDHAM, R.
1962   *Structure and Sentiment.* Chicago: Univ. of Chicago Press.

NEILL, A.S.
1960   *Summerhill: A Radical Approach to Child Rearing.* N.Y.: Hart.

NEWCOMB, W.W.
1950   A Re-Examination of the Causes of Plains Warfare. *Amer. Anthrop.* 317–329.

NIEBOER, H.J.
1900   *Slavery as an Industrial System: Ethnological Researches.* The Hague: Martinus Nijhoff.

NISSEN, H.W.
1956   Individuality in Behavior of Chimpanzees. *Amer. Anthrop.* 58: 407–413.

NISSEN, I.
1961   *Absolute Monogamy.* Oslo: Aschehoug.

OAKLEY, K.P.
1950   *Man the Tool-Maker.* London: British Museum.
1957   Tools Makyth Man. *Antiquity* 31: 199–209. Also in: *Annual Report, Smithsonian Institution* 1958: 431–445.
1962   On Man's Use of Fire, with comments on tool-making and hunting. Washburn, S.L. (ed.), *Social Life of Early Man.* London: Methuen.

O'NEILL, W.L.
1967   *Everyone Was Brave: The Rise and Fall of Feminism in America.* Chicago: Quadrangle.

OPIE, I., and OPIE, P.
1961   *The Lore and Language of School Children.* Oxford: Clarendon Press.

OPLER, M.E.
1964   The Human Being in Culture Theory. *Amer. Anthrop.* 66 (3): 507–528.

OTTERBEIN, K.F.
1967   The Evolution of Zulu Warfare. Bohannan, P. (ed.), *Law and Warfare.* N.Y.: Natural History Press.

PAINE, R.
1967   What is Gossip About: An Alternative Hypothesis. *Man: The J.R.A.I.* 2: 278–285.

PAPPENHEIM, F.
1968   *The Alienation of Modern Man; An Interpretation Based on Marx and Tönnies.* N.Y.: Modern Reader Paperbacks.

PARK, G.K.
1963   Divination and Its Social Context. *J. Royal Anthrop. Inst.* 93 (2).

PARK, W.Z.
1938   *Shamanism in Western North America.* Evanston, Ill.: Univ. of Illinois.

PARKER, A.S.
1960 Premenstrual Tension Syndrome. *Medical Clinic of North America*, No. 44 (March).

PARKINSON, C.N.
1957 *Parkinson's Law*. Boston: Houghton Mifflin.

PARSONS, T.
1951a *The Social System*. N.Y.: Free Press.
1951b Illness and the Role of the Physician: A Sociological Perspective. *Amer. J. Orthopsychiatry* 21: 452–460.
1957 The Mental Hospital as a Type of Organization. Greenblatt, M.; Levinson, D.J.; and Williams, R.H. (eds.), *The Patient and the Mental Hospital*. Glencoe, Ill.: Free Press.

PARSONS, T., and SMELSER, N.
1956 *Economy and Society*. Glencoe, Ill.: Free Press.

PASTORE, N.
1949 *The Nature-Nurture Controversy*. N.Y.: King's Crown Press.

PAULME, D. (ed.)
1964 *Women of Tropical Africa*. Berkeley: Univ. of California Press.

PAVLOV, I.P.
1927 *Conditioned Reflexes*. London: Oxford Univ. Press.
1928 *Lectures on Conditioned Reflexes*. London: Lawrence and Wishart.

PENFIELD, W., and RASMUSSEN, T.
1950 *The Cerebral Cortex of Man*. N.Y.: Macmillan.

PERICOT, L.
1962 The Social Life of Paleolithic Hunters as Shown by Levantine Art. Washburn, S.L. (ed.), *Social Life of Early Man*. London: Methuen.

PETTITT, G.A.
1970 *Prisoners of Culture*. N.Y.: Charles Scribner's Sons.

PFEIFFER, J.
1969 *The Emergence of Man*. N.Y.: Harper & Row.

PICKENS, D.K.
1968 *Eugenics and the Progressives*. N.Y.: Vanderbilt Univ. Press.

PILBEAM, D.R.
1967 Man's Earliest Ancestors. *Science J.* 3 (2).

POLANYI, K. *et al.*
1957 *Trade and Markets in Early Empires*. Glencoe, Ill.: Free Press.

PRIBRAM, K.H. (ed.)
1969 *On the Biology of Learning*. N.Y.: Harcourt, Brace and World.

PRICE, J.
1967 The Dominance Hierarchy and the Evolution of Mental Illness. *The Lancet* (July 29), pp. 243–246.

PROVENCE, S., and LIPTON, R.C.
1962 *Infants in Institutions*. London: Bailey and Swinfen. N.Y.: Internat'l Universities Press.

RAPOPORT, R.N., and RAPOPORT, R.S.
1957 "Democratization" and Authority in a Therapeutic Community. *Behavioral Science* 2: 128–133.

RAPPOPORT, R.A.
   1967   *Pigs for the Ancestors.* New Haven, Conn.: Yale Univ. Press.
RASMUSSEN, K.
   1929   *Report of the Fifth Thule Expedition, 1921–24* VII (1). *Intellectual Culture of the Iglulik Eskimos.* Copenhagen: Gyldendalske Boghandel, Nordisk Forlag.
RAUM, O.F.
   1940   *A Chaga Childhood.* London: Oxford Univ. Press.
READ, C.
   1920   *The Origin of Man and His Superstitions.* Cambridge: Cambridge Univ. Press.
READ, M.
   1959   *Children of Their Fathers: Growing Up Among the Ngoni of Nyasaland.* London: Methuen.
REDFIELD, R.
   1956   *Peasant Society and Culture.* Chicago: Univ. of Chicago Press.
REICHARD, G.
   1939   *A Navaho Medicine Man: Sand Paintings and Legends of Miguelito.* N.Y.: J.J. Augustin.
REINHOLD, R.
   1971   Bone Traces Man Back 5 Million Years. *The New York Times* (Feb. 19).
REYNOLDS, V.
   1965   *Budongo: A Forest and Its Chimpanzees.* London: Methuen and Co.
   1966a   Open Groups in Hominid Evolution. *Man: The J.R.A.I.* 1 (4): 441–452.
   1968   Kinship and the Family in Monkeys, Apes and Man. *Man: The J.R.A.I.* 3 (2): 209–223.
   1970   Roles and Role Change in Monkey Society: the Consort Relationship of Rhesus Monkeys. *Man: The J.R.A.I.* 5 (3): 449–465.
RHEINGOLD, H.L.
   1961   The Effect of Environmental Stimulation Upon Social and Exploratory Behavior in the Human Infant. Foss, B.M. (ed.), *Determinants of Infant Behavior* 1. N.Y.: John Wiley & Sons.
   1963a   Controlling the Infant's Exploratory Behaviour. Foss, B.M. (ed.), *Determinants of Infant Behavior* 2. N.Y.: John Wiley & Sons.
   1963b   *Maternal Behavior in Mammals.* N.Y.: John Wiley & Sons.
RICHARDS, A.I.
   1956   *Chisungu: A Girls' Initiation Ceremony Among the Bemba of Northern Rhodesia.* London: Faber and Faber.
RICHARDS, O.W.
   1953   *The Social Insects.* London: Macdonald.
RICHARDSON, L.F.
   1960   *Statistics of Deadly Quarrels.* London: Stevens and Sons.
RITTER, A.E.
   1955   *Shaka Zulu.* N.Y.: G.P. Putnam's Sons.

ROBBINS, L.
  1932 *An Essay on the Nature and Significance of Economic Science.* London: Macmillan.
ROBERTS, D.F., and HARRISON, G.A.
  1959 *Natural Selection in Human Populations.* N.Y.: Pergamon Press.
ROBINSON, J.T.
  1964 Adaptive Radiation in the Australopithecines and the Origin of Man. Howell, F.C., and Bourlière, F. (eds.), *African Ecology and Human Evolution.* London: Methuen.
ROE, A., and SIMPSON, G.G. (eds.)
  1958 *Behavior and Evolution.* New Haven, Conn.: Yale Univ. Press.
ROEDER, K.D.
  1963 Ethology and Neurophysiology. *Zeitschrift fur Tierpsychologie* 20: 434–440.
ROETHLESBERGER, F.J., and DIXON, W.J.
  1939 *Management and the Worker.* Cambridge, Mass.: Harvard Univ. Press.
ROMER, A.S.
  1958 Phylogeny and Behavior with Special Reference to Vertebrate Evolution. Roe, A., and Simpson, G.G. (eds.), *Behavior and Evolution.* New Haven, Conn.: Yale Univ. Press.
  1959 *The Vertebrate Story.* Chicago: Univ. of Chicago Press.
ROSE, F.G.G.
  1960 *Classification of Kin, Age-Structure and Marriage among the Groote Eylandt Aborigines: A Study in Method and a Theory of Australian Kinship.* Berlin: Akademie-Verlag. London: Pergamon Press.
  1968 Australian Marriage, Land-Owning Groups and Initiations. Lee, R.B., and DeVore, I. (eds.), *Man The Hunter.* Chicago: Aldine.
ROWELL, T.E.; HINDE, R.A.; and SPENCER-BOOTH, Y.
  1964 "Aunt"—Infant Interaction in Captive Rhesus Monkeys. *J. Anim. Behav.* 12: 219–226.
ROYAL COMMISSION ON THE STATUS OF WOMEN
  1970 Participation of Women in Public Life. *Report of the Royal Commission on the Status of Women.* Ottawa: Information Canada.
RUBINOFF, C.
  1967 *Pornography of Power.* N.Y.: Quadrangle Books.
RUSSELL, B.
  1945 *A History of Western Philosophy.* N.Y.: Simon and Schuster.
RUSSELL, W.M.S., and RUSSELL, C.
  1961 *Human Behaviour.* London: Andre Deutch.
  1968 *Violence, Monkeys and Man.* London: Macmillan.
SADE, D.S.
  1965 Some aspects of Parent-Offspring and Sibling Relations in a Group of Rhesus Monkeys, with a Discussion of Grooming. *Amer. J. Phys. Anthrop.* 23: 1–17.
  1967 Determinants of Dominance in a Group of Free-Ranging Rhesus

Monkeys. Altmann, S.A. (ed.), *Social Communication among Primates.* Chicago: Univ. of Chicago Press.

1968   Inhibition of Son-Mother Mating Among Free-Ranging Rhesus Monkeys. *Science and Psychoanalysis* 12: 18–37.

SAHLINS, M.D.

1959   The Social Life of Monkeys, Apes, and Primitive Man. Spuhler, J.H. (ed.), *The Evolution of Man's Capacity for Culture.* Detroit, Mich.: Wayne State Univ. Press.

1960   The Origin of Society. *Scientific American* 203: 76–86.

1961   The Segmentary Lineage: An Organization of Predatory Expansion. *Amer. Anthrop.* 63: 322–345.

1963a   On the Sociology of Primitive Exchange. Banton, M. (ed.), *The Relevance for Models for Social Anthropology.* A.S.A. Monograph No. 1. London: Tavistock.

1963b   Poor Man, Rich Man, Big Man, Chief: Political Types in Melanesia and Polynesia. *Comp. Studies Soc. Hist.* 5: 285–303.

SALISBURY, R.

1962   *From Stone to Steel.* Cambridge: Cambridge Univ. Press.

SALZEN, E.A.

1967   Imprinting in Birds and Primates. *Behavior* 28: 232–254.

SARICH, V.M.

1968   The Origin of the Hominids: An Immunological Approach. Washburn, S.L., and Jay, P. (eds.), *Perspectives on Human Evolution* 1. N.Y.: Holt, Rinehart and Winston.

SCHALLER, G., and LOWTHER, G.

1969   The Relevance of Carnivore Behavior to the Study of Early Hominids. *Southwest. J. Anthrop.* 25: 307–341.

SCHAPERA, I. (ed.)

1937   *The Bantu-Speaking Tribes of South Africa.* London: Geo. Routledge and Sons.

SCHILLER, C.H. (ed.)

1957   *Instinctive Behavior.* N.Y.: International Universities Press.

SCHNEIDER, D., and GOUGH, K.

1961   *Matrilineal Kinship.* Berkeley and L.A.: Univ. of California Press.

SCHNEIRLA, T.C.

1941   Social Organization in Insects, as Related to Individual Function. *Psychol. Rev.* 48: 465–486.

1956   Interrelationships of the "Innate" and the "Acquired" in Instinctive Behavior. Grassé, P. (ed.), *L'Instinct dans le Comportement des Animaux et de L'Homme.* Paris: Masson et Cie.

SCHORR, A.L.

1966   *Slums and Social Insecurity.* Washington, D.C.: U.S. Dept. of H.E.W. Research, Report No. 1.

SCHRIER, A.M.; HARLOW, H.F.; and STOLLNITZ, F. (eds.)

1965   *Behavior of Nonhuman Primates: Modern Research Trends* 1 and 2. N.Y. and London: Academic Press.

SCHULTZ, A.H.
  1961   Some Factors Influencing the Social Life of Primates in General and
         of Early Man in Particular. Washburn, S.L. (ed.), *Social Life of Early
         Man*. London: Methuen.
SCHUMPETER, J.A.
  1942   *Capitalism, Socialism and Democracy*. N.Y.: Harper and Bros.
SCHWEITZER, A.
  1948 (1913 orig.)   *The Psychiatric Study of Jesus*. Boston: Beacon.
SCOTT, J.P.
  1958   *Aggression*. Chicago: Univ. of Chicago Press.
  1958   *Animal Behavior*. Chicago: Univ. of Chicago Press.
  1962   Critical Periods in Behavioral Development. *Science* 138: 949–
         958.
SEAY, B.; HANSEN, E.; and HARLOW, H.F.
  1962   Mother-Infant Separation in Monkeys. *J. Child. Psychol. Psychiat.*
         3: 123–132.
SEAY, B.; ALEXANDER, B.K.; and HARLOW, H.F.
  1964   Maternal Behavior of Socially Deprived Rhesus Monkeys. *J. Abnorm.
         Soc. Psychol.* 69: 345.
SEBEOK, T.A.
  1965   Animal Communication. *Science* 147: 1006–1014.
SECOY, F.R.
  1953   Changing Military Patterns on the Great Plains. *Monog. Amer.
         Ethnol. Soc.* (21).
SERVICE, E.R.
  1965   *Primitive Social Organization*. N.Y.: Random House.
  1966   *The Hunters*. Englewood Cliffs, N.J.: Prentice-Hall.
SEXTON, P.C.
  1969   *The Feminized Male*. N.Y.: Random House.
SHEPHER, J.
  1971   *Voluntary Imposition of Incest and Exogamic Restrictions in Second
         Generation Kibbutz Adults*. Ph.D. Thesis, Rutgers University, Dept. of
         Anthropology.
SILBERMAN, C.E.
  1970   *Crisis in the Classroom*. N.Y.: Random House.
SIMEONS, A.T.W.
  1960   *Man's Presumptuous Brain*. N.Y.: E.P. Dutton.
SIMONS, E.L.
  1962   Fossil Evidence Relating to the Early Evolution of Primate Behavior.
         Annals of the N.Y. Academy of Science 102 (2).
  1964   The Early Relatives of Man. *Scientific American* (July).
  1965   New Fossil Apes for Egypt and the Initial Differentiation of the
         Hominoidea. *Nature* 205.
SIMPSON, G.G.
  1950   *The Meaning of Evolution*. New Haven, Conn.: Yale Univ. Press.
  1953   *The Major Features of Evolution*. N.Y.: Columbia Univ. Press.
  1966   The Biological Nature of Man. *Science* 152: 472–478.

SKINNER, B.F.
  1953 *Science and Human Behavior.* N.Y.: Macmillan.
SLATER, M.K.
  1959 Ecological Factors in the Origin of Incest. *Amer. Anthrop.* 61:
         1042–1059.
SLUCKIN, W.
  1965 *Imprinting and Early Learning.* London: Methuen and Chicago:
         Aldine.
SMITH, A.
  1904 (1776) *Wealth of Nations.* London: Methuen.
SMITH, J.M.
  1958 *Theory of Evolution.* Harmandsworth: Penguin.
SMITH, M.G.
  1962 *West Indian Family Structures.* St. Louis: Washington Univ. Press.
SMITH, R.T.
  1956 *The Negro Family in British Guiana.* London: Routledge and Kegan
         Paul.
SOLLAS, W.J.
  1924 *Ancient Hunters.* London: Macmillan.
SOMIT, A.
  1968 Toward a More Biologically Oriented Political Science: Ethology
         and Psychopharmacology. *Midwest J. of Political Science* 12 (4): 550–
         567 (Nov.).
SOMIT, A.; DAVIES, J.C.; and SCHWARTZ, D.C.
  (in press) *Biology and Politics.* Chicago: Aldine.
SOUTHWICK, C.H. (ed.)
  1963 *Primate Social Behavior.* Princeton: D. Van Nostrand.
SPARKS, J.
  1967 Allogrooming in Primates. Morris, D. (ed.), *Primate Ethology.* Chi-
         cago: Aldine.
SPENCER, H.
  1876 *Ceremonial Institutions.* (Part 4 of *Principles of Sociology*) London:
         Williams and Norgate.
SPIRO, M.E.
  1954 Is the Family Universal? *Amer. Anthrop.* 56: 839–846.
  1956 *Kibbutz: Venture in Utopia.* Cambridge, Mass.: Harvard Univ.
         Press.
  1958 *Children of the Kibbutz.* Cambridge, Mass.: Harvard Univ. Press.
SPUHLER, J.N.
  1959 Somatic Paths to Culture. Spuhler, J.N. (ed.), *The Evolution of
         Man's Capacity for Culture.* Detroit, Mich.: Wayne State Univ. Press.
SPUHLER, J.N. (ed.)
  1959 *The Evolution of Man's Capacity for Culture.* Detroit, Mich.: Wayne
         State Univ. Press.
  1968 *Genetic Diversity and Human Behavior.* Chicago: Aldine.
STAYT, H.A.
  1931 *The BaVenda.* London: Oxford Univ. Press.

STEWART, K.
1954   *Pygmies and Dream Giants*. N.Y.: W.W. Norton.
STOCK, M.B., and SMYTHE, P.M.
1963   Does Undernutrition during Infancy Inhibit Brain Growth and Subsequent Intellectual Development? *Archives of Disease in Childhood* 38: 546.
STORR, A.
1968   *Human Aggression*. London: Penguin Press.
STOTT, D.H.
1962   Cultural and Natural Checks on Population Growth. Montagu, M.F.A. (ed.), *Culture and the Evolution of Man*. N.Y.: Oxford Univ. Press.
STOUFFER, S. *et al.*
1949   *The American Soldier*. Princeton: Princeton Univ. Press.
SULLIVAN, H.S.
1953   *The Interpersonality Theory of Psychiatry*. Perry, H.S., and Gawel, M.L. (eds.), N.Y.: W.W. Norton.
1954   *The Psychiatric Interview*. Perry, H.S., and Gawel, M.L. (eds.), N.Y.: W.W. Norton.
TANNER, J.
1955   *Growth at Adolescence*. Oxford: Blackwell.
TANNER, J. (ed.)
1960   *Human Growth*. (Symposium for the Society for the Study of Human Biology, No. 3) Oxford: Pergamon Press.
TAWNEY, R.H.
1921   *The Acquisitive Society*. London: G. Bell and Sons.
TAX, S. (ed.)
1952   *Indian Tribes of Aboriginal America*. Chicago: Univ. of Chicago Press.
1960   *Evolution After Darwin*. (3 vols.) Chicago: Univ. of Chicago Press.
TERESHKOVA-NIKOLAYEVA, VALENTINA
1970   Women in Space. *Impact of Science on Society* UNESCO 20 (1) (Jan.–March).
THOMAS, W.I.
1906   The Gaming Interest. *Amer. J. Sociol.*, pp. 750–756.
THOMPSON, L.
1970   A Self-regulating System of Human Population Control. *Proc. N.Y. Academy of Sciences*, pp. 262–270.
THORPE, W.H.
1956   *Learning and Instinct in Animals*. London: Methuen.
1956   Ethology as a New Branch of Biology. McGill, T.E. (ed.), *Readings in Animal Behavior*, 1965. N.Y.: Holt, Rinehart and Winston.
THRASHER, F.M.
1936   *The Gang*. Chicago: Univ. of Chicago Press.
TIGER, L.
1966   Bureaucracy and Charisma in Ghana. *J. of Asian and African Studies* 1 (1).

1969   *Men in Groups.* N.Y.: Random House.
1970a Dominance in Human Societies. *Annual Review of Ecology and Systematics* 1 (1).
1970b The Possible Biological Origins of Sexual Discrimination. *Impact of Science on Society* 20 (1): 29–44.
1970c Biological Fabianism. *Canadian Forum.* 50: 112–117.
(in press) Introduction, *International Social Science Journal* (Issue reporting Meeting of Experts on Human Aggressiveness, U.N.E.S.C.O., Paris, May 1970).

TIGER, L., and FOX, R.
1966   The Zoological Perspective in Social Science. *Man: The J.R.A.I.* 1 (1): 75–81.

TINBERGEN, N.
1936   The Function of Sexual Fighting in Birds; and the Problems of the Origin of Territory. *Bird Banding* 7: 1–8.
1951   *The Study of Instinct.* Oxford: Clarendon Press.
1953a *Social Behavior in Animals.* N.Y.: John Wiley & Sons.
1953b *The Herring Gull's World.* London: Methuen.
1955   Psychology and Ethology as Supplementary Parts of a Science of Behavior. Schaffner, B. (ed.), *Group Processes.* (Transactions of the First Conference) N.Y.: Josiah Macy, Jr., Foundation.
1960a The Evolution of Behavior in Gulls. *Scientific American* (Dec.).
1960b Behavior, Systematics, and Natural Selection. Tax, S. (ed.), *Evolution after Darwin: Volume 1 The Evolution of Life.* Chicago: Univ. of Chicago Press.
1962   The Evolution of Animal Communication—A Critical Examination of Methods. *Symp. Zool. Soc. Lond.* 8: 1–6.
1963   On the Aims and Methods of Ethology. *Zeitschrift fur Tierpsychologie* 20: 410–433.
1964   The Evolution of Signaling Devices. Etkin, W. (ed.), *Social Behavior and Organization Among Vertebrates.* Chicago and London: Univ. of Chicago Press.
1965   Behavior and Natural Selection. Moore, J.A. (ed.), *Ideas in Modern Biology.* N.Y.: Natural History Press.
1968   On War and Peace in Animals and Man. *Science* 160: 1411–1418.

TOFFLER, A.
1970   *Future Shock.* N.Y.: Random House.

TROPP, A.
1957   *The Schoolteachers.* London: Heinemann.

TROTTER, W.
1916   *Instincts of the Herd in Peace and War.* London: E. Benn.

TUNSTALL, J.
1962   *The Fishermen.* London: MacGibbon and Kee.

TURNER, V.
1957   *Schism and Continuity in an African Society.* Manchester: Manchester Univ. Press.
1964   An Ndembu Doctor in Practice. Kiev, A. (ed.), *Magic, Faith, and Healing.* Glencoe, Ill.: Free Press.

1969   *The Ritual Process.* Chicago: Aldine.
TURNEY-HIGH, H.H.
1949   *Primitive War: Its Practice and Concepts.* Columbia, S.C.: Univ. of South Carolina Press.
TYLOR, E.B.
1870   *Primitive Culture.* London: John Murray.
1888   On a Method of Investigating the Development of Institutions. *J. Royal Anthrop. Inst.* 18.
UBEROI, J.S.
1962   *Politics of the Kula Ring.* Manchester: Manchester Univ. Press.
UCKO, P.J., and DIMBLEBY, G.W. (eds.)
1969   *The Domestication and Exploitation of Plants and Animals.* Chicago: Aldine and London: Gerald Duckworth.
UDRY, J.R., and MORRIS, N.M.
1968   Distribution of Coitus in the Menstrual Cycle. *Nature, London,* 220: 593–596.
VANDENBERGH, J.G.
1967   The Development of Social Structure in Free-Ranging Rhesus Monkeys. *Behavior* 29: 179–194.
VAYDA, A.P.
1960   Maori Warfare. *Polynesian Society Maori Monograph* (2). Wellington: Polynesian Soc.
1961   Expansion and Warfare Among Swidden Agriculturalists. *Amer. Anthrop.* 63: 346–358.
VAYDA, A.P., and LEEDS, A.
1961   Anthropology and the Study of War. *Anthropologica* (n.s.), 3: 131–133.
WADDINGTON, C.H.
1961   *The Ethical Animal.* N.Y.: Atheneum.
WALLACE, A.F.C.
1958   Dreams and Wishes of the Soul: A Type of Psychoanalytic Theory Among the Seventeenth Century Iroquois. *Amer. Anthrop.* 60 (2): 234–248.
WALLAS, G.
1948 (orig. 1908)   *Human Nature in Politics.* London: Constable.
WASHBURN, S.L.
1959   Speculations on the Inter-relations of the History of Tools and Biological Evolution. Spuhler, J.N. (ed.), *The Evolution of Man's Capacity for Culture.* Detroit, Mich.: Wayne State Univ. Press.
1960   Tools and Human Evolution. *Scientific American* (Sept. 1960).
1961 (ed.)   *Social Life of Early Man.* Viking Fund Publs. in Anthropology (3). N.Y.: Wenner-Gren Foundation for Anthropological Research.
1965   An Ape's Eye View of Human Evolution. DeVore, P.I. (ed.), *The Origin of Man.* N.Y.: Wenner-Gren Foundation.
1966   Conflict in Primate Society. *Conflict in Society.* London: Ciba Foundation, J. and A. Churchill.
1968a   *Behavior and the Origin of Man.* Rockefeller Univ. Review (Jan.–Feb.), pp. 10–19.

1968b *The Study of Human Evolution.* Eugene, Oregon: Oregon State System of Higher Education.

WASHBURN, S.L., and DEVORE, I.
1961 The Social Life of Baboons. *Scientific American* (June).

WASHBURN, S.L., and HAMBURG, D.A.
1968 Aggressive Behavior in Old World Monkeys and Apes. Jay, P. (ed.), *Primates: Studies on Adaptation and Variability.* N.Y.: Holt, Rinehart and Winston.

WASHBURN, S.L., and HOWELL, F.C.
1960 Human Evolution and Culture. Tax, S. (ed.), *Evolution After Darwin: Volume 2 The Evolution of Man.* Chicago: Univ. of Chicago Press.

WASHBURN, S.L., and JAY, P.C. (eds.)
1968 *Perspectives on Human Evolution* 1. N.Y.: Holt, Rinehart and Winston.

WASHBURN, S.L., and LANCASTER, C.S.
1968 The Evolution of Hunting. Lee, R.B., and DeVore, I. (eds.), *Man The Hunter.* Chicago: Aldine.

WATSON, J.B.
1930 *Behaviorism.* Chicago: Univ. of Chicago Press.

WEBB, S., and WEBB, B.
1894 *History of Trade Unionism.* London: Longmans, Green and Co.

WEBER, M.
1947 *Theory of Social and Economic Organization.* Glencoe, Ill.: Free Press.

WEIR, R.H.
1962 *Language in the Crib.* The Hague: Martar.

WELKER, W.I.
1956a Some Determinants of Play and Exploration in Chimpanzees. *J. Comp. Physiol. Psychol.* 49: 84–89.

1956b Effects of Age and Experience on Play and Exploration of Young Chimpanzees. *J. Comp. Physiol. Psychol.* 49: 223–226.

1961 An Analysis of Play and Exploratory Behavior in Animals. Fiske and Maddi (eds.), *Functions of Varied Experience.* Homewood, Ill.: Dorsey Press.

WESTERMARCK, E.
1903 *History of Human Marriage.* N.Y.: St. Martin's Press.

WHITE, C.L.
1970 *Women's Magazines 1693–1968.* London: Michael Joseph.

WHITE, L.A.
1948 Man's Control Over Civilization: An Anthropocentric Illusion. *Scientific Monthly* 66: 235–247.

1949 *The Science of Culture.* N.Y.: Farrar, Straus and Co.

1959 *The Evolution of Culture.* N.Y.: McGraw-Hill.

WHITING, J.W.M., and CHILD, I.
1953 *Child Training and Personality.* New Haven, Conn.: Yale Univ. Press.

WHITING, J.W.M.; KLUCKHOHN, R.; and ANTHONY, A.S.
1958 The Function of Male Initiation Ceremonies at Puberty. Maccoby, E.E. *et al.* (eds.), *Readings in Social Psychology.* N.Y.: Henry Holt.

WHYTE, W.F.
  1943 *Street-Corner Society.* Chicago: Univ. of Chicago Press.
WICKLER, W.
  1967 Socio-Sexual Signals and Their Intra-Specific Imitation Among Primates. Morris, D. (ed.), *Primate Ethology.* London: Weidenfeld and Nicolson.
WILENSKY, H.L.
  1968 Women's Work: Economic Growth, Ideology, Structure. *Industrial Relations* 7: 235–258.
WILLIAMS, G.C.
  1966 *Adaptation and Natural Selection.* Princeton: Princeton Univ. Press.
WILLIAMSON, K.
  1962 Changes in the Marriage System of the Okrika Ijo. *Africa* 32: 53–60.
WILSON, A.C., and SARICH, U.M.
  1969 A Molecular Time Scale for Human Evolution. *Proc. Nat. Acad. of Sciences* (U.S.A.) 63: 4.
WILSON, E.
  1940 *To the Finland Station.* N.Y.: Harcourt, Brace and Co.
  1960 *Apologies to the Iroquois.* N.Y.: Farrar, Straus and Cudahy.
WISSLER, C.
  1916 Psychological and Historical Interpretations of Culture. *Science* 43: 193–201.
  1923 *Man and Culture.* N.Y.: Crowell.
WITALEN, R.E. (ed.)
  1967 *Hormones and Behavior.* Princeton: D. Van Nostrand Co.
WITTFOGEL, K.
  1957 *Oriental Despotism.* New Haven, Conn.: Yale Univ. Press.
WOLF, E.
  1966 *Peasants.* Englewood Cliffs, N.J.: Prentice-Hall.
WOODBURN, J.C.
  1964 *The Social Organization of the Hadza of North Tanzania.* Ph.D. Thesis, Cambridge University, Dept. of Anthropology.
WRIGHT, Q.
  1942 *A Study of War.* (2 vols.). Chicago: Univ. of Chicago Press.
WYNNE-EDWARDS, V.C.
  1962 *Animal Dispersion in Relation to Social Behavior.* N.Y.: Hafner.
  1964 Population Control in Animals. *Scientific American* (Aug.).
YABLONSKY, L.
  1964 *The Violent Gang.* Harmondsworth: Penguin.
YERKES, R.M.
  1933 Genetic Aspects of Grooming, a Socially Important Primate Behavior Pattern. *J. Social Psychology* IV: 3–25.
YOUNG, F.
  1965 *Initiation Ceremonies: A Cross-Cultural Study of Status Dramatization.* N.Y.: Bobbs-Merrill.
YOUNG, J.Z.
  1965 The Organization of a Memory System. *Proc. Royal Soc.* 163B (Nov. 23, 1965).

YOUNG, M.
  1958 *The Rise of the Meritocracy, 1870–2033*. London: Thames and Hudson.
YOUNG, W.C.
  1961 *Sex and Internal Secretions* (2 vols.). Baltimore: Williams and Wilkens, Co.
YOUNG, W.C.; GOY, R.W.; and PHOENIX, C.H.
  1964 Hormones and Sexual Behavior. *Science* 143 (3603): 212–218.
ZEMAN, F.J., and STANBROUGH, E.C.
  1969 Effect of Maternal Protein Deficiency on Cellular Development in the Fetal Rat. *J. Nutrition* 99: 274–282.
ZUCKERMAN, S.
  1930 The Menstrual Cycle of the Primates. *Proc. Zool. Soc.*, pp. 691–754.
  1932 *The Social Life of Monkeys and Apes*. London: Routledge and Kegan Paul.

INDEX

War(s) and fighting (*Cont.*)
236; peace and, 208, 220; ritualization, 214, 217, 218–219; status, 111, 212, 213–214; symbols and, attachment to, 217–218; war machines and, 236; weapons and, 211; youth, 114–115. *See also* Aggression; Violence
Weapons, 210–211, 213
Weber, Max, 37, 47, 48
Welfare (aid): psychological effects of, 135–136; right, 135; women, treatment of, 103
Witchcraft, 186–187

Wolves, mating bond and pack formation, 61, 68–69
Work: coworker selection, 144–145; industrialization and conditions of, 127 ff.; play and, 178; schooling as, 153; sex behavior at job, 145, 201–202. *See also* Labor
Wynne-Edwards, V. C., 225

Young, *see* Adolescents; Childbearing, rearing; Mother-child bonding
Young, J. Z., 18

Zoology, 2, 3. *See also* Primates